HOOD TO COAST Memories

An Oral History of "The Mother of All Relays"

MARC B. SPIEGEL & ART GARNER

ISBN-13: 978-1984200761

ISBN-10: 1984200763

HOOD TO COAST

Memories

For Emily, thanks for the support and encouragement and joining me on this journey.
—Marc

For Anna and Emma, who make me want to go the extra mile.
—Art

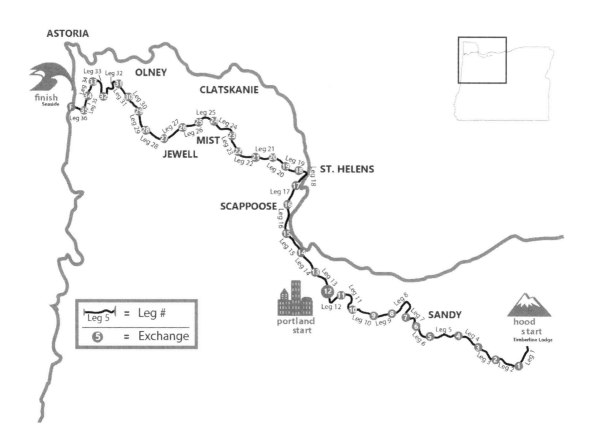

ASTORIA

OLNEY

CLATSKANIE

finish
Seaside

Leg 33   Leg 32
Leg 34
Leg 35   Leg 30
Leg 36   Leg 31   Leg 29   Leg 28
Leg 25
Leg 27   Leg 24
Leg 26   Leg 23
JEWELL   MIST   Leg 23
Leg 22   Leg 21
Leg 20   Leg 19
Leg 18
ST. HELENS

Leg 17

SCAPPOOSE   Leg 16

Leg 16

Leg 15   Leg 14
Leg 15   Leg 14
Leg 13   Leg 13
Leg 12
Leg 12   Leg 11
portland   Leg 10   Leg 8
start   Leg 9   SANDY
Leg 10   Leg 9   Leg 8
Leg 6   hood
Leg 7   start
Leg 5   Timberline Lodge
Leg 4
Leg 3   Leg 2
Leg 1

Leg 5   = Leg #

⑤   = Exchange

Contents

Glossary of Hood To Coast Terms

Captain: Primary team contact who manages the activities and requirements necessary to compete in the event, including coordinating event registration, assembling a roster of runners, arranging volunteers, gathering the required safety equipment, and organizing travel and accommodations.

Exchange: Locations along the racecourse where one team member finishes running a leg and another team member begins running a leg. There are a total of 35 exchanges along the racecourse.

Exchange (Major): Locations along the racecourse where the two team vehicles meet when the final runner in Van 1 (Runner 6) hands off to the first runner in Van 2 (Runner 7) and when the last runner in Van 2 (Runner 12) and the first runner in Van 1 (Runner 1) meet. There are a total of five major exchanges along the racecourse before the finish.

Finish: The relay finish line is situated on the beach in Seaside, north of the Broadway Street turnaround. Team members often join their anchor runner (Runner 12/Leg 36) to cross the finish line together, officially completing the race.

Legs: A designated section of the racecourse. A total of 36 legs make up the Hood To Coast (HTC) racecourse. On a team of 12, each runner is responsible for three legs, which vary in distance from just under four miles to almost eight miles.

Miles: The total distance of the racecourse is about 199 miles but can vary from year to year. Each individual runner will complete between 13 and 20 miles.

Numbers: Each team is assigned a number used by race officials to identify the team. Runners wear a race bib with that number when running.

Portland To Coast (PTC): A walking relay race that has been a part of HTC since 1991. It begins in Portland at Exchange 12 and ends in Seaside, following the same route as

HTC. Traditional teams have 12 members with each walker handling two legs. Annually, there are 400 teams that participate in the 130-mile walk.

Portland To Coast High School Challenge: A running relay race for high school students that has been a part of HTC since 1998. It begins in Portland at Exchange 12 and ends in Seaside, following the same route as HTC. Most years about 50 teams compete in the 130-mile race. The teams of 12 usually include athletes from high school cross country and track teams.

Road Kill: Term used to describe a runner who is passed on the racecourse. Some runners will keep track of their road kills and keep a running tally on their vans.

Runner: Each runner on a team of 12 is identified with a number from one to 12 and is responsible for completing the three legs of the race assigned to his or her position. For example, after starting the race with Leg 1, Runner 1 will also handle Legs 13 and 25.

Safety Equipment: Between the hours of 6 p.m. and 7 a.m. all runners are required to wear a reflective vest, have front and back flashing lights, and wear a headlamp or carry a flashlight.

Sleeping Area: There are several designated spaces for sleeping located along the racecourse, including in school gyms and fields at several exchanges. Tent City, which provides free sleeping accommodations in tents, is located at Exchange 24.

Start: The race start is located in the lower parking lot at Mt. Hood's Timberline Lodge. Waves of runners depart from the start every 15 minutes beginning around 5 a.m. and continuing through the late afternoon. An assigned time to begin running is based on the team's projected overall time to complete the relay. Faster teams will typically start later in the day, which helps alleviate congestion along the racecourse.

Team: A group of runners competing together in HTC. A team typically comprises 12 runners, and teams often have interesting, funny, or unique names.

Vans: The primary means of transportation for teams participating in the relay are vans, and each team utilizes two vehicles. After vans, the most common forms of transportation are minivans and SUVs, but all are referred to as "vans" for the purposes of the race. Van 1 holds Runners 1 through 6, and Van 2 is occupied by Runners 7 through 12. Vans are usually adorned on the outside with designs, expressions, and decorations, including the team moniker, and the names of the runners and their legs; some teams will also keep tallies of each team member's road kills on the van.

Volunteers: Teams with at least one member residing within a 100-mile radius of Portland are considered local and required to provide three volunteers for the race. Race volunteers fill a variety of roles during the relay, from assisting runners at an exchange, to providing directions along the course, to directing parking at exchanges. There is mandatory online training for volunteers.

Wrist Wraps: Slap bracelet that must be carried or worn at all times throughout the race, and is handed off from one teammate to another at each exchange.

Categories: Each team is placed in a category based on the composition, in terms of sex and age, of its runners. There are six different categories for men, women, and mixed teams.

- **Open:** Any age with at least one runner under 30.
- **Submasters:** Minimum age for each runner is 30.
- **Masters:** Minimum age for each runner is 40.
- **Supermasters:** Minimum age for each runner is 50.
- **Champion Masters:** Average age of all participants is 60 or higher.
- **Corporate Open:** Any age, all from the same employer.

Preface

WE WERE AT TIMBERLINE LODGE getting ready for the start of the 2014 Hood To Coast. Our team arrived Thursday evening and stayed at the Lodge—two or three to a room. Even though we all had images of Timberline from *The Shining* in mind, it wasn't a scary experience. However, we were all a little scared about what waited for us the next morning.

It was my first time participating in the relay. In fact, it was the very first time for everyone on our team, Agony of Da Feet. My wife, Emily, and I came to Oregon from Charlotte, North Carolina. She was our team captain and coordinated all the logistics. I was basically the team Sherpa, there to carry luggage and groceries, pack the van, do whatever else was needed, and run—albeit slowly. Our team included friends from Charlotte and runners from Arizona, Connecticut, Chicago, and Portland.

I was Runner 1 and would start the relay for our team. There were nerves before our Friday morning start time. Actually, I was slightly panicked. In the race handbook, the first leg was rated as very hard and described in the course overview as a "severe downhill." I'm not sure what I expected, but it probably wasn't this. I'd be heading down a mountain—on a really steep downhill.

As our whole team waited at the start, we spotted Bob Foote. What better way to commemorate our inaugural relay than by having a team picture taken with the event founder! Bob happily posed with our team, a few pictures were taken, and then he asked, "Who's running the first leg?" I sheepishly raised my hand. Expecting to hear some words of encouragement, I was somewhat surprised when he mentioned how difficult it was. I believe Bob's last words before he headed off were, "You better be careful."

I was worried before we even got to the start and now I was even more concerned. Crazy thoughts started dancing through my head. "What am I doing here? How did I let Emily talk me into this? Can I run one leg, let alone three?"

Next thing I knew, our start time was called. All the teams in our wave were introduced, and suddenly I was standing behind the starting line. It was me and 20 or 30 other runners. Some looked as worried as me, and others looked like they could run the entire relay by themselves. Just before we were set to begin, the announcer asked everyone to introduce themselves to another runner and wish them luck, which I did. The countdown began—five, four, three, two, one—and we were off. I ran past my teammates cheering me on and began to make my way down the mountain. Slowly and carefully, but feeling pretty good.

I established a nice, comfortable pace. Eventually, I pulled up beside a young woman running a similar pace. It turned out she was a recent college graduate and some friends had talked her into running at the last minute. It was her first time doing the race too. We ran and talked, and ran and talked. The conversation calmed my nerves. Although Emily and I did train, even breaking out our headlamps for a few evening runs, I'm no speed demon. But I wasn't gasping for air. Finally, my temporary running partner told me she needed to slow down. I thanked her for the conversation and wished her luck.

Feeling good, I continued down the mountain gaining momentum with each step. At the exchange I found my longtime friend and teammate Kevin. My first leg was finished, and in another 30 hours we'd all finish our first HTC.

What did I learn from my first time participating in the race? I learned the experience I shared with my fellow runner on that first leg is a common occurrence during the course of the relay. Runners help runners. Teammates support teammates. Teams assist other teams. And volunteers help everyone. It's about laughter and making memories and spending too much time together in a sweaty and smelly van with little to no sleep. It's about raising money for charity and remembering those who can no longer participate or who have passed away.

Everyone involved is part of a unique, one-of-a-kind community, in which even though teams are competing against other teams there's a tremendous amount of camaraderie, friendship, and benevolence. Even though it's about doing whatever is necessary to get to the finish, it's assuring others make it to the finish too. That's the spirit of HTC. There's nothing else like it, and that's why it's "The Mother of All Relays."

It's what keeps me and my team coming back year after year, and we have no plans of stopping anytime soon. And it's where the idea for this book came from after finishing the race in 2016.

I was contemplating writing another book with my friend and longtime colleague Art Garner. The first book we wrote together, *Indy 500 Memories*, was published in May of that year and we were looking for a new project. Although Art had never run the race, he had recently relocated to the Pacific Northwest and was quickly on board with the idea that became this book.

The plan was rather simple. Collect memories from runners, teams, volunteers, event organizers, and others. It wasn't going to be simply about the elite teams or the fast runners. It wouldn't focus only on the early years of the race, and it wouldn't solely highlight the relay's recent history. Instead we wanted to feature memories from the inaugural event and the early years, through the record-breaking and unique teams of the 1990s, into the 2000s and all the way to the present.

It was two years in the making, and included plenty of ups and downs, and twists and turns, much like the HTC racecourse. And much like the relay itself, there were plenty of stories to share and memories to collect.

We hope you enjoy!

—Marc B. Spiegel

Larry Dutko

Introduction

Larry Dutko is the only person to have competed in every Hood To Coast.

There is magic in the air during late August in Oregon. That's the only way to describe what brings me back to Hood To Coast every year. An event so unique and held on a course so majestic, it creates lifelong memories for the thousands who participate every year.

I grew up on the East Coast in the small ocean beach town of Brielle, New Jersey. I loved playing sports, but discovered in high school I was too light for football and too short for basketball. When we ran the dreaded mile in our physical fitness testing, however, I was at the front of the pack. I loved the feeling running provided and by 1967 I was running a 4:45 mile and covering two miles in 10:02, respectable times even by today's standards.

In 1976 I graduated college and spent two years in a van traveling around the country. I discovered the beautiful mountains, lakes and forests that Portland offered and made it my home. The city also had an active running community and it wasn't long before local 10Ks led to half-marathons, the Portland Marathon and even a trip to the legendary Boston Marathon.

That's when I met Bob Foote. He and several other friends became my marathon training partners. When Bob suggested doing a team endurance run, we all agreed to undertake the first-ever relay from Mt. Hood to the coast of Oregon. I figured with 10 guys splitting 165 miles it would be a piece of cake. But would it be exciting? Sitting in a van watching other guys run didn't sound like a lot of fun.

I ran the inaugural HTC in 1982 and along with my nine teammates was fortunate enough to win, topping a field of eight teams. Everyone seemed to enjoy themselves and agreed to do it again the following year. We won again, but more importantly, we all knew by the time we reached the finish that there was something magical about running together with a group of friends for 20 to 24 hours, being crammed into a van, and sharing stories filled with sweat, pain, tears and laughter.

For me, that magical fervor remains today. I now run with the Dead Jocks in a Box team. Even with a streak of 36 consecutive races and counting, and having run with more than 100 different teammates, the excitement begins to build weeks, and even months, before the race.

The magic is hard to explain. When running solo in a 10K or marathon, most runners tend to be critical of their time and how they finish. In HTC, however, we discovered that individual achievements were secondary to what the team accomplished. Since HTC offers each runner a series of legs of varying difficulties, there are no basic standards of measurement. Only effort and attitude counts. With three legs to run, if you have a tough climb on one, you do your best and focus on crushing your next flat leg. In the relay, you are a critical part of the *team* and every completed leg becomes a success.

I was 33 when I ran the first HTC and I've run every race since heading into 2018, when I'll be 69 years young. The answer to what keeps me going is pretty simple. It's the runners I meet every year that have changed my life, kept me fit and energized. And it's not just me. Seeing new teams each year keeps us Dead Jocks strong and still running with a competitive edge, even in our 60s. We're feeling as good as ever, even if we're a little bit slower. My goal is to run the relay between 45 and 50 times before I retire my running shoes, which should be sometime around 2030, when I'll be about 80.

If you happen to see the Dead Jocks along the course or at an exchange, please say hello. Share the magic of your HTC experience. It's what keeps me and my fellow Dead Jocks, along with thousands of others, young and energized, and what makes this event so special.

In 1969, I was a young man when I attended Woodstock. After doing HTC, I've heard and also said it many times, HTC is like Woodstock moving down the road, only much more entertaining.

HOOD TO COAST

OREGON ROAD RUNNERS CLUB

RELAY

Mizuno RUNNING SHOES

August 7- 5:oo am TIMBERLINE LODGE —— SPONSORS

5 or 10 member teams (provide own aid and transportation enroute)

course: Timberline Lodge to Glade Trail into Government Camp, Highway 26 into Zig Zag, Back roads into Sandy and Gresham, Powell Blvd. into Portland, South to Woodstock and cross on Sellwood Bridge enroute to Beaverton-Hillsdale Hy, Through Beaverton and out Farmington to Bald Peak (whew), Steep down into Laurelwood and out Springhill Rd and to Carlton, Nestucca River Road and to Beaverton and Hy, 101, South to Neskowin.

contacts: Fred Neilson   #283-1302 days; #668-9405 evening (start)
Bob Foote   #223-2390 days; #224-0268 evening (course & entries)
              608 N.W. 19th; Portland, Or. 97209
Dan Deakins   #640-5263 days & ev. (Sunday morning beach picnik

wards : Running shoes for first team (limit of 5); Meal at Timberline Lodge . for each on second team; athletic bags (Mizino) third team, T shirts for early entrants.

fee: $6.00 by August 4 and $7.00 day of race. Entry to Bob Foote, Map and course description returned with early entry (August 4 deadline). Checks to Oregon Road Runners Club please.

rules a. Enter as a team consisting of either 1-5 members or 6-10 members. If you don't have a team you may choose to get on the list and the directors will assist you.
  b. 5.0 mile legs x30 = 150 miles, (Running distance to be divided equally into 30 legs with the exception of the Glade Trail; i.e. 5.12 mile legs.
  c. Team member order for running each leg. Order is to remain the same throughout the race. If a team member drops out due to injury, etc. team order remains the same.
  d. All teams to monitor and guide their teammates through the course, If a wrong turn is made, runner must return to point on course where error was made and then resume race, Deviations from this will disqualify them.
  e. Teams to record all times for all legs: 1st leg - time leg begins; elapsed time of leg; (ie. leg Begin 6:21:56, Ends 6:56:56, elapsed time 35:00.......... Leg 2. Times along with who ran each leg must be submitted upon completion of race.
  f. There will be white lines along bo h sides of road where a "tag" and exchange of runners is to take place.

ge groups: in each of the teams (1-5 & 6-10)
  (1) sub masters - all male (below 40)   (4) masters - all male
  (2) sub masters - all female   "   (5) masters - all female
  (3) sub masters - mixed   (6) masters - mixed
           (7) all male - sub masters and masters
           (8) all female - sub masters and masters
           (9) mixed - open to any mix

ENTRY

Name _____ sex _____ age _____ ph #
Address _____ city _____ state_____ zip _____
age group you wish to enter as a team _____ (#1-9 & # On team)
Other team members _____
_____
Person acting as team captain for mailing purposes,_____
fee enclosed $6.00 per person & to ORRC   (can send for all members)
Do you need to be put on the "I NEED A TEAM LIST" ? yes ____ no ____
I want to be put on the list for 1-5 member _____ 6-10 member_____

ORRC

Promotional flyer for the inaugural Hood To Coast in 1982.

CHAPTER 1

The Beginning

THE FIRST HOOD TO COAST began on August 7, 1982, and was sanctioned by the Oregon Road Runners Club. The early entry fee was $6 until early registration ended August 4, then it jumped to $7 on race day. Teams of five and 10 runners were invited to enter, with five pairs of Mizuno running shoes to be presented to the winning team, and a meal at Timberline Lodge promised to each member of the second-place team. Teams were told to provide "their own aid and transportation en route."

The following participants in that first relay recall what it was like in year one.

Kib Dacklin was captain of the Tigard High School (Oregon) team that competed in the first and third years of Hood To Coast. He went on to play competitive Ultimate Frisbee on a national level and now lives in Utah.

Mike de la Cruz was part of the winning Hood To Coast Men's Masters division team every year from 1982 to 1987, first with the Oregon Master Milers and then with a team he put together called the Vintage Collection. He now lives on the island of Maui.

Larry Dutko was a member of the Road Warriors/Road Kill team that finished first in the inaugural Hood To Coast. He later became a member of the Dead Jocks in a Box team and is the only runner to have competed in every HTC.

Bob Foote is the founder and chairman of Hood To Coast.

Patti McDonald (formerly Foote) was married to Bob Foote from 1975 through 1995.

Jim Sapp *was a member of the Road Warriors/Road Kill team that finished first in the inaugural Hood To Coast.*

John Smets *was a member of the only Men's Masters team in the first Hood To Coast, which finished fourth overall.*

Jim Smith *was a member of the Tigard High School team that participated in the inaugural Hood To Coast. He went on to run in college at the University of Oregon and returned to be on a winning HTC team. He's now a principal at Wheeler High School in Fossil, Oregon.*

John Stirniman *was a member of the Road Warriors/Road Kill team that finished first in the inaugural Hood To Coast. He kept a diary throughout the event.*

Bob Foote: In 1980 I participated in a little event in southern Oregon called the Roseburg to Coos Bay Relay. It was about 67 miles with five-person teams and three legs of about 2.6 miles per runner. It tore our bodies up. We were just hopping in and out of this passenger car. We'd run our legs, then jump in the car, and wait for the other four guys to run. All of a sudden it'd be time to run again. We'd be stiff and sore and then we'd have to jump out of the car and literally sprint. We were all marathoners, so 2.6 miles was a sprint.

We did that race two years in a row. We were five of the fastest guys in the area and won our age group—and I think we were second overall. The thing that struck all of us, however, was that it was one of the best competitive experiences we'd had since our college days. We had never felt that camaraderie when running marathons by ourselves. Running, as all runners know, is this isolated, inner, self-discovery kind of thing. Nobody cares about your run but you.

We were traveling back from the second Roseburg to Coos Bay Relay and we were pumped. We were in this big, old beater of a Buick that housed five guys really comfortably. We were driving back to Portland and I said the relay was just too much fun to have to drive down to southern Oregon every year to do. We needed to have something up in northern Oregon and it needed to be a completely redesigned concept. Roseburg to Coos Bay was all wrong. The legs were too short and it beat you up too much.

There was total support from the other guys. They thought it was absolutely spot on.

We all knew you needed at least a five-mile leg because then you get a sense of pace. There's no pace at two and a half miles. That's just death, an all-out sprint.

Jim Sapp: We did Roseburg to Coos Bay. And it was so much fun we went back and did it a second year. Bob kind of used that as the template for how to set up Hood To Coast.

Mike de la Cruz: I was on the board of directors of the Oregon Road Runners Club and a member of the race committee. At the end of the year we would meet at Silver Dollar Pizza in downtown Portland to plan the races for the coming season. One year we were all having beers and pizza and talking about the races and someone, I believe it was Bob Foote, said, "We need to have an interesting race. Not just a marathon or a 10K. Let's go from the highest point in the state to the lowest point." And then somebody else, I think it was Dan Deakins, said, "Well, that would be from Mt. Hood to the coast." Everyone thought that would be cool and Bob took the idea and ran with it.

Bob Foote: It planted the seed to start thinking about a relay. I wanted to design something showcasing northern Oregon. It was kind of a no-brainer, the mountain and the beach. But how do we get from Mt. Hood to the coast? My idea was to avoid the high-traffic highways as much as possible and use scenic backroads as another way to showcase the beauty of Oregon.

I chose Pacific City and a little beach there called Cape Kiwanda as our destination. I grew up in Salem and that was the beach we'd go to when I was a kid. It has Haystack Rock out in the middle of the water and huge dunes you can climb up and run down and have all kinds of fun on. I loved that place.

Then I had to figure out how to get from Point A to Point B. That involved going through maps and trying to find backroads. I found Barlow Trail Road and Marmot Road, and all those little two-lane farm roads coming off Mt. Hood that skirt and parallel Highway 26 and lead, eventually, to Portland.

I finally got the course figured out and documented as much as the maps would allow. The next step was to chart the route using the criteria we had talked about coming back from Coos Bay, establishing five-mile legs. Every single leg would be five miles to the inch.

One of my big pet peeves is running a road race on a mismeasured course. Setting a personal record only to find out later that I ran my guts out for nothing because the guy measured the course driving his car. I could never forgive a race director for an inaccurate racecourse. That's their number-one obligation. I don't care if you have water or volunteers on the course, just measure the course right. I don't care about all the frills. I just want to run a course and know it's accurate and that my time is real.

With that in mind, I knew through our Oregon Road Runners Club where there was a laser-measured half-mile in Portland. They had brass pins in the road and it was exactly half a mile. I took my 10-speed bicycle down to a bike shop and had them put a surveyor wheel counter on the back with a trip meter. Then I rode my bike the half-mile and doubled it to get a mile. I did that several times to calibrate the bike exactly.

One mile was 744 tire revolutions and 12 spokes. I measured it down to the spokes. Twelve spokes. That was one mile right to the inch. Then I got a CatEye altimeter to put on my bike so that I could get elevation readings. I also had a little handheld tape recorder and a can of spray paint.

Patti McDonald: The idea of doing something fun and different in the Portland area was bandied about by Bob and his group of running friends. The next thing I knew, we were driving up to Mt. Hood to chart a possible course for these crazy guys to run from Mt. Hood to Pacific City. I had just given birth to our daughter, Felicia, in May of 1982. We owned a 1974 Dodge pop-top campervan called "the Watermelon" and we loaded up Bob's 10-speed bicycle, which was calibrated to perfection, cans of spray paint, and all the paraphernalia needed to spend a day in the car with an infant.

Bob Foote: I had done some races at Timberline Lodge and knew about Glade Trail, which is a little ski trail that goes from Timberline down to the town of Government Camp at the base of the mountain. I took my bike down the trail to measure it correctly. It was going to be Leg 1.

From Timberline I did one-mile splits. I'd get close to 744 clicks on my bike and get off and walk it to 744. Then I'd rotate it to 12 spokes. Bam! I'd spray my white mile marker on the spot. Then I'd get back on my bike and start the process over for the next mile.

Patti McDonald: I'd drive exactly five miles down the road and pull over and wait for Bob while nursing Felicia in the back of the camper. Being the perfectionist that he is, he would get off his bike and walk it, staring at the odometer until it clicked exactly on the five-mile mark, and exactly at that point a line was sprayed on the road. Then off we'd go again, another five miles down the road. This happened all the way along the pre-planned route through Portland until we called it a day and headed home to prepare for the second half of the trip the following day.

Bob Foote: When measuring the legs I'd cut tangents the same way a runner would. I'd ride on the wrong side of the road because I knew that's where the runners would be. I was facing oncoming traffic and almost got killed a couple of times by trucks coming around the corner, but I wanted it to be exact.

The early course to Pacific City was around 165 miles. To measure the course I biked 80-something miles the first day and 80-something the next day. It took all day and night.

Every quarter-mile I was taking an altimeter reading and recording it on my tape recorder. I was also dictating all the time as I was riding and recorded the whole course, turn by turn. "Slight downhill here" and then "left turn there."

There was one constant throughout the first course. There was an exchange point every five miles. Period. It didn't matter where it was, that was the exchange point. And there were some crazy exchange points.

For example, when I got to Southwest Portland I was on Beaverton-Hillsdale Highway and approaching this really busy five-way intersection at Scholls Ferry Road. I was getting close to 744 clicks on my bike and I was going, "Oh my god, don't do this to me. Don't do this." I roll up to the five-way intersection and it's at 740. I know the exchange point is going to be right in the middle of the intersection. I wait for the traffic to clear and as soon as it does, I roll out my bike, paint the spot and run, just narrowly missing a car. But I got it right.

Mike de la Cruz: Bob's markings on the highway were really important. I knew how fastidious he was and how accurate he was. If he said it was 3.2 miles to the next point; it was 3.2 miles to the next point. That's just the way he is.

Patti McDonald: The exchange where Beaverton-Hillsdale Highway intersects with Scholls Ferry Road was a disaster waiting to happen, but it was exactly five miles, so that's where the line was made.

Bob Foote: There were no official approvals to do any of this. Zero. We just went and did it. It wasn't until the third year that the cops figured out something was up. Until then we were completely under the radar.

We decided from the beginning to start the race on Friday. We figured if you start then and beat yourself up on Friday and Saturday, you'd have Sunday to go home for rest and recovery before you went back to work. We also allowed for five- and 10-person teams so there'd be more running for the runners. That first year I put out a funny little race flyer and left it at a few running stores. When the dust settled we had eight teams.

John Stirniman: The summer edition of *Oregon Distance Runner* (ODR) magazine arrived at the beginning of July and there was a short article about a new race in August, a 165-mile relay from Mt. Hood to the Oregon coast. Relays weren't new; there were a couple of four- or five-person marathon relays. This was a point-to-point relay, however, and over a very long distance. I didn't really see it as a race, although I thought it would be a fun distance workout in preparation for the Portland Marathon.

Jim Sapp: Originally, our idea was to have teams of five. I was helping Bob search for people for our team. Then we lost a runner and were scrounging around for a replacement. It was tough to find someone the week of the race. I talked to another guy I knew who was trying to put together a five-person team. I said, "I'm going to call Bob and see if he's willing to merge to make one team of 10." Bob said, "Yeah, let's merge." I didn't really know three or four of the guys on the team, but they were all faster than I was, so it was a pretty solid team.

John Stirniman: We had a team of five, but 10 days before the race things started to fall apart due to injuries. Then I heard Jim Sapp and Bob Foote also had a team of five and wanted know if we were interested in merging. *Yes!* I barely knew Bob. We had run together once on a long training run. The other four I knew only by name.

Mike de la Cruz: The first race was a big question mark. It was hard to get runners to do it because it had never been done before. It sounded really crazy and you had to do some big-time talking to convince people to run. I could explain it a little better because I was on the race committee, and I was able to get enough guys together for a team.

Jim Smith: We saw the flyer and a bunch of us on the high school cross country team were ready to do the race the first year, but we were still a couple guys short. We ended up picking up a couple of guys who were just friends. We had a basketball player, a couple of runners who weren't in great shape, and one guy who was drunk when we picked him up. We almost didn't make it up the mountain in time because we couldn't find him. We were still trying to sober his ass up going up the hill, and when we finally got there it was like, this isn't starting out so good.

Jim Sapp: The first year, we had eight teams of 10 in Hood To Coast. Most of the people did not write down a team name on the application. All of the creative team names you have today weren't around. If you look at the entry list for the first HTC, it was just a list of the names of the people on the team. However, there was one mixed team from the Tri-Cities area of Washington called N.U.T.T.S.-n-B.U.T.T.S. We thought it was one of the cleverest names we ever heard, period.

Kib Dacklin: At the start there was a team called N.U.T.T.S.-n-B.U.T.T.S. that had some women on it. The women were very good looking and very good runners, so we were all into that.

John Stirniman: Each team was mailed a course booklet. There were 33 legs and a "34th leg" of a half-mile that anybody or everybody could run. The booklet provided street directions, road maps, elevation profiles, and the rules. It was very complete.

Larry Dutko: When we arrived at Timberline Lodge we got out of the van and looked over the competition. It wasn't too threatening. Then a young kid came over and asked me, "What are you old guys doing up here?" Now remember when you were in high school, anyone over 30 seemed too old to compete in an athletic event. I replied, "We're here to win this race!" He laughed a bit and said their team was from the Tigard

High School cross country team. Young legs, yes. Lean bodies, yes. But I didn't consider them a threat to our team.

John Stirniman: Eight teams showed up, each with a full complement of 10 runners—80 total participants. Not a bad turnout for a race with such an unusual format and no history. But at sunrise, with only eight runners toeing the line, it looked pretty anemic. Bob decided to use a mass start and said we would start at the first glint of the sun.

Jim Smith: It was pretty sparse at the start, no signage, just a couple of guys milling around and asking each other, "Are you running this thing?" It was supposed to start at about four in the morning, but Bob made the decision that it was still too dark, considering the first runner would be running down the Glade Trail ski run. That was Bob's ingenious idea. Not on the road, but right down the ski run. It was probably a good idea to wait until it got lighter.

Bob Foote: The Glade Trail is nothing but big rocks and boulders. It's a really treacherous vertical trail that you could kill yourself on in broad daylight. You can't run it in the dark.

John Stirniman: The Glade Trail is an unmaintained dirt and rock road between Timberline Lodge and Government Camp. It's straight, heading directly down the mountain. It drops 2,040 feet over 2.9 miles, an average 13-percent grade over a rough surface.

Paul Kingzett was the only person on our team remaining after the other nine of us all stepped backward when we asked for volunteers to run the first leg. He said he'd skied the trail many times, but I don't know how. It is about 10 feet wide with no room for turns. I would have just accelerated downhill until crashing.

Bob Foote: We were standing at Timberline Lodge, waiting for the sun to rise. All of a sudden the sun comes up at about 5:25 a.m. and there are streaks of light cast down around the mountain. We could see. I said, "Okay, line up guys." And we were off.

John Stirniman: We see the sun, we hear the gun, Pacific City here we come. Actually Bob just said, "Go," but I like the rhyme. All the teams headed back to the parking lot, got into their vehicles, and proceeded to the first exchange.

Jim Sapp: Bob made sure everybody came down the Glade Trail. It was not necessarily the best idea at dawn, because people were coming down with a lot of "strawberries" on their legs and limbs when they popped out on the road.

Kib Dacklin: The first year was a free-for-all. Our team had three or four cars. You could drive along next to your runner and hand him water. There were no cell phones or anything like that. How we all kept it together, I'll never know.

John Stirniman: We decided to use my Plymouth Duster and Larry's van. Post-race we'd camp in Pacific City. Everything else, we'd figure out on the fly. We drove down to watch all the teams make the first exchange and there were lots of scratches and a couple of bloody legs. Bob said that perhaps Glade Trail wasn't one of his best ideas.

Mike de la Cruz: We knew the first three or four legs were downhill and would be really hard on all the runners, so we were like, "Okay, lace your shoes up tight," and off they went. The first leg was set up to run down the Glade Trail. That trail was a killer. It was a very steep decline with no smooth surfaces, just rocks. It's really hard on your feet and your ankles. Our first runner got blisters, but he survived and ran the whole race.

Bob Foote: I was doing Leg 2, so I went down to Government Camp to wait for the guys. Literally all eight people, when they showed up out of the wilderness, had blood on their legs and hands. They were all scraped up. They took some major falls coming down that thing. Afterward I knew we had to change Leg 1. I almost killed some guys on that one.

Kib Dacklin: The first two legs of the race, or about 10 miles, you're running downhill from Timberline Lodge and it's pretty hard on the body. Our first two guys really smoked it and I think we were actually leading for a while.

John Stirniman: We were shocked to be in a race with the young men from Tigard. A high school cross country team that can average 5:35 over fifty miles, even given the downhill, is a damn good cross country team. So much for this being "just a training run." We were clearly racing. But Legs 6 and 7 were coming up and a couple of our stronger runners were lining up against two of their weaker runners.

We were also racing each other. Not head to head, since each leg is unique. It's a race within the race. I imagine this dynamic was true for every team. The race was turning out to be more fun than I had anticipated.

Larry Dutko: When our other vehicle arrived at the exchange point from Portland, they were shocked to learn that the Tigard High team had about a two-minute lead. I could see the look of concern on their faces.

"Look, guys, they're kids," I said. "They can run a fast 5K or 8K in cross country, but then their legs will feel like melted butter before long. Remember, it's a long way to the coast!"

I took off, filled with adrenaline, running a slight downhill grade at just a bit over a five-minute-mile pace. Two miles down the road I could see our van, and as I rounded a corner I heard, "Four hundred meters, Dutko. He's only four hundred meters ahead."

As I closed in on my very first road kill, although the term had not yet been invented, I understood what the magic of this race would be in the future. For the first time in my many years of road racing, I was no longer a solo runner grinding out the last 10K of a marathon or the last mile of a 10K. Not that day. I was part of a 10-cylinder, high-performance engine. We all started to feel the magic of running on a team again.

Bob Foote: A relay event changes everything. Some days when you're running, demons get in your mind and start telling you to back off because you don't have it today, next time will be your day. They talk you into failure. In a relay, however, you hear the louder voices of your teammates going, "Come on, Bob! You can do it! Dig down deep!" They pull you through levels of pain you would never otherwise put yourself through.

Kib Dacklin: We definitely had some stud runners. But we also had a couple of guys who were partiers and really hungover. By their third legs they were wiped out. We came out strong, but then we sucked.

Bob Foote: Tigard High School had some really fast guys on their team. I think they had a couple of state champions. They stayed with us for basically the first legs of the race. And then they just burned out—it just destroyed them. By the time we got through one rotation, we were pretty much off in the distance by ourselves. These other teams were wherever.

John Stirniman: I hadn't thought about what runners would do between their legs. We discussed a team name. Our original name, Jim Sapp's suggestion of Half Fast Five, was no longer valid after the merger. Jim thought Road Warriors represented tenacious road racing and paid homage to the movie. I said, "It's a punny plan," meaning I liked it. Later we changed it to Road Kill, a reference to the racing and a tribute to the local fauna we kept running across.

We were like groupies following a band. After each exchange we'd throw everything into the van and drive to the next gig, then party with the other teams while we waited for the exchange. The other teams became new friends. But we were seeing fewer of them at each exchange. As we departed the fourth exchange the slowest team hadn't arrived yet. We didn't see them again until the coast.

Jim Smith: By the time we all got through our first run, those guys on the team who weren't really runners were kind of banged up and injured. Most of them made it through their second run, but after that we were down to five guys who could still run.

My most vivid memory of the event was when the five of us gathered around and decided to keep going. We had one guy run five legs, and I ran four. When you have only five guys, your rest time obviously gets a lot shorter. There was almost no recovery time.

Jim Sapp: The first year, Bob was real anal and precise about each leg being exactly five miles. However, there was one problem. Just after Portland we came along the Beaverton-Hillsdale Highway, which is a fairly busy area, to a little traffic triangle where three roads converge. The exchange point was right smack dab in the middle of that triangle and we had to make the handoff in the middle of the intersection.

John Stirniman: We're standing on the corner at the five-way intersection of Scholls

Ferry Road, Beaverton-Hillsdale Highway, and Oleson Road. The orange mark was in traffic, about 15 yards beyond the curb. Timing was critical. We needed to judge the speed of the approaching runner, take his mark at the last possible moment, and then negotiate a safe passage to the far side.

Larry Dutko: As I began to approach the complex five-corner intersection on Beaverton-Hillsdale Highway, I realized the exchange point was located in the exact center of the intersection. My buddy Gary Wilborn, who was a parole/probation officer in Portland, had told me beforehand not to worry. "I'll take care of the intersection," he said. As I approached to hand off to Gary, I could see him get out of the van, stand in the middle of the intersection, and as the light changed to green put his hands up to slow and stop traffic.

The curious and mostly courteous drivers watching us make the exchange mid-traffic must have been wondering what the heck was going on. Gary yelled something like, "It's the Hood To Coast Relay, baby, we're running Hood To Coast," although no one knew what that meant at the time. Future generations would realize it meant something very special.

Bob Foote: I remember giving instructions to the eight teams at the start of the race. "You guys have to be exact on the exchanges, right on top of the exchange points, every single one. There's only one place you have any latitude and that's down at Scholls Ferry. The line is in the middle of the street. I'll let you take your exchange on the curb, but you can't stop or start your watch until you hit my line in the middle of the street for your leg. On the score sheet I want times for every leg and I want them to be accurate. You have to give me an accurate time. Those 12 feet matter."

Mike de la Cruz: That first year it was hot. My God, it was hot, in the 90s. It was just sweaty, sweaty hot. We hadn't anticipated that. We also hadn't anticipated some of the intersections and all the trucks, especially the logging trucks. Holy mackerel. I almost got hit by one of them, and a couple other runners almost got clobbered. Some of those roads were very narrow, and when a big truck was coming you got off the road because you were going to lose to that truck.

Jim Smith: By the time we got into Portland there was no one out on the course. The eight teams had really spread out and you didn't see anybody else. Very different than today.

Bob Foote: Our team was basically made up of the 10 fastest guys in the area. Any other day these guys were my main competitors. Beat them and I win the race. Now all of a sudden we're a team. You can imagine the peer pressure. One guy runs an incredible, super-fast leg, which means I have to outdo his leg. If he ran a 25:02 leg, I'd have to go under 25 minutes on my leg. We were competing with each other, time-wise, and just killing ourselves. No one was backing off. In the third leg the guys were still hammering it. We were all marathon-type guys and some were saying, "Only 15 miles for the day is not enough. I'm supposed to do a long run today. I'm supposed to do a 25- to 30-mile run." So when one guy was running his leg, there'd be some of the other guys running the leg behind him, just to get the miles in. That was the mindset of our team. We were driven and focused.

Jim Sapp: While I was out running, I think it was my fourth leg, our van stopped in front of this house. My teammates got out and were waiting for me to arrive. A dog came out of the house and started barking at them. One of my teammates started walking down the driveway to say hello to the dog when the owner of the house came out and he fired a shotgun into the air. I was ignorant of this whole thing because I was running. I got to the exchange and my teammates were in a real hurry to get out of there after I made the tag. Then they told me the whole story. The interesting thing is I worked at Bonneville Power in Portland and I used to go out and run during my lunch hour. One day I was talking to a security guard who worked there. I'm not sure how we started talking about the relay, but it turned out he actually knew the guy who fired the shotgun. The security guard told me his friend said, "I didn't know what the hell all these guys were doing coming up my driveway."

John Stirniman: Carter Nakashima did the leg running up Bald Peak. It included 80 percent of the uphill and all the downhill. Unfortunately, the downhill is very steep and all the effort spent going up is wasted, because you're braking all the way down. We positioned ourselves near the apex of the hill, where we could watch Carter throughout his climb. From that distance you could see his legs moving, but he didn't appear to be getting any closer. As Carter approached, things got real quiet, just the opposite of our usual irreverent, loud behavior. We clapped lightly as he went past. I guess it was a subconscious show of our support and respect.

Kib Dacklin: On one of my legs I had to go up and over Bald Peak. It was something like two miles uphill, two miles downhill, and then a flat mile. When I started it my teammates said there was a runner just ahead of me and that I had to catch him. I caught him with about half a mile to go and we ended up having a full-on sprinting match to the end of the leg. I was dry heaving after that one.

Mike de la Cruz: Most of the time we were racing against a track team from Tigard High School. It was us old guys against them young guys. It was pretty competitive and they stayed with us until the last two or three legs. We finally finished ahead of them, but I give them a lot of credit. We kept jockeying back and forth and it was a fun race between two teams.

John Smets: I've run one and a quarter miles uphill in hot weather before, but it wasn't nearly so steep. This was two miles straight up. If this was an ordinary race, I would have been walking in the shade. The run downhill was shaking my kidneys. I overcame it by taking short steps. It's pretty when you stop to see where you've been, but not when you're running.

Jim Smith: We were running on gravel roads over Bald Peak with a flashlight in one hand, a car in front, and a car behind to light the way.

John Stirniman: When we got to the wine and farm country around Yamhill and Carlton, the temperature was much higher than earlier. The forecast was for the high 90s and we stopped frequently to offer water to our runners. Near a dairy farm there was another unfortunate exchange location, right next to a pond where the stench of manure, curdled milk, and ammonia was overpowering.

Later we stopped at *the* store in Carlton. The only employee, possibly the owner, was happy to see us. I asked him if we could get some water. He said we could now buy water in bottles, just like pop. I almost laughed out loud. Bottled water was an idea that was dead on arrival. No thanks. "If you could just fill our two water jugs, please." We loaded up on more junk food. As we were leaving, Mitch told the owner there were seven more teams behind us and that if he moved his sandwich board closer to the street, and wrote "Food, water, bathroom," he'd probably snag all seven to stop.

Bob Foote: My quads were blown out on the first leg. On my second leg I ran a slower pace, but my quads were just toast. The pain was unbelievable. By the time we got into our third legs we were up along the old Nestucca River, which runs out of the Coast Range. I knew what to do. I had them stop the car and let me out. I sat down in the river, which was ice cold with all the snow runoff. I just sat there for about 20 minutes and broke up all the lactic acid in my legs. I got out of the river and I was back at full strength. There was no soreness, my legs felt great, and I was ready to go again.

Jim Sapp: One thing we did that I don't think any team has done since is make it from Mt. Hood to the coast in daylight. When we hit the coast the sun had already set, but there was still a glimmer of sunlight. We still had to run from Pacific City to Cape Kiwanda in the dark. There were faster teams in subsequent years, but the starting times were staggered so those teams didn't start at dawn. And of course the race is longer now too.

John Stirniman: It was completely dark before I started the final leg and I hadn't anticipated running in the dark. We had camping gear, so I could carry a flashlight, but it was heavy and bounced around a lot. I needed something like a miner's hard hat. Our car followed close behind with its lights on and I felt better.

I'd never run fast in the dark before and it was a real rush. Everyone was waiting for me when I reached Pacific City and we jogged the final half-mile together. At the finish

Bob was standing by the side of the road, under a street light. He was holding a banner over his head that we couldn't read because the light was coming straight down from overhead. No doubt it said something inspirational. It was nearly 10 p.m.

Bob Foote: We rolled into Pacific City and there was this little parking lot and access point to the beach at Cape Kiwanda. The dory fishermen use it because you can drive on the beach at that point and launch your boats and then come back and park in the lot. We got there hours before the next team was expected and I set up my little makeshift finish line in the parking lot. I was waiting to be a one-man cheering squad. I was waiting there all night because I didn't have a clue when the next team would arrive. Finally, one by one, the other teams came trickling in.

Jim Smith: My last leg was the second to last leg into Pacific City. When we got close to the finish line everyone jumped out of the cars and we all ran, or kind of limped, across the finish together, even the guys who were banged up. That was very cool and it became a tradition for the race to have everyone come across the finish line together. We got to the finish and didn't have any plans for lodging or anything. A couple of guys slept in the camper, but most of us just slept on the beach.

Larry Dutko: Our younger, more optimistic competitors finished fifth, about three hours behind us "old guys." They were impressed that a sub-six-minute pace could be run by a bunch of "guys over 30." The respect they showed felt good and we all agreed that we had had a great time.

Mike de la Cruz: As I was running I knew it was going to be a huge success. It was so damn much fun. I had run ultramarathons and marathons and tons and tons of other races, but this one was so different. It was a great bonding experience. The guys I had raced against forever were now on my team and I was rooting them on. After that first year there were never any problems getting enough runners to form a team.

Bob Foote: Franco-American gave us some spaghetti for a little pasta feed on the beach. We also had stuffed gourmet hot dogs. They were injected with relishes and cheese and other really unhealthy stuff. That was the party. We made a little bonfire and did an awards ceremony. We had a bunch of beer, pasta, and stuffed hot dogs. The sports company Mizuno was trying to get into the running shoe market and offered to give a pair of running shoes to each member of the winning team, so we even had a few prizes.

John Stirniman: At the beach we saw the same faces we had seen at the early exchanges. Everybody was somewhat familiar with everybody else. Lots of stories were being exchanged. Since our team was first overall, we each won one Mizuno running shoe. They had only donated five pairs. Bob said he would have to see if he could get them to donate another five pairs.

Jim Smith: There was a beer company there, and they must have been expecting a lot of people because it seemed like they had a hundred cases of beer. But there were only about 80 people at the finish. The next morning they were going back to Colorado and they didn't want to take all the beer back with them, so here are all these high school kids walking around with two cases of beer. Holy @#$%! A couple of the older guys were drinking the beers for breakfast.

I don't know if I took a step longer than six inches the next day. I was so stove-up. It lasted for a good four or five days. I was so sore. Every muscle in my body, every capillary, was sore. I was just beat up. We lost some guys, but we had a ball and I still have the first T-shirt.

Bob Foote: After the race, standing on Kiwanda Beach, the first question I asked everyone was, "Do we want to do this again?" The response was overwhelmingly, "Absolutely! Let's do it again next year." Everybody just had a ball.

John Stirniman: My car was trashed. The seats were wet, and it stunk to high heaven, but we all agreed to run again the next year. No arm twisting was required.

1982 HOOD TO COAST RESULTS

1) 15:52:50 (5:45) Road Kill (Portland) – 1st Men's Submasters: Larry Dutko, Bob Foote (captain), Brendon Kelly, Paul Kingzett, Carter Nakashima, Jim Sapp, Mitch Steeves, Erik Sten, John Stirniman, and Gary Wilborn

2) 18:03:21 (6:33) N.U.T.T.S.-n-B.U.T.T.S. (Kennewick, Washington) – 1st Mixed Open: Gloria Sherfey (captain)

3) 18:19:25 (6:38) Spur of the Moment (Portland) – 1st Mixed Submasters: Ernest Hodgin (captain)

4) 18:47:07 (6:48) Name Unknown (Portland) – 1st Men's Masters: John Smets (captain)

5) 18:55:39 (6:52) Top Ten (Tigard) – 2nd Men's Submasters: Kib Dacklin (captain)

6) 20:06:00 (7:17) Rampage Sports (Beaverton) – 2nd Mixed Submasters: Tim Rhode (captain)

7) 20:12:26 (7:19) Name Unknown (Portland) – 3rd Men's Submasters: Landy Sparr (captain)

8) 21:28:40 (7:47) Name Unknown (Portland) – 1st Men's Open: Bill Elliot (captain)

```
                    HOOD TO COAST RELAY 1982


     Eight teams began and finished this first annual 165.55 mile trek
from snow to surf.  Congratulations and a warm thank you go out to all
of you who participated in this run over demanding terrain.  Those of you
who had a chance to lift his eyes above his feet and the sweltering
pavement observed some of northern Oregon's most beautiful landscapes.
As if the hills were not tough enough, the 95 + temperatures and night
running made this a supreme physical and mental challenge.

     I hope that all who participated found this to be a challenging
adventure and welcome alternative to a summer filled with "flat, fast"
10k races.  Closer and new friendships and a strong sense of group com-
radary are the major benefits of this kind of event.  Another one is
the satisfaction of digging down for and delivering that extra effort
when you really hurt because you know nine other people are depending
on you.

     No one reported getting lost, which is truly amazing considering
the length of this run.  Thanks go out to Dan Deakins and Fred Nielson
who worked jointly with me to pull this event off.  Dan did a great job
putting the picnic together, lining up sponsors, and giving us some
local support at the finish.  Likewise, Fred can be thanked for getting
us off at the start and the great lime marking at all turns throughout
the course.  We are already discussing next year's event.  Involvement
of local T.V., radio, and other major sponsors would let us expand this
event greatly.  Not only would we get more attention and recognition
for this challenge, but the awards and a totally catered picnic/party
afterwards could be greatly expanded upon.  If anyone would like to get
involved in the planning of next years race or have suggestions/criticisms
please contact me.  (223-2390 or 224-0268)

See you next year,


Bob Foote

                         TEAM RESULTS

1.  Bob Foote, Captain, Prt. 15:52:50. . .5:45/mile. . .1st male submasters
2.  N.U.T.T.S -n- B.U.T.T.S
    Gloria Sherfey, Kennewick 18:03:21. . .6:33/mile. . .1st mixed open
3.  Ernest Hodgin, Portland  18:19:25. . .6:38/mile. . .1st mixed submasters
4.  John Smets, Portland     18:47:07. . .6:48/mile. . .1st male masters
5.  Top Ten
    Kib Dacklin, Tigard      18:55:39. . .6:52/mile. . .2nd male submasters
6.  Rampage Sports           (approx.)
    Tim Rhode, Beaverton     20:06:00. . .7:17/mile. . .2nd mixed submasters
7.  Landy Sparr, Portland    20:12:26. . .7:19/mile. . .3rd male submasters
8.  Bill Elliot, Portland    21:28:40. . .7:47/mile. . .1st male open
```

Results from the first Hood To Coast in 1982.

Bob Foote at the 1982 finish in Pacific City.

CHAPTER 2

Foote Notes

***BOB FOOTE** IS THE FOUNDER and chairman of Hood To Coast, and in many respects his story of how he became a runner is the story of the relay.*

I went to the University of Oregon in 1965 on a track scholarship under the legendary Bill Bowerman. We were national champs one year. Funny thing, I was actually a high jumper. Dick Fosbury—who invented the Fosbury Flop—and I were archrivals in high school. He went to Oregon State University, and we stayed rivals all the way through the U.S. Olympic Trials. He beat me out for a spot on the 1968 Olympic Team and then won the gold medal in Mexico City.

When I graduated from the Oregon School of Architecture in 1971 I figured it was time for the real world. I needed to start being a practicing architect and be done with high jumping.

After college I got into tennis. I got into running too. Frank Shorter won the gold medal in the marathon at the 1972 Olympics, and after that everyone got caught up in the running movement. But I was into tennis hardcore, really hardcore. I'm a very triple Type A, high-intensity, really competitive person, so I'm either all the way in or nothing. I'd play tennis seven days a week. Running was more of a casual thing.

Then I got burned out on tennis. I went cold turkey one day, said I can't do this anymore. I was turning into Ilie Nastase, a professional player with a terrible temper whose nickname was "Nasty." My wife didn't even know who I was. I'd get on the court and just go crazy. I didn't like the person I became. I was so competitive that when things didn't go my way I'd throw my racquet and cuss and swear. One day I just said, "I'm done." I hung up my tennis racquet. I knew I wasn't mature enough to play tennis and couldn't handle it emotionally.

That's when I became a hardcore runner. I needed something to motivate me to stay in shape. So I bought all these books on running and used running a marathon as my carrot. I figured if I ran a marathon, even if I never ran another one, I'd be in good enough condition where I could just sort of maintain it for the rest of my life.

I came up with my own training program based on the books and said, "Okay, I'm starting from scratch. I'm going to run the Trail's End Marathon in Oregon four months from now." I started running from base level zero and within a month I was running 40 miles a week.

I was quasi-injured the entire time during my training for that first marathon. Something would break down, but I'd keep running. It would heal up and something else would go, but I kept running. I was up to about 65 miles a week as the marathon date was drawing closer, even getting in a couple of 20-milers. The target for my first marathon was three hours and 30 minutes, an eight-minute pace.

Fittingly, the marathon was in Seaside. Race day was in February of 1978 and it was raining and 37 degrees with 40-mph gusting winds. It was an out-and-back racecourse, which meant for the first 13.1 miles the wind was at the runners' backs. Then you turn around and face 13.1 miles of headwinds. Just a killer course.

Naturally, I started out running way too fast. I turned around and began fighting the wind. The gusting wind was picking people up and pushing them into ditches. All I had on were shorts and a T-shirt. At mile 21 hypothermia set in and my pace dropped dramatically, but I still had enough left in the tank. I finished the race in three hours and 31 minutes—one minute off my goal and a couple of seconds a mile off my targeted pace.

I was hooked. I should have known there was no chance I—again, Type A—would run only one marathon as a carrot to get in shape and never do it again. Not a chance.

I seriously got into running and started piling up marathons and extending myself into ultramarathons. Pretty soon I was doing 50-mile and then 100-mile races. I did the Western States 100-Mile Endurance Run. My marathon time went from 3:31 down to 2:31. I became a pretty fast runner, one of the fastest guys in the Portland area. I was really competitive and winning a lot of races, training 100 miles a week, running 30-minute 10Ks, and really pushing hard.

At the same time I opened my own architecture firm. I finished my three years of apprenticeship, passed my exams, and started my own firm. I wanted to be in control and didn't want to work for someone else. I wanted to be Number One. I was a 30-something architect consumed by running, health and fitness, and architecture.

By 1980 I was involved with the Oregon Road Runners Club, the second largest running club in the country, second only to the New York Road Runners. I was competing in all their races and they asked me to join the race committee because I had a lot of ideas and energy.

I learned how to organize and run events, and developed some manuals on how to do it right. Pretty soon they wanted me to run for the board of directors. I got on the board and by the early 1980s I was president of the Oregon Road Runners. I was getting pretty well known in the running community, and it gave me a position to sort of make my mark in road racing in the Northwest.

At the same time, I'd been running such high mileage it was becoming difficult to keep myself motivated. You can only run so many marathons and ultramarathons. I was asking myself, "Why am I going through this?"

Then the Roseburg to Coos Bay Relay planted a seed. I needed a new adventure in my life, and the idea of doing a relay was really a way for me to separate 1982 from 1981 and the blur of races before that.

The first year of Hood To Coast we had eight teams with 10 runners. After the first year I thought if we ever got up to 25 teams our race would be a true success. Roseburg to Coos Bay had between 25 and 30 teams, so with 25 teams I figured we'd be legit. That was my goal after the first year, to someday get the thing up to 25 teams.

Every time I modified the course I'd re-measure the whole thing. I think I re-measured the racecourse at least six times the first six years. I had to re-bike it every single year.

In year two I put out a race flyer and a little bit of interest started rolling in. A week before the race about 25 teams had signed up. I thought, "Great! We're there! We've done it, we've hit our goal."

Of course I should have known, the way runners are, they're all last-minute entrants. I was thinking things were pretty well capped off and finalized. Then during the next seven days, as race day approached, we found ourselves at 64 teams! Now I was panicked, saying, "Oh my God!"

I was just hammered trying to register, seed, and get all these guys in. The race was Friday morning. I pulled an all-nighter on Wednesday night, and more teams kept coming in. I had to start over to seed the new guys.

By Thursday night I hadn't slept in 48 hours. I called my teammates and said, "I'm going to be up all night again. Can we replace me? There's no way I can run." I was pissed because the whole reason I did this race was so I could run it. All of a sudden, year two rolls around and I don't even get to run in my own race. I was majorly bummed.

I sent those 64 teams out and I was almost hallucinating. I didn't know when I was awake or when I was asleep. I'd shut my car off at an exchange waiting for runners to come through and fall asleep. I'd almost fall asleep while driving and have to pull off the road, slap myself around, open the windows, and throw water in my face. I was completely out of it during the whole race.

After year two I said, "I can't do this by myself again. There's no way."

Heading into year three I knew we needed to set up a race committee to help me. Finding the people wasn't a problem. The challenge was for me to give up a little bit of the control and delegate some responsibility to others.

At my architecture firm, when a draftsman finished a drawing he'd make a print and send it to me. I'd take a red pen and mark it all up: change, change, change. "Now that's the way I want it." And they go and make all the changes. That's the way I kept total control over everything.

I took a similar approach to the race. I had my race committee of five guys. One guy was responsible for the start, another guy was responsible for the racecourse, another guy was doing some public relations, and the other guys were doing whatever. They all had their responsibilities.

After working with me for two years the whole group came to me and said, "We're resigning. We can't work this way anymore. You redo every single thing that we do or we propose to do. What you need is a clone of yourself, a five-way clone of yourself, because you don't want us to use our brains or our creativity; you want everything exactly the way you want it and that's it. We can't work that way."

My mind was moving fast and I was thinking I had two options. I could take back all the responsibility and kill myself trying to do it all; or I could let go and trust these guys to do it. Of course, I said, "Okay, I'll step back and I'll allow you guys a lot more wiggle room. I'll give you a lot more freedom."

That experience also helped my architecture practice. It taught me to start backing off and trusting people more. As HTC got bigger I had to trust other people much more. It was a great growth vehicle for me personally. I had to come miles from where I was—close-minded and control-oriented—where my way was the only way.

We continued to grow without any real marketing. Just a race flyer at the running stores and the rest was word of mouth. In our third year we had 150 teams; by year four, 238; and by year five, 405. It was getting big and out of control. It was elbow to elbow at the finish at Cape Kiwanda in Pacific City. Like sardines packed in a can. We capped it at 500 teams for year six.

By 1988 we were at 500 teams and turning a lot of others away. We had to think about a new home for our finish area because Kiwanda Beach was just too small. I was open to other locations, but in the back of my mind I was hoping Cannon Beach would work. I remembered it as this really pretty, long beach.

In searching for a new finish area I started in Pacific City and drove north along the

Oregon coastline. At every beach outlet I'd drive out and take a look. Normally the initial hit was—nope, wrong—and I'd move on. Or if it had some merit I'd start thinking about how we would get to it. Were there access points from the east, north, and south? If not, I'd move on. The path to the beach, hotels and other accommodations, all those kinds of things also came into consideration.

When I got to Cannon Beach I rolled in and thought, "Uh-oh, the access is terrible. We've only got one way to get in here. You'd have runners coming down the same roads as the vans. This would be a disaster!" I was really bummed Cannon Beach wouldn't work out.

I hadn't initially considered Seaside. I had pigeonholed it, along with Lincoln City and some other coastal cities, as either too big or as having the wrong personality. Then I rolled into Seaside and went down to the Promenade. The beach looked great. There was good access from the east, north, and south. Runners could come into town on a completely different route than the vehicles. There were plenty of accommodations. It really looked good and had a lot of promise.

Then I went to see the Seaside city officials. They wanted the runners to come into town on 12th Avenue—the most northern point coming into town with beach access. They wanted us to stay away from Broadway Street in downtown because that's where all the tourists were. They said as long as we stayed out of everyone's way we could do our little party up north and have fun. So that's the way we planned it.

Logistically, moving to Seaside was a major undertaking. It was a brand-new racecourse. These days we're always changing things, always refining and tweaking things, but nothing compared to a whole new racecourse.

We started from scratch. New exchange points and new everything. Two guys from the race committee took on the task of designing the course and they did a great job. It was a huge undertaking. And now we were looking at the course with different eyes. An exchange needed enough space for vans to park and for all the other necessary logistics. We were still using scenic backroads, but by now we were doing five-and-a-half-mile legs or seven-and-a-half-mile legs. That was plenty good enough. No more making every leg five miles to the inch.

The first year in Seaside was 1989, and we expanded to 550 teams. We finished at the end of 12th Avenue, right out on the beach. Big party. Fun party. Everybody was happy.

The Seaside people, however, came back immediately after the race and said, "We didn't see any of your people. No one was downtown spending money. Next year, we want you down on Broadway at the turnaround because we want you in town spending some money." They saw the relay was a big deal and could have a positive economic impact on the city.

That got us into Seaside and within three or four years we were up to 1,000 teams.

In 1991 I decided to go full-time with HTC. I'd had some serious health issues and a kidney transplant. I had about 50 architects working for me and three minor partners in the firm. I was working from eight o'clock Monday morning until noon on Wednesday at the architecture firm and from noon on Wednesday through Friday afternoon at HTC's offices. I was putting in 40 hours at HTC and 40 hours at the architecture firm. It was really taking a toll on me. I knew it was a scenario for not living very long.

HTC was at a crossroads. There was a small window of time where it could become really big. If I didn't do it now, the opportunity was going to be gone, and someone else would do it. I'd end up either being entrenched in the architecture firm or just dropping over dead.

I decided on HTC. I'd get really serious about it and treat it as professionally as my architecture firm because now it had to support me full-time. I called my partners in and dropped the bomb on them, "I'm taking an indefinite leave of absence that I doubt I'll ever return from." Then I went full-time HTC.

After a few years in Seaside, as the race got bigger and bigger, there was some opposition from people who lived there year round. It was an inconvenience. People couldn't move around because the streets were clogged. They didn't like having the runners in town and they didn't like the race.

Some of the merchants were complaining about the runners not spending money in their shops. They didn't buy a lot of the things Seaside tourists normally buy. They'd rather pay for good meals and hotels.

I asked them to look at the long-term benefit. From an economic impact standpoint, you've got people from all over the world coming to Seaside, and they will come back and visit the city again, and they'll bring their families. That's when they'll go into the tourist shops.

People who understood the economic value of HTC loved and embraced the event. Seaside knew they couldn't buy this kind of advertising and exposure, but still a lot of people who retired in Seaside didn't like the inconvenience of the Saturday race finish in their community.

It came to a head when the city manager asked me to change the dates of the race. They wanted us to stage it in either May or June or after Labor Day, when the kids are in school. I said, "We just can't. It has to be during the dry part of the year, and it rains until

July 4th in western Oregon." There was no way I was going to put on a race and have it snowing at Timberline Lodge. It also had to be during summer vacation because we have people from all over the world coming and they wouldn't be able to attend if the race wasn't during summer break.

We fought about the dates for several years. I'd say, "HTC is bigger than any one city. We'll leave before being forced to change the date to May, June, or September."

Finally, they decided to poll the merchants to see what dates between July 1 and Labor Day they preferred for the race. The poll indicated the weekend before Labor Day was the slowest for merchants. Nobody travels that weekend because everyone is getting ready for Labor Day and the end of summer. It was their dead weekend.

For the first 15 years or so the race was held on the weekend with the fullest possible moon. Having a full moon meant it was almost like twilight, you could see a lot better. Every year when picking the date I'd call the planetarium at OMSI (Oregon Museum of Science and Industry) and ask them, "Within this two week window in August, when will the moon be the fullest?" There was a huge advantage to being able to run with that illumination, so the race weekend bounced around.

After seeing the results of the merchant poll we agreed to compromise and make the last weekend in August our race weekend. We knew it was hard for them to plan when we moved the race dates every year based on the moon. We gave up the full moon, but we also discovered it was typically the nicest weekend of the year, weather-wise, in Seaside.

A few years later they did a study again and found the slowest weekend of the year had become one of their biggest weekends of the year. The city has more people, does more business, and sees a bigger positive economic impact on HTC weekend than nearly any other weekend of the year.

Our relationship with the city is really solid now. I tell war stories about the early years to the staff now and they go, "Hey, these guys are great to work with." In the old days it wasn't always that way, but that's in the past, and there's a great relationship now.

The game plan with my daughter, Felicia, had always been that at some point in her career, maybe about 20 years after she graduated college and was ready for a change, she would come on board to work at HTC. She'd only been out of college for a couple of years in 2006 when I called and asked her to reconsider her plan. The complexity of the race was increasing and I was getting up there in age. I didn't want to be working as hard as I was when I got to be 70. There was no other exit strategy, and I needed her sooner than planned. She agreed and said it was something she'd always wanted to do since she was a little child hanging out on the edge of the finish line stage.

She's the most detail-oriented, analytical person I've ever known outside of myself. I could never hope to get somebody from the next generation who is as detail-oriented as she is. It would drive me crazy to have someone who is more of a generalist, who blows off the details, and skips to the main things. This event is all about the details.

My role has changed in recent years. I try to see the big picture of the race as it's happening and stay out of the logistics and the staff's role in the event. I'll have input after the race about the start and the finish and things I observe that should be addressed. However, I don't get actively involved except to do all of the seeding. That's still my thing. Outside of that I just try to be available and keep my eyes open.

One thing that hasn't changed since year one is the sense of anticipation as the first waves of runners take off. HTC is a living, breathing entity. It has a life of its own and is going to do what it wants to do. It's way bigger than any of us.

When we're at the start line and the first runners take off I give a sigh of relief. Once we're on the road nothing can stop us. Anything can happen right up to that point, but when those first runners leave—it's done. It's time to relax. It's going to do its thing and the waves of runners are going to keep rolling out.

Felicia Hubber and Bob Foote

CHAPTER 3

The Early Years

THE INAUGURAL HOOD TO COAST featured eight teams of 10 runners. Founder Bob Foote believed the race would be a success if it one day saw a field of 25 teams. In year two, it appeared the number of entries would fall short of that mark. The week before the relay, however, entries started to flow in and 64 teams started the relay. Over the next few years, the number of teams jumped from 150 in 1984 to 500 in 1987 when the size of the field was capped for the first time.

Patti McDonald was married to Bob Foote, the founder and chairman of Hood To Coast, from 1975 through 1995.

The first group of crazy guys that ran the race in 1982 had the time of their life. Hood To Coast was born.

Word spread, the race grew, and we realized we had to get organized. Hard to believe, but people actually wanted to run through the middle of the night and the next day, all for the glory of having said they ran from Mt. Hood to the coast of Oregon.

For the second year we made entry forms, had people sign waivers, and printed up some T-shirts. We had no money and the race had no money, so the first couple of years the T-shirts were cheap and thin, albeit 100 percent cotton. It was all we could afford and I remember the runners complaining about the quality! I thought if they wanted better shirts, we'd have to raise the price to participate in the relay.

I was working full-time as the director of volunteer services in one of the Portland hospitals and entered all the race entries at night. I was also helping out with Bob's architecture firm and caring for our daughter, Felicia.

Running had definitely become a priority in Bob's life. Our accountant and family members held an intervention with him, trying to get him to focus more on architecture and not so much on running. In his defense, I told them running makes Bob happy and he loves it. And so, it continued. The race still didn't make any money. I remember how exciting it was after the second or third year when there was enough money left after paying the bills to buy a new odometer for his bike.

Those early years were definitely a family affair, with Felicia and me up at Timberline Lodge to help out with the start. Then we drove to Pacific City and set up a finish banner. I'd handwrite the numbers of the runners as they crossed the finish line, while keeping an eye on a two-year-old running around. There were no special perks for the event organizers. I remember spending a couple of hours in a sleeping bag on the ground in a parking lot across the street from where the runners had just finished.

Our close friends and family members served as volunteers at the start, finish, and exchanges. They would wait for the last runner to go through and then leapfrog down the course to get ready for the next wave. It was exhausting work for our friends and relatives. After a few years we realized we couldn't keep burning them out by asking them to spend a whole full moon weekend in August serving as our race volunteers. That eventually led to the team volunteer requirements.

The race quickly outgrew the small parking lot in Pacific City and the finish moved to Seaside. As the race continued to grow, so did the sales of souvenir merchandise. That became my responsibility too—T-shirts, jackets, baseball caps, posters, and Tyvek jackets. Our garage and rec room became storage areas for the boxes and boxes of merchandise that would accumulate for the race.

After working at the hospital, I'd come home, prepare dinner, and help Felicia with her homework. Then I entered each runner and volunteer into the HTC database, slept a few hours, and went back to work at the hospital.

I spent many days before each race counting T-shirts, loading boxes into rented trucks, and then driving to Mt. Hood to set up the souvenir merchandise tent. After the start we'd load up everything and drive to Seaside and do the same thing there. We'd work with volunteers until the wee hours of Sunday morning after the finish party ended.

There were some very difficult years when Bob's Lupus flared up and his kidneys failed, causing him to go on home dialysis for a year before a kidney became available. Bob's first kidney transplant wasn't 100 percent successful and after three years of trying to keep that kidney healthy, he went back on dialysis. It was another year of waiting for a donor until a match was found and another transplant happened in 1993.

Most people didn't know how sick Bob was. Thanks, however, to a great board of directors, and with help from family, friends and volunteers, the race continued to take place, and continued to grow.

Bob decided to leave the architecture business in 1991, so it became important that HTC begin to make money and provide our family with some income. We still had my salary from the hospital, which thankfully included medical insurance for our family. When Bob took the plunge to go full-time with the race, a marketing director and an office assistant were hired, and we rented office space in Portland. Up until then, all the phone calls, mail, storage, and work was done out of our home. HTC began to grow bigger and bigger each year, to the success that it is today.

From helping Bob mark the course that first year through the 1994 event, I was intimately involved in HTC, and I'm proud to say it has become the largest relay event in the world. But stress and illness can cause couples to come together or can drive them apart. In our case, the marriage ended in divorce in 1995.

I'm so proud of my daughter Felicia, who's doing a great job as HTC president and has incredible support and help from her husband Jude (HTC Race Series CEO) and a wonderful team. I'm sure the event will continue for years to come. I hope so, because I now thoroughly enjoy my HTC weekends babysitting my grandson while his parents work.

It isn't easy to share my story and there is a lot that remains unwritten. But I hope people can understand the passion, dedication, and hard work it took to take a dream and make something like HTC happen. As they say, "It takes a village."

Dan Gauger was born in Portland and now lives in Vancouver, Washington. His first Hood To Coast was in 1983, and he has participated in the event more than 30 times.

My goal as a runner was to enter every 10K, 15K and half-marathon I could find. In early 1983 I was looking for something different and heard about this new relay race. It was going to start at Timberline Lodge and end in Pacific City. Each team had 10 runners. The first four runners would run four legs and everyone else would run three legs.

I worked at PGE (Portland General Electric) and was involved in the company's running club. I put out a notice to see if anyone was interested in being a part of a team for this relay and barely managed to scramble together a full team. Some people thought I was completely mad! (And they still do.)

I remember that all 60 teams were supposed to start around 4:00 a.m. at Timberline Lodge, but we actually started a bit later—probably around 4:30 a.m. All 60 teams took off at the start and were followed by their support vehicles, everything from trucks to cars to vans to motor homes. Hardly anyone was on the roads when we were running, and porta potties were a bit scarce.

I remember running up a street in the West Hills by Gabriel Park. I also remember an exchange point out near the Colton/Yamhill area. It was real hot and we stopped near a hog farm. What a smell!

The exchange points were every five miles and some of the handoffs were a bit dicey. Parking was also interesting. When we pulled into the community of Hebo it was dark and all these vehicles started showing up. I remember a county Sheriff pulled up and asked us, "What the *hell* is going on here?"

I ran the very last leg, which was my fourth leg. I didn't realize that the last leg was an extra six-tenths of a mile. I was checking my watch and thought I was getting near the finish line based on my pace. But there was no finish line! There were only one or two other runners even remotely close and I thought I was lost. Finally, I saw the lights at the parking lot at Cape Kiwanda. It was about 12:30 a.m. There were maybe a couple dozen people hanging around. There was this one guy with a bullhorn and a garbage can full of beer! That guy was Bob Foote.

Melissa Bishop lives in Ridgefield, Washington, and is a retired Portland police officer. She first participated in Hood To Coast in the 1980s and has run in the event more than 20 times.

When I was attending Oregon State University I had a summer job with the Multnomah County Road Department. My boss at the time was a runner and had heard about Hood To Coast. He was talking about getting a team together, and as I was running at the time he asked me to join. Our team was called Fleet Feet.

That was the first year I ran HTC and I'm pretty sure it was the second year of the race (1983).

When I first heard about the event it sounded crazy. At the time all the legs were five miles. I thought, "Five miles, that's not too bad. I can do that." Afterward I realized it was a lot harder than I thought.

I'm pretty sure I ran three legs that first year, although it could have been four. I don't remember seeing a lot of people out on the course and there weren't any volunteers telling us which way to go. We had a map with the route and as far as finding the right way, I don't remember it being a really big issue. When we ran at night we held flashlights; we didn't have headlamps or reflective vests.

It was a lot of fun—I mean, I did it again! It was a lot different back then. All the teams started together at the same time. We didn't have vans. I think we used Broncos. We were all together at Timberline Lodge for the start and our team's two vehicles stayed together almost the entire course. One van would drop off a runner and then they'd leap-frog ahead, and then the two vehicles would pretty much stay together. I remember it being really tight quarters and not having a lot of space in the Bronco.

Everybody stayed pretty close together because there wasn't the congestion that there is today. We didn't have to rush like you do now and hustle to the next exchange so that you don't miss your runner. You were lucky if you even saw another runner on the road.

The first time we did it we finished late at night and there was nobody around. There were just a couple of cases of beer by a lamppost in a parking lot—and that was the finish line!

Jim Sapp *was a member of the Road Warriors/Road Kill team that finished first in the inaugural Hood To Coast in 1982.*

During the second year of Hood To Coast in 1983, we had to come through down-town Beaverton. One of our runners, Gary Wilborn, was trying to stay ahead of another team that wasn't terribly far behind us. Gary was a pretty quick runner. He was heading down one of the main streets in Beaverton. We saw the stoplight was getting ready to change, so we all got out of the van and started motioning to stop traffic in all four directions. I think everyone thought there were going to be a ton of runners coming through, and then Gary comes darting through the intersection all alone. After he passed we gave all the cars the "Go ahead" signal.

We got a lot of really angry stares, but nobody cursed out their windows. I imagine they were all thinking, "We stopped for one guy?"

There wasn't much media coverage of the race at the time. If there was any, it was done by the local newspapers and television stations close to the coast, rather than by the *Oregonian* of Portland.

At one point during the second year of the race there was a camera crew from a small town near the coast that worked really hard to get in front of us. They were trying to get some video footage of us passing the baton or of a runner taking off after the exchange.

It was a very hot day. The guy who took the baton on our team was wearing just short shorts, socks, and sneakers. He wasn't wearing a shirt because of the heat. The TV guys in the van with the camera were frantically trying to get into a school parking lot to shoot the handoff. Just as they swung their camera around and started filming, our teammate mooned us. He pulled his short shorts down halfway and ran about 100 yards before pulling them up.

It was actually more of a half-moon. I imagine the guys with the camera were going, "Oh, my God!" It may have been the first moonrise on the course.

Jerry Duncan has been participating in Hood To Coast since 1984. The Aloha, Oregon, native began running in the late 1970s to lose weight and has completed more than 80 marathons and 100 ultramarathons.

In 1983 my wife, Pat, and I were on our way back from competing in a motorcycle desert race in eastern Oregon. By chance we stopped in Sandy for lunch. We saw a bunch of runners who looked like they were in some sort of organized event and our curiosity was aroused. Since we had no idea what the run was all about, we did some sleuthing once we got home and discovered Hood To Coast. At that time the race was only in its second year.

Pat decided she wasn't interested in running a relay race. However, I was a runner at the time and was really intrigued about doing something different from the usual 10Ks and marathons. I shared what little I knew about HTC with my good friend John Hanan and he was equally excited about running the relay. We began to recruit other runners to see if we could put together a complete team. The people we talked with had never heard of a team relay and were a little skeptical of the idea, but with John's help we were able to find eight other runners who were interested in joining us for an unusual and exciting event.

As a result, we signed up our newly formed team, Achilles and the Ten Dons, to run HTC in 1984.

At 40, I was the oldest member of our team, and none of us had ever run a relay before—let alone an event that spanned two days. That's the reason we really knew nothing about the logistics required to complete a relay and had to learn many things the hard way during our first year.

We split the team among three cars the first time, with three or four runners in each vehicle. It wasn't until years later that we started using vans. Although we tried to put together a plan for our team, it was really up to each car to decide how and when to get their runners to and from the course, as well as when to meet up with the other vehicles and runners. After their first set of legs, our runners went to their homes in Portland to eat and rest, before heading back out on the course. And only the third team vehicle actually went all the way to the finish line in Pacific City—the other two cars went home after they finished their third set of legs.

Our two original team volunteers in 1984 were my daughters, Julie and Laurie. Today they're still volunteering for our team. In fact, Laurie has volunteered more than 30 times and Julie has been a volunteer for more than 20 races, and Pat has also served as a volunteer.

It was so much fun that first year that we continued to run it the next year and the one after and the rest is history. Over 34 years we've had about 120 different runners on our team and 12 of those runners have been part of our team for more than 10 years, including five who are still running on our team.

In 1988 we changed our team name to Middle Aged Crazies, and the next year we became the Devotion to the Ocean team, before switching the team name to Scrambled Legs in 1991. Our team is now You Can Run but You Can't Hide.

Rich Kokesh *is from Portland and has run Hood To Coast eight times.*

Back in 1984 no one really knew Hood To Coast. I'd just graduated from Willamette University. At the time, unemployment in Portland was pretty high, and I was working at a moving and storage company in the city.

One day this new guy came to work. I didn't know him from Adam, but we started talking anyway.

I ran track in high school and was on the track team my senior year of college. I also played football in college and had recently started competing in triathlons and a lot of 10K road races. When my new co-worker learned I was a runner, he said, "I know this guy who knows a doctor who's putting together a relay team. Would you be interested?"

This was on Wednesday, and I said, "Sure." He said, "Let me check to see if I can get you on the team." On Thursday he told me, "You're in." Then I asked him for some details. "Everything's taken care of," he said. "All you need to do is show up at St. Vincent's Hospital tomorrow night at 9 p.m. with your running gear." And that was everything I knew heading into this thing.

When I showed up at 9 p.m. Friday night, there are two Volkswagen vans in the hospital parking lot. A bunch of guys in their early to mid-20s were loading them up. I didn't know any of the guys, but I got in one of the vans and we headed to Mt. Hood. On the drive, one of the guys told me that none of them had done the race before. Then he said, "All the legs are five miles." I was thinking, "Okay, I'm good for a five-mile leg."

After that they told me, "We start at Timberline Lodge and the race ends in Pacific City." It was then that I realized it was going to be more than one five-mile leg. That was my "Aha" moment, when I finally understood what HTC was all about.

Another of my new teammates asked, "Who wants to run three legs, and who wants to run four legs?" I was looking in my bag. I had one T-shirt, one pair of shorts, and my running shoes—and that was it! Everybody else seemed much better equipped. Although, one of my vanmates did take a little pity on me and gave me an extra pair of running shorts.

The doctor who put the team together (I can't recall his name) was from St. Vincent's and had graduated from the University of Oregon. He named our team the Hayward Grandstanders, after the school's legendary track and field stadium in Eugene, Hayward Field.

Back then every leg was five miles, and the vans leapfrogged each other. We started at Timberline and headed toward Pacific City. Somebody up front had directions, but not knowing anybody I didn't ask any questions.

At the start, we stood around and waited until between 1 and 3 o'clock in the morning to begin. There were probably around 150 teams, and there wasn't really any light. We were just standing around in the middle of the night. It was dark out and freezing cold. Somebody gathered a group together and yelled, "Go." That was the start!

The first time I ran the sun was already up, and I didn't have to worry about carrying a flashlight. In fact, all my legs were during the light of day. Although when we finished at Pacific City it was just starting to get dark.

It was really fun, although it was very anti-climactic at the beach. There was a keg of beer with a pump handle and a Weber kettle grill. They were cooking some hot dogs, and each runner got a ticket for a hot dog and a beer.

We had a hot dog and a beer, and then drove back to Portland.

Jim Sapp was a member of the Road Warriors/Road Kill team that finished first in the inaugural Hood To Coast in 1982.

In 1984 we got clobbered after finishing first in Hood To Coast the previous two years. The winners were very fast runners and beat us quite handily. Their team ultimately entered an A and a B team. The B team would later become the Killer Bees, a perennial race winner in the 1980s and 1990s. There was also another team from Washington that beat us that year, but not by a whole lot.

We always took really good care of our runners. We wanted to make sure they had water when they needed it, that they wouldn't mess up the directions, and that they knew where they were relative to where they needed to be.

In the early days you could stop along the side of the road without creating a traffic jam. So we were chugging along in our van out near Carlton while our runner and another guy were going head to head. There was a place where the course was somewhat confusing and we thought our runner might turn off on the wrong road. We stopped on the edge of that road and waited for our runner. When we saw him we motioned to him that the road he wanted to turn on was about a quarter-mile ahead.

While we were stopped there, the van for the team on our tail came up and we were doing some friendly trash talking. What they didn't realize was that where we stopped we were covering up some turn markers. There were plenty of signs and arrows pointing different directions, and although the HTC course was clearly marked, there was some uncertainty as to where you needed to turn.

At the exchange they were waiting and waiting for their runner. Finally, their runner showed up and was just screaming curses. You could hear him from 50 yards out before he reached the tag. He had gone down the wrong road.

We didn't deliberately block anything, but we did take care of our runner and they didn't.

Jerry Duncan has been participating in Hood To Coast since 1984. The Aloha, Oregon, native began running in the late 1970s to lose weight and has completed more than 80 marathons and 100 ultramarathons.

My first year running Hood To Coast was in 1984. Our team was Achilles and the Ten Dons.

Just like today, the first leg was down the mountain from Timberline Lodge to Government Camp. Foolishly, I decided to be our team's first runner. However, it turned out my body build really worked for Leg 1. I could run that first leg and not worry about getting injured, unlike a lot of other people.

I don't remember our exact start time, but it was dark out. I needed some type of light, but I didn't own a flashlight. The only thing I owned that was a portable light was this multi-battery thing that was similar to a miner's light.

I carried that sucker all the way from Timberline down to Government Camp. My arm was so tired by the time I got to the bottom of the mountain. I really learned my lesson. Ever since then we've used lightweight flashlights or headlamps, and don't carry anything heavy.

Felicia Hubber grew up in Portland, moved to Montana during high school, and attended college at the University of Montana. The daughter of Hood To Coast founder Bob Foote, Felicia was just a few months old when she attended the first HTC—and she's been at every relay since. In 2006 she succeeded her father as president of HTC.

My mom was an important person in the early years of Hood To Coast, always helping my dad. There was a time, early on in the evolution of the relay, when my dad went through two different kidney transplants because he has Lupus. He had just gotten out of a race committee meeting when he had a Lupus attack. His first kidney transplant was failing. He had to go back on dialysis, and it was just two or three weeks before the race in August when he had his second kidney transplant.

The race committee was about to stage a mutiny, and planned to take over the relay. They said, "Bob is incapable of doing this event. He just had a kidney transplant and is in the hospital. We're going to take this over and he's not going to be a part of it anymore."

My mom said, "I don't think so." She's a sweet person, but you don't cross her. She did so much of the last-minute planning and finalizing of the details for the race that year. I feel like she singlehandedly saved the relay while my dad was in a hospital bed. He made it to the race, but he was obviously very weak from the recent transplant surgery.

In 1995 my parents divorced, and I remember my mom saying to my dad, "You can have Hood To Coast. That's fine. I don't want to be part of it anymore. I don't need that stress in my life anymore."

Sandy Dukat (third from left) and The Amazing Awaits team.

CHAPTER 4

Do You Want To Run A Relay?

IT WAS A SIMPLE ONE page flyer that introduced Hood To Coast to the running world in 1982. All the pertinent details were highlighted, along with some additional background regarding the event: "All teams to monitor and guide their teammates through the course. If a wrong turn is made, runner must return to point on course where error was made and resume race."

In the early days of the relay, word of mouth played a key role in spreading information about the race. Media coverage and more recently, a documentary film, along with the growth of social media, have all played roles in expanding its reach.

One's personal introduction to HTC usually starts innocently enough. A friend will ask another friend if they want to run a relay race. How much information is exchanged after that depends on how good of friends they are. The better the friends, the less is probably said.

Kirk Helzer is from Tualatin, Oregon, and is a longtime competitor in Hood To Coast with the Dirty Half Dozen +6 team. His father, Richard, ran in the very first HTC in 1982.

Our team, the Dirty Half Dozen +6, dates back to when the race was first created, in 1982. A couple of our fathers, including my dad, competed in the very first event. Most of us were in early middle school and just starting our running careers and our friendships as a group of guys.

I can remember being a 12- or 13-year-old and trying to understand the first race. We were too young to run in it, but we were fascinated by the relay. We were used to running on a track and this was something that was totally different.

It was really cool to watch. There wasn't much in the way of spectators or fanfare. It was just the runners. It was small and very different from what we would experience in later years. By the second and third year you could see it was catching on. There were more and more teams signing up and you could tell it was going to keep getting larger.

We'd been asking for several years if we could form a team as a group of kids. Then a couple of guys from our high school participated on a team that was put together by our coach. The next year our parents said we could form a team if we had parents driving and serving as chaperones.

We formed a team with runners and friends to see if we could actually do it. We knew about marathons, but this was a totally different running event. The idea of starting up on a mountain and running to the coast as a team was unique. The team atmosphere is what really interested us.

The first couple of years were a compete blur. We were just kids excited about being out there running. The energy came naturally. My dad and our coach would tell us to not run like crazy kids and reminded us we needed to pace ourselves. We didn't do a very good job of listening, but we were young and could recover quickly. It was all about the racing. We enjoyed the competitive atmosphere of going head to head with other kids for an extended period of time—pushing each other along. And it's such a fluid race, you're either passing someone or someone is passing you all the time.

We're smarter now. We know we don't still have the legs to go out and sprint. When we were kids, we were young enough and brash enough to put ourselves through it.

The core members of our team, eight or nine guys, have all run HTC for more than 25 years. Everyone has missed a year here or a year there. Our motto is, "The team will be here next year." For us the big thing is continuing every year and keeping it going. We've all grown up together from our early high school years through the adventures of college, getting married, starting families, and having careers. One thing that was always a constant was getting back together to run the race.

Some of my fondest memories of HTC are having fun ripping each other and being in awe of my teammates running splits or times we didn't think possible. It's a unique race that provides those types of opportunities that no other race ever has.

When we were younger it was a grand adventure and a lot of fun. We didn't worry about injuries or nagging pains. That was the farthest thing from our minds when we were in our teens and early 20s. Now, as we enter our late 40s and 50s, it's all about maintenance. It's all about survival and keeping comfortable. I wouldn't say it's necessarily harder, it just now requires more effort in our preparation and training, along with trying to run smart.

It's still just as much fun. It's the same camaraderie. We're still like a bunch of teenagers out for a weekend on our own. That part of it hasn't changed, and that's my favorite part.

Rob Rickard *is from Canby, Oregon, and has participated in Hood To Coast every year since 1983. He has also been a course marker for the event for more than 25 years.*

I missed the first Hood To Coast because of a business appointment, but I've done every one since then, and I've been a team captain every year but one.

I've probably been running for close to 40 years. When I was younger I got in a situation where my back was giving me problems. My doctor told me, "You need to get out from behind your desk. You need to start walking." I started walking and got bored rather quickly, so I began running. I'd been competitive all my life and participated in sports in high school and college. I started saying, "Hey, this running is fun."

I would hear about races here and there. One of the salesmen that called on my company said, "Let's go run this race next week." That's how I got started in competitive running. After that, I kept saying, "When's the next race?"

Then HTC turned up on my radar. I had heard of relays, but the only ones I was familiar with were the 4x100 or the 4x400 sprint relays—stuff that you would encounter in high school or college track and field. I was intrigued by the HTC concept.

At that time, I was a member of the Oregon Road Runners Club, and Bob Foote was the president. The club was aware of any running events happening in the Portland area. When HTC popped up, it was mentioned in an article in *Oregon Distance Runner*, the official magazine of the Oregon Road Runners Club. Back then that was how you heard about events—there was no social media to check.

Following the first year of HTC there were a couple of articles in *Oregon Distance Runner* about runners that participated in the event. That definitely piqued my interest because in all the articles the runners talked about the camaraderie and the spirit of the event. Typically when you run, you go out and run alone or maybe you run with your neighbors. But I lived out in the woods and typically ran by myself.

The *Oregon Distance Runner* magazine was my connection to running and my introduction to HTC.

John Truax *was born in Montesano, Washington, and moved to Corvallis, Oregon, when he was in high school. He ran track throughout high school and at the University of Oregon. He began working at Nike in 1990 and continues to work for the company today. He was the captain of the Nike Hood To Coast team Mambu Baddu in 1993 and 1994.*

I first heard about Hood To Coast when I was in college at the University of Oregon. I worked in the lumber mills during the summers to help pay for school because I wasn't on a track scholarship—I made the team as a walk-on. I was working in a mill in St. Helens, on the other side of the Columbia River from Washington.

I was living with the family of a high school track coach. He was actually the high school coach of my college roommate Seth Simonds, which is how I got to know him. He put together a HTC team with a bunch of teachers and friends from St. Helens. Since I was living in his house at the time, he invited me to join the team.

It was 1985, and I really didn't know anything about HTC. The high school coach explained the event. I was always looking for an adventure and thought it'd be a fun way for me to get some good training runs in during the summer. He liked the fact that I might be a ringer for his team.

Everybody on the team was in their 40s, and I was just a 20-year-old kid. Everybody was serious about running, but it was a fun team. I went along with it and really enjoyed it.

One thing I remember is sleeping under a picnic table in a park somewhere in the Coast Range. It was raining and I laid my sleeping bag out on the ground underneath the table. When I woke up, I ran my third leg. My family spent a lot of time hiking and backpacking in the woods when I was growing up, so I knew bringing a sleeping bag would come in handy—and it did.

The race ended in Pacific City, and it was a nice sunny day on the beach. Our whole team got in the ocean after we finished. I remember hanging out that night with a bunch of drunk teachers.

The next time I ran HTC was after I finished college. I was living in Portland and working in a running store. I met some guys from the Nike Portland crew, a competitive running club back in the day. They were part of an HTC team called the Killer Bees that had been around for quite a while. It was either 1988 or 1989—I can't remember exactly—but we had a good time running.

We won that year and it got me excited for the future, but the next few years I didn't run HTC because I was busy with life and starting a family.

Dave Harkin *grew up in Seattle, attended the University of Oregon, and spent four years teaching in Louisiana, Colorado, and Seattle before returning to Oregon. He and his wife, Paula, have owned and operated the Portland Running Company since 2000.*

The first time I did Hood To Coast was in 1988. It was early on in the event and I was just a kid.

I was a high school senior in Seattle. I went to John F. Kennedy High School my first two years and then Roosevelt High School my last two years. At both schools I ran cross country and track, and for as long as I can remember I was a runner and soccer player.

Most of the guys on my HTC team were Kennedy alumni. I'd met them at alumni events, where they'd come and run with the track team when I was a student. They were all at least 10 years older than me and were a pretty tight group.

There are always stories about teams with a great race plan, and then two weeks before the event the plan starts crumbling when people are injured. In this case, I'm pretty sure I was one of those last-minute substitutions where they said, "Oh, this kid can probably run those legs." I imagine they started off with a team of guys between the ages of 25 and 35 who were engineers at Boeing or teachers or whatever. Then it got whittled down to me and a bunch of older guys. It happens to a lot of teams. As the race gets closer, teams are scrambling to fill those last slots.

Back then I didn't have a whole lot of parental supervision, so there wasn't really an issue with permission like there would have been for a normal high school kid. In most cases, it probably would have been, "No way are you doing that race." However, I just told my mom, "I'm going to be gone for the weekend and I'll be back on Sunday." That was it.

I'm sure if she'd seen me running through western Oregon in the middle of the night on a road without a shoulder she wouldn't have been thrilled. Not to mention the fact that a lot of drinking went on afterward. Not for me, but for everybody else, which was pretty funny.

We had two vans, but the logistics weren't the same as today. Our vans didn't split up. We went to the start together and stayed together throughout the entire race, and we all rotated between the two vans.

One van almost didn't make it to the start. On the way to Timberline Lodge we stopped in Seattle for gas. We went to fill up the tank and discovered that the gas cap was locked and we didn't have the key! I have a vivid memory of watching a bunch of engineers trying to open it using a screwdriver and banging on it with a hammer. In retrospect, that wasn't very smart, plenty of potential for sparks. Somehow, however, they hammered it open. Since they couldn't get the cap back, they just shoved a towel in there and we were on our way.

That was the beginning of what would be the funniest road trip I've ever experienced. It involved little food and a lack of sleep, and a bunch of guys at different fitness levels running their guts out.

I ran my first leg as fast as I could run five miles because I was young. I didn't have any understanding of not going out as hard as I could, or saving something for my other legs. Neither did I have a whole lot of knowledge about warming up or cooling down.

I remember thinking on my second leg there was no way I was ever going to be able to run those five miles. By my third leg I was devastated. I was as torn up as I'd ever been as an athlete. It was just brutal. I'm sure I went from running six-minute miles on leg one to seven-minute miles on my second leg to 10-minute miles my final leg.

We stayed up all night and changed vans every third or fourth exchange because we really didn't have a system. I remember jumping from one van to the other.

I don't know where we finished in the standings, but I think we did okay. When we got to the end in Pacific City we were all exhausted. I remember thinking there was going to be a big celebration, but I literally fell asleep on the beach at 8 p.m. and woke up in the same place at 8 a.m. the next morning.

It was like my coming of age. As a teenager I was getting exposed to all this craziness—the wild party at the end, sleeping on the beach for 12 hours, and waking up completely disoriented.

It was one of the biggest things I'd ever done and the farthest I'd ever run.

Steve Hanamura was born in Upland, California, and now lives in Portland. He has participated in Hood To Coast more than 25 times and served as captain of the team I Hurt, You Hurt, We All Hurt for more than 20 years. Blind since birth, he is an avid runner and sports fan.

Sports have always been important to me. I wrestled and ran track in high school. In 1978, when I was a counselor at a community college in Eugene, Oregon, I started to take my running more seriously.

I hadn't heard about Hood To Coast until I moved to Portland. My first running guide was an ultramarathoner and she had run HTC a couple of times, which is how I became aware of the relay.

My running guide trained me to run the Portland Marathon in 1983. As my running capabilities got stronger, I began thinking about participating in the relay. When I went to work for the phone company in Portland, I didn't know 11 other runners to put together a HTC team. I suggested to the phone company, "Hey, why don't you guys form a team for HTC and let me be on the team." And they said, "Sure."

So in 1990 I was ready to compete in the relay. I wanted to do it, but I wondered, "Am

I strong enough? Am I capable enough?" I had my doubts and thought, "I'm going to be the slowest person on the team. I'm not a good runner."

I had to fight through many internal conversations before I realized, "Wait a minute. I don't have to be the best runner. I just have to be a decent runner and a good teammate." As soon as I figured that out, I wanted to do it.

In 1995 I formed my own team called I Hurt, You Hurt, We All Hurt. When I started the team, a friend and I decided that on our team if you're in Van 2 you still have to go to the start at the top of the mountain to see Van 1 take off. We also determined that if you're in Van 1, you will wait until Van 2 is done and then the whole team will cross the finish line together. At the time, very few teams would cross the finish line together with their last runner. Now it happens with almost every team.

In order to be a real team, we thought it was important to start the race with the entire team and finish the same way. It has become a requirement to be on our team. And if you want to run on our team, you also have to be at our pre-race team dinner on Thursday, stay over Saturday night in Seaside, and have breakfast with the team Sunday morning.

As the captain, I screen all our prospective runners. Basically, I tell them, "Here's how fast we are. We're competitive, but we're not speedsters. We've got runners of all levels and capabilities. Some run a mile in six minutes and others may do it in 11 minutes. We're competitive among ourselves. We're probably not going to win, but we're definitely into building community."

I saw what happened with other teams, and that's why we established those requirements with my team. Other teams I ran with didn't care about each other. The runners in one van would say, "Hey, we're going to go get a drink." And they would do that while their teammates in the other van were still struggling on the course.

In my mind that wasn't being a real team. We have people come back and run with us year after year because we care about each other and connect with each other.

While I can be selective as to who gets on the team, there's no foolproof method that everything will work out. Although one thing I can definitely say is that it's not just about the runners. We have 12 runners, but we also have two van drivers and three volunteers who are just as essential.

My wife, Becky, works as an exchange coordinator, and she's also the glue that holds our team together. She communicates with our team and sends out all the emails, and gets the food ready for our Thursday night pre-race dinner.

When I talk about our HTC team, for us it's usually 17 or 18 people, not just the 12 runners, and that's really important!

Peter Courtney lives in Salem, Oregon, and has represented the 11th District in the Oregon State Senate since 1999. He is currently president of the Senate, a role he has served in since 2003.

I moved to Oregon in July 1969. At the time, I didn't know much about the state, wasn't sure where the plane was going to land, and didn't know a soul there. Shortly after I arrived I became aware that everybody runs in Oregon. It's like they run from conception to the moment they're on the embalming table. Everybody jogs, everybody runs, and everybody is outdoors.

Somehow I heard about Hood To Coast very early on when it was first founded by Bob Foote. It immediately appealed to me because I loved team sports. Then I learned somebody from near my home in Salem was involved in the event and I took an interest.

Finally in 1991 I ran my first HTC. I'd been trying to get on a team for several years but nobody wanted me and it made me depressed. I wasn't really built for distance running. I didn't have bird legs and didn't talk the language of runners. And I didn't wear a nice running outfit—I just had ragtag gear. I looked like a disaster and didn't think anybody was going to put someone like me on their team.

Then I learned that you could put your name in a pool. If a team needed a runner they could pull someone from this pool. I didn't think I was ever going to get picked, but one day before the race I got a call. It was from a team called AGC (Associated General Contractors) and they needed a runner. They didn't know me, and I didn't know them. They just said, "Show up here." That was it!

I remember meeting the team in the parking lot of the Fred Meyer in Sandy. I found their van, walked up, and said, "Hello." They told me I was Runner 7 and would have the first leg in Van 2.

I was over the moon that somebody finally put me on their team. But, I didn't know what I was getting into at the time. When everyone on the team saw me, they were taken aback. I imagine they were all wondering why it was me who was asked to join their team. I have no doubt they were worried if I'd be able to run all three of my legs.

I'll never forget that first time! I recall running my second leg during the middle of the night. The Killer Bees was a team that dominated back in those days, and one of their runners just went flying by me. It was one of the most demoralizing times of my life, but I swore I wouldn't walk. And I didn't.

I've never walked during my 20 times participating in HTC!

Kasha Clark *is an Oregon native from the small town of Lorane. She now lives in Portland and has been participating in Hood To Coast for over half her life.*

It was August 1996 in Lorane. I was 15 and my high school cross country coach called to see if I'd been training over the summer. I fibbed a little bit and said, "Yes." He then explained that there was a team that needed a last-minute substitute runner for Hood To Coast. At the time, I had heard about HTC but didn't really know what it was all about.

I agreed to run and a few days later, since I was too young to drive, my mom dropped me off at a stranger's house on a Thursday night. The next morning we woke up before sunrise and drove the four hours to Timberline Lodge. I had no idea what I was getting myself into. I didn't pack any food and only brought some spare clothes and a sleeping bag.

I was going to be Runner 5. I distinctly remember questioning whether I was truly a runner during my first leg and swore that I was never going to run again. I remember it being really hot and miserable. The team I was on was the Guaranty RV team called the Roadtrekers—and I remember we had a nice new luxury Road Trek conversion van.

By the time the race was over I'd forgotten all about the misery of Leg 5 and was ready to run again. At the finish line I met and had my photo taken with Alberto Salazar.

I ran with the same team again the following year and then took 1998 off. After that I decided to never miss another year of HTC. I proceeded to run with various teams over the years. Usually it was with strangers who were looking for a last-minute runner. Sometimes I stayed on a particular team for a few years, until they lost out in the lottery. Then I would get picked up by another desperate team in need of a runner.

In 1999, when I was 18, I ran as the only woman on the TrusJoist Silent Floor team. One year, I was so desperate to join a team that I planned to get dropped off at Timberline the morning of the race with a sign and a backpack—just hoping that some team would need a runner. Luckily, I ended up finding a last-minute opening before settling for that frantic plea.

My commitment and dedication to this race is a part of me. My life goal is to be the person who has run HTC the most times. While I know I have a lot of catching up to do, I've been running this relay over half my life—longer than I've been driving a car!

Jeff Glasbrenner *is originally from Boscobel, Wisconsin, and now lives in Golden, Colorado. He was a member of the Hood To Coast team The Amazing Awaits in 2008 and 2009.*

I'm originally from Wisconsin. When I was eight I was involved in a farming accident. I was with my dad and we were cutting hay. I was in the wrong place at the wrong time when he turned on the machine and I lost my right leg right below the knee.

After losing my leg I was always told what I couldn't do by doctors and others. The bad thing was I accepted that I couldn't do a lot of things. Then I went to college at the University of Wisconsin-Whitewater and found a coach who believed in me and I started playing wheelchair basketball.

Through a lot of hard work I became a member of the Team USA wheelchair basketball team at three Summer Paralympics, winning one bronze medal. After my wheelchair basketball days, I began participating in Ironman-distance triathlons. In 10 years I completed 25 full Ironman-distance events, along with several marathons. Recently I started climbing mountains and in 2016 became the first American amputee to summit Mt. Everest. I've also been to Antarctica, where I skied to the South Pole and then climbed a mountain.

I like to stay active and busy, and I like pushing past people's perspectives about what a disabled person can accomplish.

I was sponsored by The Hartford, an insurance company, and did some public speaking for the company about the Paralympics and the company's involvement with U.S. Paralympics. I didn't know anything about Hood To Coast before I started working with The Hartford, but they knew I was a runner and in 2008 they asked me to run the relay. I was like, "Sure. No problem." It was an invitation to compete—and I never turn down one of those!

I showed up in Oregon for HTC without knowing anything about the event or its history. I quickly learned a lot. All of a sudden, we were with thousands of other people shuffling in and out at the starting line. It was really neat and I remember being in awe of the mountain and the whole event. It was a big spectacle and something I never knew existed—and now I was part of it.

Being in the van with my teammates was a cool experience. We were all strangers before we arrived in Portland and we quickly had to trust one another. I didn't know how any of my teammates would run and they didn't know if I could run, but we became fast friends. Everyone of us was doing our best because we didn't want to let our teammates down. We were feeding off each other, and I remember being really excited about the challenge.

All of us were struggling with our own little issues, but it was cool that there was so much positive feedback and so many people saying, "Hey, man, you can do it. I know you can do that." I remember going by a couple people and they were just flabbergasted that a one-legged guy had passed them. The running community is an amazing community because all of us have our own stories, but it's cool that we can inspire one another, and I definitely felt that our team inspired a lot of people.

It was great finishing my last leg, but I was part of a team and we weren't done until we were all across the finish line. I was happy I could take my foot off the pedal a little bit and take it all in. It was a really cool moment when the whole team got together at the finish line and we had our photo taken. It was amazing to see how many participants were there and how many spectators were at the finish.

Our goal was to finish—and we finished. Our other goal was to have fun—and we had an amazing time!

Ashton Eaton was born in Portland and grew up in Bend, Oregon, before attending the University of Oregon. He won gold medals in the decathlon at the 2012 and 2016 Summer Olympics, and established a decathlon world record at the 2015 World Championships in China. In 2017 he retired from track and field and now lives in San Francisco with his wife, Brianne. He first participated in Hood To Coast as an honorary captain for Team World Vision in 2013 and returned to the role again in 2014 and 2016. In 2017, he served as a van driver for World Vision.

The first time I heard about Hood To Coast was in 2013. I think it was at a USA Track & Field meeting. Lopez Lomong, a fellow athlete and a good friend of mine who represented the United States in the 2008 Summer Olympics, wanted to get together. He's a very charismatic guy, but also very straightforward, and we agreed to meet.

The next morning I went to breakfast with Lopez, who has a great story. He was kidnapped from his family in Sudan when he was young. He was able to escape and live in a refugee camp. And eventually he was adopted and made it to America. Lopez was really good at track, loved running, went through college, and became an Olympian.

Lopez told me all these things about raising money for clean water in the South Sudan. He mentioned there was a really great event happening that he was going to do and that I needed to be a part of it. He kept asking me, "Do you want to do it?" And I was like, "I don't really know what it is, but sure." I committed to participate in the event without knowing anything about it because of Lopez. When I asked him for more information, his response was, "Just call this guy."

The guy Lopez told me to contact was Michael Chitwood, the executive director of Team World Vision. When I called Michael a couple days later, he asked, "What did Lopez tell you?" My response was, "I don't really know. He said there's this event going on to raise money for his home country and he wants me to be involved—so I'm going to do it." Michael then told me, "Well, here's the event. We're running a 200-mile relay race across Oregon that starts at Mt. Hood and ends at the coast." At that point, I was wondering what

I had gotten myself mixed up in. Basically, that was the first I heard of HTC—and it sounded long.

I never heard about HTC growing up. I'm not quite sure how that went down, especially after I learned how long the relay was going on and how famous it was. I was surprised I hadn't heard of it before, but nobody I knew really said anything about it growing up. It could be from growing up in Bend, rather than in Portland. It also could have been one of those things where everybody knew about it except me.

Part of it was probably HTC taking place in the summer, and as a young person I was always doing my own thing during the summer. And in college, I was gone most of my summers. In fact, when we were able to participate in HTC, it was sometimes just a couple days after we got back from the Olympics or the World Championships or something like that.

Michael explained it would be great for me to join because the idea was to get people to run on teams, and these runners would then go out and solicit donations. They wanted professional athletes on board to inspire the runners and provide encouragement and make the event fun. They told me the event takes place in August, and I just needed to show up at the Sheraton Airport Hotel in Portland. The funny thing is, I knew that hotel—it's the same hotel where my mom met my biological father.

I showed up at the hotel, and they were reviewing what was going to happen. My role was basically to be in the vans and encourage the runners. At the time, Team World Vision had five teams—which meant there were 10 vans. I was supposed to jump into as many vans as I could during the relay and spend time with as many runners and teams as possible.

I remember waking up super early on a Friday morning. The start was really awesome. Everybody was getting ready to run; all the teams were supporting one another; each team was introduced; and finally the runners were taking off every 15 minutes. It was really exciting.

During the relay, I was hopping around in these vans and totally burning myself out because I didn't realize how long the race would take. That first year I probably spent 36 hours in vans. Honestly, it was really hard. I had just gotten back from the World Championships in Russia and was tired from that, and just tired from a long year of competition. Then I got to Portland and I was trying to learn how HTC works. I was trying to figure out how I'd be able to spend time with teams and vans and when people would be tired in the middle of the night. By the next day I was just completely wiped out. I remember sitting in a grass field, lying under the stars, and having all the runners come through the exchange. There were people milling about in vans, coming and going—and I was thinking, "This is a really cool event."

I tried to get to know everybody, asking them what they did for a living and why they were running. That was really good. The funny thing was, a lot of the vans had their own distinct smell! It was almost like each van was its own little community. It felt like each van had its own culture by what was written on the outside—names, slogans, and pictures. And it was the same inside. In some vans everybody was quiet and doing their own thing. In other vans people were hooting and hollering and listening to loud music and cracking jokes. I'd pop into a van and they'd be like, "Where did you come from?" It was funny, too, because by the end of the relay the dirtier and messier the vans got, the less room I had.

Sometimes it was super hard finding the vans. I'm surprised I was able to find some of the teams, because all the vans look alike. I'd be walking around in a grass field asking, "Hey, has anybody seen a white van?"

At the finish I was amazed how many people were on the beach and how big a production it was. I had a good conversation with Lopez at the finish. He was extremely thankful I had participated in the event and was saying, "I'm so glad you're here." And after I saw how much money the event raised, and how good it was going to be for clean water in Lopez's home country, I was like, "This is really all my pleasure."

The partnership with World Vision has been great for both sides. Brianne and I have been to Africa a couple times and think they do great work, and quite a bit of money is raised every year for clean water in South Sudan.

Alex Casebeer is from Salem, Oregon, and her Hood To Coast team is Chaffin Our Dream.

Our team's first year running Hood To Coast was 2016. We had 12 first-time runners. I was the team captain and thought I was very well organized. We had a team meeting and gave everybody their shirts and had everything planned out. We were packed well in advance and ready to go. I was in Van 2 and we were planning to meet up with the other half of our team at the first van exchange and start running at about 5 p.m.

We got to Sandy High School about four o'clock and I got out to begin stretching. I looked up and noticed the team next to us was a Bowerman team. You know, the team that seems to win almost every year. I was completely intimidated and said to myself, "Okay, I'm just going to do what they're doing."

I started stretching, watching them, and doing my deal. It was getting close to my starting time and the Bowerman runner was beginning to get ready, putting on his shoes and stuff. I opened up my bag, got my shirt out, and put it on. I was just about ready, and then I realized the one thing I forgot was my running shoes. I'd organized everything for the entire trip and now I was wearing my flip-flops and realizing I had no running shoes to run The Mother of All Relays.

So we all got back in the van and drove straight to Fred Meyer. I bought some shoes off the rack. We made it back in time and I was able to start my leg, but no one will let me forget that I didn't bring my running shoes.

I was a little nervous about running in brand-new shoes. But I was lucky, no blisters. I was able to get some very flexible shoes that worked out fine. I made everybody on the team sign my pair of shoes from the race and they're now our team trophy.

Holly Haggenjos *is from Vancouver, Washington. She participated in her first Hood To Coast in 2017.*

My first time running Hood To Coast I was in Van 2 and Runner 7. Since our van didn't go to the start at Timberline Lodge, my first taste of the relay was at the major exchange at Sandy High School.

I had no idea what to expect at the exchange. Even though it wasn't the beginning of the race, it was the start for me and all my teammates in Van 2. The energy and support at the exchange was just incredible. I was nervous when my teammate was approaching and I was preparing to run. However, when I stepped on the course to meet my teammate my feelings quickly changed. And as I began to run I realized that instead of being nervous I was pumped up for my first HTC. I put all my nerves aside and crushed my leg with a great time. It was truly amazing!

It was another story after I finished my third leg. I was tired, hungry, and thirsty. I was stoked we were almost finished. The start of the leg had been chaos for our team. Now I was finished running and so ready to be out of the van. But even though I was the first runner finished in our van, I had to be there to support my teammates to the finish.

The overall emotional rollercoaster of HTC was something else. My feelings changed from one moment to the next. I was nervous and antsy one minute and then pumped up and excited. At other times, I was scared and worried. I really pushed it at the end of my legs, and when I was done it was a thrill. I experienced all those different emotions and everything in between.

At the start I was wondering what I signed up for. At the finish I decided I'd be back.

Eva Deutsch *is from Bavaria, Germany, and competed in her first Hood To Coast in 2017.*

I was a semi-professional soccer player in Germany, but because of a new job I didn't really have time to continue with a team sport. I wanted to stay in shape, so I started to focus more on running.

I ran even on vacation. Once, I was in Beaverton, Oregon, staying with a friend I had met there when I was a high school foreign-exchange student. I would run there in the morning and someone saw me running on the street. She asked, "How fast do you go? What do you run?" I told her I usually run the 800 meters, some of the shorter and faster stuff.

She asked if I had ever heard of Hood To Coast, and I said no. When she was telling me about it my eyes must have gotten bigger and bigger because she said I should be on their team as a backup in case somebody got hurt. I said sure.

Two days later she called me and said somebody had a sprained ankle. She said, "I think you've got to jump in."

So I went to practice with them and ran a mile. It was actually the first time I had ever run a mile, because in Germany we count in kilometers and I had always run in kilometers. I didn't really know how to pace myself, but I must have done okay because they put me on the team.

I was Runner 11 in the race and had a really good night run. That was my favorite one.

I didn't know how to pace myself. My first leg was like seven kilometers, I think. I always have to try and translate how far I had to go. I had like 36 road kills on that one. I was just counting road kills. I was kind of fast on that one. I think I had a 7:18 pace. No wait, 6:18? I'm not sure.

But the night leg was my best. I tried a new shoe and it just made me fly. Brand-new shoes. I went to the Nike store and bought the new shoes—40 percent off! But I started to cramp up, so I went back to my old shoes for the final leg. I just wasn't used to running a long distance in a short time without breaks and then not much time to recover.

It was incredible seeing all those vans and then the people decorating them. I saw that here in the states when I was in high school, when we went to the state championship. We decorated our school bus. But I'd never seen so many private vans getting decorated.

I don't have a single regret. I'd love to do it again, anytime, every time. I didn't know anybody at the start, but our entire van, we're like old friends now. They said I should become their Facebook friend so they could tag me in all their pictures.

It was such a great experience.

Matthew Cox is from Dallas and works in the experiential marketing business. He has worked with a Hood To Coast sponsor and has also participated in the race.

I would regularly tell my clients at Dick's Sporting Goods, "Oh my gosh, I can't wait until you guys get to run Hood To Coast. I'm so jealous. I want to be on your team, but I'm managing the event."

Then they called me in 2016 and said, "Hey, you've been talking about running the race with us and we reserved a spot for you on the team." I was like, "Oh, really? There's no way I can run." And they were like, "You're not getting out of it. You're running." I realized I had to run.

Running in the race did a couple of great things for me. It forced me to transfer a lot of trust to the people who worked for me and help them grow. I really benefited from that in a way I never expected. And I got to run the race, which enabled me to experience the event in a totally new way.

It was educational because I learned how hectic and chaotic it is from a runner's perspective, which I previously didn't realize. My earlier perception was you run your race and then you get in the van, and then you're kind of on autopilot until it's your turn to run again. From my experience, that's totally not the case because you run your race and get in the van, but then a short time later you're at the next exchange, where you're cheering and high-fiving your teammates. It really is nonstop.

I knew one other person in the van very well. We were close friends. And I was familiar with another runner, but I didn't know the other runners at all. However, there was something about the challenge, struggles, and pain, along with being together in a van, where, regardless of how close you are before the race, you become a tribe. Whatever your teammates need, you're willing to help. When a teammate says, "I'm sore and tired, and I'm really hurting," you respond by telling them, "You got it. You can do it." You learn so much about each other, and you bond in a way that's not common elsewhere.

I didn't run with the team again the following year. However, when I see my teammates from 2016 they get an instant high-five. It doesn't matter if I haven't seen them in six months, it's still like, "How are you? What's happening? How are your kids?" There's just something there like a collective DNA that we built up and share. And that's pretty cool.

Nelson Farris is the chief storyteller and senior director of global HR talent development at Nike. He has been competing in Hood To Coast and Portland To Coast for more than 20 years, most recently as a member of the Nike T-Wrecks PTC team.

I ran Hood To Coast about five times and have walked Portland To Coast about 15 times. I tore my ACL and lost my ability to run, so I took up walking. I transitioned over to a walking team and it has been great. We've got ex-NFL guys on our team and athletes of all kinds. We have people who never were athletes, but are competitive, especially the women. We're all about 60 years old and that adds to the camaraderie.

The first year I ran HTC was 1996 or 1997. There were no big athletes on the team, but everybody was jogging and running, so everybody was relatively fit. We were living the dream: working at Nike and competing in a goofy race. It was, "A bunch of guys, 24 hours and two cars. Sounds like a lot of fun. Let's do it."

We didn't have a van so we were packed into a station wagon and it broke down. Everything that could go wrong did go wrong. That's part of the charm of the race. But nothing was a game-breaker. Nothing stopped us from our mission, to finish and have a big party afterwards.

The camaraderie, the teamwork, it really came together. To me, it's the inner challenge that probably exists in all of us—fight or flight. You don't want to fail because you don't want to let your teammates down. Even if you're hurting, you're not going to quit. There's some of that visceral response to competitiveness that helps everybody endure. The relay challenges you physically *and* mentally. You don't sleep. You get funky. Some people get cranky. Some people get stupid. Some people get delirious. For us it was an adventure.

The beach finish was great because you get some food, have a few beers, and stay overnight. The next day we walked down to the Pig 'N Pancake restaurant, the go-to place in Seaside for a big gut-bomb breakfast. It was great.

That was 20 some years ago. Everything was less sophisticated then. The maps were dicey and you weren't sure where all the markings were. We didn't have a timing system figured out. We didn't know what or when to eat. We didn't know what we were up against. That also made it attractive in a bizarre sort of way. Everything was done on the fly. You'd make a mistake, figure something out, make another mistake, and correct it. But we got through it and we got a medal. I hadn't won a medal in a long, long time. Then we were in the top six in our class, so we got another medal. Two medals! That was good.

CHAPTER 5

It's All Downhill From Here

TIMBERLINE LODGE WAS BUILT IN THE 1930s as part of President Franklin D. Roosevelt's Works Progress Administration. Located on the south side of Mt. Hood, about 60 miles from Portland, it was designated a National Historic Landmark in 1977. A popular ski resort and tourist attraction, it appeared in the 1980 Jack Nicholson movie *The Shining*, serving as the exterior for the Overlook Hotel featured in the film.

The inaugural Hood To Coast started on Glade Trail, a steep ski path which ended at the base of the mountain. Nowadays, the infamous first leg follows Timberline Road to the community of Government Camp and covers almost five and a half miles, descends 2,000 feet and is labeled a "severe downhill' in the course overview.

In its early years, the relay began when someone said, "Go." Today, the start features an announcer, sound system, music and vendors and every team is introduced before their first runner heads down the hill.

John Hammarley is the longtime and only public address announcer for Hood To Coast. He is responsible for introducing every team at the race start and as they cross the finish line. Hammarley is a former television news reporter in Chicago, New York, Dallas, and Portland, who now lives in Bend, Oregon. He received six Emmy Awards during his television career.

I had run Hood To Coast the second year of the event through the fourth (1983 to 1985). Bob (Foote, HTC founder) knew me from television—I was a reporter for the NBC affiliate in Portland—and I knew Bob because he was the president of the Oregon Road Runners Club. I guess he felt comfortable asking me to be the public address announcer. Or maybe he went down the list and couldn't find anybody else willing to yell into a megaphone for 36 hours!

Bob reached out and said, "This thing is getting kind of big. I think we need an announcer." Before I became the announcer, it was just someone at the start saying "Go," and there would be a volunteer at the finish saying, "Okay, you're finished." That was about it. Around year five there was a significant jump in the number of entries and that's when Bob reached out. He asked me if I would be willing to be the announcer, and of course I said yes.

I was nervous that first year because I'd never been a race announcer. While I was comfortable in front of a television camera, being in front of several hundred, if not a few thousand amped-up runners, was a whole new experience.

When I began I used a megaphone to announce the start at Timberline Lodge. That's how electronically advanced we were back then. It then jumped from using a megaphone my first year to a bullhorn the following year. For the first three or four years I'd announce all the teams that way because it was still pretty manageable in terms of the number of teams. As the event continued to get bigger and bigger it became obvious we needed a better way to introduce the teams. And that's when my job as announcer became more critical. I'm really like an air traffic controller in the announcer's booth—making sure everything goes off according to plan and on schedule.

My goal at the start is to get the crowd as excited as possible. There are plenty of people who are total relay virgins—they've never run a relay and they certainly have never run HTC. I want to get them energized. There's a little housekeeping in terms of providing details about where to run and what side of the road to run on, along with telling everyone not to pee on people's front lawns and all that stuff. There's also a good mix of safety and instruction, but it's very important for me to get everybody enthusiastic and ready to run.

When it gets close to the scheduled time for a wave of runners to take off, I have my routine. It may vary a bit from year to year and from wave to wave, but I'd say I'm announcing about 20 to 25 teams every 15 minutes, which means I'm introducing teams at the start for roughly 13 consecutive hours.

I hold a deep, loving spot in my heart for HTC and I want to share that feeling with everyone at the start.

Kathy Kaiser *is from West Linn, Oregon, and began running Hood To Coast in 2001.*

I'm not a runner. I'm a junk-food junkie who runs because I love to eat cookies my kids and I bake together. I never imagined I would run a wild relay for 17 years with my crazy college roommate who also loves to eat. But, we're still in it and we're still telling stories.

I started running Hood To Coast because one day I happened to be driving to Zigzag and got caught in traffic with hundreds of runners on the road. I didn't know much about the relay on that August day, but I wanted to be a part of whatever it was that was happening.

In 2001 our team, the Stiff Shafts from Sandelie Golf Course in West Linn, started running HTC. Like all teams, we have the most amazing people in our vans. Each year brings so many ridiculously funny moments that it's hard to keep track of them all—and picking a single event is practically impossible.

One of our more memorable moments happened in 2011 on race day. Early in the morning we were driving to Timberline Lodge for our 5:30 a.m. start time. It was a relatively simple task. We chatted and told stories from previous relays and were excited for our first runner to start the race. The wind was fierce that morning at the start line. It was raining sideways, and lightning could be seen striking the hills in the distance.

Oh, the stories of the first leg of HTC. Not everyone has run Leg 1, but those who have know what's required before getting to the starting line. What's certainly needed to run down from Timberline is a healthy dose of, "Oh my gosh, what was I thinking?" and "Will my quads ever be the same after this?" During our drive to the starting line we all failed miserably to communicate to our first runner, Randy, the process of getting ready.

It was early and we were late getting to the start. I checked in and assumed we were ready. And we were ready, except nobody told Randy what to do. Once we had parked at Timberline, everyone in the van jumped out as usual. Some of us visited the Honey Buckets and others searched for coffee. It never occurred to any of us to stay with Randy to make sure everything went smoothly. He wandered around looking for us—and for some reason we thought he knew what to do at the start. We assumed he was in the van getting ready to run, but he had no idea what to do because we forgot to tell him!

Moments before the announcer was ready to send off a wave of runners for our start time, it occurred to all of us to look around. We didn't see Randy anywhere, and it was hitting us like the rain! In a few moments we saw his silhouette standing in the dark. No vest. No number. No flashing lights or flashlight. For an epic relay, we had an epic fail. And as any good team would do we laughed and immediately got our act together. Randy asked, "Do I need a vest?" Then he asked, "What about a flashlight?" We continued to laugh and panic at the same time.

Eli ran to the van to get a vest and a headlamp. But that wasn't enough because I had to make a second trip to the van to get a race number and flashing lights. Randy was not a small man. He needed an XL in everything, and the little vest we were trying to force over his large body and belly was not the right size. It was a women's small pink reflective vest. There wasn't time to go back to the van and find a larger vest that would fit. What we had in our hands barely fit over Randy's chest and rested just above his belly. I tugged and pulled on the sides thinking that it was just twisted or stuck. Nope. It simply squished all of his upper body together. He didn't realize it was a tiny vest at the time. We hastily slapped some flashing lights on the front and back of his vest and gave him a headlamp. We then told him he was "good to go" and turned him toward the start line.

While all this was happening, the lightning continued to strike in the distance, and the rain and wind continued to drench us before we even began. But Randy took off as scheduled.

As he approached the exchange all we could see was a large man with his chest compressed into a small pink reflective vest. He huffed and puffed in the little vest all the way to the exchange. Once he finished, getting the vest off was just as much of a challenge as putting it on had been. And as any good team would be—we were still laughing!

Each year, we have countless stories to tell and events that we still laugh about. We can only hope for a lot more years of amazing miles with HTC.

Will Ferrin *is from West Linn, Oregon, and has been a regular participant in Hood To Coast.*

In 2017 I participated in Hood To Coast for the 20th time. My fondest memory happened in 2008. It was the year they were filming the movie about the race. In order to save my quads, and because it would be a lot less stressful, I decided to run Leg 1 backwards. My teammates and others are always curious when I run backwards.

I played football in high school and college. Since I was a defensive back, I would often run backwards during practice and games. I then decided to run backwards on downhill runs because it was easier on my legs. Of course, the downside to running backwards is that you can't always see where you're going. Occasionally I would run into cars or potholes and fall. Eventually I got pretty good at looking over my shoulder.

When I ran Leg 1 backwards in 2008, one of the camera crews that was there filming for the movie interviewed me while I was running backwards. Unfortunately, I didn't make the movie. But I also didn't trip or fall as I completed my backwards run.

And when we got to the finish in Seaside I was able to walk down the stairs to the beach with style and grace!

John Hammarley *is the longtime and only public address announcer for Hood To Coast. He is responsible for introducing every team at the race start and as they cross the finish line. Hammarley is a former television news reporter in Chicago, New York, Dallas, and Portland, who now lives in Bend, Oregon. He received six Emmy Awards during his television career.*

On the Thursday night before Hood To Coast starts I stay at Timberline Lodge. The race takes place during the last weekend in August, which is tourist season and a busy time at Timberline. In the early years there would be guests who had no idea the race was taking place. When the public-address system got to be very powerful and the sound would carry a long way and I would start announcing and playing music around five in the morning, guests would come down to the start and yell at me and ask what was going on. I was as kind as could be, but I had to explain to them that the largest relay race in the world was taking place. Unfortunately, they picked that weekend to get married or celebrate an anniversary or kick back and relax—and they were smack dab in the midst of thousands of runners who were amped up and ready to go.

A few years ago Timberline decided to reserve that weekend for race teams and volunteers. Now the night before the start it's all race-related people. Since then I've enjoyed walking around on Thursday night and introducing myself to teams in the dining room or at the bar. I try to playfully ask the runners I meet to come up with something embarrassing about their Leg 1 runner—something to use during introductions at the start. They get in the spirit of things and slip me something terribly embarrassing about their Leg 1 runner—and it usually makes for a really good time at the start.

Along with sharing stories about some of the first runners to hit the course, there's one special tradition I have at the start every year. Just before each wave of Leg 1 runners takes off, I ask all the runners in the start area to turn to each other and extend a hand of friendship, introduce themselves to each other, and wish each other luck. It kind of serves as an icebreaker and something I haven't seen in any other races.

When I first started announcing the relay I looked down at the runners and a lot of them were scared. At that point there wasn't a lot of history to the event. Many runners didn't know what lay ahead, especially in terms of that first leg. I just thought I'd remind them that it's a team event and that it had been my experience from running that teams helped each other. So if somebody got in trouble, I thought it was a good reminder to let them know they weren't alone.

Ashton Eaton was born in Portland and grew up in Bend, Oregon, before attending the University of Oregon. He won gold medals in the decathlon at the 2012 and 2016 Summer Olympics, and established a decathlon world record at the 2015 World Championships in China. In 2017 he retired from track and field and now lives in San Francisco with his wife, Brianne. He first participated in Hood To Coast as an honorary captain for Team World Vision in 2013 and returned to the role again in 2014 and 2016. In 2017, he served as a van driver for World Vision.

Every year I always get asked for running advice and things like that. One year, I jokingly told this one guy, "The key to running Leg 1, the downhill run, is to just let the gravity take you—don't try to slow yourself down, just hammer down." He took that advice seriously, and the funny thing is he was really excited about his time.

He told me, "Hey, I listened to your advice. I just flew down the mountain. I was passing all kinds of people."

I was like, "That's awesome. I'm surprised you didn't blow your knees out of your legs."

He said he felt great and ever since then it's been a huge joke.

Bruce Harmon *began running Hood To Coast in the late 1980s and now captains the team Old Enough to Know Better.*

I've been running Hood To Coast since 1988—30 years and counting. You'd think after all that time it would get old, but it doesn't. Each year is special and I have no plans to quit any time soon.

The first year I was Runner 1 and was also going to run four legs because a teammate had been injured. Little did I know how tough that first leg would be, even if it was just running down a mountain. I went out way too fast and about halfway down my muscles were cramping up badly. I finished, but there was no way I was going to be able to run three more legs. But that's one of the things I love about HTC: my teammates were there to provide support. They encouraged me through my next two legs, and then another team member stepped up to run the fourth leg.

In 1995 I finally formed my own team, Old Enough to Know Better. I've been blessed to share in our team spirit and camaraderie every year since then.

And, yes, one year I did finally get the chance to run a fourth leg. It was a great feeling!

Felicia Hubber *grew up in Portland, moved to Montana during high school, and attended college at the University of Montana. The daughter of Hood To Coast founder Bob Foote, Felicia was just a few months old when she attended the first HTC—and she's been at every relay since. In 2006 she succeeded her father as president of HTC.*

I remember asking my mom and dad when I was 11, "Can I run in Hood To Coast? I want to run in it so bad." They said, "Absolutely not." They told me I could run in it when

I was 14 because, "You need to be strong and old enough to handle such a big endeavor." They also felt being younger than 14 would not serve as a good role model for anyone else who wanted to run in the relay with a younger child.

Each year of the race we're asked about a son or daughter running at a certain age, and we always say, "It's up to you. Do you feel your daughter/son truly has enough running background, mileage, and ability to handle HTC? And if so, you need to ensure you'll be running on the team with them." We do not have a minimum age requirement. We leave it up to the best judgment of parents. My parents felt I could handle running in the relay when I was 14, based on my running experience.

The first time I ran the relay was on a team with my dad. I was so excited and had the same perspective a lot of new HTC runners have, wondering, "What's it going to be like?" There was a lot of excitement being around the team, hearing their questions and comments. I remember hearing their enthusiasm and thinking, "Wow! This is really special." I didn't realize that this event is so important to so many people until I was out there in the mix with everybody.

That first year I ran Leg 1 with the brutal descent from Mt. Hood and lost my big toenail because I was so psyched and ran way too fast. With a 2,000-foot elevation decline over five and a half miles, my feet took a pounding, especially in my toe box. I still loved the first leg despite that. It felt great to get to the first exchange point and hand off to my dad. I remember looking down at my left shoe and seeing the top covered in blood.

I was stiff and sore because I didn't run smart that first year. I was quite sore for my second leg, which made it not as enjoyable, but there was some vindication on my third leg. I thought to myself, "I got this. I'm almost there. This is an accomplishment." When I finished my third leg, I was super happy because as Runner 1 I was the first one done! I was able to sit back and cheer on my teammates for the remaining journey to the beach and thought, "This is pretty neat. I definitely want to do this again."

The second year, my dad and I were on the same team and unintentionally ended up running together at the start. I was with the team heading up to Timberline Lodge, and my dad was already there. I was going to run the first leg again, and my dad was running the second leg. When I didn't get to the start in time, my dad knew our start time and just took off running in my place. We got there about a minute late and he was already heading down the mountain. I took off sprinting down the mountain to try to catch him. It wasn't as easy as I would have anticipated. All the runners were sprinting down the steep descent of Timberline Road, and he was right in the thick of them all. It probably wasn't until close to a mile down the road when I finally caught up with him.

I remember telling him, "Stop, you can go back up the mountain now." He said, "No way. I've already gone this far, so I'm going to finish." We ran together for a ways, which made for another inadvertent but fun memory!

The Hood To Coast team seeding process—deciding which teams start when—is one of the most important, talked about, and often misunderstood things about how the race works. **Bob Foote**, *HTC founder and chairman, continues to personally oversee the process and talks about the history and background.*

The race seeding has always been the backbone of Hood To Coast. If the seeding works, the race takes care of itself. If the seeding doesn't work and you have overlapping groups, you have a problem. When you've got excess volume at exchange points, the best of intentions are not enough. You just get overwhelmed.

The first year of the race I just lined everyone up and said, "Go." Then we got enough teams in 1983 that I had to split the start into three groups of about 20, but there was no real science behind it.

After that I was always messing around with the seeding and the start times, trying to get us into Pacific City at the right time. The first wave of runners went off at 11 p.m., with staggered starts until about 4 a.m. Teams would really complain if they didn't get an 11 p.m. or a midnight start time. They didn't want the 4 a.m. start time.

Everything was done manually, no computers. The calculations on how fast a team was going to be or how to anticipate their finish, time-wise, was all done the old-fashioned way.

I looked for a way to analyze team speeds, and since a lot of people were running 10Ks I asked the teams for those times or estimates for all their runners. Of course, I knew there would be some falloff from the times over the course of the race, and I tried to incorporate that while calculating the finish times and seeding the teams.

If the teams gave me accurate data—like computers now, good data in, good data out—I had some running within five seconds of my predicted time. Five seconds. I wouldn't tell a team its predicted time until after the finish, and I used to have a contest to see which team would run closest to its time.

In the late 1980s and early 1990s we had some real problems with sandbaggers, the guys who wanted to get early start times. It was simple math and they figured out the slower the team, the earlier their start time. They'd turn in really inaccurate times so they could start early, finish early, party earlier, and get home early. My seeding mechanism began to fall apart because of those crappy times.

We instituted a rule in 1986 where if you ran within one hour of your anticipated finish time you got a finisher medal. If your team missed it by more than an hour you got nothing, zip. Everyone wanted the finisher medals. They would cry and make excuses about why they missed their time, but it was a black-and-white rule at the time.

The race results were published in the 1990s on about four pages and we had this infamous back page for the sandbagger awards. We would identify the worst offending teams and rank them from first down to 40th place. I'd write, "For all the teams that abided by the rules and provided honest times to help make this race run efficiently and smoothly, these are the people you have to thank for saying they're more important than the race and the quality of your experience. They chose to cheat and give intentionally inaccurate times so that they can finish early in the race and take the race away from you guys who legitimately should have been finishing earlier." It created big-time peer pressure.

The one-hour finisher medal was a big hit with the runners and eliminated the sandbaggers almost immediately. It represented a sense of accomplishment. To go home without it was a sense of failure. We had the finisher-medal rule for a number of years until it pretty much cleaned up the problem.

When I started working with a computer I built some Excel spreadsheets and algorithms that allowed me to study all the 10K times. I did lots of analysis of race data and found a bell curve—I call it the deterioration factor. It showed, not surprisingly, the better the runner the less deterioration there was in 10K speed over the course of the race. Someone who runs a 10K at a five-minute pace probably can run our race at about a 5:10- to 5:15-minute pace for all three of his legs. A person whose best 10K pace is nine minutes and 30 seconds is probably going to end up running at a 12-minute pace. He's going to fall apart because he doesn't have the same conditioning as an experienced runner. I pretty much dialed in the deterioration factor for any given speed group and used that as part of the seeding process.

Then in 1991 I made a big mistake, a major screw-up. I decided to start the slowest teams in the first wave and the fastest teams last. We had never tried it before, but I just decided to go slowest to fastest.

It was a total and complete disaster. I wasn't sophisticated enough in my calculations. The thinking was that the teams would spread out, but you've got to remember that the slower teams were being constantly overtaken by the faster teams.

Late in the race, at major Exchanges 24 and 30, all of a sudden there were five or six waves of runners hitting at the same time. It blew up the exchange points. There was epic road congestion. People couldn't get to the exchanges because vans were stopped and backed up for miles. Teams had to let their next runner out and have them jog up to the exchange point so they'd be there in time. It was a total disaster.

At the finish that year people were swearing at me, calling me names, and flipping me off. They were pissed because it was a terrible race. The whole race was in danger of going down the tubes.

On Sunday there was still a hostile crowd at the awards ceremony, waiting to hear what I was going to say. There was no way I was going to try to skirt the issue. Excuses are baloney, and I'm not an excuse kind of guy. It was my fault. I screwed up. I went up on stage and said, "Number one, I apologize for the huge disaster that happened. It was totally my fault, 100 percent my fault. The slowest to fastest seeding was a complete mistake."

I asked everyone to give me a chance. "If you trust me, come back next year and it's going to be fixed. And if you decide not to come back, I understand." We did have some registration falloff the next year. It wasn't as traumatic as I thought it would be, but it fell by more than five percent. I knew the next year was my last chance. If we screwed up again, that would be it, there would be no coming back.

I was already working on some solutions. One was to create some alternate routes for the vans, so on the latter legs the vans with no runners on the course would take a different route. And only one van from each team would be allowed on certain parts of the race-course. The other van would have to detour around.

Obviously, a new seeding system was needed. I was working with a new Excel spread-sheet and algorithms, but there was still a lot of manual time involved in the process. It took me days to do it. I took all the teams and their anticipated finish times and looked at different scenarios.

I assigned start times based on the algorithms and then manually charted every team through the racecourse to see where they'd be at any given time. I'd look for where waves of runners would overlap and where there could be trouble spots. Then I'd experiment with some different variations. Try these start times and those start times. I kept changing it around. It was just trial and error. I literally went through more than 100 different scenarios before I finally came up with something that worked.

The next year we implemented the changes and it was acknowledged as our best race yet. The new seeding system worked. We had a good race.

Fast forward to just a few years ago. We found a manufacturing software program designed to maximize product output by tracking and managing all the conveyor belts supplying parts as part of the production process. It's designed so all the parts arrive at the right time and the right place for maximum output and greatest efficiency. Nothing gets jammed up.

Our staff thought that the program could be adaptable to HTC. Instead of conveyor belts we had teams. I outlined and designed a program using our algorithms and had an engineer and programmer put in coding to make this new program work for us.

The program takes every team and all 12,000 or so runners into account. It seeds the teams so in any given wave we have teams with runners of different speeds. We'll have teams with a 5:30-mile pace and teams with a 10-minute pace in the same wave. When that wave takes off, it dissipates. The program then tracks every team through the entire course to see where they're overtaking each other. It studies the congestion points on an individual team basis, rather than on a wave basis. It can see the maximum density at any given exchange point. It won't allow you to exceed a certain maximum density or it will kick it out and reject it.

It's called "The Trial" and it runs through the entire race field in one sweep. The more it runs, the better the outcome because it always saves its best solution and throws away the worst. It keeps running through 15,000 permutations and that's scenario one.

I'll study things like how many teams does it have in the early start waves and if there are some big groups bunched together at the start. Big groups in an early wave are always a concern because they hit some of the first exchanges really hard. If we have a backup there, we'll never overcome it. I'll analyze and adjust the data and then start over and run another 15,000 permutations from scratch. That's scenario two.

I had a special computer built with a solid-state drive and the fastest chip that exists for a desktop. It's screaming fast and runs 24 hours a day when it's processing the programs. It never stops. In about 10 days we'll get eight or nine scenarios. Then we'll take what we think is the best one.

I keep the computer at home and don't use it for anything else. Once a year I pull it out and run it. That way it never gets corrupted. I never open anything on the internet with it. It's protected, like a pure little lamb.

With today's seeding process we can look at a major exchange that is potentially a big congestion area and see how many teams pass through during every one hour increment. I can also study the density of how many teams are coming through a given exchange during an entire 24-hour cycle.

I'll analyze and rank each scenario, awarding points in different areas such as volume and congestion. It needs to be objective, not emotional. Whichever scenario scores the most points, that is our seeding for the year.

Now when I talk with teams at the beach I hear, "Smooth race, no backups that we saw." Or maybe from another team we'll hear, "At noon, at Exchange 30, we hit a backup." Sometimes there will be little bubbles like that and we'll try to address them for the following year.

I still do all the seeding. It takes me about 10 days, with the computer cranking 24 hours a day. It's pretty tedious, but it seems to work!

The Cereal Killers living up to the team name.

CHAPTER 6

What's In A Name?

FOR MANY TEAMS PARTICIPATING IN Hood To Coast, the most important task after assembling 12 runners is selecting a name. That team name will identify and define a team throughout its journey from Mt. Hood to the Oregon coast. Once a name is selected, it becomes the team's moniker for the "The Mother of All Relays," whether it's just a one-time occurrence or a longstanding group that has participated for 20 or 30 years.

In most cases, the name reflects the core values, location, or the team's running ability – or lack of running skills. A team name may also elicit a laugh, a gasp or a smile, or even carry a subliminal message that other teams need to figure out while running down the road. Whatever the name, it usually offers a glimpse into the dynamics of the team.

John Hammarley is the longtime and only public address announcer for Hood To Coast. He is responsible for introducing every team at the race start and as they cross the finish line. Hammarley is a former television news reporter in Chicago, New York, Dallas, and Portland, who now lives in Bend, Oregon. He received six Emmy Awards during his television career.

One of my favorite things about Hood To Coast is the team names. They usually can be broken down into a few different categories—bathroom humor or sexual innuendo, and names related to whatever news personality or event has captured the people's attention that year. I remember when the dot-com craze was in full bloom there were a lot of dot-com team names.

There will also always be some team names that are a play on words with teams trying to get me to mispronounce their name so it comes out as something raw and off-color. However, after all my years as the announcer I'm usually pretty good at catching them.

Over the years I've enjoyed the team name Naked Love Pretzel. The past few years, I've really liked the team My Couch Pulls Out, But I Don't. I also like Off Like a Prom Dress. Those are a few names that stand out.

One thing that will almost always happen, especially for teams that haven't done HTC before, is they'll come up with a boring team name at their first organizational meeting. That's what they'll put down on the entry. Then they realize that half the fun is in the team name. Those are usually the teams that come up to the announcer's stand before the start and yell, "Hey, instead of calling our team the Acme Brick Company can you call our team Off Like a Prom Dress?" And it's fine with me.

One of the great things about the relay is that it's formal enough to make sure the race runs smoothly, but it's also a fun race. It's about having a fun weekend. If people have the inspiration and come up with a new team name—I'm happy to announce it at the start line. Of course I tell them I can't promise to remember their new name at the finish.

I pride myself on having a pretty good memory, so I can usually remember the changes. Lots of times the team will remind me just before they cross the finish line, "Hey, don't forget we've changed our team name." Team names are one of the highlights of my time as the announcer. When I announce the team names for each wave of runners at the start everybody gets real quiet and ready to laugh when they hear a name they love.

There have been a couple of instances where I've had to say, "I'm just the announcer and I'm just reading this team name." There also have been times when I've given a sort of parental advisory message before I announce a team name, but I do it with a smile. By and large it's pretty much an adult crowd and I figure, "What the heck." If a team wants to come up with a really off-color team name for 24 to 36 hours or however long it takes them to finish—they have to live with that team name. It's no skin off my back. After all these years I'm happy to make a fool out of myself and announce it to everyone.

***Brian Adams** is the associate dean of graduate programs at the Pamplin School of Business at the University of Portland. He took part in his first Hood To Coast in 1992.*

I first heard about Hood To Coast when I read a story about the Killer Bees team in the *Oregonian*. I decided to put together a team because it would be a unique challenge and a way to keep in shape. And that's why we keep coming back: it's a one-of-a-kind challenging and fun team-oriented event.

Our team name is Naked Love Pretzel. You think a name like that would have a special meaning, but it doesn't. For our first team meeting back in 1992, we met for dinner and a few beers. We were throwing out different team name suggestions for about 30 minutes. Someone on the team yelled out, "Naked Love Pretzel."

And it was the best name we had!

Larry Dutko was a member of the Road Warriors/Road Kill team that finished first in the inaugural Hood To Coast in 1982. He later became a member of the Dead Jocks in a Box team and is the only runner to have competed in every HTC.

As this was the first endurance race we had ever run using a team concept, we figured we needed a team name and started the race calling ourselves the Road Warriors. Given that our team goal was to average sub-six-minute miles for all 150 miles of the race, which included a difficult set of climbs over the Coast Range, we knew it would take a road warrior mentality to win.

For the record, that name only lasted about 90 miles into the race.

Leg 16 required running up, over, and down the backside of Bald Peak. This leg incorporated an ominous, nearly three-mile steep climb up the front side of the mountain. After making it to the top, a runner was faced with about a two-mile downhill grade that averaged 17 percent.

That leg was brutal on the quads and the knees, as well as all the other body parts. It made the downhill leg at the start from Timberline Lodge to Government Camp seem like it was almost flat. After watching our runner come grimacing into the exchange after Leg 16, we decided Road Warriors did not reflect the true nature of the race.

From that point on, our team name was changed to Road Kill to better reflect what was required to run the event. We decided you had to be ready and willing to suffer to compete in the relay. And after leaving Portland we also noticed there was a higher incidence of dead critters on the road, which only added further support to our new name.

The course was a killer and we were now Road Kill!

Scott Thompson is from Beaverton, Oregon, and is a founding member of the Dirty Half Dozen +6 team, which has competed in every Hood To Coast since 1986.

In middle school there were six of us who decided to start a running club that we called the Dirty Half Dozen. A couple of us knew each other from running in grade school. Back then running was a big deal and a couple of the dads even had track clubs.

We were just a bunch of kids who decided running was what we wanted to do. We liked to go up on the trails and have dirt ball fights. There was a duck pond near our middle school that we'd run to. The initiation into the Dirty Half Dozen was that you had to wade into the pond until your head went under water. That's where the dirty part of the name came in.

In 1986, the first year we competed in Hood To Coast, there were only 11 runners on a team, so we called ourselves the Dirty Half Dozen +5. When it switched to Seaside and everyone added a runner, we decided to keep the name and just make it +6. Some people wonder why we don't call ourselves the Dirty Dozen, but it started out as the Dirty Half Dozen and we want to hold on to that beginning.

Devrie Brennan hails from Moraga, California, and now lives in Lake Oswego, Oregon. She is an orthopedic physical therapist who has completed Hood To Coast 15 times.

Back in 1997 my husband ran this crazy relay race called Hood To Coast. At the time I was a novice runner. After watching the men cross the finish line for two years, all the wives were inspired to form our own team. In 1999 the Bondo Babes were born. As you can tell by the name, we were sponsored by an auto body repair shop.

I fell in love with the race and a few years later I took over as team captain. Since we no longer had sponsorship, I decided to change the team name. In the HTC community a team name means a lot. It lets people know what kind of team you have and what your team is all about. Some teams raise funds for charity and others have sponsorship or are corporate entries. And then others, like my husband's team, are just 12 fun, raunchy people. Their team name is No Gu Btwn the Legs.

Our new team name is pretty simple, UGATAWANNA. What does it mean? "You gotta wanna" translates to every facet of life. It means if you want to succeed, you have to want to.

UGATAWANNA has inspired us over the years. Years back, running as new moms, some of us had to "pump and dump." One notable memory was when we traded breast milk for a beer. Apparently they just *had* to have milk in their coffee. Hey, you gotta wanna, right? Another time we noticed one of our teammates returning from the Honey Buckets with only one sock. When asked what happened, she said she noticed too late there was no toilet paper. Again, you gotta wanna! A few years later one of our dear friends from my husband's team passed away from cancer and we ran in his honor that year. You gotta wanna. RIP Big Al!

There have been 35 different members of team UGATAWANNA over 15 years. Never once were we disappointed by a new recruit. The most surprising team member was when a co-worker's girlfriend, Marianne Dickerson, agreed to run with our team. She was older than all of us and said she had slowed down over the years, but we didn't care. Well, "slowing down" is a relative term. She ran seven-minute miles and was the fastest runner on our team. It turns out that she was a career marathoner who had won a silver medal at the 1983 World Championships in Finland, beating the favored Russian at the finish line. Runners can be humble people! Runners are nice people too, and the level of friendliness multiplies during HTC. People are never hesitant to lend a hand, including helping a team to find their bird when it flew the coop. (Not sure why anyone thought running with a bird was a good idea, but whatever inspires a team!) It also includes paying for someone's coffee at an exchange because they forgot their money or handing out toilet paper when the Honey Buckets are empty. Cars need jumper cables, runners hitch rides with other teams, and toothpaste is shared. There are so many nice gestures during the race.

I am forever indebted to the teammates who have run with me over the years. They have given me many, many fond memories and experiences that I will forever cherish. I love this race for the camaraderie between strangers and friends, along with the push to persevere and achieve your own goals and the goals of the team. You gotta wanna!

David Murphy was born in Liverpool, England, and attended Western Kentucky University. He competed internationally in both the 5,000 and 10,000 meters and was a two-time winner of the Falmouth Road Race in Massachusetts, as well as runner-up in the 1984 New York City Marathon. He moved to Portland with adidas in 1993 and put together the Rolling Thunder team that competed in Hood To Coast in 1994 and 1995. Now he lives in the San Francisco area and consults on various sporting events.

The team name Rolling Thunder was a tribute to our former adidas America, Inc. CEO and leader Rob Strasser. That was his nickname. Sadly, he passed away from a heart attack in 1993. In a previous working life he had been the Nike head of marketing and had a very close relationship with Phil Knight. But things changed and Rob moved forward with a new leadership challenge in bringing adidas America to Portland. He was a giant of a man with a booming voice and personality to match. That's where his nickname came from, and it was a perfect name for our Hood To Coast team.

He was absolutely one of the greatest characters in the industry you would ever wish to meet. He was a real swashbuckler and would get after it 100 percent. We were like a bunch of pirates in many ways. At adidas we didn't have the luxury of massive budgets or infrastructure like at Nike or another big corporation. Many times we put plans together, like deciding to run HTC, and then moved into action without overthinking it. We would roll up our sleeves and do it.

We had permission to do a lot of things that were fun and very competitive. It was a great time. A man like Rob created so much enthusiasm and support for us to take risks. He'd say, "If you want to be the best and win, you've got to take risks." He was that type of inspiring, honest leader. Today that type of get-after-it attitude is missing from many corporate environments.

Max Woodbury is from Portland and became a C-6 quadriplegic in 1996 from a fall while working at a Superfund cleanup site. He has competed in Hood To Coast multiple times and captains the Pimps 'n' Gimps team that consists of both wheelchair athletes and able-bodied competitors.

Originally our team name was Runners & Rollers. It included me, another wheelchair dude, and a visually impaired woman. The rest were ABs (able-bodies). After seeing all of the adult humor painted on team vans, I realized our name was a bit tame. We also saw plenty of guys wearing dresses and women wearing lingerie. To add a little spice to our team name, I looked for something silly to rhyme with my self-endearing term *gimp*. I also thought it would be fun to have a team costume. That's where Pimps 'n' Gimps came from. We could have been Cripples & Nipples, but that might have been pushing it. To make the event even more fun we decided everyone should dress up. We got some great wigs, and my wife sewed up some shiny capes with "P/G" on them. We can always find our team because of the capes.

Brendan McNassar is from Beaverton, Oregon, and participated in his first Hood To Coast in 2014.

For health reasons I began running in 2014. In April of that year I ran my first-ever race, a 5K. Then, just four months later, I participated in Hood To Coast for the first time with a team from work.

In 2015 I was preparing to again run the relay, except this time I joined a new team.

In Van 1 were a group of labor and delivery nurses. I was in Van 2 with friends and family of the team captain. While the runners in each van knew their teammates, neither van knew the runners in the other van.

Being in Van 2, I had a leisurely breakfast Friday morning and then gathered my race bag together. I went to the laundry room to get a couple shirts from the dryer. That's where from under the washer crawled the most enormous European house spider I'd ever seen. I swear it looked like it was half-tarantula.

For some unexplained reason I decided to trap it using a small Tupperware container and then put the lid on it. My wife and kids were still asleep, and one of my teammates was about to pick me up. I remembered catching butterflies as a kid and putting an alcohol-soaked cotton ball in with them to ease them from the world. I did that same thing with the spider and stuck it in my bag.

I wanted to share this experience of awesomeness with someone. When my teammate showed up, I pulled the spider container out and showed her. "I found this spider." She seemed a little nonplussed. I continued, "You know all the nurses will probably be interested in this. It's biology and life sciences stuff, right?" She looked at me like I was crazy! In all fairness, she was right to do so. I then stuffed the Tupperware back in my bag and forgot all about it.

When we got near St. Helens, we had a hotel room where our Van 2 grabbed something to eat, showered, and took short naps. When Van 1 arrived, we would head out and hand off the room. Before we left I looked through my bag in the hotel parking lot. I then realized the ridiculousness of bringing along the spider. I was about to throw it into the bushes before I thought twice and put it back in my bag.

At the end of the race we had a couple rooms in one of the motels along the Promenade in Seaside. I had quietly taken the spider down to the beach and cast him into the wind. We walked past all the devastation from the storm that had blown down the finish line and into the warm comfort of our motel rooms. We sat around and celebrated with food and drinks and shared stories and experiences from the race.

It was then that the teammate who picked me up to start my HTC journey told the rest of the group about my spider. We laughed. Under normal circumstances, you tell a story and laugh and that's it. However, our laughter continued to get bigger and soon we were all doubled over. We all couldn't stop laughing as she regaled us with the tale of my huge spider and how I thought the nurses would "dig it." She marveled at how ridiculous it was that I "packed a spider."

The next day I was feeling pretty sore. I thought it might have been from running the seven miles of Leg 35 that was a wind tunnel that year. My wife told me something funny and I laughed. I also doubled over in pain. I realized my soreness came entirely from the fact that I had laughed so much the previous night.

We all had such a great time that when we signed up to run again in 2016 our new team name was #packyourspider.

Jack Folliard *is a retired attorney who worked 33 years officiating Pac-12 college football games. He has run Hood To Coast more than 25 times.*

We were looking for a sponsor for our team and on a lark called the Big Sky Brewing Company in Missoula, Montana. They said they'd be happy to help. Since one of their great beers is called Moose Drool, we decided to call our team the Drooling Moose Migration. We wear moose antlers and everything we do has a moose theme.

Our motto for the race is, "We migrate to hydrate." It just means that after the relay we trot to the beer garden to hydrate!

John Howarth *is an engineer from Beaverton, Oregon, who has participated in Hood To Coast 10 times.*

Over the years our team has changed. We began putting a team together at the company where I worked and incorporated the company name into the team name without much creativity. Eventually, many of the runners from the company moved on, although a few of us still continued participating in Hood To Coast.

As new faces continued to join the team, there were more and more opinions regarding the name of our team. We decided the team name had to change. It was time to come up with a flexible team name. We needed a name that would remain consistent but that would also incorporate the thoughts of our new teammates.

Thus a new team name was born—Some Days I Run Because. . . . What's so special about that name? Well, every year our team members provide the reasons they run and we then vote to select the top six reasons. Each year the reasons change, but the team name always remains the same.

The reasons have been at times real, not so real, and outlandish. It provides us with an opportunity to be creative yet still be part of something that will hopefully continue for a lifetime. What are some of our reasons for running? Here's a quick list of a few of the reasons:

SOME DAYS I RUN BECAUSE . . .

it Beats the Hell Out of Burpees

I Have No Vitamin D Left

I'm Free-Range, GMO- & BPA-Free

Sex Isn't an Option

to Avoid Social Media

to Get the Right Selfie Angle

to Keep Portland Weird

to Hit Another Food Cart

Fewer Potholes Than Driving

to Shake Off the Hangover

Beer Is Good

a Mile Feels Like 26.2

Zombies Eat the Slow Ones First

it Sounded Like a Good Idea at the Time

it's All Fun and Games Until Your Jeans Don't Fit

Of course, the relay always ends with a beer, and the reasons always end with beer too. So . . . Other Days I Drink is always last on the list of reasons every year.

Katie Olson is from St. Helens, Oregon, and captain of the Team Annie! Hood To Coast team.

Team Annie! is all about my daughter. She has a lot of medical complications and was only expected to live about two years. She's nine now and is an inspirational and amazing kid.

A few years back one of the nurses who works with her suggested we form a Hood To Coast team. I thought it was a great idea. We dedicate the team to her every year.

We think about Annie a lot during the race. In 2017 we wore pink shirts because she wanted them to be pink. We even made the men wear pink shirts. They were proud to do it because Annie is such a cool kid.

Annie always wants to be at the finish line, but she can't because she walks with a cane and it's a little hard for her to come to the beach. She cheers us on over the phone while we're running, and we take lots of pictures of the team during the race and send them to her.

It's inspirational for all of us!

Linda LaBash *began running in 1990 while attending the Oregon Police Academy for probation and parole officer training. She is an original member of the Heart 'N Sole team that has run Hood To Coast more than 25 times, and has also run more than 25 marathons, including six Boston Marathons.*

Back in January 1991 a friend rounded up 12 local women runners to form a Women's Masters team to participate in Hood To Coast. We couldn't agree on a name for our team—the names were all over the board! However, the one name that we could all live with was Heart 'N Sole. That was the beginning of a team of women runners that would last for decades and is still here today!

There were no pace requirements. We were just a bunch of women who had a passion for running, and running was our lifestyle. Some of us were marathoners, many of us were age-group winners, and some of us were slower than others. All were accepted!

We were surprised in our inaugural HTC when we placed first in our division. We continued to place in the top three every year thereafter. Over the years some members of the team dropped off for a variety of reasons and we made friends with new additions. As we aged on the run our conversations took on the changes in our lives—children marrying, becoming grandparents, marriages, divorces, health issues, and even retirements.

Of course running was always in the conversation as we talked about upcoming races and supporting each other. When the last of us turned 50, we moved up to the Women's Supermasters division. Though we have slowed down, we still place in our class.

There are three original Heart 'N Sole teammates—Ardy Dunn, Sandy Overstreet, and me. In 2015 we celebrated our 25th anniversary and invited every woman who had ever run on the team to get together. It was a special and emotional celebration, complete with photo albums from the 25 years. Our team's 25th HTC was indeed special, with wind, rain, lightning, collapsed tents in Seaside, and no finish line on the beach!

As we continue to run the relay, our ages now in the 50s, 60s and 70s, there's no reason to stop!

Adam Morris *is an attorney from Wayzata, Minnesota, who participated in his first Hood To Coast in 2014.*

When we were getting ready for our first race in 2014 we were really kind of groping around trying to figure out a team name. All the teams in the relay have names, although anyone who knows anything about the race knows that goes without saying. The pressure to have a good name is palpable, especially when you're a team captain.

Our decision was random and not really well thought out, but at the end of the day we had to land on something. People generally reacted very positively to our team name, Baba Ganoush. The name comes from the movie *Wedding Crashers*. It's a term of endearment in the movie and not the Lebanese food, which I'm sure, is quite lovely.

If you picture Owen Wilson's goofy face, not to mention add in a few classic lines from his work, it's not difficult to smile when you hear "Baba Ganoush." Finishing a close second in our team's name selection was one of Vince Vaughan's lines from the same movie, "Just the tip." However, we deemed that too risqué. Although, once we saw all the team van decorations at the race start, including several vans adorned with panties, we realized we may have been too conservative in our choice. But it all worked out in the end.

For one thing, it turns out Baba Ganoush is a spectacularly fun thing to holler at a teammate or just yell for no reason at all. The "oush" syllable in particular makes the yeller feel manly, with its low, long, ominous tone. At the same time, shouting, "Baba Gee!" has a real lightness to it.

It's also a fun thing to write on a T-shirt. I'm not sure how many of the other team names we'd want on a shirt when we're walking into a restaurant. Our name was kind of an inside joke. It doesn't mean anything to anybody else on the planet, and we liked that aspect of it as well.

The lesson we learned is that naming your team is like naming a child, maybe more important. At least the child can grow into a name. On the other hand, a team name somehow seems more absolute and defining, since all 12 members have to live with it.

What I like about our name is it fits our team. The unserious personality of our team fits the name, or has come to fit the name, which feels lighthearted and silly. But we're not trying too hard to shock anybody, and we are just as focused on the run as on the humor.

Lillian Mongeau Hughes *lives in Portland and is an education journalist. She first participated in Hood To Coast in 2008 as a last-minute substitute and returned in 2016 and 2017 to captain all-women fundraising teams.*

She Persisted was our team name for the 2017 relay. The name came from the brouhaha around Senator Elizabeth Warren being asked to stop talking when she read a letter aloud to a full Senate chamber about Jeff Sessions that was written by Coretta Scott King, the widow of Martin Luther King, Jr.

While none of us wanted to make our team name overly political, the fallout from that event inspired all of us—women in our thirties—to remember the importance of keeping on keeping on. Whether running, raising children, breaking glass ceilings, or pushing for social change, we persist because of those who have persisted before us.

We hope we honored them with our 2017 Hood To Coast team.

Martha Estes *is from Bainbridge, Washington, and has been part of the Portland To Coast team Mr. Toad's Wild Ride for about 15 years.*

I think it was our team's second year participating in Portland To Coast. We were riding in one of the vans when we saw this ceramic toad flying through the air. We all thought that it was really funny. Ever since then the name of our team has been Mr. Toad's Wild Ride.

Team Mr. Mojo Risin'

The 1994 Nike Mambu Baddu team heading to the finish line.

Chapter 7

Elite Feats

IN ITS EARLY YEARS, HOOD To Coast was primarily an event for experienced runners seeking a unique challenge, something other than traditional 10K road races and marathons. In the late 1980s and the early 1990s, sports apparel and shoe companies used HTC as a showcase for outstanding runners using their products. The relay featured elite runners from across the U.S. and around the world including Olympians, world record-holders, college All-Americans and major marathon winners, all vying for an overall first-place medal. The peak of the so-called "shoe wars" occurred in 1994 and featured a clash between elite teams from adidas and Nike.

Black Flag was the surprise overall winner of the 1990 Hood To Coast, ending the reign of the Killer Bees and overcoming what was, on paper, a superior SportHill Eugene squad. The team was assembled by **Dave Frank,** *a former steeplechase runner at Stanford University and now a math teacher and cross country and track coach at Portland's Central Catholic High School; and* **Joe Rubio,** *a former NCAA Division II All-American in the 5,000 meters and now owner of the Running Warehouse online shoe company based in San Luis Obispo, California.*

Dave Frank: I grew up in Portland and went to college at Stanford. I moved home and was training with some guys who were always talking about Hood To Coast. This was 1986. Matt Cato asked me to run with his team and I said yes, it sounded like fun. Later that spring I was visiting with a teammate of mine at Stanford, Jeff Atkinson. He set the school record in the mile that still stands today, and I mentioned HTC to him. Jeff said, "Screw that. We'll get our own team and we'll kick all their asses up there." So we put together our own team and we got beat bad, just destroyed. We had no idea what we were doing. We didn't think about having food or water in our vans. We hadn't considered that we wouldn't be able to get gas at 3 a.m. out in the middle of nowhere. We had no idea what we were doing, but we still finished, I think, in third place.

I moved back to the Bay Area, and a few years later Matt called again and asked me to do HTC. I said yes again. This was 1990. A team called the Killer Bees had won the race four years in a row and Matt was forming a team called Black Flag to exterminate the Bees.

Then almost the exact same thing happened. I mentioned it to Jeff and he said, "Screw that. We'll get our own team. We'll kick their asses." When I told Matt I was defecting again, he suggested we just take over his team. A couple of his guys were hurt and they were down to just five runners. They were already registered and had a sponsor. But I said no, we're going to do it on our own. Then he mentioned their sponsor was the Portland Brewing Company, who had donated a keg of beer. I said, "Matt, for you, we'll do it." So we became Black Flag. It wasn't our idea, but that's how it started.

I was a member of what was then the Reebok Aggies Running Club in the Bay Area, along with Joe Rubio, and we recruited a number of our Aggie buddies and some other guys for the team. We put together a pretty darn good team with some well-known guys and some other guys who weren't as well-known but were *really* good. I kept trying to explain the race to the other guys and they kept saying, "What do you mean we have to run three times and sleep in a field at 3 a.m. with thousands of other people?"

Joe Rubio: We left after work on the Thursday before the race. Everyone had jobs, and while we could take one day off, we couldn't take two or three days off. I drove up from San Luis Obispo with a couple of guys and stopped in San Francisco at about 10 p.m. to pick up another runner. Then we got a burrito and hit the road. Drove all night to Portland and showed up at Dave's mom's house in the morning.

Dave Frank: I was the only guy who was local. All 11 of the other guys drove in. They arrived about 9 a.m. and slept for a few hours at my mom's house, just sprawled out on couches, on the floor, or in my sister's bedroom, wherever they could sleep.

Joe Rubio: Dave and I didn't sleep. We looked at the map and came up with who was going to run which legs and our running order. We knew which guys were in the best shape and which guys were not as fit as they could be. We tried to piece it together that way.

Dave Frank: Even though I had done it before, I wasn't much better prepared. We didn't have all the stuff we needed. I borrowed a van from a cousin who worked at a car dealership. We had a driver for one van and the guys who weren't running in the other van would have to alternate driving.

Joe Rubio: On the drive to Timberline Lodge, Greg Whiteley, who was fourth at the

Olympic Trials a couple of times in the 1,500 meters while running at Brown University, said, "It's stupid that we're named Black Flag and we don't even have a black flag." So we stopped at a Safeway to get a flag. We bought a guy's black apron. I think White-ley gave him 20 bucks for it.

Dave Frank: Greg stole the dowel rod out of my sister's closet and threw all her clothes on the floor. She was pissed, but we had a flag pole. We taped the apron to the pole and had our black flag. We also bought a piñata of a bee and hockey masks like Jason wore in the movie *Halloween* so nobody would recognize us. We started at 11 or 11:30 at night that year and both vans went up to the start. We all had our hockey masks on and people were looking at us like we were crazy, which we sort of were.

Joe Rubio: We put the bee piñata on the ground, grabbed some sticks, and beat it to death.

Dave Frank: I knew a few of the guys on the Killer Bees, but I wasn't close to any of them. As it turned out, we didn't really race them. We beat them by about an hour. But there was a new team from Eugene, Oregon, that had a whole bunch of good runners everyone knew.

Joe Rubio: Jim Hill had run for the University of Oregon and had a company called SportHill. He had been a two-time PAC-10 cross country champion and an NCAA All-American, and was very, very good. He put together a team which included Art Boileau, another University of Oregon runner, who was a two-time Olympian in the marathon and a two-time winner of the Los Angeles Marathon. They had Don Clary, who was a U.S. Olympian in the 5,000 meters and had competed in the IAAF World Cross Country Championships. Pat Haller, Brad Hudson, and Peter Fonseca, who had all finished among the top 20 in the NCAA cross country championships the year before, were all on the team. Brad is a prominent coach now and ran about a 2:13 marathon in high school; and Peter eventually became a 2:13 guy. They had Matt McGuirk, who was a University of Oregon All-American in the steeplechase.

Dave Frank: They had a stacked team. A few of our guys were known. Jeff (Atkinson) made the Olympic finals in 1988 in the 1,500 meters, but he wasn't really a long-distance runner. We had Marc Olesen, who broke four minutes in the mile in high school in Canada and captured the 1985 PAC-10 cross country title while at Stanford. We had Harry Green, who was a seven-time All-American distance runner at the University of Texas. We also had a whole bunch of guys you never heard of—Kevin Ostenberg, Rob Anex, Mike Livingston, and Victor Santamaria. We had some people who were really good and we had some people no one knew about. A bunch of 30-minute 10K guys. Thirty minutes is really solid, but a guy like Don Clary was a 28-minute 10K guy. So I don't think anyone would look at our lineup and think we were capable of winning. Beating the Killer Bees was a reasonable goal, but the level of talent on the SportHill Eugene team was far beyond ours. They had a whole bunch of guys who were, on paper, definitely better than we were. But we didn't really care. We just wanted to race.

Joe Rubio: The really cool thing about the race was the lead switched at least 17 times between the two teams. We ran at about a 5:03 mile pace for the whole race.

Dave Frank: Since I had done the relay before, I was "the voice of reason." I told the guys, "On the first leg, you can't run all-out. You got to save something. On the second leg you can race as hard as you want and then just hope you have something left for the third leg." Pretty much everyone ignored me completely and just went out and ran as hard they possibly could. Even doing that, after about seven legs, we were down by four or five minutes. They had Art Boileau running and we had Rob Anex. Rob who was a very good runner, a 2:18 marathon guy, but Art was a 2:11 guy. We figured we would be down by seven or eight minutes after the leg. We still have no idea what happened. Somehow Rob made up about two and a half minutes and we were only about a minute and a half behind. We started catching up here and there and by Leg 12 we were leading.

Joe Rubio: It went back and forth after that. I remember watching the sun rise and looking off in the distance for the runners. We could see Mike Livingston, and behind him was this other flashlight coming at a really high pace. It was Brad Hudson and he beat Mike. Then Mike came back on his third leg and beat Brad, putting us ahead for good.

Dave Frank: Mike put together a big last leg. He vowed to do it after his second one, saying, "There's no way that guy's beating me next time. I'm putting a minute on it."

Joe Rubio: When they were doing strides on the last leg Brad made a little comment to Mike, something like, "It's on." Mike's a hothead and that was all he needed. He just blew Brad away. Killed him.

Dave Frank: Back then there weren't a lot of rules regarding the vans. So we would leapfrog the vans. We put all the even-numbered runners in one van, and the odd-numbered guys in another. You were able to run your leg and jog a little bit to loosen up because you weren't in a hurry to get to the next stop. After my first leg I saw one of our vans go by. Then I saw the other van coming and looked right at it, and it drove right past me. I asked the guy I was running against, I believe it was Don Clary, "Don, can I get a ride in your van?" And he said, "Yeah, of course." So I rode with the SportHill team after my first leg until I could get back to my team. I got left behind again on my second leg and rode with Art Boileau's parents, who were fielding a team too. It was just crazy stuff.

Joe Rubio: That's the culture of most competitive runners. It's to strive together. It doesn't mean kick the crap out of the other guy. It means work together to try and get things done. We're all in the same boat. We're trying to help each other get better. We also knew that when the thing was over we were going to get drunk together and share stories and lie to each other.

Dave Frank: Even though those guys had better numbers than us and their personal records were better, they might not have all been in the same shape that they were at their peak. I got to believe that a few of their guys weren't quite as fit or didn't take it as seriously as they might have. Once we got going we sort of felt like we had something to prove, maybe more than they did. They had a lot of big names . . .

Joe Rubio: . . . I honestly don't think that was it. If I had actually known who those guys were beforehand—I mean I kind of figured it out as we were going—but we were just out there racing. The tough part about going to big events is that you put people on pedestals because of their past times and accomplishments. We didn't have those pedestals. We just had a bunch of knuckleheads who didn't know who Don Clary was or didn't know who Jim Hill was. We were just running.

Initially, we were just going up there to have a good time. Most of us had no idea what HTC was all about or what it meant. But when we started racing—it was on. It was an amazing back and forth. I wasn't looking at the rosters and going, "These people are way, way better than us." We were going back and forth, and back and forth, and back and forth. And finally, we broke away. I remember running my last leg. That was when you could drive alongside your runner. I'm out there hammering and the guys roll up beside me and they're yelling, "Come on, come on, come on." I just looked over and said, "Get the %#@$ away from me. Leave me alone." I was on the job.

Dave Frank: A lot of the race is run in the middle of the night and when you get the handoff you just start running. You can't really tell who anybody is and you can't make out any faces even if you did know who they were. You just take the handoff, find your rhythm, run as hard as you can, and then hand off to the next guy.

We ended up winning by seven or eight minutes. That year was the first year since they began staggering the starting times that the wining team was the first team to cross the finish line. At some point in the middle of the afternoon we passed the last slow team out on the course. We were starting the last go-round and Jeff Atkinson pulled out a bunch of disposable razors and shaving cream and said, "We gotta shave for this last leg. We gotta get clean."

Joe Rubio: We had this keg of beer from our sponsor. HTC didn't want the beer inside the fenced area. So we put the keg outside the fence and had the nozzle coming through the fence. We shared it with everybody who wanted some, and if they were female and moderately attractive they got as much as they wanted.

Dave Frank: Then it got confiscated. A police deputy showed up and said it was illegal. It was empty by then, so we didn't really care. Until the next morning, when we realized we had promised to bring it back to the Portland Brewing Company.

Joe Rubio: I slept on the beach that night. Where did you sleep?

Dave Frank: My cousin loaned us a tent, which disappeared at some point. Some of the guys slept in the vans. The women's team that won was called Chicks that Crank . . .

Joe Rubio: . . . We called them the Chicks that Spank . . .

Dave Frank: . . . And some of our team slept on the floor in their rooms. Some guys also slept on the beach.

Dave Frank: We showed up for the awards ceremony the next morning and to a man we were wearing exactly what we had worn to finish the race the day before. Nobody had changed. No showers. We were clean shaven, but we didn't look particularly good.

Joe Rubio: We were a motley crew, to say the least. But we did set a record that stood for several years until the Nike and adidas teams came along. For a bunch of ragtag guys we did pretty well.

Dave Frank: We finally figured out that we had to get our keg back. We had guys who had to be back to work on Monday and had to drive to San Luis Obispo or San Francisco. So we went to the police station to get back our keg. There was a deputy there and he was not going to give it to us. We didn't have a receipt. He was being a real pain in the ass. Finally the sheriff came in and asked the deputy what was going on. The deputy explained the whole thing, making us look like a bunch of bad guys. The sheriff looked at us and said, "So you ran the race, right?" And we said, "Yeah, we ran the race." And he says, "How'd you do?" And we said, "Well, we won." He goes, "You won the whole thing?" And we said, "Yeah, we won the whole thing." He looked at the deputy and goes, *"Give them their keg back."*

Joe Rubio: We had some people with a lot of great running accomplishments. And I would say that, to a man, that was a really positive event. We had a really, really good, positive experience.

Dave Frank: I've experienced a lot of great things in the running world. I ran in three Olympic Trials, but I would say winning HTC might be my all-time favorite running memory. Doing it with your friends and suffering together, that makes it way more special. I've been lucky to do the relay maybe a dozen times now. It's fun every time, no matter if you run on a fast team or a not-so-fast team. Whether you run eight-minute miles or five-minute miles, people are all sort of going for the same thing, and I find that to be really enjoyable.

Joe Rubio: It was one of the best experiences of my life. It really was. We went up there and we weren't really a team. When we came out of it we were a damn good team. I don't think there's any person on that 1990 team who wouldn't look back on that and go, "That was #@$%ing awesome." Maybe the details get a little fuzzy, but memories don't. There was absolutely no plan. That's difficult for some people to grasp. It was just a bunch of jackasses going up to run a race. That's all it was. There wasn't any plan to win the thing or do anything spectacular. That was the cool thing about it. It was just like, shoot, I don't know—it was like Woodstock or something.

Dave Harkin grew up in Seattle, attended the University of Oregon, and spent four years teaching in Louisiana, Colorado, and Seattle before returning to Oregon. He and his wife, Paula, have owned and operated the Portland Running Company since 2000. In 1988 Dave participated in his first Hood To Coast

My second time competing in Hood To Coast was when I was a runner at the University of Oregon.

These guys put together an awesome team full of Olympians and national champions, along with guys who ran at the University of Oregon. It was an amazing team fronted by Jim Hill, the owner of SportHill Athletics. It was a highly visible team led by Jim, who qualified for the Olympic Trials and ran a sub-28:00 10K when it wasn't fashionable to run that fast.

Jim put together this dream team and then, of course, like every other team, they lost someone close to the race. That's how I joined the team.

At the same time, I remember another team that was put together in San Francisco that came to run the relay that year. They were called Black Flag. Today they're a pretty legendary team.

All the guys on our team and Black Flag were established runners, including some Olympians, others who participated in the Olympic Trials, and several marathoners.

I was easily the slowest guy on our team, by a lot. Probably by two minutes over a 10K. There was a ton of pressure on me to do well because it was a real grudge match between two teams with all these guys who had raced against each other for the last eight or nine years.

Although I ran track at the University of Oregon, my third leg was probably the hardest I'd ever run in my life. I had all these guys counting on me in this huge race. I distinctly remember getting the handoff and being tied with Black Flag. With five legs remaining we were dead even, but we ended up losing by about two minutes.

It's a phenomenal memory because it was an amazing race to the very end.

John Truax was born in Montesano, Washington, and moved to Corvallis, Oregon, when he was in high school. He ran track throughout high school and at the University of Oregon. He began working at Nike in 1990 and continues to work for the company today. He was the captain of the Nike Hood To Coast team Mambu Baddu in 1993 and 1994.

In 1993 I was captain of the Nike Hood To Coast team Mambu Baddu. I put the team together with Matt Cato, who had run the race with the Killer Bees for many years. We combined forces and reached out to people we knew in the running community. The team was pretty much all local guys from the Portland area, including some former members of the Killer Bees and some people from Nike. Our goal was to put together a team that could win HTC—and we did.

I remember picking up our runners as we were heading toward the race start at Mt. Hood. I think Matt was driving, and he either misjudged a turn or ran into a curb, and we popped a tire in Portland. That was the beginning of our adventure that year. We were in a bit of a panic because we were already running late and had to quickly switch out the tire and get up to the mountain to start running.

I think I came up with the team name Mambu Baddu, which in Swahili means, "The best is yet to come." I was talking to some people who knew Swahili, including Martin Keino, who at the time was doing an internship at Nike. Martin's father, Kip Keino, won two Olympic gold medals for Kenya in distance running. Nike had a big group of Kenyan athletes who were doing really well back then. We always tried to think of some different names for our shoes, and sometimes we had names that originated in Swahili.

The name Mambu Baddu just kind of stuck. I don't remember any other names we were contemplating. We kind of wanted a fresh start with our team in 1993 because it was a blend of different people and teams.

There wasn't any pressure on us that year. It was just the drive the guys on the team had. We all wanted to win it, and that's what we set out to do. I think Bucknell University had a team that was pretty competitive over the years, a bunch of alumni who would come out and run the race. They won it a few times and had some battles with the Killer Bees over the years. Our goal the whole time was to win it with a bunch of Oregonians.

David Murphy *was born in Liverpool, England, and attended Western Kentucky University. He competed internationally in both the 5,000 and 10,000 meters and was a two-time winner of the Falmouth Road Race in Massachusetts, as well as runner-up in the 1984 New York City Marathon. He moved to Portland with adidas in 1993 and put together the Rolling Thunder team that competed in Hood To Coast in 1994 and 1995. Now he lives in the San Francisco area and consults on various sporting events.*

I was the running promotions manager at adidas in 1994. We were a relatively new company in Portland and had many employees who had moved from other cities to join us. We had seen the results of the 1993 Hood To Coast, when the first-year Nike team Mambu Baddu was the overall winner of the relay.

My boss, Adrian Leek, came to me one day and said we needed to put a team together to compete against Nike in HTC. At the time, we were new Oregonians and trying to get established right in Nike's backyard. We liked to have a lot of fun and push their buttons any chance we got—in a good way.

We were all extremely competitive and we loved to go head to head with Nike, whether it was in business or in any event in any sport. It was a very good rivalry. It was a great time in the history of running. We enjoyed shaking things up.

We pitched the event to several elite adidas athletes as a completely amateur event. I said, "Why don't you come out for a fun weekend. You can use it as a training run. It will be like an off-site get-together before your fall training starts. And, oh yeah, you'll be going head to head with Alberto Salazar and the Nike Mambu Baddu team."

That's how we put the team together. It was a tough time of the year for most elite athletes because they were just finishing off the track racing season. We also had a couple of runners coming off injuries, and things like that. Just as Nike did, we had tremendous athletes on our team. They understood they were coming to compete in a tough race, a race they'd never done before. It's a very unique race. Three legs and running through the night. You don't normally present that type of event to world-class runners, but they all accepted the challenge in good stride.

We were late getting our entry in, and I believe Bob Foote probably informed Alberto that we entered a team. Alberto then went to work making sure Nike had the best team possible, which led to a very exciting head-to-head contest.

It was definitely an adventure. We got started late with our planning and just finding vans was a challenge. No vans were available in Portland, so we had to widen our search.

We ended up going and picking up our vans in Salem, Oregon. At that point, beggars couldn't be choosers, but those vans were awful. They shouldn't have even been allowed on the road.

I was the team captain and driving Van 1. We met at adidas in Portland before we headed off to Mt. Hood, and everybody was in a good mood. We were at the start and everyone was getting ready to head down the mountain. I got in the van and turned on the ignition. Nothing! It was dead. I tried it again and it was just not happening. The team was out doing their warm-ups and getting ready, and our van wasn't going anywhere.

I looked over at the van on our left. All the runners were chuckling away, realizing we were adidas and our van wasn't going to start. I said, "Jumper cables, guys?" Lo and behold, they had jumper cables. So we were very lucky and got the van fired up. Our first runner departed and off we went. I kept the van running all the time, right up until we had to fill it up with gas.

We had no familiarity with the course and what was happening. There were a couple of occasions where our runners went off course. We had to scream and shout at them to get them back on course. We lost some time early on because of that. Would it have made a difference? Who knows? I can't say whether or not going off course would have shaped a different outcome. Maybe a lack of experience hurt us a little bit. Maybe other teams had a little advantage because they'd done it before and knew some of the logistical issues. But as far as getting after it and having a great competition, it was tremendous.

We really thought we were going to win, but Nike pulled away with three or four legs remaining. It was a tremendous race because it was head to head the whole way. It was just back and forth, back and forth. A real duel—the type you would expect. It was great athletes going at it in the spirit of competition. It was pure competition—two teams just duking it out. There were a couple of places on the course where Alberto and I crossed paths and we tipped our hats to each other and smiled.

What surprised us the most was just how hard it was. It was a big surprise to all of us—the runners, the van drivers, and all the team supporters. Everyone ran their hearts out though. Because of the season, it wasn't a time when our runners were all in peak fitness, but, our guys gutted it out.

And it was a blast. I can look back on it fondly now and say it was a great thing having participated in HTC. I'm sure all the Rolling Thunder team members remember it fondly, as well, even though they probably still hate me for bringing them out to the event and making them run so hard every single leg.

Running is truly an individual sport, but if you bring people together on a relay team and the team is dependent on your effort, you tend to step it up a notch. There were some moans and groans in the vans at times. Especially before the third leg, after each runner had already run two legs and was ready for a massage and a shower. Now they had this clown Murphy telling them, "Okay, are you ready to go again?" It was a very unique experience, but again, because of the nature of the event, everybody pulled together and got after it.

There weren't any hard feelings afterward. We were very disappointed not to win— and tired. We gave everything we had, but it turned out it wasn't our weekend. And that's the way it goes.

It was a tremendous race, and in the end the stronger team won. If we came back and ran it a month later, maybe there would have been a different outcome. It was that type of race. Maybe with a bit more experience the outcome might have been different. You just don't know.

There wasn't a single Rolling Thunder runner who couldn't say they gave it everything they had. You could see it in their faces when they finished each leg. We were a very close team, and I was very privileged to work with them. We had a very strong team spirit the whole time. They were all very proud to represent adidas and performed their best. They were great athletes, as were the Nike athletes.

After the awards ceremony we went back to the house we rented in Seaside. I have a vivid picture in my head to this day of the entire team lying on the grass out in front of the house asleep. They were just out. It wasn't until dinner time and the other post-race festivities started that they came back to life.

The next morning we headed back to Portland. I was driving the van and the boys were in the back. Keith Dowling from the team was riding shotgun. He suddenly looked over and said, "Dave, is that smoke I see coming out of the engine?" We pulled over and jumped out because the engine was on fire. Everyone was laughing.

We managed to douse the flames from the engine, got our gear out of the van, and put our thumbs out. A very kind HTC team of nurses from a Portland hospital saw us, pulled over, and gave us a lift back to the city. Our van was left on the side of the road for the rental company to collect at their own expense. Let that be a lesson. Get into the queue to get a van early. Make that your first and foremost task.

The next year, 1995, was different. Some of our athletes had different competitions or commitments already confirmed for that time of the season. Alberto, as competitive as he is, was a complete win-at-all-costs type of guy. But in 1995 he sort of went over the top and was flying people in from all over the world. He went wild. So the race wasn't as exciting. It wasn't the same head-to-head competition, and it didn't have the same shine on it.

That 1994 race was the one with the real drama. It's the one to remember!

John Truax *was born in Montesano, Washington, and moved to Corvallis, Oregon, when he was in high school. He ran track throughout high school and at the University of Oregon. He began working at Nike in 1990 and continues to work for the company today. He was the captain of the Nike Hood To Coast team Mambu Baddu in 1993 and 1994.*

At Nike in 1994 we heard adidas was putting together a Hood To Coast team called Rolling Thunder. We stepped it up that year with help from Alberto Salazar. It was the first year Alberto ran on the team. He was coming back from some injuries, but he had just won the Comrades Marathon, the world's oldest ultramarathon. Alberto was kind of making a comeback as far as just competitive running. I asked him to join our team. Alberto said, "Sure. That sounds fun."

Alberto helped us bring in some runners from outside the local Portland crew. Jon Sinclair and Dan Held were brought in to run. Tom Ansberry, who had already moved to Portland and was training under Alberto, joined our team. Tony Williams was a runner in Seattle who became part of our team.

Seth Simonds was another member of the team. He and I were college roommates and great friends. Seth had competed in the steeplechase at the U.S. Olympic trials in 1988 and 1992, and was living in Eugene, Oregon, while still trying to run competitively.

Seth actually broke his arm about a month before the race and was still in a cast during the event. At the time, Seth was living in a tent and training in the Cascade Mountains all summer long and that's where he broke his arm. He came down out of the mountains to run the relay with us. He had to take a few weeks off from his training before the race because of his arm and he wasn't in great shape.

I distinctly remember Seth's last leg that year in the Coast Range during a foggy morning. Seth got the stick from Alberto with the lead on his last leg. We were waiting for Seth to come into the next exchange, and all of the sudden an adidas guy came out of the fog ahead of him. We were like, "Oh, no. What's going on?" Seth had run Leg 1 and just flown down the mountain, but his feet were shredded from running downhill. We started counting the difference. The clock kept running as the adidas guy came through. Ten seconds passed and then fifteen seconds. After twenty seconds, all of a sudden, we could hear Seth. We couldn't see Seth because of the fog—but we could hear him breathing. He came rolling in through the fog, just gasping for air. He lost the lead to the adidas team by close to 20 seconds on his last leg. What stood out for me was hearing Seth and not seeing him come through the fog—it was eerie!

That basically tells the story of the battle between the two teams. It was back and forth throughout the entire race and throughout the night. I don't think there was ever a time where either team had a sustained lead.

I was Runner 4 and we were still behind when I began running, but I held my own and maybe even gained a few seconds. I was running against Danny Lopez, who was a team-mate of mine at the University of Oregon. He competed for the U.S. in the steeplechase at the 1992 Olympics in Barcelona.

I remember the one-two punch of Dan Held and Tom Ansberry that got us back in the game. They really made a difference and ran unbelievably in their last legs. Dan was our next-to-last runner.

Alberto was the anchor (Runner 12) and he had a pretty sizable lead when he started his final leg. He was running against Todd Williams, who was one of the top Americans in the 10,000 meters for many years and a two-time U.S. cross country champion. We were all a little worried because Alberto was not the same as he had been back in the day, but he was running fairly well. His lead was about 20 seconds, maybe a little bit more. It was a good ending and we were all really happy that Alberto held him off.

We just rented two white vans and were stealth—we didn't decorate the vans or anything. Maybe we had a small Nike flag, but that was about it. Our two vans stuck together the whole time. It was small enough back then that you could do that. I remember Alberto yelling out the window at our guys. He was shouting encouragement, "You got to do this. You got to hold it together." It was pretty intense. There was also no sleeping. We were going. There was a lot of pressure to defend the HTC title that we won in 1993.

At the finish we parked the two vans and the whole team was waiting for Alberto to hit the beach and we had a small red Nike flag. We gave the flag to Alberto as we all ran the last half-mile to the finish together. Then we all passed the flag around as we were running down the boardwalk in Seaside. Even our van drivers ran with us to the finish. There was a pretty big crowd there cheering us on and it was fun to cross the finish line together.

During the race we didn't realize how important it was to win. Obviously we wanted to beat the adidas team, but we didn't realize how closely Phil Knight was watching the results and following along until it was over. For him, it was more than just a running race. It was a business battle. For us, it was a battle against other runners, but for him it was like we needed to take them down—we took them down in business and now we needed to take them down in HTC.

The adidas team had motivation because of Rob Strasser, who was known as Rolling Thunder. He had passed away and it was a chance for those guys to pay tribute to him. Rob had history with Nike before moving to adidas. Nike was not happy about him leaving to go to the competition. It was definitely deeper than just 12 guys running against each other.

It's competition. For our team it was all about competing and trying to beat people. It wasn't that we didn't like these people. It's just like brothers tend to be—you turn it on and off. You can be friends after the race, but during the race there's no friendship. I mean there's friendship, but it's definitely blocked during the competition. It's hidden for 15 or 16 hours, or until it's over.

I don't want to use the word hatred, but we definitely had a strong dislike for the Three Stripes, and they had a strong dislike for the Swoosh.

After the race Nike threw a celebration out on the patio on campus. It was one of those rare, all-employee meetings at Nike, and it was to celebrate our win. We came running out wearing our team warm-ups. Alberto was given a convertible BMW for the victory. We all got leather coats that said Mambu Baddu on the back and had our time on the sleeve. I still have mine!

A few days later, adidas took out a full-page ad in the *Oregonian* showing a black convertible with its hood up and some comment. I don't remember exactly what it said, but something like, "we're going to take you down."

After 1994 I stopped running HTC because it got a little too competitive for me. Not necessarily the competitive atmosphere but the level of athletes that were being brought in. I think we got caught up in it a little bit and took it to another level, which was beyond my ability. I believe we brought in some runners from Kenya and some other people, and it got a little too out of control.

Bob Foote *is the founder and chairman of Hood To Coast.*

After the 1993 race adidas threw down a challenge and said they were going to beat Nike in the 1994 Hood To Coast. And of course Nike said, "No way. That's not going to happen."

An adidas team was put together featuring many of their world-class runners—guys from all over the world. The team featured 12 of the very best runners they could muster. At the time the decision was made to form a team, Rob Strasser was the CEO of adidas of America. He was a former big guy at Nike and had been with the company during the early years. When he left Nike there were some bad feelings, and I heard it was a bitter separation. One of the first things Rob did when he became adidas CEO was to move the company headquarters to Portland.

The opportunity to beat Nike seemed to be personal for Rob. His nickname was "Rolling Thunder" because he was this big, tall presence. Although he passed away before the 1994 race, the elite adidas team was named in his honor and became adidas Rolling Thunder.

Phil Knight seemed to also take this challenge to heart. He said, "There's no way we're going to lose to adidas." Nike reached far and wide to put together a team of top runners. Alberto Salazar was on the team, and helped handpick the other members of the team. Alberto is extremely detailed, exceptionally organized, very analytical, and he'd run the relay in the past. He helped pick the perfect combination of runners for the team. The Nike team was called Mambu Baddu, which means "the best is yet to come" in Swahili.

It was a back-and-forth race between the two teams, and it really came down to the last two legs. Nike was holding a slim lead and had two of their best runners to run the final two legs, including Alberto as the anchor runner on Leg 36. Those guys just blistered off unbelievable times, maybe around a 4:20 pace, on the last two legs.

It was just an unbelievable event.

A few days after the race, they closed the entire Nike campus and had a big party. There were thousands of people, including employees and their families, and I was invited to attend. I remember someone from Nike talking about the spirit of the company and what Nike had accomplished by beating adidas in HTC. He said something like, "We are challenged from every direction all the time, and it's in our culture to never give up and never back down to a challenge." Then the Mambu Baddu team was called up to the stage.

About that time a black BMW convertible started rolling by as the crowd watched. It stopped right in front of the stage. Phil says, "I'm starting a new award this year and it's going to be called the Alberto Salazar Spirit and Inspiration Award. This first year we're going to give this award to Alberto. This car is a thank you from Nike for your efforts to put together a team to win HTC." They gave Alberto this brand-new convertible and it just blew everyone away. It was unbelievable.

It was probably a mistake for me to be there because I saw exactly how important our relationship is with Nike, and being a part of the company's culture. Nike said they bring in all these foreign teams from Asia and Europe, along with senior officials, vice presidents, and heads of departments to Oregon for a week and give them an education in the spirit and culture of Nike. They also visit Hayward Field in Eugene, where many legendary track and field events have taken place, and culminate the week with all the teams running in HTC.

It showed me that the relay was a big part of Nike's corporate culture.

Steve Bence *made his initial appearance in Hood To Coast in 1985 and since then he has participated in the event 28 times, split evenly between running and walking teams. In 1977 he began working at Nike and still works for the company today, while also serving as the unofficial historian for Nike's involvement in HTC.*

In 1993 John Truax was the captain of a non-corporate Nike Hood To Coast team called Mambu Baddu that won the Men's Open division—and the overall race. After the Nike victory that year, adidas quietly plotted to bring together some of their best runners for an elite team and steal the race in 1994. Alberto Salazar heard about the adidas plan and arranged to bring in some of the best Nike runners from around the U.S. to form a team.

The two teams, Nike's Mambu Baddu and Rolling Thunder from adidas, went head to head for almost 16 hours in the closest—and fastest—race in event history. Mambu Baddu crushed the course record in 15 hours and 56 minutes, averaging less than five minutes per mile en route to the victory. It's the Men's Open division record that still stands today. (The following year, Mambu Baddu competed in the new Men's Elite division and broke their own course record, which still stands today.)

On the Monday after the race, Phil Knight honored the Mambu Baddu team on the Nike campus. The Salazar Award was created to recognize a Nike employee who "did the right thing." Salazar was the first recipient of the award and received a brand-new car. Phil introduced all the world-class runners on the team and asked them about their experience competing in HTC, and their answers went something like this . . .

"I loved it! Running is usually an individual sport and I had the opportunity to run as a team."

"I hated it! I'll never do it again and I wouldn't recommend it to anyone."

"I'd run it again. We covered 200 miles of beautiful Oregon scenery."

"This was the hardest thing I've ever done."

"It was worse than a marathon. I basically ran three hard 10Ks over ten hours with no real rest while in a packed van."

Bob Foote *is the founder and chairman of Hood To Coast.*

There was a team from Boulder, Colorado, that battled the Nike Mambu Baddu team in 1993. The group from Boulder was an elite team with many amazingly fast athletes. They called themselves the Rocky Mountain Oysters.

Jon Sinclair, who had several American records in road races, was on the team, along with England's Steve Jones, who set a world record in the marathon. Another runner on the team was South Africa's Mark Plaatjes, who won the marathon at the World Championships earlier that month.

The team from Boulder came to Hood To Coast to take on and try to defeat Nike Mambu Baddu. Even though it was a horse race all the way to the end, the Mambu Baddu team's previous experience in the relay is what really helped them prevail.

I saw Mark and all his teammates at Timberline Lodge before they started. I couldn't help it, so I went over to Mark and introduced myself. After talking for a while, I had a question for Mark. I said, "You just won the marathon at the World Championships a few weeks ago. You're the world record-holder in the event. Why are you guys here at HTC?" It just didn't make any sense to me.

Mark responded, "Wherever we compete around the world there's always talk about Hood To Coast. We've been talking about it for years. Outside of the Olympics, we've been told it's the best competition anywhere in the world, and we always wanted to do it. At our Super Bowl party, we made the decision that this was going to be our year."

And Mark added, "For 51 weeks of the year I run to put food on the table. One week a year—it's my week—and this year I chose Hood To Coast to be my time."

They were doing it on their own—for the sheer joy of competing in the purest form. It was a great compliment to us that they would choose to run with nothing at stake except pride and great competition.

Jason Humble lives in Sherwood, Oregon, and works in footwear development at Nike. He was a member of the track and field team at the University of Oregon and first ran Hood To Coast in 1986.

I ran a couple of years with the Avia corporate team. That was fun. Pete Julian, who was a great runner and now coaches the Nike Oregon Project, was on the team.

Not everyone is right for team competition. We had one guy on the team who was a duathlete and was running professionally. He was a rather arrogant person and thought he was going to roll onto this corporate team and be *the guy.* I was only about a year out of college at the time, but I'd been doing the race for a number of years and knew how to do it.

Pete was just starting his professional career and still really fast. This other guy was talking about how great he was going to be during the race. Someone mentioned that Pete was pretty good and this guy pretty much pooh-poohed that. So Pete went out on a seven-mile leg and averaged about 4:40, and this guy didn't like that. He didn't want to be second fiddle on the team—he wanted to be the king.

Depending on what you're going after and who's leading the charge, things on the better teams can get pretty serious. The Killer Bees were another really serious team and all their runners had certain times to hit. If you didn't hit your time, the team captain, or whoever was running the show, would be riding your ass. They would say, "Hey, you were supposed to run 4:48s and you only ran a 4:56 on your final leg. That's not good enough. We just lost four or five seconds." On those teams it would get a little aggressive at times.

I really enjoyed the competitiveness of the event. My nickname in school was "Not So" (Humble) and it was well deserved. I was, shall we say, fairly confident in myself. I'd let people know how well I was going to do.

At that time I knew a bunch of the guys who ran on the Killer Bees. I told them I wanted to run with them the next year and they told me I had to try out—that there was a time trial. I started thinking to myself, "What the hell do you mean there's a time trial? I don't need to time trial. I'm better than half the guys on the team."

Ultimately, I did the time trial. I made the team relatively easily and was then competing against friends who had been my high school teammates and had gone on to other colleges or teams. So it was a lot fun and there was lots of banter back and forth.

That year a team from Colorado, the Rocky Mountain Oysters, came out to do the race. Steve Jones, who held the world record in the marathon for a time, was on the team. Mark Plaatjes, who won a gold medal in the marathon at the World Championships, was also on the team, along with a handful of other professionals.

There was a leg that went through Damascus at that time, right along Highway 212, where there were a lot of fairly good rolling hills. It was at night and I was moving along pretty good, running about five-minute miles.

I started hearing this heavy breathing coming up behind me. I was thinking, "No way in hell is somebody catching me at this pace." I started running a little harder, but the breathing behind me kept getting closer and closer. Finally, I looked back and it's Jones. He just goes hammering by me up this hill. I was blown away. Here I was averaging about five-minute miles and he just hammered me—he must have been running 4:42s. I was totally shocked.

Later on, I was sitting on the tailgate of a truck chatting with Plaatjes and Jones. I was bitching at Jones for making me look bad out there. It was a lot of fun, the bantering and the camaraderie and the chance to be with those really good runners. Guys you wouldn't normally have an opportunity to talk with or compete against. I was just getting out of college and was thinking about giving this running thing a go, so it was great to get to talk to those guys.

Kirk Helzer *is from Tualatin, Oregon, and is a longtime competitor in Hood To Coast with the Dirty Half Dozen +6 team. His father, Richard, ran in the very first HTC in 1982.*

Some of my favorite Hood To Coast memories are of the different legs and the different battles, whether it was going over Bald Peak or running through the Coast Range or just grinding and competing and going up against some of the elite teams.

One of the things I'll always remember is running head to head with Olympian Mary Decker, and losing to her. And besides, my teammates wouldn't ever let me forget it!

It happened in 1996 during the "shoe wars," when Nike, Rebook, adidas, and others were sending these super elite teams and runners to compete in HTC—high-gun runners and professionals. Not only were the teams fast, they also generated exposure and created interest in the event. It was fun for us to see elite runners. It was also a year when the Olympics were taking place, which was always exciting for us as distance runners.

Nike had put together an elite women's team with some of the best road racers who were competing at that time. Decker was probably their top runner and had just come back from the Olympics. She was about our age, and we had grown up watching her career, along with her trials and tribulations as a competitive runner. Now she was making a comeback.

We knew we were going to have a tough time matching Decker's team's speed. We were a few years past our really competitive days, but we still took pride in beating as many teams as possible, and we had never been beaten by a women's team. It was a good challenge for us to try to beat a hand-picked elite women's team.

They started out behind us, and we knew if they caught us and passed us, we wouldn't be able to stick with them. I was running Leg 12 heading toward downtown Portland. As I walked up to the exchange before my leg, I noticed I was going to be racing Mary. Our runner came around the corner about four seconds before their runner made her way around the corner. I knew it was going to be close and I'd be going head to head with Mary Decker. Of course, my whole team was there yelling, "You *cannot* let her beat you."

I took off and tried to build a little bit of a gap. We were both probably running a 5:20- or 5:30-mile pace. Then she came up behind me and we dueled for a little bit. We might have exchanged a few words and I may have said something to her about trying to make me work a little bit. Then she just took off and passed me.

I knew I'd never hear the end of it if I didn't keep her in sight, so I tried to make sure she didn't get too far ahead. I ended up finishing about a block behind her. There were no words exchanged at the end of our "duel." We might have exchanged looks, but I doubt she was even aware of what was happening.

Her team ended up beating us by about 45 minutes and a few places in the overall standings. We would see them from time to time along the course. It was a lot of fun for us to go toe to toe against that team, watch them, and try to chase them. It was all about the competition.

One of the great things about the race is you can go head to head with, or get passed by, an elite or professional runner, someone that you wouldn't normally get to run with. In a normal race, you just wouldn't have that opportunity. But in HTC it happens all the time.

Ann Trason, *from Auburn, California, is considered one of the world's all-time top ultra-marathon runners, setting more than 20 world records. She won the Western States 100-Mile Endurance Run in 1995 (one of her 14 victories in that prestigious event) and followed it up a few weeks later with her only appearance in Hood To Coast.*

I can't tell you how flattering it was to be asked to be part of the Nike Women's Elite team in 1995. They had some very fast people on the team. I was like, "Wow, they want me to be on *that* team?" I was an ultrarunner in training for much longer races, so I wasn't able to train specifically for Hood To Coast. I looked at it as more of a tempo run than anything else.

I remember everyone took it quite seriously. *Oh yeah,* very seriously. I believe adidas beat us that year, and then Nike came back the next year and won. Nike doesn't like to lose and took it very, very seriously. I could feel the pressure, and I felt like I was in over my head.

When I looked at the rosters and saw who was on the adidas team, I knew we were in trouble. I mean, you can see the times and do the math. I may be an ultrarunner, but I'm not *that* stupid. I wasn't sure how much magic we could pull off, but I didn't think it would be that much.

I treated the event pretty much like an ultra. Of course, I didn't mind the longer legs and I liked running at night. I thought it was pretty funny that some people were complaining about running with flashlights because that's what ultrarunners do all the time. And the race certainly got people out of their comfort zone. I gave it everything I had. I made all my splits. But I kept wishing I were faster.

Of course we were disappointed that we lost, but I thought the party at the beach was fantastic.

In some respects, an event like HTC is more like an ultramarathon experience—being up all night and using flashlights to run—than going out and hammering a 5K or 10K in the daylight.

The organization was terrific. I put on races now and it's a lot of work. All the people, the permits, making sure everyone is prepared and does what they're supposed to do. You've got to be serious about the safety stuff. They seemed to have really good volunteers and good race staff.

It's amazing it's stayed on this long. That says a lot about the organizational skill and the people who put it on. I really applaud what they're doing.

I loved how people would write on their vans and have fun team names. That was really cool. It seemed like the type of event where you get together with your buddies once a year and that's the only time you see them. That's fantastic.

I was asked to do it again a couple of other times, but I'd probably have done the whole thing solo before I ran again as part of a team.

If I were to do it again, it would definitely be for fun, not competitively. I like big parties now. I've been there and done the other stuff. Partying is a lot more fun.

Steve Bence *made his initial appearance in Hood To Coast in 1985 and since then he has participated in the event 28 times, split evenly between running and walking teams. In 1977 he began working at Nike and still works for the company today, while also serving as the unofficial historian for Nike's involvement in HTC.*

I still call myself a runner even though I haven't been able to run for almost 20 years because my knees are shot. Hood To Coast taught me that running is more than just a physical activity; it's also a mindset, and it has been an important thread throughout my life.

I took over as the captain of team Nike Tarahumara for about 10 years from founder Mike Franklin. Recruiting the right runners for the team was always a priority. The Tarahumara team competed in the Corporate Mixed Division, so I had to select from Nike employees and field a team with six men and six women. My goal was to find men who could run a mile in between five and six minutes, and women who could run a mile in between five and a half and seven minutes.

In the early days, finding men to join the team was relatively easy. Nike had a lot of former male collegiate middle- and long-distance runners, including several All-Americans, a few Olympians, and even an American record-holder. However, in the 1980s it was difficult to find women who were distance runners. There were very few women who worked at Nike who could run distances because most of them were in school during the 1970s when Title IX was just ramping up and women weren't yet allowed to run distances. The Olympics didn't even allow women to race in distances over a mile until 1984. So the women on our team had very different backgrounds, including fitness dancer Darcy Winslow, former University of Oregon runner Ellen Devlin, lunch-time runners, and athletes from other sports. Compared to other teams, the women on Tarahumara were extraordinary and the team's biggest competitive difference.

I even asked my sophomore-year University of Oregon roommate, Paul Geis, who competed in the 5,000 meters at the 1976 Summer Olympics, to join Tarahumara. Paul, who had trained with and competed against Steve Prefontaine, wasn't running the way that he'd like at the time, so he offered to drive a van, which he did for several years.

I always liked to point out that our team was so good that we had Paul Geis, an Olympian, serve as our driver.

In 1983 the goal of team Tarahumara was simply to have fun, which they did with a Winnebago and plenty of beer. Reportedly, they finished dead last, but they didn't care. A surprising thing happened the following year: corporate divisions were created, and Tarahumara managed to finish first in the Corporate Mixed division.

Mike Franklin wanted to continue winning and started to replace the team members leaving with the best runners he could find. I joined the team in 1985, when the primary goal was still to have fun and keep as many runners from year to year as possible. A second goal was to win the division, which happened while I was with the team in 1985 and 1986.

Each year, our team was slowing down and in 1987 we were upset by Hewlett Packard, when they brought in runners from around the U.S. It happened the same year that Tarahumara ran its slowest race, an average pace of just over seven minutes a mile. Since our primary goal was to have fun, the second-place finish shouldn't have been a problem. However, we all agreed that second wasn't any fun and vowed to return to winning in 1988, which we did.

In 2006 Tarahumara had another disappointment, losing by one minute to a team from GE.

After hearing about Tarahumara finishing second to a GE team, Nike vice president, and former Tarahumara runner, Dave Taylor challenged future teams with an email:

"NIKE should NEVER, NEVER, NEVER lose in a category in which you choose to field a competitive team. NIKE is a sports and fitness company (which evolved from a RUNNING company for those that may have forgotten). I think GE makes light bulbs. Don't say, 'We didn't lose, we were beat by a recruiting process.' Say, 'We screwed up and it won't happen again.' When you start to feel good about second place, well . . . you may as well quit trying."

CHAPTER 8

Teams

IT TAKES A TEAM TO tackle the trials and tribulations of Hood To Coast. Many feature long-time members and longstanding traditions. Others have runners that meet for the first time the day before the race. Some are made up of family and friends and the relay is an annual ritual, perhaps the only time the teammates see each other during the year. Other teams evolve from the same neighborhood, high school or college, and see each other on a regular basis. No matter the makeup of a team, they share a common goal—to finish the trek from Mt. Hood to the Pacific Coast. Each knows the keys to success include communication, collaboration and cooperation, or in other words, teamwork.

Jeff Boly is from Tacoma, Washington, and has been competing in Hood To Coast since 1985. He is a co-founder and captain of the Mr. Mojo Risin' team now running in the Men's Supermasters division.

Neil Greeley, a friend of mine from high school cross country, did Hood To Coast in 1984 and came back raving about how much fun it was. A year later he was looking for recruits and I said yeah. We had an incredible time and I got the bug. I was really impressed with the whole concept of relay racing and the camaraderie. We had to do it again.

We were one year out of high school and pretty unorganized. Back then registration and everything else happened on the same day at Portland State University. We walked in and there was Bob Foote and a couple of other people. It was the last few minutes of sign-up and we were like, "Hey, we'd love to do the race. Is it too late?" He said, "No problem. Just sign this stuff." That was the beginning of our team.

When we got back in the car we were high-fiving and talking about running the race.

We flipped on the radio and "L.A. Woman" was playing. At the time we were all really big fans of the Doors and Jim Morrison. The song has a refrain that keeps repeating, "Mr. Mojo Risin'." So Neil said, "It's a sign, a sign from Jim. We have to name the team Mr. Mojo Risin'." That's how the name came about.

For the next several years, we recruited random people. Anybody we could convince to do it. We really didn't want to tell them too much because we knew it was going to be a slog and most of the guys were not really runners. We'd say, "You want to do this really cool thing?" That worked with a couple of guys and we kept going from there. It became my thing. At that point I was at the University of Santa Clara and I would tell people about it and was able to get a few more team members. Some people caught the bug and you could see a core group developing.

Finally, in 1994, I was at a party and a bunch of us guys stayed late and we're sitting around shooting the bull. I convinced several of them to run HTC and that's when it took off as a more serious team. We started to get guys that were more competitive.

It never got *too* serious. We were never really *that* fast. More like a top-20 team. But we were having a blast and I realized, "Wow, this is my thing." It became the centerpiece of my life. I had this thing to do every year that kept me in shape, gave me goals, and netted me amazing, lifelong friends. It created this tradition and here we are now—more than 30 years later.

Music is a central theme for our team. We love music. The first year we would sit on top of the van and wait for our runner to go by and we would play music out of a boombox. We had a lot of fun with that and were surprised and intrigued by how it motivated other runners.

I ended up with an electrical engineering degree and was into wiring stuff, so I built a really powerful car stereo. We'd carry boomboxes on our shoulders and run alongside our runners as they passed by. As we got older and we ended up with more money and more time, we realized this was something to keep going year after year.

We started buying stuff to outfit the van. We have a Yakima roof rack system with a generator and a really powerful sound system. We keep it pretty mellow during the night so we don't get in trouble. We're always worried that we're going to disturb somebody and get banned. During the day, however, when you're out on those country roads and you're slogging through the middle of a run, it's amazing when the van comes around a corner about a half-mile back and you can hear the music just blaring. It provides incredible motivation.

It's the same for everybody. We're going down the course blaring tunes and everybody is shaking their fists, "Yeah!"

At first it was the Doors all the time. Then we played a lot of classic rock. Fortunately, some of the guys on our team are musically inclined and up to date on what's current and popular. We play a wider selection now and really try to get the crowd going.

It's kind of a DJ thing. We come into a major exchange on Saturday and there are a thousand people there. It looks like New York City in the middle of nowhere Oregon. People everywhere, barbeques are going. It's 11 a.m. and we're blaring U2's "Beautiful Day" and everybody loves it. Then we see a state trooper and turn it down a little bit.

We also began stopping along the route. On some teams you get in the van and you don't move until you have to get out again at the next stop. A lot of people just sit in the van the whole time because they're exhausted. We didn't think that was much fun and started buying a huge supply of water and juice cups. We set up our own portable water stop on almost every leg and hand out water to runners passing by.

The amazing thing about this race is that you're both a participant and a spectator. We try to run as fast as we can as participants and we love cheering everyone on as a spectator. We also go to Costco and buy a big box of cookies in little packets and throw them to the volunteers as we go by. At 3 a.m. those volunteers are going, "Why the hell did I sign up for this thing?" All of a sudden someone comes by, tosses them some cookies and says, "Hey, thanks for volunteering." It makes their day. We try and carry the energy from the music and the drinks and the cookies all the way from Mt. Hood to the coast.

As we got more organized, my brother developed a logo for our team. It looks like the crosswalk guy, only he's running out of the darkness and into the light. It's like you're going out one door and through another door, another Doors tie-in. Most of the guys have a tattoo of the logo on their leg and one of the guys even has a big one on his back. We also have coordinated uniforms with bandanas, all with the logo.

For us, the relay has turned into a five-day guys weekend. It's all about having a blast. We fly in on Thursday and stay at the same Courtyard Marriott. We have a ritual dinner at the Spaghetti Factory. We go to Fred Meyer and buy all of our stuff. We outfit the van with slogans using stick-on letters and window stats we have printed. It looks pretty professional. We put the thing on top that carries the sound system and we have all this lighting. It's like Halloween, and every year we add a little bit more.

We stay Saturday and Sunday night in Seaside and leave Monday. We love the beer garden, but we're not as active now in our 50s as we were when we first started.

We also have team awards. The Jim Shirt is the highest award. We've got this crazy button down Jim Morrison shirt and whoever does the most outstanding thing each year gets the Jim Shirt. Then the Dong Shirt goes to someone who does something stupid or is a jerk. One year I had this crazy idea of screen-printing our team shirts myself and I messed it all up. That's called the Dong Shirt.

I'm the only one who's never missed a year. A couple of other guys have missed one year and have competed in about 30 relays. Then there's a core group from 1994, a bunch of guys who have been there ever since, a good 20-years plus.

I'm getting to the point where the training is hard. I mean it really hurts, but I keep thinking back to one of our runners, Brook Boynton, who was still running strong at 52 when he was killed. Then I think maybe we should become more of a recreational team. We'll still train but not try and kill ourselves in the race. Show up and do it for fun.

But I know I'll keep doing it until I can't run anymore, whenever that is. I want to be the last man standing, where they're helping me up on the stage going, "This guy has done HTC for 50 years."

Peter Courtney *lives in Salem, Oregon, and has represented the 11th District in the Oregon State Senate since 1999. He is currently president of the Senate, a role he has served in since 2003.*

After running with the same team in 1991 and 1992, I was dumped without even being told. The next year, the local newspaper in Salem called me up and said they were putting together a team. For two years, I helped them organize their team.

It was a big moment for me when I decided to form my own Hood To Coast team. Nobody wanted me on their team, so I decided to have my own team. I knew if I was the team captain I would always be able to run. I was working at Western Oregon University at the time and named my team Peter and the Wolves—combining my name with the name for the Western Oregon athletic teams. We had T-shirts and thought running for the school was the greatest thing in the world.

I recruited some real fast runners from local races for the team—runners you'd see when they took off and not again until they finished. I had a hot team—even though I was the slowest thing. I'd take off like a sprinter, but after 60 yards I'd be a turtle.

I recruited one runner from the great Nike Bowerman team in Eugene. I said, "I'd like to put you on my team." Everybody told me, "You're never going to get him." And he said, "You know what. I'm going to run for you, Peter." He loves our team more than anything and he doesn't have to worry about the pressure. I remember the first time he ran with us he beat the van on one leg he was so fast.

I had six men and six women on my first team. We had runners in their 20s all the way up to runners in their 60s. There were track stars and marathon runners and students from Western Oregon. I was so proud of the makeup of our team, the range in ages and backgrounds and speed.

Everyone loved being on our team. We had some great athletes and some really fast runners. Yet they loved being with me—the old geezer. And they loved being on my team, which I thought was quite a compliment.

We had traditions too. When we got to the finish, everybody on the team, including our two van drivers, escorted the last runner across the finish line. Afterward, we all went out for pizza together. Then we got in our vans and drove home, but we always stopped at the Dairy Queen on Highway 26. We did that because we couldn't say goodbye to each other. We wanted to hang onto each other for as long as we could. We knew when we said goodbye we wouldn't see each other for a year.

We didn't want to let go. The feeling after finishing HTC is like no other. You're exhausted, spent, and hungry, but you've got great memories and can't wait to do it again because there's nothing like it in your life. When you find something special like that, however you came to it, you want to hang onto it.

Larry Dutko *was a member of the Road Warriors/Road Kill team that finished first in the inaugural Hood To Coast in 1982. He later became a member of the Dead Jocks in a Box team and is the only runner to have competed in every HTC.*

After five years my original team had basically dissolved due to running injuries, busy careers, and other family issues. Only Mitch Steeves and I were left from the original team that won the very first Hood To Coast. Meanwhile, the race had grown from eight teams to more than 500!

Mitch called to tell me he knew some guys forming a new team and suggested we join them. Fortunately, they were looking for some experienced runners. Plus, my 1984 Dodge van was available and already filled with some good race karma. So we were elated to be asked to join the team.

The team was called Dead Jocks in a Box. They put self-made coffins on top of their vans to store sleeping bags and other equipment. Within the first couple hours of the ride to Timberline Lodge for the race start it was apparent they were happy to add Mitch and me to their group of 10, and we were just as happy to have made new friends. And by the time we reached Timberline—that HTC bonding worked again—it was like a family reunion.

I started running this race in 1982 at the ripe old age of 33, and I'm very fortunate to be healthy and still running with my Dead Jocks team.

Over the years I've probably run with well over 100 teammates. Many are no longer running and we've lost some to health issues, but so many others are still good friends.

When you're in a van with a group of people for 25 to 30 hours something magical can happen. That may not always be the case, but I have a chest full of memories that seem to keep me young and healthy.

Marlon Gorden *has participated in Hood To Coast more than 10 times and his goal is to run every leg of the event. The Vancouver, Washington native has completed two marathons and more than a dozen half-marathons.*

In 2006 I started running. At first it was just for fitness, but it soon became a passion. The 2007 Hood To Coast was just my second competitive running event. That year I was a substitute on the legacy Old Enough to Know Better (OETKB) team captained by Bruce Harman. When I laced up my running shoes I had no idea that it would become an epic race for the ages.

On the eve of the start of that year's race we were challenged by the vaunted Dead Jocks in a Box team and captain Larry Dutko. The first team to cross the finish line would receive a cheeseburger lunch from the losing team. Our team started seven hours ahead of the Dead Jocks. And as fate would have it, it all came down to me—a relay rookie—to bring it home for OETKB.

We took note of the Dead Jocks' van with its frightening coffin on top entering the exchange in Mist as we were preparing to leave for our final set of legs. Our eyes locked on each other and we all knew then that it was going to be a close finish. They were an elite team of six-minute milers. Our pace, depending on the runner, was between eight minutes and 12 minutes a mile.

Off we went from the Mist exchange, totally exhausted but full of hope that we could fend off the mighty Dead Jocks for those cheeseburgers. We started clicking off that last set of legs and there was no sign of the Dead Jocks in our rearview mirror. Finally the baton was passed to me for the journey to the finish—and a date with destiny. My vanmates knew that the Dead Jocks were probably lurking just behind us and they urged me to go as fast I could, shouting encouragement at me from the van. I was feeling pretty good, or as good as an HTC rookie can feel after absolutely no sleep and with two legs of all-out running already completed. I cranked out eight-minute miles toward the finish line—as painful as they were.

The van went on ahead to the finish about halfway through my final leg to witness what would become a legendary ending. I had no idea who the final runner was for the Dead Jocks. Therefore I needed to be wary of any runner passing me and avoid becoming just another road kill for the Dead Jocks.

Finally the end was near. I started to sprint and saw my OETKB teammates standing on the left just before the finish line. They were shouting, "The finish line is over there!" I gave it one last burst of speed. The Dead Jocks' van was there as well and Larry yelled "There's our guy! He's got it!" But as I was crossing the finish line one of my OETKB teammates, who just happened to be Larry's sister Lynn, corrected Larry and screamed, "There's OUR guy!" (She was talking about me!) I was just a shoulder ahead of the Dead Jocks' runner, who was blasting to the finish line at a six-minute-per-mile-or-faster pace. It was total chaos and bedlam at the finish line, but the result was clear—OETKB was victorious by a mere second or two!

After all the dust had settled, we thoroughly enjoyed that cheeseburger lunch with the Dead Jocks where we shared our memories of the race. Now we annually relive our memories of that 2007 race within a race—which has become a priceless remembrance.

Rick Jaspers *is from Longview, Washington, and participated in his first Hood To Coast in 2017 with the legendary team Dead Jocks in a Box.*

When I was younger it had been a dream of mine to run Hood To Coast. However, by the time I was 25 I had quit running. It wasn't until I was in my 50s that I got back into running. At that time I would run an occasional organized race, mostly small and local events, but an epic event like HTC was no longer on my radar.

Then in early August of 2017 I was asked to replace an injured runner in an event that was coming up in a few days. Reluctantly, I agreed despite not having run a single race the entire season. The race was the Crawfish Crawl and it was part of the HTC Race Series. It was a relay race with each team having four runners. Each runner ran three legs of two miles. Despite my apprehension, our team of men in their late 50s finished second out of 25 teams.

A little less than two weeks later I received a call from one of my teammates from the Crawfish Crawl. Unfortunately, he had injured himself and needed to find a substitute to run HTC, which was only eight days away. He asked me to fill in for him on his team, Dead Jocks in a Box. Although I was concerned about my lack of preparation and my ability to perform at the level that would be expected, I couldn't pass up the opportunity.

My first run was Leg 2, which started at Government Camp and dropped 1,500 feet over the course of 5.6 miles. I felt strong and kept up a relatively good pace.

In the past I had always been a lone wolf runner. I ran because I loved getting out on the road and challenging myself. I seldom ran with anyone else and always thought of running as a personal journey. But as I passed one runner after another, I recognized that I was driven by being part of something bigger than myself—I was part of a team. I finished my first leg without being passed by another runner.

For my second run (Leg 14), I was heading out of Portland on Highway 30 late at night. The damage done by the constant pounding of the downhill leg, which I had completed some eight hours earlier, seemed to be minimal, so I tried to push the pace. I would set my sights on a flashing light up ahead, speed up a little bit, and then overtake the next runner. This is what's lovingly referred to as road kill. I lost track of how many runners I passed on this leg, but again I made it to the exchange point without being passed by another runner.

During the race you spend a lot of time in a van and this gives you time to get to know your teammates. Through our conversations it became abundantly clear to me that these other guys on the team were serious runners. Most of them had run multiple marathons as well as many shorter races. The last several years I considered myself to be an avid runner, but now I was wondering if I could even call myself a runner at all. My so-called training just didn't match up with what these guys were doing.

Since I was running an additional leg, I still had two legs to complete and was worried how things would play out. What if I couldn't finish one of those runs? I decided that giving up was not an option—not so much for my own pride—but for the sake of my team that had put so much time and preparation into doing well in the race.

After a night of no sleep, I took off on my third leg. It was then that I realized that my quads had had enough when with every stride they tightened in pain. I just had not prepared myself for this race. The good thing was that it was a short leg of less than four miles. Even though my legs hurt, as I continued they didn't get any worse. Surprisingly, I passed dozens of runners and again no one passed me.

As I started my fourth and final leg, I was keenly aware of two things. First, I had seven miles to go on a coarse gravel road in the heat of the day with legs that continued to protest every step. And second, I was going to have to give it everything I had just to finish.

In the back of my mind I was thinking about the fact that I had not yet been passed by another runner. But as I told a few of my teammates, I was in survival mode now and my goal was just to finish the leg and not worry about a good time.

My legs ached, the miles dragged on, and my mouth was dry. Still, I was passing quite a few other runners. At about the halfway point I started thinking about not being passed. This was actually doable. Yet this was also when my quads protested the loudest. A silent battle raged on between my mind and my legs. I used every little trick I knew to convince my legs to keep moving.

Finally, as I crested the top of a hill, the exchange came into view maybe a quarter of a mile down the road. I glanced back and a runner I had not passed was just a hundred yards back. I pushed with everything left in the tank. I couldn't risk the time it would take to look back again. I thought I could do it, but with 150 yards to go my record was dashed as the runner effortlessly glided by.

After I passed off the baton following my final leg I was met at the exchange by two guys from my team. One gave me an Oreo which I could barely swallow with no moisture left in my mouth. I hobbled to the support vehicle, which was quite a ways from where I had finished running.

When my mind and body began to recover from what had transpired I wasn't filled with the disappointment I expected. Instead I realized I had just participated in one of the greatest relay races in the country. I had given it everything I could possibly give and had contributed to the team's effort to do its very best.

I don't know if I have any more HTCs in my future, but I do know that the memory of this one will stay with me for a long, long time.

Larry Dutko *was a member of the Road Warriors/Road Kill team that finished first in the inaugural Hood To Coast in 1982. He later became a member of the Dead Jocks in a Box team, and is the only runner to have competed in every HTC.*

One of the more unexpected developments of Hood To Coast as it grew in popularity during the first five to eight years was the arrival of international teams, many of which were very competitive.

One of our first head-to-head matchups was with a team from Italy, a bunch of crazy guys who were out to beat us. One of their runners was really fast, but what was unique about him was after every leg he would come over to us to practice his English—and he was always smoking a cigarette. We told him smoking would slow him down, but he continued to bury our runner on every leg he ran.

Since then, the Dead Jocks have been approached by international teams from China, Japan, Sweden, England, and even New Zealand.

In 2015 at Leg 30, where you can always get a fresh-grilled burger, I was talking with some Kiwis who told me they decided to come to Oregon and run the race after seeing the documentary about the race. They also mentioned they were hoping to run into the Dead Jocks!

Much to their surprise, I told them I was an original member of the Dead Jocks. Then we made a bet that one of our runners would catch their team during the last six legs, even though they started several hours before we did. The bet was set for a beer at the finish. On Leg 34 we saw their runner just ahead and we made the road kill, again much to their surprise. But it was all in good fun.

In retrospect, adding international teams to this unique race seems to make the world appear smaller—at least when you're out on the road!

Scott Thompson *is from Beaverton, Oregon, and is a founding member of the Dirty Half Dozen +6 team, which has competed in every Hood To Coast since 1986.*

I've been competing in Hood To Coast most of my life.

In 1985 our high school cross country coach at Sunset High School in Beaverton, Dave Robbins, put together a team he called Robbins' Renegades. The team was made up of some of the guys he used to run with and some of the older kids on our team. At the time we were just sophomores, about 15 years old, and we wondered why he didn't pick some of us to run, too. When you're that age you think you can do anything!

They ran in 1985 and did pretty well, so in 1986 a group of runners in my age group, between sophomore and junior years, decided we were going to run, too.

Everybody we were around ran, and a couple of the dads had competed in HTC, so it was fairly easy to talk them into it. Maybe the moms were a little more concerned because we used to start at about 1 a.m. and they worried about us running through the night and not getting enough sleep or getting enough to eat. They had a lot of concerns that we didn't really care about. Every year the moms said, "Oh my gosh, I can't believe you're doing this again."

We graduated from high school doing this race and then went off to different colleges, but we'd always get back together for the last weekend in August to do the race. Then we all graduated college and slowly started getting married. Some teammates' jobs took them away and others even went overseas. One guy joined the Army, so he was in and out of places around the world. Every August, however, no matter where we were, it was, "We've got to get together and do this." Everybody knew they needed to get home that weekend.

In 2017 we finished year number 32 without missing a race. We had nine of the original Sunset High cross country runners and three other guys we've picked up over the years. One has been with us for over 20 years. Another has run with us for probably 18 years, and the other has been on the team for 12 or 13 years. But the original nine runners are all Sunset guys who are 25- to 30-year veterans of the relay. The average age on our team is about 48, and we've been running together for 32 of those 48 years. It's been a huge part of our lives.

We've been fairly competitive and we've kept pretty good records. For all 32 years we've averaged six minutes and 28 seconds per mile for the 6,000-plus miles we've run. Obviously, some of the early years were much faster. But it was just a couple of years ago that our average per mile was the same as our very first year.

Every now and then someone will miss a year, but everyone in the core group is getting closer and closer to running 100 legs. Soon one of our runners will pass that mark. I think it may be hard to find a team with more guys running that many legs and running that pace.

For five or six years, my two brothers also ran on the team, which was a highlight for me. Being able to hand off to your brother is pretty cool.

On our 30th anniversary we re-created the first exchange ever for the Dirty Half Dozen. I ran the first leg again and handed off to the same guy for the second leg. Handing off to my teammate Kirk Helzer 30 years apart was very cool. It was a special memory.

Someone on our team said his ultimate goal is to run HTC for 50 years and then retire. I guess we have about 18 years to go before we can put our shoes up on the rack and say we're done!

Steve Bence *made his initial appearance in Hood To Coast in 1985 and since then has participated in the event 28 times, split evenly between running and walking teams. In 1977 he began working at Nike and still works for the company today, while also serving as the unofficial historian for Nike's involvement in HTC.*

A big growth year for both Hood To Coast and the number of Nike teams participating in the event was 1989. That year the race outgrew Pacific City and the finish line was moved to Seaside, and the number of teams grew from 500 to 750. At Nike I brainstormed with fellow colleagues about how to field more than just the single Tarahumara team. The result was six Nike corporate teams entering the relay in 1989, including five Mixed teams and one Men's Open team.

The key to increasing the number of Nike teams was finding new team captains. Throughout the summer, as we were preparing to move to the new Nike campus, a group of us met at a local tavern on Thursday afternoons. Over a few pitchers of beer, we made plans and agreed to hold ourselves accountable on the follow-through. We probably overthought it because we figured out how to get things like T-shirts, hats, vans, and hotel rooms at the beach, which we charged to the different Nike cost centers that we handled.

Several months after HTC, I was feeling pretty proud of the six teams that participated in the event. I started thinking about how to increase the number of Nike teams, which would allow more employees to share this great experience.

Marla Murray, who captained the team One Time Only, even signed up for a second year—despite the fact that her team's van tipped over while they were parking and a Portland news helicopter circled overhead and documented their plight for its television audience. Marla was determined to get the relay right and signed her team up again, but this time her team was called One Time Only, Again.

So, I was feeling pretty good. That is, until I thought I'd been fired!

Del Hayes, a senior vice president who was on the Nike Board of Directors and the man who hired me in 1977, summoned me to his office just before Christmas. I had no idea what he wanted and approached the meeting with extreme nervousness. Del said he caught wind of what we were doing with HTC and asked the accounting department to pull any financial documents that referenced the relay. He spread in front of me this collection of Nike purchase orders and invoices for everything ranging from T-shirts to entry fees. I truly thought it was my last day at Nike!

Del asked me to explain all the invoices, which I did—emphasizing that the relay was a great opportunity and experience. The event spoke volumes about Nike's cultural running roots, and employees who participated passed along great reviews.

Then there was a deafening silence—which lasted way too long!

Finally Del laughed and let me off the hook. He said what we were doing was perfect, but we didn't need to go underground. He asked me to build out a HTC plan for 1990 and said he would pay for it. I put together a plan, with a rather urgent request for Nike to pay for eight teams in order to secure our entries. Four weeks later the check was sent and our HTC participation was officially endorsed by senior leadership.

But Del had a second condition. We had to include his daughter Kathy on our team—which was an issue. The problem wasn't her running. She was a great runner! At the time, Kathy held University of Oregon records at 3,000, 5,000, and 10,000 meters. The problem with Kathy participating was that she wasn't a Nike employee and couldn't run on a corporate team.

Two years later we crafted a solution. We formed an Open Mixed Nike team called Team Swoosh, which was composed of an impressive list of mostly former distance runners from the University of Oregon. Although Kathy Hayes didn't run, Team Swoosh easily won their division and set a course record that I think is the longest standing event record.

Brianne Theisen-Eaton *was born in Saskatoon, Saskatchewan, Canada, and attended the University of Oregon, where she won six NCAA championships in the heptathlon and*

pentathlon. In the 2016 Summer Olympics, she won a bronze medal for Canada in the heptathlon, becoming the first Canadian to ever earn a medal in that event. She retired from track and field in 2017 and now lives with her husband, Ashton, in San Francisco, where she is a board-certified holistic nutritionist and practices functional medicine. She first participated in Hood To Coast as an honorary captain for Team World Vision in 2016 before running the event in 2017.

After participating in Hood To Coast as an honorary team captain, I thought it would be fun to actually run the event and not just ride in the van. When I retired from track and field, I knew right away I should run the race. There wasn't a reason not to participate anymore, and it's something I always wanted to do. Soon after I retired, I committed to running the Chicago Marathon with Team World Vision. I'd already been training for the marathon and decided participating in HTC fit in perfectly.

I already knew all the World Vision people because I had been involved in HTC and had also gone to Africa with them quite a few times. When I told them I wanted to run, they called me and said, "Okay, you're on this team and you'll be in Van 1. What legs do you want to run?" I had no idea what to tell them because I'd never run it before. They sent me a course map and said I could pick whatever I wanted. I decided to be Runner 3, which meant I'd run around 18 or 19 miles over three legs. I wasn't going to pick the hardest legs—which I think is what you get as Runner 5. I was not doing that one!

There was another woman on our team who was a distance runner and she said, "I'll happily be Runner 5 and do the hardest legs." I wasn't going to argue with her and let her have those legs. I'm not a distance runner and for me it would be hard enough to get through 18 miles in 24 hours.

What was really cool was there were people on our team who had never before competed in the relay. There were 10 World Vision teams in the race and we were ranked as the second fastest. Our first couple of legs everyone was taking it real easy because you're always told not to go all out at the beginning. I think we actually took it a little too easy and I said to the team, "I think we should try to be the fastest World Vision team. I know we're ranked as the second fastest and pretty far back, but I think we should try to win."

The guy who ran the first leg, the downhill from Timberline Lodge, admitted he took it pretty easy on his run. Later he told me he had trained for a marathon a year earlier and it had been a horrible experience. He never got through it and didn't have much confidence in his running anymore. After our team collectively decided we were going to run as hard as we could to beat the other World Vision teams, he told me he had never before had so much fun running. He regained confidence and his love for running returned. And he was going to train for another marathon. It was one of my best experiences from the race—seeing somebody who was a little defeated and who had to be convinced to partic-ipate leave the event with a totally different idea about running.

I didn't believe saying we should try to beat all the other World Vision teams would be inspirational, but I thought it was just me being "typical, competitive Brianne." But it wasn't just me—the rest of the team was like, "Yeah, let's try to win." Then this guy saw everybody else going for it and he was encouraged to do it too.

It was fun to run because I actually felt like I accomplished something when we fin-ished. Being able to get pictures with your team at the finish, drink beer and eat, and all that kind of stuff—it's just different as a competitor. You feel more a part of the team than when you just ride along in the van. And to be honest, when I rode along in the van, for some reason I was much more tired. You don't have the adrenaline and you really have no reason to wake up. When you're running it's like, "Oh, I have to get up and get ready for my leg." So you wake up and get ready.

When I was honorary captain, toward the end of the race I sat in the back of the van half asleep. I felt like I experienced so much more as a runner!

Tim Dooley *is from Gresham, Oregon, and has been running in Hood To Coast since 1989. This memory was originally published in* RaceCenter *magazine.*

Until recently reunions never exerted much of a pull on me. Maybe it was the moves of my teen years that dulled the reunion urge, but most of the time I feel like the present is a pretty good place to be. That unsentimental stance evaporated in 2006 as I found myself frequently reminiscing about past Hood To Coast adventures.

Fifteen years of captaining my company's relay team had come to an end when my job was eliminated. Life went on, and while I adjusted to my new path I missed those sleepless race adventures and the friends I had left behind. That's when the reunion bug hit me and I decided to see if others were similarly afflicted.

To my delight, my exploratory emails resulted in a resounding "yes" from equally nostalgic teammates. That set the stage for the Return of the Asphalt Warriors in 2007. The 12 of us embarked on a quest to recapture our former teams' magic. Old memories began to give way to exciting new possibilities and it didn't take our reunion team long to find that the special chemistry still remained firmly intact. Like many reunion-goers, most of us had lost a step or two, but that didn't matter to a team that valued the journey's quality even more than its speed.

We were determined to milk every moment of the experience. For more than 26 hours we cheered each other on and formed human arches for runners to pass through while the theme from the movie *The Natural* (when Robert Redford hits the game-winning homer) trumpeted from our vans! Along the way we addressed our own personal unfinished business. Nancy from Ohio added three new relay legs in her quest to eventually run all 36. For John Jellybeans the event meant beating the torturous 1,000 foot climb of Leg 20 and realizing his post-knee surgery dream to run HTC one more time with his friends. He did both in style.

I faced some physical challenges of my own, having selected my legs more on memory and pride than good sense. As I undertook my grueling final leg, I waved my vanmates ahead to the next exchange with instructions not to stop for me. While I wanted them to avoid traffic delays, I also expected some suffering on my climb and wanted to do it in solitude. And suffer I did. With each turn of the road the grade only got steeper, and though I felt spent I concentrated on trudging forward in as steady a fashion as possible.

Finally, experience told me that the summit of the leg was just ahead. As I rounded the corner and gathered myself for the final push, there ahead of me stood 11 Asphalt Warriors yelling and whooping it up like there was no tomorrow. They had disobeyed my orders to drive ahead, and if I'd had the strength I would have smiled. A lump formed in my throat as I felt my own unfinished business evaporating. As I passed the cheer brigade Sunny Tim yelled out, "Andy Carson from Channel 12 is just ahead. Catch him!" That did force a smile. I didn't have the strength to catch Andy Griffith, let alone Andy Carson!

Helped by those cheers, I eventually finished my leg and the Asphalt Warriors did go on to appropriately cross the finish line together. Maybe we can't go back in time, but once in a while it's possible to recapture some special magic of the past if you're making the journey with great people.

Rob Rickard is from Canby, Oregon, and has participated in Hood To Coast every year since 1983. He has also been a course marker for the event for more than 25 years.

I've competed in every Hood To Coast race except the first one in 1982, and I'm still looking to add more to my total. And I've been the team captain for all but one of those years. I've been on some really competitive teams. We set an age-division record that stood for several years and we were usually in the midst of the competition.

We've kind of mellowed a bit in recent years. I'd say now our attitude is mostly, "Let's have fun, and if we're competitive, great."

One of the experiences that really stands out happened back in 1991 or 1992. On the Thursday before the Friday start I got a call from one of our runners who had just blown out his knee and wasn't going to be able to run. He was one of our quicker guys, so I was really concerned.

I called one of my other teammates and he knew of somebody who could run with us. I went into Friday thinking we had a full team. Well, it turned out when everyone showed up at my place we didn't have an extra man. In the Mixed Masters division you can start with fewer men, but you must have six women to start.

We started with five men and six women. After our first set of legs, one of the women got sick from vehicle fumes. She could only do one leg.

Now we had three guys doing an extra leg to cover for the runner who was injured, and now we had two women who had to do an extra leg to make up for the one runner who got sick.

We had a great bunch and stopping was never an option. They were all pretty hardcore runners. When we faced an obstacle, we found a way around it. In years past and years since, whenever there was an injury, there's always been someone to step up and say, "I'll run the extra leg." Men or women, it didn't matter. Both were just happy to contribute to the overall team success.

We wound up setting a course record that year that stood for four years. We just had a phenomenal time with the synergy and the energy each person brought. No one complained about running an extra leg. Everybody contributed and it was just a fantastic event.

In March of 2017, at the age of 74, I was diagnosed with something called Polymyalgia rheumatica. It's an inflammatory disorder that causes muscle pain and stiffness, and it basically hurts all my muscles. From my knee to my neck, I'm in constant pain if I'm not on some pretty heavy medication. However, when I'm on the medication it makes me weak and I gain weight.

I told the team before the 2017 race, "Hey gang, why don't we find a sub for me. I'll see that everything is taken care of, but you guys can be more competitive and have more fun without me." To a person, they all said, no, we'll run it with you.

We did the event and I was the slowest person on the team, which was a bitter pill for me to swallow. I wish I were faster, but that's the reality of getting older and encountering some of the challenges we face.

I loved every minute that I was out there. The team said they wanted to keep things together and told me, "You're still a part of the team as long as you can run without hurting yourself." That was real special to me!

Michael Gritzmacher is from Portland and now lives in New York City. He was a Hood To Coast volunteer in 2009 and began participating in the event in 2012.

I was born and raised in Portland—graduating from Central Catholic High School and

Oregon State University before attending graduate school at Lehigh University and then moving to New York City.

Growing up less than a mile from Portland's Springwater Corridor Trail, Hood To Coast was always an annual event that tore through our neighborhood at the end of summer right before school would start up again. In 2007, before my sophomore year of high school, my parents, aunts, and uncles started a team—the Rear Enders. I remember being enlisted to paint subtlety inappropriate slogans on the team vans—slogans that I pretended not to understand in front of my parents.

The following year, one of the runners on my parents' team suffered an injury just before the race. My sister Alyssa, a senior in high school at the time, joined the team. Not to be left out, two of my friends and I volunteered at Exchange 31 for the team. That was my first real experience with the organized chaos that is HTC. We were on the side of a highway at 2 a.m., deep in the mountains between Portland and Seaside, with no cell service. There were thousands of runners and plenty of vans cruising by us—and it was crazy and awesome.

Fast forward to July of 2012 and I get a text at work from a distant cousin. The text said, "Had someone drop from our HTC team. Are you interested in running?" Bear in mind, I hadn't run once that summer. However, I immediately replied, "YES!"

I was 20 and, even with only a month to train, figured it would not be a problem! I was Runner 6 that year in a van full of people 10 and 20 years older than me—and whom I barely knew. The team was Team 8 Hammers and 4 Rubys On the Go. Sure, I was incredibly sore afterward and discovered a crass side to my older cousins that I never knew, but it was worth it. I had the time of my life and was hooked!

Alyssa and I decided to start a team for 2013 with a group of friends from college. Alyssa was studying journalism at the University of Oregon, and I was an engineering major at Oregon State. To this day I'm still not quite sure how we convinced 10 poor, flakey college kids to commit $115 one year in advance to run somewhere between 15 and 20 miles over a day and a half and live in a car with five other sweaty, tired, and grumpy humans. And Ducks (Oregon) and Beavers (Oregon State) alike, no less! This was the beginning of what will someday be known as the greatest team in race history—Tight Butts and Sweaty Nuts.

Tight Butts and Sweaty Nuts ran the following three races as well. Our friends got just as excited about it as my sister and I did, and every year we've added something extra to our team presentation. We make team T-shirts every year. We've also added team flags and our own logo! In fact, in 2016 we even added magnets with our team name and logo to slap on other vans.

Every race we also film pre-run and post-run interviews with each runner, random van shenanigans, and the celebration at the beach. One of our teammates compiles all the footage into a short documentary. The night before we start at the top of Mt. Hood our team watches the video and we all relive the memories from the previous year.

I've been living on the East Coast now for our last two races, and people always look at me in shock when I tell them why I'm flying home for 72 hours. They say something like, "So you're flying five hours to go run 18 miles and sleep in a van?" I guess when it's said like that it may sound a little crazy. But for us, especially now that we've all graduated college, the race provides the opportunity to get together once a year and see each other.

In 2016 we had team members fly in from Australia, California, New York City, and Pennsylvania, as well as make the drive from Seattle. It gives everyone on the team an event to train for in the summer and a reason to stay active.

Although we didn't make the lottery cut for 2017, you can bet the Tight Butts and Sweaty Nuts team will be back. Where else in the world can you and your 11 best friends run down a mountain, through a city, up and down another mountain, and into the ocean?

Steve Bence made his initial appearance in Hood To Coast in 1985 and since then has participated in the event 28 times, split evenly between running and walking teams. In 1977 he began working at Nike and still works for the company today, while also serving as the unofficial historian for Nike's involvement in HTC.

Of all the years that I've participated in Hood To Coast, only one year has my team had the unique problem of everything going *right*—including being 28 seconds ahead of our predicted finish time. It was boring. But every year we've found a place to spend Saturday night near the beach, where we've relived the previous hours and laughed at what went wrong. You can learn a lot about yourself and others from how you handle what seems like a crisis at 3 a.m.

Here are a few examples of things that went wrong during the relay.

The traffic lines leading up to the exchange points were extremely long and we heard it didn't get any better. Four of us in the van still had to run, and it seemed impossible to get us to our exchange points on time. The four of us jumped out and jogged to the upcoming exchange. The first runner stayed at the exchange, and the three remaining runners hitchhiked to the next exchange, and so on until we were all at our respective exchange points. The van picked us up when it could, we didn't miss a hand off, and we tallied another team Tarahumara victory.

Andy Mooney lost the skin off the soles of his feet running the steep downhill first leg. He somehow managed to finish the next two legs, but by the time we drove back to Portland Andy was in enough pain that he had to be carried from the van to a nearby bush to relieve himself.

Bob Harold uncharacteristically screwed up by tipping the van in a ditch while trying to park on the side of the road. We knew he screwed up because he said so in a stream of profanity from the driver's seat. After calling a tow truck, Bob and I leaned against the van looking up at the stars during the 4 a.m. stillness. We were just standing on the side of the road waiting for somebody to come pull us out of the ditch. Bob then asked me, "Do you think people will forget this?" I said, "Bob. We're not going to let you forget."

Patrick Cross is from Hillsboro, Oregon, and started running when he was in his late 20s. He has been a regular participant in Hood To Coast.

The first year I ran Hood To Coast was in 1985 with a team from Newberg, Oregon. At the time, my wife worked there and I ran with that team for two years. Later, I hooked up with a team from Hillsboro and ran with them for a couple years. After that I ran with three different teams.

Finally I started my own team, which has been around for more than 20 years. In all my years running HTC I've only missed the race twice. Once it was because I broke my ankle playing softball (1990), and the other time was for the birth of our wonderful daughter (1987).

My team has had runners come and go, but for 22 years we've had a core group of five runners. About half of our team is from out of state, including runners from Louisiana, Texas, and Washington. Our team is made up of men and women, and the ages range from early 30s to late 60s. I'm the oldest!

We all get along and everyone has a great time. Actually, I should say most everyone gets along. A few years ago we had one runner who was a last-minute replacement. We thought she was going to be fine, but she got sick after her first leg. We later found out that she had taken something she shouldn't have before running. From that experience we learned to never find a runner to add to your team at the local laundromat!

Our team name is Growing Older . . . But Not Up. It's the title of a Jimmy Buffet song, and we think it kind of explains our team.

Candi Garrett grew up in Portland and now lives in Newberg, Oregon. She has partici-pated in Hood To Coast more than 25 times.

My best friend, Melissa, used to run Hood To Coast when it ended in Pacific City. She ran with a bunch of work buddies and it sounded like a blast. In the late 1980s my mom and I went out to watch her team run through Portland.

I thought, "Gosh, this would be cool to do." At the time I worked in a shipyard with a fun group of people. In 1989, the first year the finish moved to Seaside, I put a team together. I really didn't know what I was doing that first year with all the logistics and everything else.

That team included people I worked with and a few friends and some friends of friends. Our company sponsored us the first couple years. The company paid our entry fee and bought our team T-shirts. We borrowed vans. At the time, tents with tables and chairs on the beach were available at the finish, and the company even paid for that for a few years.

Then the shipyard closed and because my team was no longer sponsored I started choosing a different team name every year as I continued to be captain. I'd just think of something different each year. Eventually I came up with the name Sustain the Pain, and that's been our team for a long time. We have a couple runners who have been part of our team for 15 or 20 years, and we have a solid core of nine or 10 runners. It's a pretty consistent group, which is really great.

It's funny how I've found runners to join our team. Once I went to a birthday party for one of my best friends. I met a guy there and somehow we started talking about HTC and I said, "Do you want to be on the team?" And he joined the team. My old next door neighbor was invited to run one year and she had a friend who also ran with our team. My neighbor only ran one year, but I've kept her friend on the team—and now we've become great friends. That also happened with another gal: she and a friend joined our team one year, and then her friend stayed on our team for several more years.

My friend Melissa, who first got me interested in running the race, ran with our team for several years. Then she had a couple kids and took some time off from the team. When her kids got older, she came back to the team.

The year of the big storm in 2015 was my 25th year running the race. At the exchange at Sandy High School, when our whole team was together, my teammates presented me with a special running jacket to recognize my 25 years participating in the event. The jacket included my name, "Captain Candi," with the words "25 years Hood To Coast." Needless to say, it was a total surprise—and I cried. I was so touched that my friends did something so special. They know how much I love HTC and what it means to me each year.

Linda Burgard *is from Portland and has been running for almost 40 years.*

In 1984 I started running Hood To Coast on a Mixed team. Then we formed a Women's Submasters team. And eventually I ended up on a Women's Supermasters team.

My team stayed together for years, with new women being added as others dropped out. One of our teams was called Submasters of the Universe; the name came from one of my son's Masters of the Universe toys. Other team names included Sole Sisters and Divas.

One year I was part of a team called Wild Woman, but I only ran with them one year. There was one team member who was just far too competitive for my taste. My most recent team was Kick It Hens—made up of the older women from the team Kick It Chicks. I continue to run on a team with five of the ladies from my earlier years, including one friend I've been running with for over 30 years.

The first year I ran HTC there were 150 teams. We were allowed to have someone with us during the night and we had someone who rode with us on a bike. When we started running in the Women's Submasters division we would regularly come in first or second in our class. One year we came in second and they were only giving awards to the first-place teams due to the low number of entries. But the owner of Portland Running Company had some awards made up for our team. Back then we didn't have all the technology that there is available today and we used our own watches and stopwatches. Boy, if one stopped we were in trouble! That's why we always had two watches going.

Then there was the "year from hell," when the course finish was moved from Pacific City to Seaside. During the last few legs that year we had to run a mile with clipboard in hand to the exchange because of the traffic. After that experience I swore never to run the race again, but then all the women on our team wanted to do it again and I decided to stick with my teammates. Another year I remember that every porta potty was full during the last few legs.

The race has grown so much. It's great to see all the enthusiasm and camaraderie among all the teams. As the years have gone by I've gotten slower and hurt in places I didn't think would ever hurt. However, I keep trudging on and am part of the older generation participating in the event in hopes that I can inspire and instill that keeping active keeps us young.

Greg Johnson is from Knoxville, Tennessee, and has been running since 1981.

In 2010 I got a chance to join the Knoxville Track Club's Hood To Coast team when a friend backed out. It was a team contending for the overall race title, and, at 52, I was well past my prime, not to mention the slowest runner on the team.

I had known about the relay for a long time, but being on the East Coast I never thought there would be a chance for me to participate. Then about eight weeks before the race, I found out I'd finally get my chance. We were eating breakfast after a group run when one team member said he couldn't go to Oregon. There were faster runners in the area available, but I happened to be in the right place at the right time—and the team said I would be a good fit. Even though I was no longer able to race the young guns, I was still fast for my age.

I was Runner 8 in Van 2. I averaged 5:41 for my first leg and 6:38 for the dreaded, dusty Leg 20. Shortly after finishing my second leg I fell into a deep sleep in our van during the middle of the night. We didn't have phone service for quite a while before I was awakened by a text.

It asked, "Are you with Knoxville Track Club team?" But my phone didn't identify who sent the text. I replied, "Yes," and waited for a response. Soon I got a second text that said, "Meet me in Mist behind the porta potties for a massage if you need one." I had no idea yet that Mist was a town. I busted out laughing and woke up everyone in the van. Of course I responded to the text with a question, "Who the #&^@ is this?"

The simple response was, "Patrick." He is a longtime friend who sells the running massage sticks you see everywhere and had been set up along the course. We laughed so hard I thought we were all going to cry.

Our team finished second overall and I got to run a difficult mountain leg. My Tennessee mountain training definitely came in handy in Oregon.

I've run for over 35 years and participating in HTC was definitely a highlight of my running career.

Adam Morris is an attorney from Wayzata, Minnesota, who participated in his first Hood To Coast in 2014.

In terms of how our team got together, it hasn't been the same 12 guys every year. There are maybe eight guys who make up the core of our Baba Ganoush team. We've had a couple guys fall out with injuries, and a few who wanted to try other events.

There are really three of us who put the team together. Neil was my best friend from high school and was the best man at my wedding. I first heard about the race from him about a decade ago. And I practiced law with Patrick in Washington, D.C. When we got into the race for the first time in 2014, we had this moment of, "Well, now we have to find some guys for our team. What kind of people are we looking for?"

We quickly landed on the type of people we wanted for our team. Above all, we wanted people who would be fun to be in a van with for 24 hours. Beyond that, we were interested in running ability. Somebody who wasn't doing any significant training wouldn't fit with our team. Though we're aging, we're all competitive and we always race with the goal of finishing among the top teams in our division (and beating a couple of competitors that shall remain nameless). Finally, we had a "no assholes rule." We didn't want someone who was going to be easily frustrated with the team or the traffic or the weather—because nobody needs that.

We all kind of fanned out to put our team together. Patrick had a friend, Phil, who I actually knew pretty well from D.C. It turned out Phil was a big runner. Patrick asked, "How about Phil?" I thought Phil was a funny guy and replied, "Let's get Phil." Then Neil and I found a couple of guys in Minnesota, where we're both from, and from nearby Chicago. Patrick was originally from Louisiana and reached out to a few friends he had run with in high school. And it grew from there. We had a conference call with three people and then another call with six people and finally with our full team. We made sure everybody was on the same page.

What we ended up with was a team with competitive runners, tennis players, hockey players, and cyclists.

Maybe the funniest story about the composition of our team happened in 2017 when we needed a new recruit due to injury. There was a guy on our team who lived in Lafayette, Louisiana, but was originally from Rhode Island. He had some running group friends in the Northeast and said, "I think a guy I know will be great. Let me ask him." I replied, "Good. I trust you."

This new fellow's name was Tim and he joined our team. Now, we all live in different places, so we're always using email and conference calls to coordinate all the race logistics. When we get to Portland, the Thursday night before the race start we all meet up at a brewpub before heading to dinner. It's the first time our team is together in one place.

Tim looked over at me and said, "Hey, Adam, nice to see you again after all these years." I was a little surprised and said, "You look familiar, but where do I know you from?" It turned out Tim was the twin brother of a very good friend of mine from college, and many years ago we even hung out a little bit.

It was a small-world moment—and now Tim is part of the story too.

Bob Harold is the former chief financial officer at Nike and has been competing in Portland To Coast since 1996.

Portland To Coast has been a tremendous experience, but I'm beginning to fall apart. I started doing it when I was 48 and I'm 70 now.

The first year I was a little leery. Talk about being unprepared. I had no idea what I was getting into. I remember walking my very first leg. The van leapfrogged ahead of me and I was just walking. As I caught up to the van, one of my teammates leaned out and said, "Bob, this is called a *race*. Pick up the pace." I was just walking and wanted to finish my five miles. I wasn't really aware of time but that comment was a slap in the face and from then on I realized it *was* a race.

A few years later we hired a walking coach who taught us the proper race walking technique and that was really an energy saver. It taught us the mechanics of walking fast. We had the coach for upwards of 10 years, and she really whipped us into shape. Even as old as I am, I got to be a lot faster than in previous years. We learned how to properly use our arms, as well as our leg strike and foot strike. It's that stride behind your body that really provides the power for a walker. Just learning all those mechanics and training with those mechanics made a big difference.

You can't help but be a little competitive. It's a race, and Nike's name is involved and you really want to perform for your teammates. For a while we were training hard and putting that kind of effort in, and we stacked up pretty well against other teams. Our team finished in the top three in our division almost every year. We've won it several times and finished as high as 15th overall a couple of times.

But it's not just about the race—it's about the people you do it with. It's a fun experience and we have such a good time. You really bond with the people you're in a van with for hours and hours.

A few years ago we came up with something called a "fart machine" because, let's face it, farts are funny. It's a remote controlled unit that we usually put under the seat of a new teammate. At the right moment we trigger it and it makes the appropriate noise. It creates a hilarious situation.

We've also used it at one of the major exchanges in Mist. We know homeowners there who allow us to pull onto their property, and we pitch a tent or bring in a motor home. So we have a pretty nice situation compared to most of the other teams. That allows us to set up some portable chairs along the road and watch the walkers pass. We also set up the fart machine beside the road and hit the remote. Most people take it the right way, and we think it's really funny. We've had a lot of fun with that fart machine.

To be honest, after every race I think we all ask the question, "Why are we doing this?" There definitely is some pain involved, and I think every year we say, "Okay, this is it." But when it's over and done, almost everybody signs up to do it again. You're relaxed and having a beer and feeling like, "Wow, I did it again." In the long run, it's just flat out fun.

The race creates such a memorable time in your life. It leaves you with a *gee-whiz* moment. "Wow, I did that? Amazing."

Talia Prosser *is from Carlton, Oregon, and competes with the Portland To Coast team Below Standard.*

After we completed our first segment our van stopped so we could shower. I left my shoes there. I didn't realize it until I went to walk again.

I needed to find shoes at the last minute or I would have had to walk in slippers. Fortunately, my friend wears the same size as me, so it worked out perfectly.

Except now I get blamed for the stink in the shoes.

Kim Breedlove *is from Portland and first participated in Hood To Coast with her company team in 2015.*

I work for Tripwire, Inc., a software company based in Portland. We've been lucky enough to have our company team selected to participate in Hood To Coast three times, beginning in 2015. It's the primary team-building event at our company and our volunteers are also employees.

We select our runners from all the different departments at the company and have runners from sales, marketing, IT, and other departments. In addition, we always convince one or two executives to join our team as well. In 2017 we had two executives join the team, including one who flew over from Germany.

What do we love about HTC?

The incredible course that has it all, including the mountains, prairies, and the coast. The camaraderie and friendly competition among thousands of runners, all with the same goal. Running in the moonlight through the peaceful Oregon countryside. Sleeping in the middle of nowhere in tents and fields. A lack of sleep and the lines at the Honey Buckets. The team spirit that features costumes, decorated vans, and funny team names. Crossing the finish line together as they announce our team. And cowbells!

Ultimately, it's a great time and a wonderful opportunity to get to better know your colleagues. How can you not get to know your teammates when you're cramped in a van together for 30 hours?

We're already excited to do it again and again!

CHAPTER 9

How It Works

DURING RACE WEEKEND, IT'S EASY to see what Hood To Coast is all about. There's the start at Timberline Lodge and the finish line on the beach in Seaside and some 15,000 participants. There's the racecourse itself, along with exchanges, volunteers, spectators and Honey Buckets. But how does it all come together? Behind the scenes, HTC requires a year of preparation and planning, from the day thousands of applications begin flowing in, through the lottery and seeding process, course preparation and hundreds of other details until the last tent is struck on Seaside beach the week after the finish, when it all starts over again.

Jude Hubber is the Hood To Coast Race Series chief executive officer.

When Felica (Foote) and I got married in Montana I had never heard of Hood To Coast. She said her dad (Bob Foote, HTC founder) did something with running, but I didn't ask much about it. Even when I learned a little more, I still wasn't really sure what it was all about. At the time, we were living in Montana and it just wasn't on our radar.

When Felicia's dad asked her to come to Oregon to help manage the race, it came down to whether or not I could find a job in the area. When I landed a job in animal pharmaceutical sales, it was a no-brainer because Felicia wanted to get back to Portland. At the time, I still didn't know much about the race, so it didn't really enter into our decision-making process.

Even though I wasn't working there, the relay became a huge part of my life. Felicia was working all the time, and no matter where we went, somebody wanted to talk to her about the race. Then I started doing a few things for HTC, like helping with packet pickup and volunteer training. Then, when the person running the front desk at the HTC office decided to retire, I thought I could do that job. However, I had to show I could do it. Bob made it real clear that Felicia was my boss and that he could fire me if things didn't work out—but I'd still always be his son-in-law.

My love for the relay was never about the running. It was always about being part of a team. I was only on the track team in high school because our football coach made us sign up. I was too slow to say I actually *ran* track. After high school I really missed being involved with team sports. You get that experience back with HTC.

I ran the race with Felicia and a bunch of friends from Montana once and just loved it. It was a mind-blowing experience. She was involved with the race by then, but I wasn't and wanted to experience it. I got to see what people were talking about. Basically, it was 30 hours of laughter with people I'd known most of my life.

There's something about the relay that I'm not sure we'll ever really understand and was never really planned. The goal was never to make it into a 1,000-team event. It just grew organically. The culture was built by the teams.

Originally, when you thought about HTC you thought of a race from the mountain to the sea. Now it means being part of a team. People want to participate in that type of event. As long as there is a team component—that's what's important.

In the 10 years I've been working with HTC, the biggest change we've seen has been in the gender of the runners. When I first started, the majority of runners were men. Now about 70 percent of the runners are women.

In the past 10 years, we've also extended our reach. Social media has had a big impact on that. There were probably 20 countries represented in the race 10 years ago. Now there are people from more than 40 countries participating.

My responsibilities have changed over the years. It used to be I had a cell phone and was the 1-800 number. If there was a concern in the community, they'd call my phone. I still like to come to the command center during the race to be involved with the radio and help out however I can.

When someone from the community calls, it's important they know we're listening. I'm from a small town and understand that the race may be a burden on some small communities. Even though it's only one day, it's still a burden. It's important we have someone answer the phone and respond to people—to let them know we listen and care.

I remember one year we went out with bags the day after the race and just picked up poop when someone complained. I'm not sure it was all human, and some of it might have been there for years, but it was important to get it all.

Those communities are pretty good to us when you consider what we're doing, how long we're there, and the amount of noise we make.

I've made many friends through the race. For instance, I get a letter every year from a woman who had cancer and says HTC is the reason she's alive today. That just blows my mind—to think her goal throughout her treatments was to get back to the relay. Now she runs it every year. Stories like that have been life changing, for them and for me.

Cassie Negra is the Hood To Coast office manager and oversees the registration lottery for the race. She previously handled marketing and sponsorships for the organization.

I've pretty much done everything with Hood To Coast. We all do everything and help out when and where we're needed.

When I first started I was answering all the emails and taking all the phone calls. I heard all the complaints. I've learned over the years that runners are different than most people. They all have an agenda and I've learned to work with them.

Ever since I've been here I've taken care of the lottery. It's so much fun I kept doing it even when I changed jobs. I don't want to let anybody else handle it.

All the teams have to have their applications postmarked on the same day. If they're postmarked the day before or the day after, they're out. That immediately cuts down the number of entries we have to choose from.

For the next week or so it's like Christmas, we get bundles of mail every day. The out-of-state and out-of-country ones take a little bit longer to arrive. But we don't care when they get here, as long are they're postmarked on the right day. For more than a week the mailman comes in our office every day with big bins full of entries.

We probably get four or five hundred entries a day. We open each one and make sure there's a check included. Then we separate the HTC entries from the Portland To Coast entries.

As soon as we get them all, we identify the guaranteed and veteran teams and then we just start choosing envelopes randomly. We'll grab about 25 envelopes and put them in different piles. Then we'll enter them into the system. We scan the QR codes on the applications, but we have to assign each application a number manually. Obviously, it takes some time.

I love the ones that are decorated. Some are covered in stickers. Every square inch of the envelope is covered in stickers. Everything you can imagine. Smiley face stickers are a favorite, but just about anything else that you can think of. It helps attract attention. Sometimes people will send goodie bags. Last year we got a huge box of candy. It had to be 10 pounds. They got in!

Being a local team helps. We need a lot of teams within a 100-mile radius so we can get all the volunteers we need. We also try and allow all the international teams in the race. Once a team is accepted into the system they get an email saying, "Congratulations, you're in the Hood To Coast Relay."

Then we let those teams that didn't make it into the race know. There are probably about a thousand teams that don't make it each year. That's about 12,000 people.

We don't get a lot of complaints from those who don't make it. Most people are really good and understand that it's a lottery and that you're not going to get in every year.

Teams that have been declined can go into a special lottery the following year, if they follow the instructions. When a team is declined, they get a letter telling them to write either "Declined One Year" or "Declined Two Years" on the outside of the envelope. We try and choose all the ones that have been declined two consecutive years because we don't want anyone not to ever get in. If they follow those instructions, they'll get in for sure after a couple years.

Making your envelope pretty certainly helps a team get selected. It's surprising how many people put their entire application into one of those tiny stationary envelopes. Those just get lost. Sometimes when you're thumbing through the envelopes you don't even see them. You don't need to send anything with the application. But making the envelope bright and colorful and big, so it stands out, can really help.

Felicia Hubber grew up in Portland, moved to Montana during high school, and attended college at the University of Montana. The daughter of Hood To Coast founder Bob Foote, Felicia was just a few months old when she attended the first HTC—and she's been at every relay since. In 2006 she succeeded her father as president of HTC.

We get huge amounts of mail during the annual team application lotteries for Hood To Coast and Portland To Coast, and there have been some really interesting submissions.

About seven or eight years ago we received an application from Afghanistan. It was a box that arrived about a month after the lottery, and the return address was from a military base in Afghanistan. The box was covered in this brown and glossy paper, and when we opened it up, there was this cool Afghan fabric inside.

A U.S. Army soldier had sent in an application from Afghanistan while he was deployed. He had a really cool story about why he and his team wanted to participate in the race that was touching and inspirational. The postmark was from a military base and was three or four days after the lottery deadline.

We read their application and thought it was astonishing that these service members wanted to put together a team to compete, from literally the other side of the world. The team captain put in a lot of effort to mail the application from Afghanistan with a personalized, handwritten note and picture that was taped to the inside of the box. The team members were all in Afghanistan, including a couple Afghans, when the application was sent. However, the military service members expected to be back in the U.S. in time for the race.

Even though the race was sold out, everyone in our office agreed: "They're in. It's a must." It was just so inspiring and cool, and obviously we wanted to support them.

Jude and I caught up with their team at the finish. For almost a year, it had been in the back of our minds to connect with them during the race. We made sure to meet and congratulate them at the finish line, and they were all such super nice, inspiring people.

There was another team with a military connection that participated in the event somewhere around 2008. I believe their team name was 360 Goes 180, and the team included an Army soldier who was stationed in Iraq. He couldn't actually participate in person, so the rest of his team ran the course, and we worked out an agreement for him to participate remotely from Iraq. It took a lot of coordination, but he ended up using a treadmill that was programmed with the distances and elevations of the HTC legs for Runner 11. He also ran one of his legs outdoors at the Iraqi base when it was about 100 degrees. I saw a picture of him, and there was a tank behind him as he was running. He did all three of his legs remotely, which was pretty cool. It was another neat way to support the military service members.

We've received other interesting race applications too. Some packages are colorful shoe boxes illuminated with batteries like a Christmas tree. People attempt to bribe us with food or other goodies, too. We've received applications containing gourmet cookies and beautiful chocolates and candy. A lot of teams will include pictures of their team and a cool, personal story about why they want to participate.

It's always fun to see the creativity and what people think will make them stand out from the typical plain white envelope. However, the lottery is based on a system selected by state population. We also need to have at least one person from 80 percent of the teams be from within 100 miles of Portland, in order to have 3,600 volunteers spread out over the event's nearly 200-mile racecourse.

Michele Beyer *is from West Linn, Oregon, and avoided running most of her life until agreeing to run a race with a friend in 2011 when she was 48. The following year she participated in her first Hood To Coast.*

The most prominent memory I have of Hood To Coast is mailing in the entry form for the lottery. I'm the one who always completes the registration for our team. It's very stressful! The first year I registered my team I wrote about five checks, just to make sure it looked perfect—and there wouldn't be any trouble cashing it. If they can read it I know they'll be able to cash my check.

It's silly, but what can I say—I want to make sure everything is just right. I don't want to do anything that will put us in the rejected pile, even though it has happened twice. I really don't do anything special to the application. In fact, quite the opposite—I just try to fit the registration into the pack.

Each year, I take the envelope into the post office, but I don't drop it in the mailbox out front. It has to go into the inside mail slot at the West Linn Post Office. That way I know it will be postmarked that day.

One year, I was out of town on the day applications had to be postmarked, so I asked my husband to mail it. His immediate response was, "Why can't you take it with you?" I said, "Well, because it has to get mailed from our post office in West Linn." He said his reaction wasn't because he didn't want to do it, but rather because of the stress of making sure he didn't forget.

I did leave him instructions though!

Felicia Hubber *grew up in Portland, moved to Montana during high school, and attended college at the University of Montana. The daughter of Hood To Coast founder Bob Foote, Felicia was just a few months old when she attended the first HTC—and she's been at every relay since. In 2006 she succeeded her father as president of HTC.*

We now have restrictions regarding team vehicles. In the early days, the sky was the limit. Some teams even used motor homes during the race. They took up so much space at the exchanges and on the course that my dad and staff decided they could no longer be used. There was always concern about trying to park these massive vehicles on muddy or steep embankments in the Coast Range. The likelihood that a motor home was going to get stuck was pretty high, compared to a passenger van. Thus, a decision was made to put some limitations on what teams could drive on the racecourse.

Today, team vehicles can't be longer than 20 feet, and the maximum height is eight feet, three inches. We sometimes allow for a slight accommodation if a vehicle is not going to meet the specifications, but it's extremely rare. For the most part, a team needs to have at least a six-passenger vehicle. Many teams rent vehicles that seat eight or nine people, or even larger passenger vans.

If you're trying to pack six people in a sedan, good luck. It's going to be a tight-quarters experience. In the early years of the race, that definitely happened.

Bob Foote *is the founder and chairman of Hood To Coast.*

For the first four years of Hood To Coast, from 1982 to 1985, a simple hand slap was used to perform an exchange between two runners.

In 1986 I discussed the idea of using a baton for the runner exchanges with a friend of mine, Vernon Lee. We were both architects. Vernon volunteered to produce batons according to my specifications, and the decision was made to introduce batons to the event.

I bought one-and-a-half-inch diameter, white PVC tubing in eight-foot lengths. We then used a hacksaw to cut the PVC tubing into 12-inch pieces, which we used to create a baton. Each baton was spray painted, and a clear, peel-off logo was affixed around the baton.

It was a very daunting manual process that first year to produce batons for the more than 400 teams participating in the relay.

One problem we had with the batons was that they would get sweaty. Some runners would even stick them down their shorts so they could run hands free. Just imagine the reaction of women runners waiting for the baton handoff from a male teammate only to see him pull the baton out of his shorts! Really gross. There had to be a better solution to allow hands-free running.

One day I noticed my daughter, Felicia, had a skinny, colorful Slap Wrap bracelet on her wrist. At the time they only existed as a type of children's fashion accessory, and could only be found in toy stores. I really studied Felicia's bracelet. When I straightened it out, I saw it was stiff and rigid—which would be ideal for a handoff. I also saw that if it was slapped across someone's wrist it would change shape and wind itself around the wrist. I thought, "Wow, hands-free running!"

I researched the manufacturer, contacted them, and explained what I wanted. The Slap

Wrap was too thin and weak for our needs. It needed to be much wider and have a stronger aluminum core so that it wouldn't fall off. In addition, the surface needed to be made of a vinyl material to allow for the printing of custom graphics. I told them if they could produce my custom order, I would buy 500 of them. They were excited and went to work developing a prototype. After a few mock-ups, we created the final design for the wrist wrap first used in 1989, and still used today.

I should have patented the idea. It created a brand-new business for the manufacturer and helped them make a lot of money.

Felicia Hubber grew up in Portland, moved to Montana during high school, and attended college at the University of Montana. The daughter of Hood To Coast founder Bob Foote, Felicia was just a few months old when she attended the first HTC—and she's been at every relay since. In 2006 she succeeded her father as president of HTC.

I was in elementary school in the late 1980s. It was probably fifth grade when kids wore those Slap Wrap bracelets. They had different patterns and designs and came in a plethora of colors. It was the cool thing for kids to wear at the time, and I had a bunch in different colors and styles. I would wear a different one every day to match my clothes, and all my friends did the same.

My dad saw us wearing these slap bracelets to school and thought, "Wouldn't that be a great thing for us to use during the relay to exchange from one teammate to another? Instead of having to hold a slippery piece of PVC pipe as the relay baton, a bracelet could just be slapped on the wrist of the next runner, just like my daughter's bracelets."

My dad implemented that for Hood To Coast in 1989, and from then on we've been using a variety of different kinds of wrist wraps in the relay.

There was one year we almost didn't use the wrist wraps. I vaguely remember one race when we left them back at our office in Portland. My dad or someone else realized it before the first wave of runners were supposed to start. Someone, it may even have been my mom, had to race up the mountain with the box of wrist wraps and hand them out as quickly as possible right before that first wave took off.

Rob Rickard is from Canby, Oregon, and has participated in Hood To Coast every year since 1983. He has also been a course marker for the event for more than 25 years.

Bob Foote, to his credit, has always been very fastidious about making sure that the Hood To Coast course and mile markings are correct, including all the exchanges. He wanted the entire route marked so everyone would know where they were on the course.

Originally a gentleman named John Kelly, who's not with us any longer, was one of the course markers. One day he talked to me and said, "It's just too big of a job for me." We decided to split the work. I marked the course from Timberline Lodge to the Spaghetti Factory, which was about a third of the way into the race. John would then mark from there to the finish.

Years ago we used to mark every mile of the course from the start at Timberline to the finish in Seaside. Then ODOT (Oregon Department of Transportation) and some of the counties the course runs through got involved making marks on the road for construction and other things and they were concerned about our markings for the race. Now we just mark from Exchanges 13 to 31.

As we get close to the event and I'm planning to mark the course, the first thing I do is start paying close attention to the weather. If it's raining, the marking paint will just disappear. So I need good weather to mark the course.

Before marking the course, I go out and mark the exchanges. Usually, it takes one day to mark the exchanges. We use one color paint to mark the exchanges and another color to mark the course, and we have a logo and numbering series specifically for the exchanges.

I'll use a mountain bike and wear a GPS to mark the course. The bike is fitted with a Jones Counter, which is mounted to the hub of the bike's front wheel. It's the way most running courses are measured, and it's the same method Bob used when he first laid out the route. I ride the bike and after one mile I get off the bike and make a mark. I continue that process until I get to the next exchange. Then I zero everything out and start over again.

My wife works with me. She drives my truck and drops me and drives ahead a few legs to a nice, safe place to pull off the road. When I meet up with her, I have an energy bar and drink some water. She drives ahead again and I get back on the bike. That's the formula we follow.

The way the course is marked has evolved over the years. We used to use standard marking paint, but we're now more environmentally conscious and utilize marking chalk, which typically disappears in three or four weeks. So now we can't just go out and mark the course in June when the weather is nice and the traffic is down. We have to mark the course within certain time limitations.

There's a team that marks the course with me, and then I'll go out and make sure they've addressed all of the mile markers. I report back to Felicia Hubber (HTC president) when we're ready to go, so the team at the office knows the course is marked and ready. Once in awhile there's a last-minute change, and I'll go out and make that change.

Each year, we measure the course to make sure we're accurate. Many runners have a GPS watch to measure their legs, and there will be feedback every year from runners who say a certain leg was too long or too short. But we know that the mile markers are pretty accurate from year to year.

Bob Foote *is the founder and chairman of Hood To Coast.*

The race grew from eight teams in 1982 to 64 teams the following year. We had no volunteers on the course. Having all those teams making their own way through the course was pretty rough for them. They didn't get lost, but there was a safety issue that started coming into play. There was no way, however, that you can recruit volunteers to go stand out in the Mt. Hood wilderness at 3 a.m. They're not going to do it. There was just no way.

We couldn't continue to grow the race unless there were volunteers on the course to support the runners. Either the race would be limited to 25 teams and there wouldn't be a need for volunteers, or the teams would have to provide some volunteers in order to let the race grow.

We included the volunteer requirement on the entry forms—three volunteers from teams within the Portland area. That was pretty risky at that time. No race had ever required the participants to provide volunteers. We told them the volunteers would work only four hours and we'd try and provide options on where they were going to go.

The volunteer thing could have blown up. There could have been a mutiny. I didn't know what to expect. The runners could have said, "Bull$@#%! We're not going to give you volunteers. We're paying you money. You should get the volunteers for us."

There wasn't a single phone call or letter. Not one team complained or protested. They got it. This was everyone's event, and this was how they could help. They were all on board. I went, "Wow! What a lifesaver." The race could have disappeared just on that move alone.

Terry Lassisse *is from Billings, Montana, and can usually be found during Hood To Coast volunteering at Exchange 26 in the middle of the night.*

The first time I volunteered it was for my sister's team while I was still living in

Portland. I enjoyed it so much I kept coming back, even after I moved to Montana. The event really takes a lot of planning and it's much better organized now than when I first started volunteering

My shift usually starts about nine at night, but I'm there by six. I can help with the setup and get the lay of the land. I stay there until the next exchange leader shows up, about 6 a.m. Only once has the next person failed to show up. That time people from the race came around and relieved me.

The volunteers usually arrive with a great attitude, and they're almost always excited to be there. They're pleasant and want to help. I tell them it's okay to encourage the competitors and cheer them on. Personally, I enjoy seeing the different vans and how the teams have decorated them and what they've written on them.

For a while you're standing around in the dark and nothing's happening. Then the walkers start to come through and things begin to pick up. Some of the walkers look exhausted. You wonder if they did any training. Others are exhausted *and* starving.

One thing I remind everyone is that the later it gets, the less people see. Everyone is tired. Many of the van drivers are also running or walking in the race, so they're really tired too. You even have to remind people to get out of the road. Sometimes I might get a little bossy when it comes to keeping people out of the street, but hopefully that doesn't happen too often. Our main goal is to make sure everyone is safe.

We've had a number of incidents over the years. One year someone kept driving real fast past our group while we were trying to set up. Another year people were firing guns up into the hills. And another year this guy was jumping out of the trees and scaring walkers. Usually we just call the organizers or the police and they get them to stop doing whatever they're doing.

A few years back we spotted a young black bear running across the field that was being used as the van parking area. Of course we warned everyone who pulled in to park. That year we didn't have any problems with people trying to sleep out in the field!

Probably the biggest challenge is when people come to us who can't find their team. They're usually freaking out. When that happens we ask them to stay put while we try to track the team down. Cell phones don't work very well in our area, but we're equipped with radios and can usually find the team fairly quickly.

Sometimes it's not just the competitors who are unprepared. One year it was so warm during the day that I didn't bring my regular warm coat. But it can get very damp and foggy out there at night and I started to get hypothermia. I had to climb in one of the fire department vehicles they had there just to get warm.

I tell people volunteering for the first time to come prepared for any type of weather and to just have fun. Get there early. Get a feel for the event and what you'll be doing. And then just enjoy yourself.

*Nike has been involved with Hood To Coast since the event's second year and was instrumental in establishing the Portland To Coast race for walkers. Two of the company's longtime competitors are **Lisa McKillips**, assistant to the chairman, and **Nelson Farris**, chief storyteller and senior director of global HR talent development. Both are members of the PTC Nike T-Wrecks team.*

Nelson Farris: Nike has been involved in some manner with Hood To Coast since the second year of the race (1983). I don't think we were even aware of the race the first year. Since then we've worked with the relay to help make it a better, safer race. I don't want this to sound arrogant, but Nike doesn't need the publicity. What we've always wanted to do is help make it a better event.

We sponsor it, and the tradeoff is we're going to bring people from around the world to compete. For us, it's all about participation. To bring in talent helps grow the event. It also allows Nike to participate in an event that shares the spirit of our corporate culture. We want to win, we want to compete, we want to work as a team, and we want to play and have fun. HTC provides all those opportunities.

Lisa McKillips: The company really gets behind the race. There's always a huge event on campus the Thursday before the event. We have 1,200 people on Ronaldo Field, where we host a pasta feast with beer. Every Nike team that is competing is introduced and we take photos and pass out team jerseys. We make custom shirts that are unique to each year's event and unique to Nike. Nobody else gets them.

Nelson Farris: People come from all over to do the relay. They want to get out there and go through 24 hours of no sleep, running three times, rain, darkness, cold, heat, and dirt—all the things that make it a great event. We started bringing in international people so they could experience what we knew was a unique, competitive, and physical event. They have to train and qualify overseas, so we have really motivated people who come in from Taiwan, Sweden, and many other places around the world.

One year the guy in charge of sales decided to bring the entire Nike sales force to Portland for its annual sales meeting. He knew what HTC and PTC were all about and he wanted the sales geeks to be a part of it. We had about 800 people involved, and they really embraced it. They had runners, walkers, van drivers, and volunteers. They did everything and they were fully immersed. Afterward, you heard the stories, "I'm a sales guy. I don't work out, and I never thought I'd get into the relay. Oh my God, I actually did it and had so much fun."

Lisa McKillips: It keeps everybody active, which is one of our company goals. It gives people a reason to be out there training and to stay active. Department teams become running teams. It's something the whole company gets behind. Everybody knows when it's going to happen and there's an excitement that builds around the event. People participate or volunteer and some just go down to the beach to cheer at the finish.

Nelson Farris: Nike is a competitive, collaborative, team-based culture, and this race emphasizes all of that. Our mission statement is, "To bring inspiration and innovation to every athlete* in the world." The asterisk means that if you have a body, you're an athlete. In the relay you see every body type you can imagine out there. Good for them! You don't have to be a jock. Anybody can run or walk, especially if you have the right team and the right chemistry.

Our company attitude also is if we're going to enter a competitive team in HTC, then we're going to compete to win. The rest of us are going to go out and do the best we can and compete at our own levels. We try to beat our times and we support each other. If you're going to put the Nike name on it, no matter what division you're entered in, you'd better compete because we're not a *C* company. We don't have a *second-place* mentality. We've lost a few, but if you look at the records, we've won almost all of the competitive corporate divisions. And everybody knows they represent Nike. So you can't go out there and be a jerk. No jerks allowed.

Lisa McKillips: Any team that's been doing HTC or PTC for any length of time has its own rituals. We're the T-Wrecks because we're all old. We have these giant dinosaurs that we put on the roofs of our vans and we mount them on Thursday afternoon, before we go to Ronaldo Field. The dinosaurs are outlined in reflective tape, and at night you can see them coming a mile away. Everyone knows when the dinosaurs are coming.

Nelson Farris: That's part of the charm, the fun, the celebration, the getting into it, the play. It's a little bit childish, which is healthy and good. It all makes for a wonderful event. It's also serious in that you've got to be serious about getting organized. That's the biggest challenge because there are so many pieces to it.

Lisa McKillips: When you're in the van, it doesn't make a difference if you're a receptionist or a vice president. When you're in the van, you're a competitor. You're a teammate, period. What happens in the van stays in the van. It makes a big difference in our working relationships. We've all done it so many times, and we've known each other for so long, that it's like being in the van with a bunch of brothers and sisters.

Nelson Farris: For a lot of people, the relay is akin to running your first marathon, because running three times or walking twice in 24 hours is like an endurance race. You get no sleep and your body's whacked. You hear, "My God, I never thought I could do this." You hear that all the time. Little breakthrough moments for people who didn't think they were physically capable of doing the race, who trained with their teammates and then you see it and hear it all the time, "I just did it!"

Felicia Hubber grew up in Portland, moved to Montana during high school, and attended college at the University of Montana. The daughter of Hood To Coast founder Bob Foote, Felicia was just a few months old when she attended the first HTC—and she's been at every relay since. In 2006 she succeeded her father as president of HTC.

My race routine varies a bit each year, but I typically have a pretty good system for seeing many areas of the racecourse. On Friday morning I get up at 3 a.m. and drive to the race start at Timberline Lodge, checking the set-up of the first five exchange points on my way up the mountain. After staying at the start for a couple hours, I make my way down the racecourse, checking in with all of our course coordinators who manage different sections of the course. I want to see the exchanges right before they open to ensure that equipment and the parking areas are set up correctly, as well as that the exchange volunteers and leg volunteer monitors are in place. When I reach Exchange 6 in Sandy I take a break to grab a bite to eat. Then I proceed to Exchange 7, and then check every one through Exchange 12.

Teams often get to Exchange 12 earlier than their anticipated times, and team vehicles like to hang out there, so I'll talk with the exchange leader to make sure parking is set up correctly and according to plans. I also like to make sure the volunteers are deployed in the correct locations for Leg 12 because there are a lot of turns toward the end of the leg.

Then sometimes I see the Portland To Coast High School Challenge start, and go to Exchange 13. I'll then check every exchange through Exchange 17 near St. Helens. After that, I try to take a short nap. Then I'll follow the course all the way to Exchange 24. It's probably around 10 p.m. when I get to Exchange 24 and from there I head straight to Seaside.

I'm up on Saturday morning around 6 a.m., because the first running team comes in around 7 a.m. I stop at the temporary bridge we have over Highway 101 and talk with the owner of the construction company that puts the bridge together for us. Then I'll check to ensure all the volunteer placements on Leg 36 and at the shuttle parking are good. Finally

I go back to the finish area on the beach, and I'm usually there the rest of Saturday, unless the course coordinators need extra help on the last two legs.

I'm traveling the course by myself most of the time, although a couple years ago I brought my husband's father along. Jude (Hubber, HTC Race Series CEO) is at the finish area on the beach starting on the Wednesday before the race. He's helping the production company set up everything according to plan, as well as ensuring Seaside city officials and businesses are happy and ready for the influx of runners.

Participants come up at the finish area on the beach to express their enthusiasm for the race and tell me about their experience. I always take notes and ask questions like, "What did you think about this part of the course? Did this exchange work? How was the heat?" Or they might tell me about the line for the Honey Buckets at a particular exchange. I'm always thinking about the constructive ideas and suggestions from race participants and volunteers. The feedback we get from their insight is invaluable to the continual improvement each year.

I'm not keen on doing TV interviews. I let my dad or Dan (Floyd, HTC COO) handle those. I help with a few announcements at the finish party and the awards ceremony, but I prefer to stay out of the limelight.

After the culmination of the race, we are so tired but at the same time elated from the stories we hear and the success of the race. Then we go back to work Monday to start our analysis of the race, looking for possible improvements as we plan the next year's Mother of All Relays.

Cory Comstock *is the chief executive officer of the Full Sail Brewing Company, which makes Session Premium Lager.*

When we began our sponsorship a couple years ago we were excited to work on an event that had both a really important cause attached to it and a passionate group of attendees and followers.

It also made sense for us because it's a natural fit. Much as Hood To Coast has been an annual tradition in the state since 1982, Full Sail has been an integral part of Hood River and the overall Oregon community since our founding in 1987. We believe our race sponsorship gives HTC the feel of a real community event, which the relay would sacrifice if another brand from outside of the state were involved.

From the activation of the beer-pouring system on the beach in Seaside to custom tents, beach towels, kites, hats, team jerseys, and team sponsorships, we've put a huge effort into making the finish line an amazing experience for all the participants and every-one involved in the relay.

For the runners, the finish line is epic. There's a massive crowd of people and it looks out over the ocean.

Crossing the finish line as a team is an amazing occurrence, and a big part of that experience is celebrating together in Seaside. There's our beer garden, corn hole, a DJ during the day, and a live band at night, and sand sculptures. It's almost like a wedding where you've worked the whole year to make this event happen, and there are plenty of nerves, along with anticipation and excitement. It's incredibly rewarding to see it all come together and to watch the athletes who've worked so hard enjoy the festive finish line atmosphere.

Being part of this event is huge for us because there's a real emotional connection made with all the participants. When teams have been running for 25 or 30 hours and cross the finish line after something so awesome, to crack open a Session beer creates a solid memory.

From a participating perspective, there's a real team bonding experience for Full Sail with the teams that compete. We have participants from every department—from the pub and production to the lab team, sales group, and office staff. Some of our team members participating were already runners, but others signed up for the experience. Of course, during the race you become close with your teammates. People you normally see and talk to at work are now sleeping in a van next to you and sharing deodorant. When you cross the finish line, it's special when your Full Sail "family" is there to congratulate you and celebrate.

From a sponsor's perspective, what really stands out is the incredible transformation of the beach. When everything is set up, a stretch of the Seaside beach turns into a dynamic, bustling little micro-culture celebrating what the runners have accomplished and the money raised for charity.

It's a fantastic event with so much personality and positive, communal spirit on dis-play, along with great costumes, uniforms, and van decorations. It all makes HTC a great fit for Full Sail Brewing and Session.

Matthew Cox is from Dallas and works in the experiential marketing business. He has worked with a Hood To Coast sponsor and has also participated in the race.

I became involved with Hood To Coast when one of our company's clients became a sponsor of the race. Our company helps clients with experiential marketing, and when

Dick's Sporting Goods decided to sponsor the event, we got involved. We then worked together with them to create meaningful experiences at the event.

Our first year was 2014. The sponsorship came together only six weeks before the race. I received a call and was told, "Hey, we've got this really cool opportunity. It's a 200-mile race and we need to build a tent hotel in the middle of the forest. Can we do that?" My response was, "You bet. Of course we can do that."

I quickly jumped on the phone and called Jude Hubber (HTC Race Series CEO) to try and learn everything I could about the race. After Jude and I talked, I had more of a basic understanding of the event. I understood it was a relay race with 12 runners and two vans. Van 1 did the first six legs of the course and then Van 2 did the next six legs, and the two vans leapfrogged each other all the way to the finish. There was one location where the two vans connected, Exchange 24, where the runners in one of the vans usually spent a couple hours sleeping in the middle of the night. The exchange was located in Birkenfeld, a rather remote area about two thirds of the way through the race.

We had space at Exchange 24 and our first year we set up what we called Slumber Village. Basically it was just 150 two-person backpacking tents. We allowed runners, race volunteers, and others to use the tents like a free hotel. If a tent was available, we would check you in at the registration area, and you could stay as long as you wanted. When you were done with the tent, you just checked out. Then another group could check in and use the tent.

I don't know exactly what our expectations were, but there was something unique and special about Slumber Village right away.

Originally we were thinking of using maybe 50 camping tents. But in our conversations with Jude he said we weren't even going to scratch the surface with that quantity. Jude said it was a great idea to have the tents available, but he mentioned there were more than 10,000 runners. With some quick math we figured out even if all the tents were double booked, we'd only have space for 100 people to sleep at one time. And if we turned over the tents three or four or even five times, we'd really only have space for maybe 500 people at the most. It was determined that 50 tents would not be that impactful. That's when we decided to really ramp it up and how we settled on 150 tents.

Logistically there were plenty of challenges that first year, including no cell phone service. We also weren't going to be able to use electrical equipment because there was really no source of power in the area. If we had anything to build construction-wise, we'd have to bring in our own generators. And that's how it evolved into being tents.

Getting the word out to all the runners was another challenge, but we figured out how best to do that with the help of HTC. Every team receives two race handbooks, one for each van, which provide detailed directions and maps, along with other vital information. Fortunately the plans for Slumber Village came together just in time to be included in the handbook. HTC also sent emails to every team captain providing the details of Slumber Village. Information about the tents was available at packet pickup, where teams collect their race numbers, T-shirts, and other gear. HTC was doing everything they could to promote it the first year.

For those people who didn't know about it that first year, it was a really cool surprise when they arrived at Exchange 24. We had a ton of people who thought it would cost money. Many people asked us how much it cost to check in to a tent. When we told them it was free they were just blown away!

After the first year we learned even more about the event. Although that first year was like dipping our toes in the water, we were really happy with everything. However, we made a couple key changes for year two. We increased the number of tents from 150 to 400, which more than doubled our occupancy. In addition, we changed the name to Tent City because all the runners were calling it that.

Now there are times during the race when the tents are not fully occupied. But every year there are also six or seven hours when the tents are packed and there's a waiting line of between five and 25 people to get in. Overall, right now we feel like 400 tents is a pretty good number.

Along with the tents, in the last couple years we also created a sleeping bag-only area between the tents and the forest. We wanted to create additional space in an area away from vehicles and people. So if tents weren't available, we wanted another safe place for people to go to kind of get away from everything.

And that's really how Tent City has grown and where we stand today.

Dave Harkin *grew up in Seattle, attended the University of Oregon, and spent four years teaching in Louisiana, Colorado, and Seattle before returning to Oregon. He and his wife, Paula, have owned and operated the Portland Running Company since 2000. In 1988 Dave participated in his first Hood To Coast.*

I think Hood To Coast sneaks up on people. Seasoned runners know what they need to do to train and get ready. However, all the rest of the people who get roped into the race don't realize what they're in for, even when the relay is just three or four weeks away.

So every year around the start of August, just three or four weeks away from the relay, we see a phenomenal amount of people who start to panic. They come to our stores for all kinds of advice and all kinds of everything. They come in for counseling sessions. They come in to talk about how they got roped into doing it. Virtually half the people I talk to who are doing the relay for the first time have been convinced by their friends that it's a great idea and they should do it. Generally speaking, they hear it's a party or something like that and decide to do it. Hardly any of them—and there are a lot of first-timers every year—have actually even run a half-marathon. They have no idea what they're in for.

I have the same conversation over and over again with customers. I'm asked questions like, "How is HTC? How does HTC compare to the fill-in-the-blank half-marathon? How does HTC compare to a 10K?" That's funny because it doesn't compare to anything. I don't think you can really even put it up against a marathon. It's just its own thing.

You can make it easy or make it hard. Most teams in their first year don't know how to make it easy. It's very unique. Although with the growth of other relays the recipe has changed a little bit and people know more about them, where to go and how to prepare.

I think it's super difficult. I've never talked to anybody at the race that said, "You know, I wish I would have run my first leg faster." No one ever says that.

They always run too hard, get drained out, eat horribly, and don't sleep, before getting to the beach. Then it takes about 15 minutes for them to think about it and decide they want to do it again, which is always awesome to see.

Matthew Cox is from Dallas and works in the experiential marketing business. He has worked with a Hood To Coast sponsor and has also participated in the race.

In 2014, our first year as a sponsor with Hood To Coast, there were two Dick's Sporting Goods corporate teams participating in the race. One team included six runners from Dick's corporate office and six runners from the Portland area who worked at local stores.

One member of the team from Dick's corporate office was running his second leg during the middle of the night. It was his first time at HTC and he didn't really know what to expect. At this point, runners were stretched out along the course. After he started running he didn't see anybody in front of him or behind him. He started thinking he was seeing eyes in the forest, and he was certain it was either Sasquatch or a wolf or something like that. So he pulled out his phone and started making a video. It was like his last will and testament.

He made the mistake of sharing the video with the rest of the team, and it was hilarious. In it he's talking about the eyes in the forest like, "I'm sure it's a wolf or something. It's going to eat me. It's maybe a bear or a cougar." In reality, it actually looked like a dog or raccoon or opossum.

The following year, he came back and ran again. A woman who I worked with was really into arts and crafts, so I asked her to make a two-foot-tall replica of Sasquatch. It was made of papier-mâché and covered in fake fur. She did a really good job. It was this little Sasquatch stuffed animal, and it was going to be a gag gift.

I gave it to him in front of everybody before the race started. Well, he's a good sport and thought it was hilarious. And he carried it around the whole race, and many people wanted to get pictures with the replica Sasquatch.

I saw that and thought, "There might be an opportunity here. The Pacific Northwest is totally the land where Sasquatch lives, if there is a Sasquatch."

Heading into the third year of the partnership between Dick's and the race, I talked to Jude (Hubber, HTC Race Series CEO) and Dan (Floyd, HTC COO). I told them, "We want to go to a Hollywood costume shop and get a Sasquatch costume made. Then we're going to make a bunch of videos with Sasquatch sightings along the racecourse, and we're going to anonymously release them leading up to the race. We'd love for you guys to send an email out to all the teams about these wild animal sightings, and let them know to be careful when running." Jude and Dan were on board with the plan.

We made all these videos and got tons of views. I'm actually the guy wearing the costume in the videos, which makes me laugh.

There was a guy who worked for me who was six-foot-eight. I had him wearing the costume at the start. I'll never forget this. He was wearing the costume, although he hadn't put the head on yet. He was sitting in the back of van and he said, "Do you really think people are going to want to take photos with me?" I told him, "Trust me. Put the head on. Let's go." So he threw the head on, the van door opened, and he stepped out. He made it about four feet before runners were coming up saying, "Oh my gosh! It's Sasquatch!" They all wanted to take pictures and thought it was a great joke.

And so we've carried Sasquatch forward from there and now every year the Dick's Sporting Goods Sasquatch makes an appearance at HTC.

One funny note is that in 2017 we had to replace the original guy who dressed up in the Sasquatch costume because he was scheduled to attend another event for us in Pennsylvania. I had to find someone else to wear the costume, and there are not a lot of six-eight guys out there. The best I could do was a guy who was six-four. It was still pretty good, but not quite as impactful.

Sasquatch always spends time at the start and the finish, as well as at different exchange points. Every year what we do with Sasquatch gets a little bigger, even if the actual size of Sasquatch gets a little smaller!

Team UGATAWANNA in 2017.

Vans heading up the mountain to the race start at Timberline Lodge.

CHAPTER 10

Vans On The Run

MOVING FLEET OF FOOT IS just one key to Hood To Coast. The race also requires two vehicles to move teams along the course in a timely manner. Typically a team of 12 is split in two, with six individuals in each vehicle. In the early years, with smaller race fields, sedans and luxury motor homes were common and teams even used three or four vehicles. For some teams, only the vehicle holding the last few runners would actually show up at the finish.

As the race grew and traffic increased, limitations were placed on the size and number of vehicles allowed. Nowadays, the most common vehicle is a van, whether it's the family minivan, a nine passenger van or something slightly larger. Sedans are almost nonexistent, although SUVs still appear on the course. Designated drivers are popular too, although some teams still rotate runners through the driver's seat.

Whatever the mode of transportation, some teams also go to great lengths to decorate and personalize their vehicles prior to the race, often incorporating the team name or logo in their handiwork.

Devrie Brennan hails from Moraga, California, and now lives in Lake Oswego, Oregon. She is an orthopedic physical therapist who has participated in Hood To Coast 15 times.

The 2017 race marked my 15th time participating in Hood To Coast. That year my team, UGATAWANNA, rallied around me to support my battle with breast cancer. I had surgery and finished radiation just six weeks before the event.

As I was running Leg 6 heading into the exchange in Sandy, I saw an accident with a fire engine down the hill. I thought the worst, that maybe a runner had been hit by a car.

As I approached the accident, I saw one of my teammates standing on the side of the road. Perplexed, I asked why she was there. She said the BRT got rear-ended. I looked off to the side of the road and, sure enough, our team's Suburban that we nicknamed the "Big Rolling Turd" (from the movie *RV*) was smashed to bits in the back.

Shocked by what I saw, I asked if everyone was okay. The rest of my team came over and said they were all fine. They told me to keep running and that they would meet me in Sandy at the exchange. I hesitated a bit, but they all insisted I keep running. I was anxious the rest of my run and hoping no one was more injured than they realized. I was also hoping that we could drive the BRT to my house so we could switch vehicles. I didn't want to stop running. This race meant a lot to me as a symbol of mental and physical recovery from my cancer, but I would defer to what was best for my team.

After seeing the accident my thoughts were sad. I wondered if my teammates were going to start feeling the effects of the collision and be unable to run or too freaked out to continue. As I continued running I didn't want to dwell on the unknown and tried to keep my focus on the scenery.

A few acts of random kindness by racers and race officials helped me finally connect with my teammates after about 45 minutes waiting at the exchange. A race volunteer let me borrow her phone to call my teammates. Thank goodness I had written down a teammate's name and phone number on the back of my bib. These days who remembers phone numbers? The race volunteer was very concerned when I told her the story of what happened and even offered me a ride back to my van if they couldn't move it.

When I finally found my teammates at the exchange I held my breath as I asked if everyone was still up for running. Their immediate response was, "Of course!" Not a single runner wanted to stop. They said if I could go through my breast cancer treatment they had no business quitting the race. It made me all warm and fuzzy inside realizing these women had my back knowing how important it was for me to finish the race.

Since the BRT was hit from behind, most of the damage was in the back end. The firefighters removed the metal quarter panels from above the rear tires because on impact they flared out like wings. The engine was fine but the frame was pretty bent—there was a strong pull to one side. If you turned the wheels more than 30 degrees there was a horrible screeching sound. It wasn't too bad, because most of our drive was in slow traffic on a Friday afternoon. We all held our breath whenever we made a turn. We drove back to my house in Lake Oswego and switched to my smaller Yukon.

We ate a nice meal and took showers and never looked back. Everyone on the team agreed our race would continue as planned. A little neck soreness wasn't going to stop any of my teammates. We actually finished the race only 15 minutes later than our official projected finish time, and being superstitious we never did give the Yukon a nickname.

Later I learned more about the people that rear-ended the BRT. They were not runners but had just come from a wedding during the race. The driver's brother married his girl-friend at an exchange. I think the groom ran Leg 1 and the bride ran Leg 2 and they were married at the exchange. The driver and his girlfriend were heading to the reception somewhere in Sandy and had all the decorations in their Grand Cherokee. The decorations included empty beer bottles, with the labels removed, holding flowers. From the impact of the accident, the beer bottles flew from the rear of their vehicle and landed on the dashboard. When the police showed up at the scene it looked like there was some heavy drinking happening. Since I was running and missed everything, I can only imagine the amount of time that was spent proving the beer bottles had been empty long before the accident.

Bryn Mathison *grew up in Beaverton, Oregon, and now lives in Irvine, California. She first participated in Hood To Coast in 2012 and has run the event multiple times.*

My second year running the epic Hood To Coast was in 2013. Our team name, which was selected by our captain, was 99 Problems but a Run Ain't One. That name would end up being changed by the time we finished in Seaside.

We were in Van 2 and all had gone well with our first legs. We were tired, but we were feeling good. We were sleep-deprived, but we were feeling good. It was smelly in our van, but we were still good.

I was Runner 12 and it was my turn to run. Off I went to run my second leg. I finished strong but couldn't find my teammates or our van at the exchange. Where was our van? I waited, and then waited some more. Finally after a very long wait I saw a teammate coming my way. She'd been sent to get me. And that's when I learned that the dreaded had happened! It was a worst case scenario in all our minds—we had a broken-down van.

Apparently after I was dropped off the van wouldn't start. We were in Mist—a beautiful place to be but we had no cell service. And our van was dead on the side of the road. What would we do? We walked down the road holding our cell phones high in the air until we were able to get service. Malaika, my sister and teammate, called the owner of our dead van—our dad. He lived in Beaverton, in the house I grew up in, which was more than an hour away from where we were located. The phone call went straight to voice mail. My sister left a message letting him know his van had died and asking him if he would please let us borrow his minivan. And could he please drive right now to Mist and find the closest auto repair shop, because that was where we would definitely be waiting.

He was our only hope to finish the race! Would he get our message? Was he available? Could we borrow his minivan to finish the race?

Our second call was to AAA. They came to tow our van away. However, there were six runners and one tow truck driver—and the tow truck could only fit two people in the cab. So we did what anyone would do on no sleep with sore muscles and stressed-out minds. The remaining four runners had to lie down in the back of the van while it was towed to the repair shop. We thought it was a brilliant idea! It was not. After many miles of winding roads we arrived at the closest repair shop with two of our runners throwing up from the ride in the van. Then the repair shop confirmed our worst fear—the van was dead, *really dead.*

Just as we received that news out of the corner of my eye I spied a blue Toyota mini-van pulling into a parking space. Dad to the rescue! We couldn't believe it. He had received our message and was coming to our aid. It was all hands on deck as we pulled our gear out of the broken-down van and put it into our shiny new minivan. We didn't care that we were going from a 12-person van to a seven-person minivan. We didn't care that our van breaking down meant we didn't get any rest. We didn't care that we had no decorations on our tiny new van. We were back in business. We quickly drove to the next major exchange and prayed that Van 1 didn't have to wait long. Remember—there was no cell service.

We arrived at the next exchange and Runner 1 had been waiting for only 45 minutes. Just 45 minutes—that's all! We could make up that time and we did. We finished our last legs strong—only 12 minutes off our predicted finish time!

What did we change our team name to after all our van troubles? How about 99 Problems and a *Van Is One.*

Dennis Masi *was a longtime college basketball coach in Connecticut who relocated to Portland with his family in 2016. He participated in his first Hood To Coast in 2015.*

We were in Van 1 and it was just past 10 p.m. somewhere between Exchanges 15 and 18. It was dark and there were runners along the side of the road. I was being extra safe, driving slowly—very slowly. Out of the darkness, I suddenly saw behind me the flashing lights of a police car. My mind and heart raced! What had I done? Was a runner injured? As I pulled to a stop, I clued my teammates into what was happening. We were all a little concerned as the officer walked up to the driver's window.

"Hi, officer," I said, as I rolled down the window. "Do you know the speed limit?" was the response from the officer. "No, sir," I responded. "I was trying to be extra careful and watching for runners, so maybe I was going a little fast without realizing it," I stammered. "Fast, not exactly," said the officer. "You were going too slow—so slow, in fact, that it's unsafe." And with those words, my teammates burst into laughter. Who had ever been pulled over for driving too slow during Hood To Coast?

The officer let me off with a warning, but each year my teammates enjoy reminding me to drive a little faster.

Rich Kokesh *is from Portland and has run Hood To Coast eight times.*

In 1984 we had two Volkswagen buses for the race, but we had a problem with one of them during the race. In those days, the two vans would leapfrog each other. We were heading to an exchange that was partway up Bald Peak, just before you get to the state park. It was one of the steeper hills we had to climb during the race.

It was the middle of the afternoon and we were in our Volkswagen bus, which was air-cooled. We had it filled with five guys and everyone's gear. It was during the middle-of-the-afternoon heat and we were just slowly crawling up this big hill in the bus we had nicknamed the Iron Lung.

We stopped at the transition and the engine was hot. We got back in our bus and it wouldn't start. This was way before we had cell phones and all that stuff. Our other van took off and we had no way to contact them. We couldn't get our van started, and we were on this narrow, uphill country road with ditches on either side.

Luckily, I was the proud owner of a Volkswagen bus and knew exactly what had happened—it had overheated. I told the guys if we could turn Iron Lung around and point it downhill, I could get it going. I'm not sure they believed me, but all five of us were on this big, narrow hill trying to push this Volkswagen bus back and forth, and point it downhill.

I knew all we had to do was get it rolling at about five miles an hour, pop the clutch, turn the key and it would kick over. Unless you owned a Volkswagen you wouldn't know that.

That was the one major event we had to overcome that year. We had to resuscitate the Iron Lung!

Scott Thompson *is from Beaverton, Oregon, and is a founding member of the Dirty Half Dozen +6 team, which has competed in every Hood To Coast since 1986.*

When we first started competing in the race we were about 16 and only a few of us were licensed to drive. We realized that we were going to have to get a vehicle or two and we knew our parents probably wouldn't want us wandering around for the weekend. So every year we had to talk at least two parents, if not three or four, into driving. For years we did that, talking parents into driving and letting us borrow a vehicle, until we were old enough for them to let us take a car. It probably wasn't until we graduated college that we did it by ourselves.

One of the challenges every year is coming up with vans. In the early years it was, "What kind of van are we going to get? How are we going to get six guys in a van?"

One year it was an old Volkswagen van. It was one of the years when we had a little bit of sponsorship from adidas. We had some pretty cool sweats and shoes and we were really decked out. Only the van had a gas leak, so when we got to the top of the mountain everybody smelled terrible. We were afraid we'd catch on fire from the gas fumes.

Another time, one of the guys had a girlfriend whose parents had a huge van. It was like we had gone to heaven. It even had a refrigerator.

Then there was the year, before there were limitations on vans, when we had a delivery truck. We put a couch in the back along with some mattresses. That was probably the coolest van, but I don't think they're legal anymore.

One year somebody donated some jackets to our team. They were some of the first jackets made from reflective materials. The jacket company wanted to have this woman ride along with us to document the race and write an article about the team. We said okay, but we didn't have a very big van. She only made it to Portland before she bailed. She'd had enough.

Jerry Duncan *has been participating in Hood To Coast since 1984. The Aloha, Oregon, native began running in the late 1970s to lose weight and has completed more than 80 marathons and 100 ultramarathons.*

I think this happened around 2000. Our team was about to take a handoff at the exchange in Scappoose. It was the middle of the night and as we drove by Scappoose High School we dropped our runner off at the exchange point (which wasn't illegal back then). We then drove into the school parking lot.

My teammate Randy Fleenor and I jumped out with the timing clipboard and headed to the exchange, which was located on the other side of Highway 30. Since it was around 1 a.m. and there was no traffic, Randy and I crossed in the middle of the street—not at a crosswalk. Just as we got to the exchange, we were confronted by a man who appeared to be a "Rent-a-Cop" and who challenged us for jaywalking.

Since he was armed and seemed "official," we answered his questions. He wanted our driver's licenses, van registration, and team name so he could have us disqualified. Since our runner was only about 10 minutes out and we had the clipboard and needed to note the handoff time, we respectfully argued that we would be more careful if he would let us go. Instead he had us stand facing his vehicle—which was parked at the exchange—and put our hands on the roof so he could frisk us for weapons. He told us to stay in that position while he got on his radio and supposedly was checking to see if we were wanted on some police database.

We stood there for about five minutes until a couple real policemen walked by and asked what we were doing. When we told them what had transpired and that we really needed to witness our runner's handoff, they told us we could leave and they would deal with the Rent-a-Cop.

At that moment our runner came into the exchange and handed off to our next runner. We noted the time on our clipboard and all three of us dashed back across Highway 30, being sure that we were not jaywalking. We got to our van and took off.

We were a little worried that we might be disqualified, but when our team arrived at the finish the problem we had in Scappoose was never mentioned!

Julie Saboe is from Beaverton, Oregon, and began running Hood To Coast with her team in 2010.

Every year after our Legacy of Sore Muscles team finishes Hood To Coast I clean out the van and find several items that have been left behind. Then I send a "lost and found" email to the team so everyone can claim their belongings.

In 2012, the third year our team participated in the relay, I found some sexy, black lace panties in the van. Interestingly, when I sent around the email about what was left behind that year no one claimed the panties. We had a co-ed team and our van included four women and two men.

Although we were never able to prove it, we believe the panties belonged to a woman who ran with our team just that one year. Two of us on the team proclaimed that we don't wear panties while we run—there's no point in causing extra friction—so we don't even bring panties. And the other woman in our van said they weren't hers. The fourth woman on our team, the one who joined us only for that year, was silent on the topic and didn't respond to the email. We think she was just too embarrassed to come forward and claim the panties. Of course we also teased the two guys in our van that the panties could have belonged to one of them!

Since no one claimed the panties, the following year I brought them back (after I washed them and stored them with our other race gear) and hung them on the rearview mirror of our van. I said, "These panties will be part of our van until someone claims them."

The tradition and fun surrounding the panties has grown over the years. Now every year before the race I start getting asked questions like, "Do you still have the panties?" or "Are the panties coming back?"

As we're loading up the van each year the race cannot "officially" start for our van until we have ceremoniously placed the panties on the rearview mirror and documented the ceremony with plenty of pictures.

Over the last couple years, our second van has tried to match our awesome panties display by asking members of other teams for donations to hang on their van. Although they've received some interesting responses to their requests, they haven't received anything truly worthy of being used to decorate a van.

Did I mention that we work for a pretty conservative healthcare organization and drive one of our company's vans in the race? The display on the rearview mirror is pretty risqué for our company's reputation, but still the panties live on!

Ashton Eaton was born in Portland and grew up in Bend, Oregon, before attending the University of Oregon. He won gold medals in the decathlon at the 2012 and 2016 Summer Olympics, and established a decathlon world record at the 2015 World Championships in China. In 2017 he retired from track and field and now lives in San Francisco with his wife, Brianne. He first participated in Hood To Coast as an honorary captain for Team

*World Vision in 2013 and returned to the role again in 2014 and 2016. In 2017, he served
as a van driver for World Vision.*

I didn't mind driving a van in 2017. I wanted to spend time at Hood To Coast in a
different role than just offering support and encouragement.

I was trading off with somebody else in the van, and I actually liked it. It was much
easier on me because I wasn't jumping from van to van, and had just a single responsibility with one van. I would say it's a thankless job—driving out there in the middle of the
night while everybody else sleeps. Maybe I shouldn't say it's a thankless job. It's just a lot
tougher than it seems. I wanted to be a driver because I thought it was going to be really
easy, but in some ways it's worse.

People always ask me if I'm running when they see me during the race. Everyone just
assumes that if I did run, I'd be really fast. I think in 2018 I'm going to run for the first
time. Once I do that I'll have experienced the full gamut of HTC.

My good friend Lopez Lomong, the former Olympian who got us involved with the
relay, always says, "Hey, man, you should run." I think he likes to run with people and
encourage them, instead of just running on his own. I do remember one time we passed
him running while we were in a van, and he was just flying by people. I was laughing
because I thought the people he was passing would be like, "Who is that guy?" I wanted
to tell them, "Don't feel bad. He's an Olympian."

Hopefully, if I do run, Lopez will run with me too.

Max Woodbury *is from Portland and became a C-6 quadriplegic in 1996 from a fall while
working at a Superfund cleanup site. He has competed in Hood To Coast multiple times
and captains the Pimps 'n' Gimps team that consists of both wheelchair athletes and able-
bodied competitors.*

Every year on the day before the race, I go pick up our van from Performance Mobil-
ity, Portland's local adapted vehicle company. They donate $300 for the rental of what we
affectionately call "Little Piggy." They also spend nearly two hours removing the rear
seats, which is important so we can put a futon mattress in the back for sleeping.

Little Piggy is a raised four-wheel-drive monster diesel with nitrous oxide for added
power when it needs that extra oomph. It also has an accessible lift, six-way wheelchair
seat base and hand controls.

Sharing a van with people for two days straight can be tough. My first year, I was in a van with only one friend, who received a call after his first leg that his dad had unexpectedly passed away. After dropping my friend off with his family, we had one of those unique bonding experiences. Even though none of us knew each other, the situation forced us to fight through an uncomfortable silence and try to lighten the mood. By the end of the week-end we were giggling at everything like it was our first childhood sleepover. We were lucky. I've heard horror stories about "blind date vans."

Now that I'm a van leader who chooses the team, I've found it more important to find people I enjoy spending time with rather than finding the fastest runners. My van includes friends that I've had since before my spinal cord injury accident about 20 years ago. These are people who I don't feel guilty asking for assistance to transfer me to and from my handcycle. They don't mind strapping the handcycle on top of Little Piggy and bringing it down when it's my turn.

Paul Cummings *works for the National Affordable Housing Trust in Columbus, Ohio.*

A few years back my Van 2 teammates and I were enjoying a leisurely pre-race meal before heading out to the first major exchange at Sandy High School. We were planning to meet Van 1 around 9 p.m. As one of the last teams to start the race that year, we had time to enjoy a relaxing dinner before our 24 hours of running. However, in the middle of our meal I got a call from one of my teammates in Van 1 with a disturbing message: "We have a problem. Our van is smoking and overheating."

At that point I'd run Hood To Coast more than 20 times. When I was younger it was as a college student on teams trying to win the race. More recently, and for this race, it was with a fundraising team called Running for Shelter that raised money for nonprofits working in affordable housing. As a fundraising team, and one that had raised almost a million dollars for the charity through the years, it was important to keep our commitments and finish the race.

Apparently the 12-passenger van we rented made it to Timberline Lodge for the start before the team realized there was a problem. It started leaking oil profusely in the parking lot. The team tried to fix the van, but in the end they determined it couldn't be driven.

As we strategized our next steps, one of our local runners offered us his family's minivan. Now with a replacement van available, we called our teammates in Van 1 and told them to find any ride they could down the mountain and to complete their first six legs.

Luckily, other teams stepped up and helped our runners get down from Timberline to start their legs. To this day we still laugh at the fact it was easier for the women on our team to find rides than the men. We took Van 2 up the mountain to collect some of our teammates, picked up our other team members finishing their legs, and then regrouped in Sandy, where we gave Van 1 their new race vehicle.

When our Runner 7 began it was clear we were near the back of the field, which wasn't good. Time was not on our side. As one of the last teams to start, and because of our van problems, we were now at risk of being swept off the course by race officials after starting our set of legs 30 minutes later than scheduled.

Later that evening our fears about where we were in the field were confirmed. While waiting in the dark for our runner to come into Exchange 9, we could hear the race volunteers on their walkie-talkies. They were getting the bib number of the last runner and being told to shut down the exchange after that runner passed. Everyone in Van 2 began to panic because it wasn't our team's bib number that was called out, meaning our runner was still somewhere out on the course in the dark. We pleaded with the volunteers to keep the exchange open until our runner finished the leg, and they did give us a little extra time.

Then, as one of the team captains, I gathered my teammates and shared what I hoped would be a motivating message, "There's no way we're going to get swept off the course. Everyone needs to dig a little deeper and find something extra to help us get back in this race." I'm no Knute Rockne, but I could see from the look on people's faces they agreed.

What happened next is one of the highlights of my running career. To a person, everyone on our team found an extra gear and ran faster than projected. We were probably behind 1,000 teams at Exchange 9 before we began to make our move. Initially we were passing one or two teams here and there. As we made our way through the middle of the course, we continued to pass more and more teams. Finally, over the last 30 miles, we picked off plenty of teams.

In the end we had too many road kills to count and ended up finishing around 150th overall. Our team felt a tremendous sense of accomplishment—not only for running fast but for running with optimism despite the knowledge that for some of the race we were just in front of the staff preparing to close down the course.

From this experience I learned a couple of good lessons: First, trust yourself and your teammates. We faced adversity, came together, and every person found a way to give something extra. Second, pay the market price and rent commercial vans. It may cost more, but the peace of mind is definitely worth it.

Tiffany Pachl *is from Vancouver, Washington, and is a member of the Hood To Coast team* *Feezy Feet.*

I've done Hood To Coast about eight times, and my mom has done it about 14 times. My first year as team captain was in 2017.

We called all the rental places and they wanted about $800 per van for two days, and we didn't have much money, so we decided to try and buy a couple of vehicles at auction.

We had a whole year to plan. We were going to get two vehicles for the race and then resell them afterwards and get our money back. No one on the team would have to put out any extra money. We got them super cheap, too, although it ended up kind of backfiring.

We took the vehicles to a friend who was a mechanic. He said he'd fix the oil and timing and handle whatever else needed to be done. Afterward, he said we were all good and ready to go.

As we were heading to the Hawthorne Bridge and getting ready to sleep some because we'd been up all night, I got a call from one of the girls in Van 2. The van was smoking from underneath the hood and they were wondering what to do.

That's when a Good Samaritan pulled over and picked up all their stuff and brought it to the bridge. Two other teams offered to take our runners to their next exchanges. Our runners were waiting a little bit, about 45 minutes, but our team kept going.

The Good Samaritan was just a random lady who was driving by. She saw that our van had pulled over and was smoking. She had previously volunteered for the race, her sister had run it, and she knew all about the event. She said, "I'll help. I have a truck. Anything I can do to help you guys." She helped out for about two hours. A tow company then took the van to the next exchange. They were so helpful.

Everyone was so great. I've never experienced anything like that. It was just crazy and fantastic.

We had eight new runners that year, but even with the broken-down vehicle, everyone said they wanted to do it again. I don't know if we'll try and buy the vehicles at auction again. As of now I'm saying no. We'll try and rent vans. After all is said and done, however, maybe.

Nikki Neuburger *is a Portland native and attended Oregon State University, where she* *walked on to the women's volleyball team and became team captain. After graduating in*

2004, she joined Nike and was a longtime marketing executive at the company until early 2018, when she became the Global Head of Marketing at Uber Eats in San Francisco. She is a regular Hood To Coast participant.

There's always a fun rivalry between our team vans. No matter that you're all on the same team and working together to do a good job, each van always seems to irritate the other. Whether it's a missed exchange, not answering a text message fast enough, or maybe they sandbagged a little bit and they're running much faster times than predicted. After you've run the relay for a long time, those things become predictable.

All those things can be handled well, but occasionally people have meltdowns. I certainly remember our van sleeping through an exchange when there was no cell service in the field near Mist and someone who had just ran the leg of their life having to stand at the exchange for 15 minutes waiting for us.

One of the most stressful jobs of the team captain is to keep everybody happy. Not just in regards to the difficulty of their legs, but also who is in which van. You don't want anyone to feel like they're stuck in the bad van or whatever. There are a lot of different personalities to navigate.

There are a lot of couples who participate in the race. My partner, David, is on my team, along with two other couples. Just balancing that can be a challenge. Do you put all the couples in the same van or mix up the couples between the two vans? How do you make sure nobody feels slighted regarding their van assignment? That can also be part of the fun. Often what seems like a big deal at the moment, in the grand scheme of things, really isn't that important. And outside of being Runner 5 or 9, there's really not much difference. They're all hard!

Mandy Biedenweg *is a paramedic from Portland.*

The 2017 Portland To Coast was our first race. I think it was the first time for everyone on our team. It was an awesome experience, but we had a lot of challenges.

We left town with a borrowed van that was making a really strange noise, although the people who had used it before us said it would be okay. We borrowed it from a non-profit organization and there must have been some miscommunication because the people who owned it didn't realize there was a problem.

We probably got asked, like, a billion times, "Hey, do you know your van is making a really strange noise?" We'd tell them we knew and kept going.

By the time we got to Exchange 15, however, we figured out we weren't going to be okay. Something bad-bad was wrong. So I called my husband. Fortunately, we had a smaller team, so he brought our SUV out and took half our team on. We tried to drive the van back to Portland, but it blew up on the I-405 overpass. We sat on the freeway for about two hours waiting for a tow truck.

Once the tow truck arrived we convinced the driver to drop the van off and then take us to get our other SUV so we could get back on the course and catch up with the others. We barely made it to Exchange 18 in time, but we did and everybody started walking again. We even bought a hat at the finish line for the tow truck driver because he lost his trying to help us on the overpass.

We thought about quitting, but we had come so far. We called every rental car agency in Portland and couldn't find a van. So we just kept going. It turned out to be providence that we had a smaller team because we could fit in two five-passenger vehicles. It was tight, but we made it work.

If we come back, we'll have a different van, that's for sure. I think I'll go and try to reserve a van right now!

Merritt Richardson *graduated from Oregon State University and worked as an auditor at an accounting firm before taking a job at Nike in 1989. After working at Nike for 28 years, she recently retired. She has participated in Hood To Coast and Portland To Coast as a volunteer, a runner, and a walker.*

When we had an eight-person Portland To Coast walking team, we had issues with logistics because of restricted areas on the course. Our first year as a team, we were trying to figure out how to get our walker out of a restricted area. Tensions were running high in the van because we were lost and didn't know exactly where we were going— and we backed the van into a tree. It wasn't anything serious, but we all had this anxiety about where we needed to be and where we were going. About halfway through the event we realized we didn't have the right people in the right vans to make everything work.

We didn't have a designated driver, so everyone on the team took turns driving. And there was a lot of yelling and screaming, "No. Go here. Go this direction. Turn here." Our driver at the time was tired and we were all pretty stressed out, especially since we were trying to get a good finish time. We were trying to make sure we were in the right place.

Hitting that tree helped us realize we needed a really good plan for the vans, and starting the following year we had a great van plan.

Amanda Grayson *is from Portland and is part of the Portland To Coast team To The Beaches.*

We had done Portland To Coast for three or four years when we ended up as the top fundraising non-corporate-sponsored team for Providence Cancer Center in 2016. Although we raised about $25,000, it still turned out to be one of those years when everything goes wrong.

We were having a good time, but before we could get the second van to Exchange 18 it broke down out in the Linnton neighborhood on Highway 30. We were all standing at a gas station wondering what we were going to do next.

Out of the blue I decided to call Enterprise Rent-A-Car. We explained what was happening and they said they'd hook us up. They even gave us a weekend discount so we didn't have to pay a huge amount for the rental.

We had to go to St. Helens to pick up the new van, so our poor walker had to keep going. We got another walker on the course, but they had no support. That walker eventually ended up hitching a ride with another van to the next exchange, where we finally got everyone back together.

The next morning when we were meeting up at the next van exchange, I missed the exchange and drove right past. We then had to turn around, go back, and find the other van.

After that, when it appeared things couldn't get any worse, we locked our keys in the van. When we finally got to the coast, one of our walkers ended up cutting her foot on a piece of glass on the beach. It turned out she was fine, but it was just one of those years where every single thing that could happen absolutely happened to us.

We were a little wishy-washy on whether we really wanted to do it again after all our troubles. But because we raised so much money for Providence, we got an entry into the event the following year—and we decided to come back and do it again.

Bob Harold *is the former chief financial officer at Nike and has been competing in Portland To Coast since 1996.*

We started out with one Portland To Coast team called the T-Wrecks, the Nike Dinosaurs in 1996. We picked the name because we were, and are, all old people. In 2002 we added a second team, T-Wrecks Too, the Nike Dinosaurs. We compete in the Mixed Super-masters category, and we've been in that division for a number of years. We're all associated with Nike in some fashion. We either work there or are the spouses of people who work there or formerly worked at the company.

During the race, when you're in a Suburban or a big vehicle like that with your teammates for so many hours, you get kind of rummie. You make observations about other people that are probably inappropriate in most civil conversations.

One of the funniest moments I remember involved my teammates Lisa McKillips and Leon Roberts. Lisa is a very nice person who never has an unkind word to say about anyone. She was driving as we left one of the transitions and she rolled down the window to say a very sincere "Thank you" to the volunteer guiding the vans in and out of the exchange. Leon heard her and said, "Hey, he's a &\$#@head, just like the rest of us." In exiting the next exchange, Lisa again rolled down the window and said a polite "Thank you" to the volunteer. Then Lisa rolled her window back up and we heard her say under her breath, "#@\$%head!"

Most teams decorate their vans to help identify them, and many of them are quite well done. A couple years ago we built a dinosaur to put on the roof of our vehicle. It was holding a cane, and the cane was in the shape of a Nike swoosh. One year each of our vans had a dinosaur on the roof. One of the drivers decided to stop at an ATM. Well, the ATM had a roof over it and as we came up to the machine, the dinosaur's head was knocked off.

We rebuilt the dinosaur and made it with a more modern look. A few years later I was driving and two of my teammates told me to cut a corner, and we ended up in a school playground. This time, I knocked the dinosaur's head off.

It's hard to believe, but that's happened twice.

Heather Hazen-Gross *is from Poulsbo, Washington, and is part of the Mr. Toad's Wild Ride Portland To Coast team.*

One year we were waiting for Van 2 to arrive. They were coming down to meet us at the exchange in St. Helens, but they got in an accident on the way. The bumper of a truck in front of them fell off and they hit it. Everyone was fine, but the van wasn't.

When I finished my leg, the team stopped me and said, "You'd better sit down. We need to tell you what's going on. We may have to do the whole thing, just the six of us." Then they told me about the second van.

I said, "Okay, let's do it, let's do the whole thing ourselves. No break." We were prepared for that.

But the other van ended up getting one of their team members to call their mother in Seattle for help. The mother drove down in this giant Lincoln Continental or Cadillac-type car, loaded them all up, and brought them down to St. Helens. They made it with just a split second to spare, threw their walker on the course, and off they went.

They traveled around the whole course in style, in this Cadillac-type car. No décor, they just put a number on it and got going.

It was scary for a little while, but fortunately we didn't have to do the whole race ourselves.

Ian Durias and his family in 2017.

Kathy Kaiser and her daughters (left to right) Kaitamaria Pounds, Karra Kaiser and Annika Pounds in 2017.

CHAPTER 11

All In The Family

FAMILY IS A RECURRING HOOD TO Coast theme. For many, the race is a family affair and passed down from generation to generation. Fathers and mothers run together. Sisters and brothers form a team. Parents, children, and even grandchildren, join together on the trek across Oregon.

When parents retire their running shoes, it's not uncommon for their children or other relatives to take their spot or inherit the team. The team name may be tweaked, a new captain may be named and some runners may change, but it's essentially the same team. And during family gatherings and over holidays, the relay remains a major topic of conversation.

Laura Neilson *is from Dayton, Oregon. She ran her first Hood To Coast in 2014 and has participated in the event every year since.*

In 2013, at 63, my mom, Carol Barker, had run Hood To Coast 13 times and was usually the captain of her team. At some point during her running career, each of my four siblings ran on her team. I was the only one of her children who had never been on her team.

Carol was contemplating retiring from participating in the relay. However, when Carol's 13-year-old granddaughter mentioned she wanted to run HTC on my mom's team, my mom placed her plans on hold. She said she would run the race again in 2014, but it really would be her last time. I had started running, and HTC had always been on my bucket list. After hearing my mom was going to run the race one more time, I called my siblings and we all decided to run together with her.

In the span of an hour, my four siblings (Beth, Erin, Dan, and Charlie), two granddaughters (Sadie and Elan), one son-in-law (Erik), and I all called Carol and asked to be

175

on her team. Of course she said yes and was delighted to have a family team. We rounded out the team with her nephew (Kyle) and two friends (Jessica and Meg) who were considered HTC family. My dad even joined the team as the volunteer coordinator at an exchange. We named our team Mom's Last Legs since it would be her last year running the relay.

Our family spent the year leading up to the race competing to see who could log the most training miles in a week. We created a spreadsheet where we entered our weekly mileage. We even managed to run together a few times leading up to the race. I spent the year anxiously anticipating the race. I was so excited!

It was an amazing experience. Our family had a blast, and my mom loved running with everyone.

As it turned out, the relay is addictive and Carol's "last time" turned out to be her second-to-last time. In 2015 she passed along the team captain duties to me, but she still was running her favorite race.

I've been running HTC ever since, and my only regret is I didn't do it earlier so I could have run with my mom for a few more years.

Mike de la Cruz *was part of the winning Hood To Coast Masters division team every year from 1982 to 1987, first with the Oregon Master Milers and then with a team he put together called the Vintage Collection. He now lives on Maui.*

After the first couple of years of running Hood To Coast I started my own team, the Vintage Collection. We had the best Masters-class runners in the Northwest. One of the advantages to being on the Oregon Road Runners Club board was I knew all the good runners. I called them and asked, "Would you please be on my team?" And they all said, "Oh yeah. I'd love to." I was so proud of that team, it was a real jewel. One year we had eight of the top 10 finishers from the Oregon 10K Masters race in Lake Oswego.

I was a reasonably good athlete in high school, when I was on the cross country and track teams. But running marathons is a solitary thing. When you're running on a relay team, everyone is dependent on everybody else. You push yourself to a point where you would normally quit. Then you say, "I can't quit, the other guys are all depending on me." You push yourself a little bit harder than normal. It's amazing how your teammates can help you through difficult situations.

I treasure those memories because my teammates were so good. I was just a middle-of-the-pack runner and there were so many other runners better than me, but I was happy to be their captain and do everything I could to make sure we could get to the finish.

We won the Masters division several years in a row. We never lost. I feel good about that. When you work really hard and you accomplish your goals, especially if it's a team effort, it's a really good feeling. It's not an individual thing. It's for your team, and it's just really great.

After a couple of years my son, Michael, started running on a team with some of his friends. They formed their own team called the Dirty Half Dozen +5. But we never ran on the same team.

As the years clicked by, I moved from Oregon to Hawaii. That's when my son called a few days before the relay and said they needed a runner for their team, they had just lost a runner. My son's teammates said to him, "Mike, get your dad to run with us." So in 1991 I had the honor of running with my son and the rest of the Dirty Half Dozen.

I was by far the slowest guy on the team. They had guys from the University of Oregon cross country team, for crying out loud. They were really good. But I had more fun in that race. It was just unbelievable.

I got in the van to start the race and they were playing heavy metal music and had it cranked up really loud. I was a little old for heavy metal, in my late 40s at the time. It was driving me crazy for the first two or three legs. Then I started thinking, "This isn't too bad." By the time we finished the race I'd been listening to it for about 20 hours and got to the point where I kind of liked it.

So I was riding in this van with all these young guys I adored and listening to heavy metal. Naturally, they were different than a Masters team. Two totally different worlds. We'd drive past our runner and they'd holler out the window, "Take no prisoners. Take no @#$% prisoners." I said, "Whoa. We're getting a little excited here, aren't we?"

That race was so special to me. My son ran the leg before me and got to hand off to me and that was just unbelievable. It was a special, special moment in my life. I felt so blessed.

The camaraderie is everything. Competition is great, but I would say only about 10 percent of the teams out there are really competing to win their division. The rest just want to finish, have a good time, and bond. And that's a great thing, because it's a feeling of accomplishing something as a team.

For me to experience that with my son was absolutely out of sight!

Karra Kaiser was a high school student from West Linn, Oregon, when she participated in her first Hood To Coast in 2015.

I waited several years to get my chance to run the Portland To Coast High School

Challenge. My mom has been running Hood To Coast for over 15 years, and my sisters ran the High School Challenge throughout their high school years. Now it was my turn and I was the youngest person on the team Horizontal Runners. I was incredibly nervous and excited at the same time, but determined to do my best.

I really don't like running when it's hot outside, and when you're 13 going out to train with your mom or sisters isn't really that much fun. But each time they would go, I laced up my sneakers and joined them. My first race was in 2015. It was my first chance to prove to my sisters that I could do what they do—although not as fast. My sister Annika really didn't want me on her team because I was the youngest runner, and more importantly I was her little sister.

I didn't really know what to expect. My mom would tell stories each year when she came home from HTC, and she talked about the race for weeks or even months. Her stories were so funny. Lots of times they were about other teams and the silly things they did out on the racecourse. I wanted my chance to collect stories and memories like my mom, and to eventually get to captain my own team.

Three members of my family were in the 2015 race. My mom had her team, and I was in the first van on my sister's team. The weather wasn't exactly perfect for running in August, but I was totally fine without any super-hot days or the heat wafting up from the pavement. When I heard that it might rain during the race I was thrilled. As the first runner, I felt like I had to zip along on Leg 1 and not dawdle to the next exchange. I managed to do okay and made it to the exchange without any problems.

I have no idea what time we started running our second legs, but it was dark and it certainly felt like Oregon because it was raining! It wasn't just raining—the wind was howling and tossing branches through the air. Tree limbs kept falling down where we were headed and then there was the deafening KABOOM of thunder. It was night time and it was raining and there was thunder. All I could think of was how incredibly cool it was to run in what seemed like the middle of nowhere during all the rain and thunder. I was good with all of it because I think running in the rain is so much better than running when it's hot.

Not only was there rain, wind, and thunder, the lightning started when I was about a mile from the exchange. The wind seemed to get stronger and stronger, and several big branches crashed down on the road. I heard trees cracking in the woods. It never occurred to me that I could get hit by a branch. I was "Lightning Leg Girl" and felt like a superhero out there. Nothing was going to stop me from finishing my leg. Except if the lightning came any closer I might have stopped! Then it crossed my mind that if I stopped or jumped in someone's van for a ride to the next exchange, I would be breaking the rules! This was my first relay and I was going to do everything possible to get to the next exchange.

By the time I reached the exchange, I was soaking wet. So was everyone else. I was smiling because I finally had my story! I could tell my mom everything that happened during my second leg. I felt like I really accomplished something and on the back of my medal from that race I engraved the date and the words "Leg 1 Lightning Girl."

I'm always up for a challenge, and that was certainly one I'll remember for a long time. And it's a story I'll tell as I continue to run this amazing relay. Like my sisters, my goal is to have my own team as an adult and carry on the family tradition. I'm hoping for a year when I can be on the same team as my mom and my two sisters. Now, that will be a great story too!

Annika Pounds *is from West Linn, Oregon, and first participated in Hood To Coast as a high school student.*

Hood To Coast isn't just a race. It's a lifestyle, a memory, and way of life. It's a beautiful thing that crazy people of all ages do once a year. Many of my friends think I'm crazy for doing it and question me for wanting to run 200 miles just for fun with a bunch of other people. For me, the relay isn't about time reliving my high school cross country days or abusing my body—it's about memories, funny stories, and grand adventure.

Growing up, the race seemed like a big, scary event that my mom would do every year while my sisters and I would stay with family friends. She would come home and tell us stories about runners, vans, and what happened to her team. We were always fascinated by these people who would show up at our house once a year, relive past races, and share stories, and who couldn't wait to go be slightly miserable for a weekend. The older I got, the more I wanted to run HTC and be like my mom. I wanted to share ridiculous stories with others, run during the middle of the night, and be a part of something legendary.

Once I entered high school, I knew I would have a chance to run on a High School Challenge team, as a member of one of 50 high school teams of 12 running from Portland to Seaside. I only had to convince my mom to let me sign up, and I'm pretty sure my mom was more excited than I was when I asked if I could run.

During my third year on a High School Challenge team I learned the importance of cracking open a window in our team's yellow Suburban. While at the major exchange in Mist, we found our second team van easily because it was bright yellow. As we approached the vehicle, all the windows were fogged up! We opened the door and were practically knocked out from the stench that was released from within. The combination of high school kids, stinky clothing, terrible food, smelly socks, and just bad everything.

I could only question what happened to the baby wipes. Did they ever change their running clothes? Why didn't someone crack open a window? And I thought, "Oh my goodness, this is so disgusting!"

From my first high school team to my first "real" team in 2017, I have felt honored to be a part of this relay each year. I don't think I'll ever be a fast runner, but I have no need for speed. The race has impacted my life in so many ways. It has encouraged me to actually go out and run a little before I show up on race day, and it has given me a chance to create my own memories.

Ian Durias *is from Portland and joined his wife and daughter on a Hood To Coast team in 2017.*

In September of 2017 my wife and I dropped off our firstborn at college. We knew this was coming, but I was wondering if I didn't spend as much time with her as we could have or should have the summer before she left home. I was in the midst of starting a business and wasn't around as much as usual. Work was taking even more time, energy, and attention. It was a bittersweet moment to drive away from the girl, now a woman, whom we had spent nearly our whole married life with.

Before taking her to college, however, the three of us were able to run the 2017 Hood To Coast together. Our team, A-O RIVER!, had run it four times before, but this was the first time my wife and I ran together with our daughter. The three of us did nearly all of our training runs together. Sometimes it was all three of us running together. At other times it was our daughter and my wife or me and our daughter.

My first run after dropping her off at college was an emotional one because our daughter wasn't there, so we couldn't run together. It was during that run that I realized how much time we actually did spend with each other over the summer because we put in many, many training miles together preparing for the relay—talking, sweating, and encouraging each other.

On that run, though sad and missing her, I found myself thankful. Grateful for running and how it can bring a family together. And to top it off, HTC was magic as usual, but the magic had a weight of significance that I hadn't expected.

Tim Dooley *is from Gresham, Oregon, and has been running in Hood To Coast since 1989. This memory was originally published in* RaceCenter *magazine.*

The 2 a.m. hour was well past my bed time, but it was the 2009 Hood To Coast and there would be no sleep this glorious race night! Our team, Return of the Asphalt Warriors, was almost halfway through the journey to the beach when, as our van pulled up to the next exchange, I faced a decision. Should I run?

The question was prompted by the opportunity to run a leg with my younger daughter, Andi. She was running her first relay, and I was tagging along as team driver after being sidelined by medical complications. But four weeks before the race my doctor cleared me to begin "light running." While it had been too late to re-enlist as a runner, I still harbored the hope that I could accompany one of our runners on a leg. When Andi heard my pre-race daydream, she quickly shot back, "You're running with me!"

That was the tentative plan, but once the race started the subject was not mentioned again. Everyone was aware of my medical history, and no one wanted to put pressure on me. The truth was I was doing a little internal waffling myself. I wondered whether I could keep up with Andi, but as we piled out of the van, the lure of the father-daughter opportunity was too enticing. I had to go for it! And as Andi heard the news that I was going to run, the pleased look on her face dispelled any lingering doubts.

About that time, a 20-something runner from another team walked by us trumpeting his latest exploits. He said, "And then this strong runner came up on my shoulder. But I said no way—this is my race! And I just annihilated him! Yaaaah!"

I smiled to myself. What a difference a few years make. Any "annihilator" aspirations that I ever had were long gone. Now it was going to take some extra adrenaline just to keep up with my daughter.

Suddenly, our team's incoming runner rounded the corner and Andi took the handoff. I caught up with her and we headed off into the back-road darkness of St. Helens. Andi was running well, and I strained to keep up. I was privately grateful that this was her second leg. My escort-runner idea might not have worked if she were fresh!

Except for the periodic sightings of other runners, we had the leg to ourselves as vehicle traffic had been diverted in another direction. While the leg was just a little over four miles long, it featured a steady elevation gain, which proved to be more challenging than anticipated. While Andi and I commiserated about the climb, we managed to maintain a steady pace and drew encouragement from each passing mile. As we passed the halfway mark I tried to savor every moment of this special father-daughter time. I'd had the pleasure of sharing similar running experiences with my dad and my older daughter, Carolyn, and they too were part of my internal memory book. This one was all Andi's, though, and as we ran through the quiet darkness I thought about how proud I was of her.

Then, all too soon, the lights of the Columbia County Fairgrounds loomed in the distance, signaling the end of our leg. As Andi mustered a final finishing kick, I peeled off into the crowd reveling in the experience. I would always remember this run. Shared moments on the road with those closest to us are true gems in a running life.

Joyce Judah *is from Scappoose, Oregon, and worked in the financial industry for 40 years before retiring. She participated in her first Hood To Coast in 1991 and ran the relay 10 times.*

It was a Friday in 1982. I asked a co-worker what he was doing over the weekend. He told me he was running with a team from Timberline Lodge to Pacific City—and he was starting after midnight!

Being a recreational runner all my life (I was 28 then), I was intrigued. As the years went by, I followed Hood To Coast, but knew it was mostly for elite runners. I lived in Scappoose, and my parents lived in Olney. I grew up in Astoria and worked in Seaside. When I visited my parents I took Highway 202. So the course was familiar to me, and I always enjoyed watching the race.

In 1989 I was watching the runners go by in Olney and told myself, "I can do this!" The following year my husband and I were finally going to participate in the race, but I had to send my husband out to run the race alone. We had been training together, but I got pregnant—go figure. In 1991, six months after our daughter was born, we finally ran HTC together. Over the years we ran the relay together 10 times, with our final race in 2009.

Eventually we passed the baton to our daughter in 2010, when she was 19. The first couple of years were a little hard on her, as she couldn't get into the beer garden at the finish party on the beach. She had done all the work, but we were the ones enjoying the party!

For us it was always a big family event with parents, siblings, children, and friends involved, and it created a lifetime of great memories.

Morgan Powers *is from Beaverton, Oregon, and participated in the relay several times before taking a job with the Hood To Coast organization as the director of design and development.*

I grew up around the race. I lived in a cul-de-sac where all the parents and kids were friends. It was like a big family. One of the annual traditions was Hood To Coast. We'd have barbeques, van decorating parties, and all sorts of fun things around the event. As kids, we didn't think anything about the neighborhood team name being Buns and Hoses. It took us a little while to figure that one out.

Pretty much all the parents would participate. Sometimes one parent would run and another would drive. Others would babysit the kids for the day. And sometimes the kids would go down to the beach and watch their parents finish. It was fun to experience and a strong memory from my childhood.

All the kids knew this was the weekend for parents. When the parents came back after the relay, they'd have all these inside stories and jokes. One year the team decided to get matching shorts. Well, the shorts were a little too short for some and my neighbor's dad endured some chafing problems. When he got back home on Sunday, there was a poster stuck on his garage door of a crime-scene body with shorts taped on and chafing cream spread everywhere.

In 2014 we turned that team into a parents and kids team, although by then we were really young adults. It was a lot of moms and daughters, and fathers and sons, on the team. I'd never run cross country or track in school or anything like that, I just ran primarily for exercise. This was a fun escape to share with other people.

We mixed up the vans so people weren't always with their families, even though we were really all one big family anyway. I'd grown up around these people for 20 years, but you definitely see a different side of them when you spend 20 or 30 hours in a van together—running, getting no sleep, and not taking showers. It was a blast!

In 2016 I decided to put together my own team with my friends, none of whom had ever done the race. It was eight of my friends from high school and three of our moms. It was still kind of a family thing, but only three people had run the relay.

Being able to share the experience with people who had never done HTC before was a lot of fun. We had one guy on the team, and he was worried about where everybody was going to change. I told him, "Wherever you can find a place." People have to get used to the fact that it's kind of like camping and you're out there on your own.

We had one girl on our team who was not a runner. She bought new running shoes a week before the race. When she met us in the parking lot before we started, she said she had lost her soles. Not her soul, but the actual inserts for her running shoes. Although she did no training and had no soles in her shoes, she survived. But she'll never do it again.

We always used a minivan and never had the luxury of using a large 15-passenger van. Space was always extremely limited. I always sent out a packing list before the event, but a team with 11 girls had a tendency to over pack. One friend showed up with three duffel bags. Another teammate said she was going to bring her portable boiling water pot to make soup or ramen. I had to explain to them that it didn't work that way.

One of my best discoveries for the van was to get a holder that fits on a trailer hitch to put your cooler on. That's always a piece of advice I give first-timers: put your cooler outside so it doesn't take up space and you have easy access to it. Sleeping in a van is also possible, but personally I just rely on Red Bull.

There's something about the sun setting and the thrill of the night. It gives me chills. The leg I run at night is always my favorite part of the event by far. It's peaceful and quiet. You run a little bit faster because you're kind of scared. There's an extra sense of security when you see someone's red flasher off in the distance. For me, it was always nice to see that.

It's also kind of spooky because during the middle of the night is when the elite teams start to pass everyone. You don't hear them coming, then all of a sudden they just zoom by. It's definitely a reality check.

One year, I could hear footsteps behind me for about five or 10 minutes. I could tell someone was close, but I was wondering why they weren't passing me. I finally turned around and said, "If you want to pass me, pass me. This is my pace." They said I was setting a good pace. I told them to run with me and we ended up talking for the rest of the leg. That was fun.

A few years back, the parents' team changed its name from Buns and Hoses to Road Kills for Cancer. For every road kill they make during the relay, they donate a dollar to cancer research, and many of their friends and family match that donation. They raise a couple thousand dollars a year and have done it for a few years now. It's starting to catch on with other teams and we hope to see that become more of a movement.

Dave Underriner *is the former chief executive for the Oregon region of Providence Health and Services, the primary Hood To Coast sponsor. After 35 years at Providence he joined Kaiser Foundation Health Plan and Hospitals of Hawaii as president in April 2018.*

Hood To Coast is certainly a unique experience. It's a great way to celebrate the diversity of Oregon and to engage people from throughout the country and around the world who come and run the race. It's all pretty amazing.

I ran the race three times when I was in my early 30s and didn't run again until my mid-50s. The first year I ran with people I didn't really know. It was just a friend of mine and a group of folks he knew. I was a little faster back then and it was a lot of fun, although at times very painful.

The second year I ran, I got cramps after my second leg. I still had my third leg to go and was thinking, "How do I do this?" But because you're part of a team and want to pull your weight, you gut it out and make it happen. The experience of running with a team and being in a van with your teammates throughout the event is like nothing else you'll ever do. Some people say running the relay is like running a marathon. I don't know about that. I'd be bored to death running 26 miles—*if* I could run 26 miles. I've never been bored on a leg of HTC.

Then, when I was in my 50s, my daughter ran the race and said, "You've got to run this again." I was like, "I don't run like that anymore. I'm older." But I took it as a challenge and we started training together. It was fun doing it with my daughter and sharing that experience.

I was Runner 12 that year, and Leg 36, the very last leg, seemed to go on and on. I was tired and thinking, "Come on. It's got to end soon." When I finally got to the Promenade in Seaside, all five of the other runners from our van, including my daughter, were waiting. They were in flip-flops, but they started running with me. It was all impromptu. When you run down the Promenade, all the people cheer and holler, and it gives you a sense of what you've accomplished as a team. That was pretty cool.

There was also a sense of being able to accomplish something together with my now adult child. I was proud of her, and she was sort of proud of me too. It's not very often when your kid actually says they're proud of you. It was cool that we were able to do that together.

Merritt Richardson *graduated from Oregon State University and worked as an auditor at an accounting firm before taking a job at Nike in 1989. After working at Nike for 28 years, she recently retired. She has participated in Hood To Coast and Portland To Coast as a volunteer, a runner, and a walker.*

At Thanksgiving my family would always share stories about what happened over the past year. My brother-in-law was always asking me about stuff going on in my world, and he always wanted to know more about my experiences with Hood To Coast or Portland To Coast. We have a niece from that family, who as a little girl was always listening to those stories. She's now an adult who works at Nike and has been participating in HTC. She told me that listening to my stories about the relay years and years ago was an inspiration. She was already a runner, so her joining a team was really just a natural thing. I don't think she needed me to serve as an inspiration. But she has told me she remembers hearing my stories about the relay at Thanksgiving. At the time she was hearing my stories, she was just a kid. Now she's an adult and has her own stories.

Now when I see my niece, I always like to hear about how she and her team did during the relay. It's something we can talk about and share experiences from. I'm happy she's part of a team and just loves it, much the same way I thoroughly enjoyed all my different experiences with HTC and PTC.

The fact that the relay has gone on long enough it's now starting to reach other generations is something I love.

Scott Parker *grew up in Portland and lives in Bozeman, Montana. He first ran Hood To Coast in 1998 and is the author of* Running After Prefontaine: A Memoir *and* Run for Your Life: A Manifesto.

In 2017 my sister put together a family Hood To Coast team. It was our first family team since 1998. After the race, many of us found ourselves seated around a table recalling the original team and the strange legacy of our Uncle Joe.

"You'll hear my name echoing on most every leg along the route."

—Joe Parker

Mary, sister: "True, Joe ran cross country at Grant (High School, Portland). Then when Ralph and I were living in Eugene and Joe was a student he'd run over to our house, but that might have had as much to do with drinking beer and watching the Ducks with Ralph as it did with running."

Martha, sister: "Big Bad Joe. I think the thing he loved about running was leaving his sweaty shirts and socks around for Mary and me to pick up. If that gives you some indication."

Sally, wife: "Joe ran Hood To Coast more than a dozen times in the eighties and nineties, for a while on a team called the Lemmings. I remember one year his team estimated its time badly and at the end of the race was the only team left on the course. When they finally came in, the beach party was shut down. All that was left was a half-deflated, two-story Spuds MacKenzie flapping sadly in the wind."

Brian, nephew: "Growing up, we were always hearing Joe talk about Hood To Coast, so eventually we decided to put together a family team. Except Joe ended up being injured and couldn't run with the team. So he drove the second van and was basically in extreme team-manager mode the whole time."

Scott, nephew: "We were kind of a motley bunch. Katie just quit one day, deciding she hated running. Jerry kept trying to convince us to ditch the van and ride five bicycles alongside our runner. Brian claimed at one point, speciously, I think, that he'd never run more than three consecutive miles. In any case, we weren't what you'd call experienced runners."

Katie, niece: "Yeah, okay, I quit that year. But to this day I'm the only one organized enough to fill Joe's shoes as a team manager—as evinced by the year Scott put a team together."

Scott: "Joe's into planning. Some have said a little too into planning. (The same could be said of Katie, one imagines.)"

Gina, niece: "He really did line us up in his kitchen before the race to practice hand-offs. Now, keep in mind the caliber of runner here. We would pace average like ten-minute miles."

Sara, friend of Gina's: "And then there's the clipboard. Gina was a mess about the whole clipboard thing."

Gina: "Even now I can't see a clipboard without breaking into a sweat. Someone in our van wasn't recording the times. And Joe had made such a big deal about the impor-tance—no, it was more like the sanctity—of the clipboard. Whatever happened on the course, the clipboard was not to be compromised. I really thought Joe might throw me off the team when we got to the next van exchange and he found out what happened. I asked Sally what to do and she said to just make up the times. Joe would never know."

Sally: "Gina was recording times but forgot at some point to keep it up. Her voice was practically shaking when she said, 'What will Joe say?' I shrugged and said, 'Oh God, Joe will be just fine.'"

Katie: "From Timberline to Seaside you have to be Total Race Face all the way. I learned that from Joe."

Scott: "And then didn't he do some weird thing where he tried to convince one of our runners she was injured and that only he could sub in for her and then run across the finish line?"

Sally: "We were at one of the van exchanges and he had his running clothes on. I remember saying to him, 'Honestly, you're so eager to run a leg it sounds like you're hoping someone gets hurt.'"

Brian: "He laced up his shoes and jumped in the race. Except our runner wasn't even injured so she just kept running and they ended up running side by side."

Sally: "Gina and Sara played this song—"

Gina and Sara: "I'll see you when you get there, if you ever get there!"

Sally: "And we all learned it and were singing along with the windows down. Then we saw Joe standing on the sidewalk with his clipboard just shaking his head at us. Nineteen years later, here we are!"

Julianne, daughter: "I was too young to run in 1998, (and I swear I would have run this year if I hadn't hurt my knee!), but back to Joe: Would this be an appropriate occasion for talking about his foot fungus? Do you guys wanna hear about that?""

Erin Gibbs is from Portland and runs with the Hood To Coast team Kult Kevorkian.

I am the child of Hood To Coast runners and have been around the race my entire life. In 2017 I finally took over the team when I turned 24.

It's been interesting to watch and be part of the event. It was always fun to hear everyone's stories, but now I get to experience them firsthand.

My mom wouldn't let me run the race until I was 18 because when you're running at night it's—you know, she's a protective parent. I wanted to run in high school, but my school didn't have a High School Challenge team. Instead, I volunteered. Then I wanted to do it in college, but my orientation weekend was the same weekend as the race, so I didn't get to do it then either.

The year after I graduated from college I started doing it. I recruited some of my friends and classmates. My dad likes to say, "They're younger, but they're slower," which is entirely true. When my parents first started competing their mile times were like 7:30s. Some of their teammates even did six-minute miles and I think the slowest runner ran eight-minute miles.

My first year I ran 14-minute miles. I did the puke and rally.

It's way more insane than I ever thought it could be. You hear the stories about the various legs, how you have to run this leg or that leg, and this leg is the hardest. Over the years, as I've continued to run, I've been putting off running Leg 5 and Leg 6, but they're coming up. I'll probably have to run them at some point.

I couldn't help being a newbie my first year. Now I'm a wily veteran, as my dad would say, which is kind of funny. It's been a lot of fun running with my mom and dad. I got to do the first leg, and I've been interviewed by a TV station during the race. It's been exciting getting to wear the colors and be part of the team.

One year, we were supposed to meet someone but we couldn't remember where. From there it went downhill and we started shouting at each other for the rest of the race, "Where are we meeting again?" Only not so nicely.

But maybe the best part of the relay is that it ends. You're sleep-deprived and probably nutrition-deprived by the end of the race, but everything is funny. Everyone is laughing. You're like, "Hey, you only have one shoe on. Hey, you have one of *my* shoes on." At least at the finish everyone is delusional and happy, rather than delusional and grumpy.

Trista Blanchard is a mother, wife, sister, nurse, and runner from Braintree, Massachusetts. She participated in her first Hood To Coast in 2010.

On Christmas in 2009 I received a present from my sister and the card inside said, "Get ready to run!" She asked me to come to Portland and run the 2010 Hood To Coast. I didn't know anything about the race and there was no information in the package about what it was other than the name. That was probably a good thing because I may have skipped it if I knew more.

In 2010 I began the year as a single parent with three beautiful girls. It was not ideal, but it was necessary. I was *not* a runner! Nope, this did not sound like fun. But soon I was training to run that August. I ran to counseling and then ran home. I ran to clear my head and then ran some more. I ran to take a break from work and from my children.

When I arrived in Portland that August I made a commitment to myself not to walk a step of any of my three legs. Our team was Racing Bears for Beer and I was Runner 1. I ran every step of all three of my legs, and four years later I came back for more.

I finally found my community! All the time now, I beg friends, co-workers, and complete strangers to join a relay team. I'm stronger and faster than I believed I could be, and I'm a finisher! And by not walking a single step of that first HTC, it helped me discover that I can do anything.

Angenie McCleary grew up in Portland and has lived in Sun Valley, Idaho, since 1999. She participated in Hood To Coast five times before forming her own team in 2004, and she has served as the captain of that team every year since.

Hood To Coast is a real family event. Every year, my brother puts together a team in the Men's Submasters division and I field a team in the Women's Open class. And my sister-in-law is a regular member of my team for the race. Even though my brother and I aren't on the same team, it's a really special experience for my whole family.

My parents live in Portland and also have a beach house in Cannon Beach. On the Thursday before the race, my parents host my team at their home in Portland. Then on Saturday after the race, both my brother's team and my team stay at my parents' beach house. It's quite a sight having at least 30 people all spending the night in the same house!

My brother and I both hope that one day his daughter and son, my niece and nephew, will run on our teams.

Felicia Hubber *grew up in Portland, moved to Montana during high school, and attended college at the University of Montana. The daughter of Hood To Coast founder Bob Foote, Felicia was just a few months old when she attended the first HTC—and she's been at every relay since. In 2006 she succeeded her father as president of HTC.*

My first paycheck from Hood To Coast came when I was 15. I worked in the office as a summer intern during high school. I was responsible for inputting all the team applications and participant information into the computer system. It was way, way before we had online registration. There were usually two summer interns and we would both handle all the data entry. It would take forever, especially with all of the additions and substitutions, but it had to be done. I remember doing that, getting my first paycheck, and being really proud—even though the check was for a small sum. I don't even remember how much it was for, but as everyone knows after getting their first real paycheck, it felt like my hard work had paid off and I had earned it. I felt a sense of gratitude about it and was proud to be part of an event my dad started and my mom helped build.

When I went to college, I gravitated toward other interests. I was planning to be a microbiologist and thought, "Maybe someday, way down the line, 20 years from now, I'll get involved in some capacity with the race. We'll see." My first two years in college I studied microbiology before realizing, "I don't really enjoy the chemistry aspect of microbiology. Do I really want to do this?" I still had a love of the sciences but changed my major to business administration because I knew I could do anything with that. I was an honors student in marketing and management at the University of Montana, where I met my future husband, Jude.

After graduating in 2005 I worked as a publicist for an agency in Montana that represented a lot of large clients in the state.

In the summer of 2005, right after I graduated college and was planning a wedding with Jude, my father was diagnosed with stage III melanoma. I remember my dad saying his diagnosis was a real wake-up call for needing to think about succession planning and what was going to happen in the future. I remember my dad calling me when Jude and I were at the football stadium in Missoula watching the Montana Grizzlies play. We were talking about his cancer and I was planning to visit him in a few weeks.

Then he said, "Would you be interested in coming on board? You're the only person I can see doing this, and doing it the right way." I didn't even think about it. When he asked, I responded, "Of course. Of course, I'll be there."

Jude and I got married, and then I began working at HTC in April of 2006, maybe eight or nine months after that first conversation with my dad. For about my first year officially working at HTC, my dad and I had desks side by side, just a couple feet from each other. He would show me exactly what he did, literally from start to finish—the full plan for what he did for logistics in planning and meetings each month. Fortunately, one of the good things about him being a Type-A personality is he kept great notes detailing how he produced the relay. I was able to utilize his notes and learn from him and adapt it and move the relay experience forward in new ways. My dad was a great teacher. Obviously, we each had our stubborn battles along the way, but that was inevitable. My dad would explain, "This is how we do it." I would ask, "Why are you doing it that way? I see us doing it more easily this way and think it would streamline the process. Why don't we do this instead?" His answer would at times be, "No, this is how we've always done it."

It was tough at first, but I tried to respect the fact that he started this event. I didn't by any means want to trample over the background and history of the event and what had been learned thus far. However, I also wanted to express the point that, "Let's look at this from a different angle. Maybe it can be done in a better or more efficient way."

He eventually came around and realized, "Wow, I can leave this in the hands of Felicia." Additionally, a few years later when Jude (HTC Race Series CEO) and Dan Floyd (HTC COO) became involved, my dad recognized it was going to be fine. "I don't need to micromanage," my dad said. To his credit, he realized that, which is great. Some people never do.

It was tough because I was only 23 when I started—still a young adult. I'm sure I was rude to him at times. He was always telling me, "You're my daughter. We need to have a good relationship as father and daughter." Any work issues we had stayed at the office when we would go home. At the time, we lived next door to each other. Sometimes we'd go home and have a family dinner together, but wouldn't talk about work. We didn't let work conflict with our father-daughter relationship, which we both continue to see as the obvious top priority over anything work related.

*Since participating in their first Portland To Coast in 2004, the Soleful Strutters have used song and dance to capture the imagination of race participants as well as a first-place finish in 2017. Original team members **Bernadine Clay** and **Karen Talton** share their memories along with current walker **Tammie Swinson** and team captain **Georgann Pierce**.*

Georgann Pierce: Bernadine's niece, Sharon Steen, was a volunteer massage therapist for Hood To Coast in 2003. She noticed there wasn't any team of color participating and decided to put together a team of African American women. For us it was more like the *real hood* to coast race as North and Northeast Portland was considered "The Hood," back then.

Bernadine Clay: She didn't see any walking teams of color either. She said, "How about we get started? Let's do this." We didn't know it was going to grow so fast. We came up with the name and suddenly everybody wanted to be a Soleful Strutter.

Karen Talton: Sharon had that vision. The word got out we were having a meeting about doing the walk and there were 50 or 60 ladies in the room. It started people thinking about getting more fit. It certainly got me thinking that way. To start doing exercises again and training. That alone generated enthusiasm.

Bernadine Clay: The news about the team spread by word of mouth. We had a minister on the team and that took care of the church. There were a lot of educators who helped reach the schools. There were trainers. We had someone to reach everyone.

Georgann Pierce: The African American Health Coalition is an organization in Oregon that helps African Americans with health disparities, diabetes and problems associated with high blood pressure. It offers educational classes to the African American community and provides tools and resources to help improve overall health and wellness. The African American Health Coalition was one of our initial Portland To Coast team sponsors and has been a great supporter by donating money to help cover our expenses and help keep our dream alive.

Bernadine Clay: We started with 24 people that first year, including drivers and volunteers. It has grown to be a huge family. Some of the original team members still participate. I was a walker on the first team and I'm a volunteer now. Besides the race, the team does fundraisers and throughout the year we strive to join community efforts by participating in community walks and health fairs.

Georgann Pierce: I've been teaching fitness classes for Parks and Recreation for over 30 years and this gave me the opportunity to scout for new and upcoming walkers to join the Soleful Strutters team. It started a fitness movement going on in the community and everyone wanted to be part it. We want to encourage and inspire other African American community members to take a healthier lifestyle and join us in our walking endeavor.

Bernadine Clay: We always have a theme song. The first year it was the theme from *Rocky*. We would sing it to each other, and that's when people first noticed us and started asking, "Who are these ladies singing?" We went to dinner one year after the race and there were one or two other teams in the restaurant and they started singing the *Rocky* theme. We also had a chant. We'd go, "Step-by-step, side-by-side, show them what you're working with." You know, kind of sassy like, "Show them what you're working with." We were much younger then. We danced and we sang and did little steps and had so much fun. It . . .

Georgann Pierce: . . . It brought us together and I think it brought more excitement to the race. Now we're dancing at the start line. We do the Cupid Shuffle and everybody joins in. It gets everybody loose and ready to go. During the race we have music and we dance and encourage people while they are racing. We're always lively. That keeps everyone loose. At Exchange 18, where our volunteers are normally stationed, they dance and get other people to join in. It's just awesome.

Karen Talton: It also helps take away the worries and the fears that you might have about walking at night or whatever is on your mind. Not just our team. It brings everybody together and that generates positive energy for everyone.

Georgann Pierce: Now we have our Soleful Strutters theme song, *"From Portland To Coast, from Portland To Coast, Soleful Strutters are the most, Soleful Strutters are the most."* And, *"From east to west, from east to west, Soleful Strutters are the best, Soleful Strutters are the best. Na, Na, Na, Na, Na, Na."* We sing our theme song at the finish line. All of us come across together. We're all family. All our volunteers, our drivers, the kids who come out to support us, we all cross the finish line together. We take pictures together as a whole team because it takes everybody to make it happen. Our volunteers, our drivers, people who get things prepared for us, the kids who come and support and help when we need volunteers. It's all encompassing. That's the beauty of it. What I really love is how people connect.

Karen Talton: We were on the front page of our community newspapers, the *Skanner News* and the *Portland Observer*, that first year. They did a feature on our team. It was a big deal. We took a stack of papers out to the exchanges at Mist and Jewell to show everyone there were black women walking. A team of all sisters. After that, everyone wanted to be on the team.

Georgann Pierce: The team would always meet before the relay at Reflections, this coffee shop that's been in the community forever. Gloria, the owner, would open up her business at 4 a.m. so we could all meet, load up, have coffee, get together and pray. We always have one of our mothers come and send us off with a prayer.

Bernadine Clay: When it came time for that first race I was in a panic. We didn't know what to expect. It was totally new to us. I had to walk at night and was just scared to death and started to get anxiety attacks. It was going to be 1 o'clock in the morning. Oh, I was so scared. Our sister team, The Strutting Sole Sisters, was out there too, but I didn't know where. When it was my turn I just went off into the darkness. Oh my God. I was scared. Then I heard, "Okay sister. Let's lock, step and go." And it was the person from the other team. She was right there and I didn't know it. The two of us went on to the next exchange, and then two more went walking off together. But the anxiety and fear about walking at night, oh my.

Karen Talton: It wasn't only walking with someone that made it easier; it was the relationship you developed with God while you were out there in the dark.

Tammie Swinson: I had a similar experience when I first walked in 2008. I was walking a leg along a forest road for about eight miles and I was by myself. There were phone lines along the road. You've also got this beautiful vista of the hills and trees. For me it was really symbolic of my relationship with God. Things were going on with my family at that time and I needed that. The telephone lines were my connection. I could talk to Him at any time.

Karen Talton: We've all been through family issues together. We've had deaths in our families and everybody experiences personal grief. The things our children go through, we share that together and are there to support one another.

Bernadine Clay: We feel safe with each other. We can express ourselves and show our feelings because we are among people who won't use that against us. They support us and that's why we're a family.

Georgann Pierce: If there's someone who is in need or going through something, everyone helps out. I always say, "Many hands make light work." So when there's a need, if everybody does a little bit of whatever their personal touch may be, then it all comes together and it's all good. We're a family. We know how things go together. It's an instinct for us. I thank God for the meaningful relationship we have formed.

Bernadine Clay: I'm a cancer survivor. Georgann kept me on my feet when I was at my lowest, after I just had chemotherapy. "Come on Mama Bernadine, you can do it," she'd say and it'd get me so mad.

Georgann Pierce: Mama Bernadine was always race-ready. We were able to support her because she was part of the Soleful family. She was not alone. Right now, we have two of our members who have suffered with breast cancer and are cancer-free. Several times we thought maybe this was our last year, maybe we wouldn't do it again. But then you realize it's bigger than you or me.

We get competitive too. We train hard as a team. We do a boot camp and try to walk together three or four times a week. We have training walks on Monday and Wednesday and then on Saturday do a longer walk of between six and eight miles. We also include core, technique training, speed training and strength training. Our motto is, "We train hard to win easy." In 2017 we took first in the new Washington HTC walking race and also won our division in PTC when we went head to head with the Manic Mommies throughout the race.

Tammie Swinson: It's what real teamwork and being part of a team means. Even on a track team, you're an individual. In the relay you're competing for your team and trying to make your body function, to make it happen for the team, despite all the aches and pains and being cramped up in the car.

Georgann Pierce: Tammie was always talking in my ear about a team of all brothers, an African American men's team, and we put it together in 2012. A mixture of young and old. There were kids in high school, college kids and coaches. They finished first in the Men's Masters walking class and there was a big story about them in the papers. I mean, they were celebrities.

Tammie Swinson: My son Justin Johnson and his friends kept saying they wanted to do the race, but they would just sit back and watch. Finally they said, "We're doing this next year." It took a lot of work because, of course, whenever the guys do it, it becomes our project. Trying to make sure they've got their T-shirts and their vans. And then having a houseful of young men all over the place.

Georgann Pierce: The first year the Soleful Strutters sponsored them, the Soleful Brothers. We paid for the registration to help jumpstart their team and secure a spot. They started a couple of hours behind us, and oh my gosh, they passed us! One good thing, they trained with us and that gave us something to shoot for. It helped raise our level. Justin was the captain and he brought in some of his coaches from high school including Leon McKenzie, LaVon Pierce, Marcus Irving and John Mays and some of his old high school track teammates. It was like a collaboration of teachers and students and they ended up walking together on the first Soleful Brothers team.

Tammie Swinson: Especially the coaches. They thought their days of participating in team sports were over. They saw they were able to get out there and do something besides coach. It meant something special for everyone

Georgann Pierce: We're planning a Soleful Strutters reunion dance for anybody connected to the teams. The Soleful Strutters have impacted a great number of people in a positive way. We try to keep the community engaged and they will always have an open invitation to participate in our team training and community walks. We really want to reach our families and friends and make this like a family affair. People show up with their kids at our training and walks to participate. They're skipping along with us and it's like an outing for them. A few years ago the daughters of two of our teammates went to school dressed as Soleful Strutters for Halloween, so we have up-and-coming Strutters in training. It's a win, win on all levels.

The late runner addition to Scott Parker's team in 2005.

CHAPTER 12

Teammate Tales

IT TAKES A TEAM TO complete the journey, and in most cases each squad is comprised of 12 runners. When spending 15 to 35 hours of quality time in a vehicle with several teammates, there are quite a few things you learn about each other. It's an optimal opportunity to explore the behavior, habits, and peculiarities of your fellow runners. It's also a chance to talk and catch up, along with reminisce and share. It's a true bonding experience. Sleep is often a last option.

Before the race start, first-time runners may think they may know each other. Afterwards, they most certainly know each other better and most everyone remains friends—although some better than others.

Scott Parker *grew up in Portland and lives in Bozeman, Montana. He first ran Hood To Coast in 1998 and is the author of* Running After Prefontaine: A Memoir *and* Run for Your Life: A Manifesto.

On the Thursday before the 2005 Hood To Coast I got a phone call from our Leg 1 runner, who was dropping out with some lame excuse. We had one day until the race and no one to run down the hill from Timberline Lodge.

I called my sister and said, "Hey Coach, who can we get on such short notice?"

She went through her network of Portland runners, but everyone by then was either already on a team or had to work.

Resigned to making do with eleven runners we started packing our bags and thinking about a pasta dinner. Then Joe called. He was my college roommate who had run the relay with us a few years before. He was in Portland for the night and on his way to our favorite local bar, Produce Row Cafe.

By the time I met him there, hours had passed, enough for a few beers at least. Would the alcohol work for me or against me? I hugged Joe, declined a cigarette, and hit him straight off with, "What do you think about getting up in the morning, driving up to Mt. Hood, and running almost six miles straight back down?"

His eyes steadied on me as he considered his response. A strange sequence of ruminative grunts emerged from somewhere behind his sternum. Suddenly he banged his fist on the table and shouted, "I'm in! Buy me a beer."

Our start time was noon, but Joe wanted me to pick him up early. As he approached the car I looked out the window and took in the tall, unshaven, and presumably hungover man in jeans and cowboy boots, and said, "There's my Leg 1 runner."

Taking the passenger seat and squinting over his aviators, Joe said, "First stop, Goodwill."

Why Goodwill? That would be for the running clothes: a Team USA No. 25 singlet from the 1980s, it turned out, and almost-matching shorts barely longer than underwear.

"Next stop, shoe store," said Joe.

It is generally considered unwise to race down steep mountains in brand-new shoes. But what can you do if your other option is cowboy boots?

And what to make of Joe at the start line! What did the other runners think of this strangely dressed man with his thin, hairy body barely covered, his tube socks and his large dark glasses? It's possible few expected it when Joe blazed down the mountain first in his wave of runners—his long, gangly stride accentuating his rail shape.

But those of us who knew Joe weren't surprised by his performance. Nor were we surprised when after the exchange he removed a shoe to reveal a blood-soaked sock and, underneath that a big toe sans nail. Nothing a can of Olympia Beer wouldn't fix.

Rob Rickard *is from Canby, Oregon, and has participated in Hood To Coast every year since 1983. He has also been a course marker for the event for more than 25 years.*

Sometimes being on a competitive team and finding substitutes for injured runners was a real challenge. You hated to have to call somebody and say, "I'm looking for a runner. What's your pace?" But it became that type of situation. And when it got closer to the race start, it really became a challenge. Sometimes you would find people who would say,

"Oh, I run a seven-minute mile." Then they would run their first leg and you'd find out that wasn't the case.

One time I ended up with a runner because a race sponsor asked me if he could run on our team. He was somebody who knew somebody in the Hood To Coast organization. I believe he was from Iowa. He repeatedly assured me that he ran seven-minute miles, but he ended up really running eight-minute miles. Stuff like that was always challenging.

One of the most difficult substitutions I had happen occurred back in the early 1990s. I had a really good female runner from Eugene. We were scheduled to start at about 7 p.m. on Friday night. She called me at eight on Friday morning to tell me her physician recommended she not compete—so she was dropping out. In the co-ed division we were in at the time, you had to have the same number of male and female runners. Her dropping out created an imbalance.

Her parting shot after telling me she couldn't run was to let me know of a lady in Eugene who might be interested in running. She gave me her name and phone number. At that point, I didn't have any other options, so I called this woman. Her name was Jane. I asked her if she wanted to join our team. She said, "Well, I just got out of the shower because I finished my six-mile run this morning, but I've always wanted to do it. I'll be there in time to meet the vans and go to the race start."

When you get a substitute runner under those conditions, you never know what you're getting. But Jane was great! She was steady and ran well. She even fell on her first leg, but she just taped it up and did her other two legs. She was a super lady!

Jane actually was on the team for several more years after that because not only was she a good runner, she was a good teammate. Spending more than 20 hours in a van with sweaty people means you really, really have to have a positive attitude, or it makes for a miserable event. Jane was a great teammate and always contributed—doing whatever needed to get done.

She was a super sub who became a regular part of our team.

Devrie Brennan *hails from Moraga, California, and now lives in Lake Oswego, Oregon. She is an orthopedic physical therapist who has participated in Hood To Coast 15 times.*

Margi (Barrie) was a new mom in 2001 during our third Hood To Coast race. It was the early morning and we were in Van 1 getting ready for our last set of legs (25–30). It was the stage of the race when you stop caring about what you look like. The van stinks and everyone is gritty from the salty residue of sweat. Everybody is loopy from the combination of fatigue, Gatorade, and PowerBars.

Margi had just pumped before her run, but she didn't have time to dump. Our teammate Sibs (Marianne Siberell) came in to the exchange with Margi waiting to take off. This being Sibs's last run of the race, she was ready for her obligatory end-of-race beer. We had one problem, though. We forgot to load our post-race reward—a six-pack of beer into our van.

As Sibs was cooling off in the back of the van she noticed Margi's milk that had yet to be dumped. As Sibs was on her way to dump it out of the way of foot traffic, she was simultaneously and unashamedly asking other runners if they had extra beer. A van close by was pouring coffee from a large thermos and someone asked if they had cream. Sibs was about ready to dump out Margi's milk when she responded, "I do!" After clarifying that it was breast milk, someone commented, "Cow's milk, breast milk—it's all the same." But Sibs wouldn't let it go without a price. "It will cost you," she said. They just happened to have beer on hand.

And that's how we traded breast milk for beer!

Marla Briley *is from Austin, Texas, and ran her first Hood To Coast in 2007.*

Having participated in Hood To Coast many times as a member of the Fat Cheetahs team, it's only natural that I have loads of great memories. One of my favorites I'd call "Run, Fatboy, Run."

Do you remember the English actor Simon Pegg? In one of his movies he's really out of shape and training for a marathon. While training he wears inappropriately tiny shorts. What does that have to do with my memory?

Every year we have new people join our team. This usually happens because someone from the previous year can't make it back. This particular year, the new guy was Edgar. His plane was delayed and he literally arrived just as we were piling into the car to head up to Timberline Lodge.

He was scheduled to be Runner 4 or 5. He was supposedly one of our stronger runners. However, all the way to Mt. Hood he didn't utter a sound. He actually slept through the first few legs of the race while the rest of us were busy cheering on our fellow Cheetahs. I got the impression that this guy was going to be a total dud.

Then, just before it was time for Edgar to run, he hopped out of the van and started to warm up. He then pulled off his basketball shorts and underneath was a tiny pair of shorts with the words "Run Fatboy Run" on the butt. Right then I knew I had misjudged Edgar and that he would be one of the funniest people I've met during my HTC experience. And he was!

He just needed some time to warm up!

Brianne Theisen-Eaton was born in Saskatoon, Saskatchewan, Canada, and attended the University of Oregon, where she won six NCAA championships in the heptathlon and pentathlon. In the 2016 Summer Olympics, she won a bronze medal for Canada in the heptathlon, becoming the first Canadian to ever earn a medal in that event. She retired from track and field in 2017 and now lives with her husband, Ashton, in San Francisco, where she is a board-certified holistic nutritionist and practices functional medicine. She first participated in Hood To Coast as an honorary captain for Team World Vision in 2016 before running the event in 2017.

This really weird thing happened to a runner with one of the World Vision teams in 2017, my first year running Hood To Coast instead of being an honorary team captain.

This team had a runner who had never participated in the relay before. He was running Leg 1, the long, steep downhill from the start. We met up with this team in Portland after everybody in our van finished their legs. We were grabbing something to eat and we saw this guy from the other team, and his knees were all bloody and skinned. We asked him, "What happened?" He said, "I don't know. I finished running and felt perfectly fine. Then I tried to get out of the van at the next exchange and my legs didn't work." His team got him crutches and he was hobbling around, but he could barely put any weight on either leg. He said his legs felt numb and they just weren't working. We kept saying, "He needs to go to the hospital."

It turned out he had something called rhabdo (rhabdomyolysis), which sometimes happens after really intense workouts. It's basically a lactic acid buildup in your muscles, and it poisons your body. He had to stay overnight in the hospital to get rid of it.

It was crazy. I'd never seen anything like that before.

Randy Gibbs is from Portland. He ran his first Hood To Coast in 1989 and his last one in 2015, when he ran out of knee cartilage. He was one of the founders of the Kult Kevorkian team.

About 10 years ago we had a runner, Aaron, from FedEx on our team. He was supposed to work the Friday of Hood To Coast. Instead, Aaron got a note from his doctor saying he couldn't go to work. Then he ran the race with our team instead of going to work.

That year, as it happens, we were on the front page of the *Portland Tribune*. There was a big article about our Kult Kevorkian team and an even bigger picture of Aaron crossing the finish line with all of us. He was in his tie-dyed shirt, and our team's pirate flags are in the background.

When he went back to work on Monday every inch of his work area was covered with copies of the newspaper. There must have been a hundred of them!

Jake Bittner lives in Leesburg, Virginia, and participated in his first Hood To Coast in 2017.

After all the post-race festivities at the beach and our hotel in Seaside on Saturday, followed by a good night's sleep, our Agony of Da Feet team headed back to Portland Sunday afternoon. We soon found our way to one of the many great local breweries in the city.

As we settled in with some beer and food, the veterans from our team started telling stories of years past. It having been my first year on the team, I was fascinated listening to the stories about some of the runners who had been part of the team, including how far people travelled to get to Oregon and the seemingly random connections that led them to joining the team.

As we sipped our pints, a story was told about the first year the team did the race in 2014. Everyone on the team was new to Hood To Coast, but the team did have a couple of experienced runners. One of those veteran runners was a great athlete who took the most difficult set of legs, but the team had kind of lost track of her in the past few years. Her name was Juda—which I noted was an unusual name. It was also a name I had heard before.

After recounting how she was an avid triathlete and had used the relay as a "cool down" after completing an Ironman in Idaho the weekend before, I thought, "Hmmm, that's weird. The Juda I know is a triathlete too." Then they mentioned that she had worked for Newton shoes. At this point, a small inkling turned into a bright shining light bulb.

I happen to run in Newton shoes, and the reason I do is because Juda sold me my first pair. Although she called Arizona home when she ran with my teammates in 2014, she was now living in Virginia. And she was working in a triathlon store in my back-yard—or actually on the ground floor below my townhouse. In fact, before leaving for Oregon, I bought another pair of running shoes from Juda and she "delivered" them to me by calling out my name—and then throwing them up to me while I was on my balcony.

What a small world and a crazy connection! Now Juda has reconnected with the team and is likely in for another HTC.

Marla Briley is from Austin, Texas, and ran her first Hood To Coast in 2007.

In 2016 we had a new team member join our Fat Cheetahs crew. His job was very demanding and he was on conference calls up until we were out of cell phone range, as we neared the start of the race at Timberline Lodge. He was a very composed and well-spoken person, so you can imagine our reaction when we hear him tell his colleague during one of the calls, "So and so is running around like his chicken is on fire." We busted out laughing!

For the rest of the race that was our mantra. As we passed one of our runners we'd all yell out the window, "Run like your chicken is on FIRE!"

Randy Gibbs is from Portland. He ran his first Hood To Coast in 1989 and his last one in 2015, when he ran out of knee cartilage. He was one of the founders of the Kult Kevorkian team.

About 20 years ago we're running the race in a heat wave. Our best runner, John, starts the race and he's just screaming down Mt. Hood. He's coming into the exchange, where they just repaved the roads. It's probably 100 degrees outside. And John is from Newport, Oregon, so he's never run in anything over 75 degrees. We finally collect him and he's spent.

We drive to my house after we finish our legs and shower. We have something to eat and get ready to go to the next exchange to start another round.

We get to the exchange and John is doing all these pre-vomit things. I finally say, "John, you're done. I know you don't want to be done, but as captain I have to make the call and you're done." John wants to go on, but he's still doing these pre-vomit things. I tell him, "John, every time you do one of those, everybody in the van gets closer to getting sick."

We left him in Scappoose. This was before the internet and cell phones. We left him at the high school with two quarters and a liter of water and drove away in *his* brand-new van. The brand-new van his wife didn't want him to take!

We changed the name of the team that year to 11 Runners and John. He never did make it to the finish in Seaside. Even now I'm not clear how he made it home, but he came back to the team again and we ran more than 20 years together.

*Steve Hanamura was born in Upland, California, and now lives in Portland. He has participated in Hood To Coast more than 25 times and served as captain of the team I Hurt, You Hurt, We All Hurt for more than 20 years. Blind since birth, he is an avid runner and sports fan. Steve's wife **Becky Hanamura** is a longtime HTC volunteer and currently serves as the Exchange 12 leader.*

Steve: In 2015 I had a different running guide, and I think he was more scared about the race than I was.

Becky: Steve's friend Dick wanted to run with him and be his guide. He had run with our team in the past and came back in 2015.

Steve: He just wanted to run with me.

Becky: Dick wanted to be Steve's running partner. I was at Exchange 12. Steve and Dick were supposed to be running into that exchange. I was waiting and waiting, wondering, "Gosh. What happened? Where are these guys?" In the past, Dick had a history of misreading signs and getting lost on the course. My brother and sister-in-law were working with me at the exchange. Finally we saw them coming in and my brother hollered, "Hey, it's wrong way Dick." And as Dick got closer he had this huge bandage on his forehead and a big, black eye and bruising on his face. Well, they were running and Dick tripped and did a face plant on the pavement.

Steve: He looked horrible. It happened in a neighborhood and one of the residents came out of their house to help and bandaged him up. We stopped for a long time. It was actually quite scary.

Becky: It was bad. His face was really swollen.

Dick's daughter and son-in-law had driven over from Longview, Washington, to see him at the finish. I had to call his daughter, who is a nurse practitioner, to let her know what happened. I said, "Just so you don't freak out when you see your dad at the finish, here's what happened."

Steve: He was bound and determined to continue running, but after that his family told him he was done.

The Monday after the race Dick walked into the college class he was teaching in Colorado. His students were all looking at him funny. Dick said to his students, "I don't look too good, do I?" He then explained what happened.

Tahni Kalina is a clinical social worker from Yakima, Washington. She participated in her first Hood To Coast in 2006 and has run the event more than 10 times.

I was first invited to join the Drooling Moose Migration team in 2006 by my best friend from the University of Oregon. I was going to be a substitute for someone who couldn't run. I had recently taken up running to get in shape, but I certainly didn't consider myself a runner. I decided to take on the challenge even though I was not familiar with the race and had no idea what was in store.

My first run was Leg 4, which was a long run and a hot one. When I finished the run my big toe was feeling a little weird and I had some major blisters developing. My second time running was during the middle of the night and it was both scary and exciting.

After I finished my second leg and removed my running shoes to put on flip-flops I noticed that my toe was feeling a bit numb. As I climbed over the middle seat to get into the third row of seats in our Suburban I accidently caught my toenail on the seat. My entire toenail came up and was now just attached at the base—and it was bleeding profusely. My seatmate in the back was also a rookie on the team that year. He was just waking up as I shrieked. He yelled at me to push my nail back down and then commented that it was disgusting. None of my teammates were sure what to do, but everyone told me to put on a Band-Aid.

We went to the first-aid station at the next exchange. The medics told me they could lance the blisters but there wasn't much they could do with the toenail. Being that it was my first time on the team, I didn't want to be a lame teammate and have someone else run my last leg. However, I also couldn't put on my shoe without excruciating pain.

That's when my trusty rookie teammate came up with a genius plan! He cut out the space for my big toe in my running shoe and I ran (or mostly walked) my final leg with a crazy, disfigured shoe. That move secured my place on the team to this day, as well as the place of my shoe-altering teammate, Michael, now lovingly referred to as "Mik-eGyver."

I keep running the relay every year because of my teammates. We have a solid core of the best people I know and call each other our "48-hour best friends." Some of my team-mates are my longest and dearest friends, while others have more recently become some of my most treasured friends.

We suddenly lost our longtime teammate Eric—much too young. The number of HTC teammates that attended his service was remarkable and demonstrated the amazing power of the race to forge meaningful relationships. Our team has been through divorces, cancer, and the loss of a spouse. We also celebrate new jobs, children, and grandchildren. We run together, support one another, and always show up when it counts. I love each and every one of my teammates.

And finally after 12 years on the team I have finally decided to call myself a runner.

Mary Oakes is from Portland and has run every leg of Hood To Coast at least once during the more than 15 years she has competed in the event.

I think this happened in 2006, the 25th anniversary of Hood To Coast. Lew Johnston, a longtime member of the Killer Puffins team was receiving an award that year for being one of only two runners who had participated in the race every year.

It was a wonderful weekend! Our team of Killer Puffins included team captain Elaine Sibley, along with runners Ken Travis, Paul and Sue Fitzpatrick, Paul Duncan, Larry Byers, Rhonda Rambo, Chris Owens, Keith and Marsha Barnden, Jim Sapp, Lew, and me.

Lew started us off on Leg 1. Our team wore special shirts celebrating Lew's accom-plishment. We had "Lew's-a-Puffin" proudly emblazed on our shirts. The weather was nice and my pace was also pretty nice, under seven minutes a mile. Oh, to be young again!

Every year, we rented the same house at the beach to celebrate our Puffin Family—runners, van drivers, and all our volunteers. It takes all of us to make it happen. There's always plenty of pasta and wine. I remember getting up early Sunday morning, before everyone else, and walking down to the beach to reflect on a magnificent weekend. I watched all the tents from the post-race party get broken down, except for the area where the awards presentation would take place.

Later that morning, after ample coffee, we all ventured over to the awards area to celebrate Lew. He received his award with fanfare and awe. We were all so proud of Lew! And it was fun watching the young ladies hover around Lew—and he loved every second of it!

This reflection honors our forever Killer Puffin, Lew Johnston!

Jean Ice in 2016.

CHAPTER 13

Overcoming Adversity

ANCIENT CHINESE PHILOSOPHER LAO TZU, said, "A journey of a thousand miles starts with a single step." Although Hood To Coast is not a thousand mile journey, it does start with a single step. Competitors often face adversity along the way. Overcoming these obstacles, whether physical or mental, is all part of what the relay is all about.

Jean Ice grew up in Austin, Texas, and has lived around Portland for more than 50 years. She first became involved in Hood To Coast in 2000.

In February 2006 I was a healthy 60-year-old lady running a half-marathon. In March I was diagnosed with late-stage ovarian cancer. I had massive abdominal and colon surgery in April, and then did 18 rounds of chemotherapy from May through September. Between my 15th and 16th rounds of chemotherapy I ran Hood To Coast.

It's so awesome that the race sponsors the fight against cancer, and it's even more awesome that a cancer patient is able to run the relay.

After my surgery I was barely able to walk down the hospital hallway dragging the "tree" with all my medical tubes. Sadly, the thought of running at that time seemed impossible, but HTC was still four and a half months away. I was released from the hospital after eight days and instructed to wait eight weeks before running. My treatments were to start in May—three-week cycles with regular chemotherapy in the arm on the first day. I was also undergoing a new process for ovarian cancer patients—chemotherapy directly into the abdominal cavity on the second and eighth days.

Thirteen days of feeling bloated and tender left only eight days when I could run, but my team rallied around me. We had run the race six years in a row and sweated bullets every October until our team was selected in the lottery. Our team included my son Darryl and daughter-in-law Vida, plus close friends and co-workers. It's a great team of caring people.

As soon as I got home from the hospital I began to walk and eventually worked my way up to 20-mile weeks. By the end of June I had begun to run slow three-milers on my good week of each three-week cycle. By early August I was up to five-mile runs, albeit slow ones.

After my last chemotherapy cycle before the relay, my teammates Doug and Dave joined me in practicing Leg 4, from Rhododendron to the weigh station. I was wearing a baseball cap over a cheap running wig with the top cut out for coolness. Then a semi-truck drove by and blew my cap off, leaving me on the side of the road looking like Friar Tuck. After Doug quit laughing, he chased down my cap!

When the big day arrived, which was during my good week in the cycle, there was the usual excitement. My goal on Leg 4 was to make it without walking. I relaxed and found that the seven-mile leg was actually fun. And I even remembered to hold onto my cap every time a semi-truck rolled by!

There is absolutely no doubt that my focus on this magical event helped me get through chemotherapy and gave me the strength for healing.

I had been given two and a half years to live and it's now nearly 12 years later. I have to give many thanks to my family and all my friends. And I have to thank HTC for making all this possible.

Michael Ann McIlvenny is from Albany, Oregon, and worked for 30 years as an educator and administrator. She was a Hood To Coast volunteer for many years before participating in the event in 2017.

After being a race volunteer for about ten years for teams from the Pacific Northwest, I finally got the chance to participate in the event for the first time in 2017. At the time, I'd only been running for about four years.

I was so excited to join the Life and Death Brigade team. I trained hard and worked diligently to plan my runs and improve my endurance. Although my training times were usually 30 to 45 seconds faster per minute, I really wanted to stick to averaging around 10 minutes a mile during Hood To Coast.

Everything was perfect during the race, and I accomplished everything I set out to do! What I didn't know was leukemia was brewing in my body. Less than a month after the race I was diagnosed with Acute Promyelocytic Leukemia (APL). My medical team was amazed that a 53-year-old woman could do as well as I had running HTC considering my health. What I do know is that training for the relay made me stronger and in the end healthier to fight my cancer.

When at the OHSU Hospital for treatment, I've been able to see Mt. Hood and know that I ran Leg 1 in the relay just as I planned. Then I can walk down the hall and see the Hawthorne Bridge—knowing that I ran over the bridge and along the river on Leg 13.

These landmarks inspire me to get healthy, and I plan to run the relay again—stronger, faster, and much healthier.

Julie Concannon *is from Portland. A former runner, she first competed in Portland To Coast in 2016.*

I ran for many, many years. One of my last races was the Athens Marathon. It had been one of my goals.

After that race I knew something was wrong, but didn't know what. I had an MRI and the doctor diagnosed me with spinal stenosis in the L4 and L5 vertebrae. It showed I had only 10 percent of the nerves in my back.

The doctor was really cool. He said some people with the condition still run with it and I'd just have to find out what made me healthy and happy. When we started talking about whether I should continue running or stop, the doctor said research shows about half the people stop and half the people keep going. For those who keep going, it's often a good thing.

Basically, I made the decision to keep exercising. I walk every day. I walk up hills and I walk down hills. And that's the reason I decided to walk in Portland To Coast.

I'm really competing with myself. I'm not competing with others. The last hill I did during PTC was between a ten-and-a-half and an 11-minute mile. That's better than some of the runs I've done. I've decided I'm going to be healthy and I'm going to be doing this for the rest of my life. Every time I can do this, it means I can do this! It's a wonderful thing.

But I still love good competition and road kills. Going up a hill or down a hill, getting a couple of kills is always a good thing.

My teammates are very supportive, and that makes it special. I was a newbie in 2016 and when my team invited me back I was thrilled.

John Banks *is from Gresham, Oregon, and has been involved in Hood To Coast for more than 10 years.*

In 2006 I ran my first Hood To Coast. At the time I was a competitive triathlete and cyclist. I joined a team that needed a runner and didn't know many people on the team. After that experience, I decided to put together my own team. My team would be made up of my friends and would compete for a spot on the podium.

Our first team in 2007 was Hard Soiled Legs. We competed in the Mixed Open division and our team consisted of six men and six women. My roommate Kelly Andrews, who was one of my best friends, was looking forward to running his first relay. However, during the summer of 2007 Kelly was in a car accident that almost took his life.

In the accident he suffered a traumatic brain injury and had to be airlifted to the emergency room at Portland's Legacy Emanual Medical Center to undergo brain surgery. He spent over a month in the hospital recovering and was unable to join our team in 2007. When Kelly was discharged from the hospital he had lost more than 20 pounds of muscle mass.

Not only did he overcome his injury, but he was able to train and join us for his first HTC in 2008. In addition to that he started his first year of dental school at Oregon Health & Science University that same year, even though he was advised by doctors to defer his enrollment a year. He's now a dentist and has been a part of our team ever since—even taking over as team captain.

One of my favorite memories is watching Kelly run. It's an annual tradition for him to strike a unique pose—shirt off, arms flexed, legs high and a big smile—each year when pounding the pavement. By looking at a picture of him posing, you'd never know where he came from and what he had to overcome.

Kelly always does his best to rally the troops each fall and put together another great year. I'm looking forward to participating in the race many more times with him!

Michael Gilliland *is originally from Cincinnati and now calls Hillsboro, Oregon home. He participated in his first Hood To Coast in 2017.*

In 2009 I had gastric bypass surgery. At the time I weighed 460 pounds. In the spring of the following year I woke up to noise outside my window. I was living in Cincinnati, where I was born and raised. What I saw were people of all shapes, sizes, and ages competing in this running race—which I later learned was the Flying Pig Marathon. I made a cup of coffee, sat on my porch, and watched all the runners pass. Then it hit me—what I needed to do to keep the weight off was run.

I always worried about putting weight back on. I told myself that next year I would do the marathon. Well, I actually signed up for the wrong race and instead ended up running my first 15K. Although I really had no clue what I was doing, I was proud of myself and cried at the finish.

Then I made my first trip to Portland. On my way back to the airport, the light rail stopped to let runners cross the tracks during a race. Right then I decided to move to Portland. Although seeing the race was not my initial reason for the move, it did solidify why I needed to be in Portland. If the city was going to stop public transportation for a race, then it was a place I needed to be! Three months later I had saved enough money, found a job, and moved to Portland.

In 2014 I ran my first race in Portland, a 10K. I didn't know anyone and was all alone at the start wondering if I really belonged. I had no clue about the right shoes or attire and didn't know about hydration or fueling. I ran by myself while my husband waited for me at the finish. While he was waiting, one of his co-workers was crossing the finish line. She asked my husband if he was running. He said, "No, but Michael is running."

My husband's colleague, Jill, became my running partner. Wow, what an interesting turn of events. Along with Jill, my husband had several other co-workers who ran, and they invited me to join them. I had made it to Portland and now I had a new running family open their arms to me. I decided I was never looking back. A few years later and I've now run a few marathons, numerous half-marathons, countless relays, and many 5Ks and 10Ks. My life is full!

After moving to Portland I heard about Hood To Coast and thought, "Wow, what an opportunity." I also knew it was hard to get on a team. Then, in 2017, a friend had a medical issue and was not able to run, and I was given a chance to participate.

My team was Dawn to Dusk and I was going to be Runner 5 in Van 1. Being new to Oregon, I had never been to Mt. Hood and was excited to be there for the start of the relay. I was like a kid in a candy store, not only at the start, but running and driving through many places I'd never been before.

Oh my goodness, my last leg. I had never trained for anything that intense. As I reached the top of the mountain after a long uphill climb, my fellow runners and teams were applauding and cheering. It was quite an accomplishment. I wanted to break down and cry at the top of the mountain, but I waited until I passed everyone and was continuing down the hill. I was so happy it was my final leg.

At the beach in Seaside, all 12 of us crossed the finish line together. Everyone on the team was a complete stranger to me when we started, but now they all felt like family. I loved taking pictures with my team, and the beach, beer, and food. It was an amazing experience.

Katrina Roberts *is from Vancouver, Washington.*

Being extremely overweight my entire life, never in my wildest dreams did I think I'd be able to be a participant in Portland To Coast. I thought it would be awesome to take part in the relay, but I couldn't even walk up my stairs without ending up completely out of breath. It was a pipe dream!

A few years ago, after several health problems, I decided to take the necessary steps to get rid of the severe obesity. Complete, dramatic, and necessary life changes happened. Over the next three years I lost 170 pounds and was consistently walking between three and six miles several times a week. A friend asked me if I wanted to join her PTC team. I was scared, but decided I was going to do it. It was the new me!

A few days before the relay I suffered two strokes in my eye, and my doctor nixed any strenuous activity until more tests. It was devastating that I couldn't be a part of PTC. However, secretly I was relieved. I was afraid of not finishing and letting my team down.

The following year I was back on the same team. I increased the distance of my regular walks and really pushed myself because I was still terrified of letting my team down. Even the day before the relay I tried to talk myself out of participating. In my head I couldn't do it.

Although I still had 30 pounds to lose, I was not going to let my team down! My first walk was on Leg 20. Oh my gosh, I was convinced I was going to die! The incline, the dirt road, and more incline. I kept telling myself I wasn't going to die until after I finished. No way would I let my team down. Through Legs 20, 28 and 36, I kept telling myself I would finish and that I could do it!

One of the greatest accomplishments of my life was crossing over the finish line. I did it. I can do hard things. I didn't just cross the finish line. I crossed the starting line—the line that showed I can do anything.

Gordon Bookless *lives in Portland and has been involved in Hood To Coast for more than 20 years.*

I played rugby for 20 years in the United Kingdom. When I moved to Portland I was looking for a team sport and stumbled upon Hood To Coast.

Ever since 1996 I've been running the relay. I've run it with many different people, some whom I've known for many years and others I shared a brief moment of time with while completing a shared goal.

My most amazing experience happened in 2015. I was waiting for my wife, Anne, at Exchange 15 when my phone rang. It was a New York phone number, so I didn't answer it. A minute later my phone rang again and it was the same number. This time I decided to answer the call. The guy on the other end said, "You don't know me, but your wife just passed us and asked me to call to let you know she fell. She's okay but may be a while getting to the exchange."

I quickly got everyone on our team together and we jumped in our van. From the driver's seat I said, "We have to go back and find her." I didn't realize our next runner had gone to the Honey Buckets and wasn't in the van! We drove back along Highway 30. It was dark and someone in our van said, "There's no way you'll see her." At which point I yelled, "There she is!"

I did a quick U-turn and pulled up behind her. She was babbling a bit and bleeding from her leg. We got her in the van, and I donned my running shoes and finished the last three miles of her leg. When we got to the exchange she was asleep in the back of the van. Obviously the shock had set in. I then ran my Leg 17.

Like any true HTC veteran, Anne wasn't fazed by any of this and rallied later on to run her last leg of more than six miles. What a trooper!

Felicia Hubber grew up in Portland, moved to Montana during high school, and attended college at the University of Montana. The daughter of Hood To Coast founder Bob Foote, Felicia was just a few months old when she attended the first HTC—and she's been at every relay since. In 2006 she succeeded her father as president of HTC.

In 2012 there was a fire at the Les Schwab Tire Center in St. Helens, which forced us to change the Hood To Coast course. I remember being out on the racecourse Friday afternoon and getting a call from the Portland TV station KGW. They asked, "What are you going to do about the fire in St. Helens?" I'm like, "What fire?" Nothing about a fire had come through on our radios yet.

At the time I was in Portland at Exchange 12, but I quickly left and headed to St. Helens. You could see the smoke from several miles away. It was a tire fire with big, black, billowing smoke. It was massive. I still don't know how it started, but it burned down the entire facility. It burned down to the ground. Fortunately, no one was hurt.

It happened right between the last Portland To Coast walkers coming through the area, and the first wave of runners coming through Portland. We were blessed it didn't happen when the participants were closer to St. Helens. We had less than an hour, however, before the first runners would get to that area and needed to figure out a plan fast.

Thank goodness for Google. I pulled Google Earth up on my phone and looked at all the side streets and roads in the area, circumnavigating around the fire. We came up with as straightforward a detour around it as possible, and received approval from Columbia County, the fire department, and the police to put it in place. It went about a mile out of the way, but our runners and walkers wouldn't have to breathe any of that terrible black smoke.

We were in Columbia County, but there were not many resources available. Their police department had been cut back and they had only three officers on duty and available at the time. I'm not sure exactly where they all came from, but there were many officers from other jurisdictions who came out to help. At every major turn of the detour there was a police officer and race official directing runners. We had every detour turn in place before the first runner came through.

Everyone applauded the amazing effort of the police and the Oregon Department of Transportation for enabling us to introduce a course detour on such short notice. They could have said, "No changes can be made to the course. Stop the race. This isn't going to happen. We've got other things to worry about here."

The police and town officials worked together with us, and it was almost as if the runners were just on their normal path. Everyone saw the smoke and knew a large fire was occurring, but as far as the runners were concerned, it was just part of the challenge and adventure of participating in the relay.

Audrey Keller is from Milwaukie, Oregon, and has competed for the Hood To Coast teams The Footprints and 12 Honeys in a Bucket.

It was more than 20 years ago. I was waiting to start my leg, take the bracelet, and get going.

The other runners started coming in. One runner crapped right in front of me, and then another threw up on my feet. He didn't acknowledge a thing. That poor guy was sick— really sick. He was a serious runner. I think he was with a Nike team.

But you ignore things like that during Hood To Coast. You just keep on going. That's all there is to it.

I've fallen a couple of times. You just pick yourself up and keep going. I actually made my time or beat it by a couple of minutes because I was so upset after falling.

Our team started out as The Footprints, and that was our name for about 20 years. Now we're the 12 Honeys in a Bucket. Those are horrible things, but they're a necessity and we're very glad when we find them. I don't care too much for the team name, but our team flag has the name on it, so we go by it.

Bill Frith *has competed in every Hood To Coast since 1985 and is one of the founders of the Dirty Half Dozen team, one of the longest-running teams that still has its same core of runners since 1986. He lives in Tigard, Oregon.*

Hood To Coast is the distance runner's *Amazing Race*, or in some cases, *It's A Mad, Mad, Mad, Mad, World*. You expect things will go sideways on the course and can count on exchanges with porta potty lines longer than those for the latest popular movies. Traffic can logjam for miles and only a desperate hitchhiking thumb or running extra miles before your leg starts gets you to the next exchange in time.

That's all part of the race. It's like one of those reality TV shows, except the pretty girls are all sweaty. If it were just a race, it wouldn't be as much fun. So when there's a diversion along the way, it makes the race better. I hate to admit it, but the more obstacles you beat, the better.

I've run every race since 1985. Three of us from that team started the Dirty Half Dozen +5 in 1986. In 1989, the race changed its route and destination, adding one more runner. Easy enough. We'll become the Dirty Half Dozen +6. One year we even finished in the top 10. That was years ago when we were in our 20s. Most years we are in the top 20 or 30, although that doesn't really matter as much when you're racing against age and health. As a team we've run well over 1,000 legs and a lot of us are closing in on 100 individual legs. Those are all great achievements. But being part of this long-running and now running scared team is the most rewarding part about the relay.

My memories aren't really about the race, however, they're about the people. Some of us have been friends since grade school. We're a bunch of guys who have stuck together for all these years and a lot of them are my very closest friends. We've been through trials and tribulations, triumphs and failures, divorces and death—all kinds of good and bad. In the end, we're still a team.

I was a good student in both high school and college. I was the student body president, a fraternity president and had plenty of extra-curricular activities. But I learned more from running with those guys than anything else. I learned about toughness and discipline. I learned how to win, how to lose, how to set goals and how to reframe and retool your life. You learn it's not just about you; it's about the guy next to you too, because you're only as good as the last guy on the team. That's what this event has done for me.

Every year HTC is the very first thing that gets put on my calendar. I still have a Day-Timer calendar in which I write down people's birthdays. I have hundreds of birthdays listed from the pre-Facebook era. I put down the rodeos and rock shows, the horse races and beer chases and other events I plan to attend. But the very first thing that goes in my new planner every year is the weekend of the relay.

I had two kids born in August. I made sure everything was taken care of in advance and that family would be around, because I was going to be gone Friday and Saturday and back on Sunday of race weekend. The race is one heckuva tradition. And while there might be a team name that's been around longer than the Dirty Half Dozen +6, there aren't many original runners remaining on those teams. My hat goes off to those runners that have kept their teams going all these years. It ain't easy when your bones tell you "no" and your stubborn heart tells you to "get up and go."

Then there are the other teams that we run against. They're not our enemies. They are companion competitors and we enjoy dueling with them. They're good people and not just some woodenheads that get in your way. One year they might beat us and the next year we might beat them. It's fun to have that tradition with guys you count on seeing every year, even if we never know their name. They're like us, running in the rain on the weekends and early pre-dawn mornings, getting ready for this goofy thing we do once a year.

It's remarkable and patently Pacific Northwesternish that there's something like HTC bringing all these people together. It's not just about the event. It's about the team. It's about one team—your team. Then multiply that by over 1,000. The event is just the excuse to watch the same movie over and over, each time with a different outcome. It's made special by the people who are part of it. Most people last about three years and they say, "The hell with this." But there's a bunch of us that aren't quite that bright and carry on. I suppose some people round out their character that way.

There are certain sports that provide you with an individual work ethic and some sports where you develop a team ethic. Running the relay provides both. You're the one that puts one leg in front of the other. Nobody else is responsible for that. But you draw on the strength and support of others. It seems every year someone has an injury or a health issue and you don't dogpile the guy. You give him support. They do their best and then you pick up the slack. We've had guys put in amazing splits to make up for the guys that aren't having a great year.

My worst year since I first ran the event was in 2017. Personally, I've struggled with my weight for years. I'll be thin one year and less than thin the next. That year I'd been under a lot of stress and put on 50 pounds. I was the slow fat guy on a fast team. Still, my team supported me and we finished together.

It hasn't always been like that for me. Some of us have our ups, downs and sideways times. A few years ago I ran 6:30 splits. In 2017, I ran 9:30 splits. Years earlier I could walk backwards on my hands and go faster than that. When you're that heavy as the result of the cold dish that life sometimes serves you, you feel every extra pound with every stride. But I didn't get grief from my teammates. The expectation is you do the very best you can and the team will take care of the rest.

There are two great moments I'm really proud of that happen during the race. The first is when the whole team comes together at the beginning of race weekend. People come from great distances to be a part of this team weekend. One teammate would come from his Army base, even when stationed in Afghanistan or Iraq. One guy used to come back from Korea, where he worked. Others come from out of state. So it's a special moment when all my longtime friends and teammates come together.

The second great moment is when we cross the finish line and the team shenanigans continue. After we take pictures and soothe our road war wounds with some hopped up barley elixir, we continue pursuit of our own traditions. We like going to Pizza Harbor restaurant in Seaside and scaring away the polite families with small, impressionable children, with our caveman table manners. All the while, we're talking big about staying awake until 7 p.m. and partying with people half our age. Every year it's a proud moment. Twelve go in, 12 come out.

In the end there's always something to celebrate. We celebrate the individuals who have really stepped up. You focus on the positive and look to next year to do better.

CHAPTER 14

Night Running

MOST RUNNING EVENTS TAKE PLACE during the day. Hood To Coast, however, is not like other races. Even the fastest teams competing for the overall victory are forced to run through the night. Running with a headlamp, a reflective vest and flashing lights, in complete darkness, is a regular occurrence in the relay. It's often a new experience for many runners. It's also a tremendous challenge and a time of solitude. There may not be another runner nearby during the evening hours, although there may be the glint of light from a runner far off in the distance. After running through the darkness, many come to believe the night time is the right time for a run.

Brianne Theisen-Eaton was born in Saskatoon, Saskatchewan, Canada, and attended the University of Oregon, where she won six NCAA championships in the heptathlon and pentathlon. In the 2016 Summer Olympics, she won a bronze medal for Canada in the heptathlon, becoming the first Canadian to ever earn a medal in that event. She retired from track and field in 2017 and now lives with her husband, Ashton, in San Francisco, where she is a board-certified holistic nutritionist and practices functional medicine. She first participated in Hood To Coast as an honorary captain for Team World Vision in 2016 before running the event in 2017.

In 2017 my night run came early, around 10 p.m. Our team was trying to run as fast as we could, so I wasn't slowing down or talking to anybody. I remember everyone had on those reflective vests with blinking lights. As I was running I was telling myself, "Okay, see that one light up ahead, go and pick them off." After I picked them off, then I did that with the next one, and the next one. I remember it being quiet—just really quiet and dark.

I had trouble with any sort of pace because it always felt like I was running faster than

I really was, and that threw me off a little bit. Even though I wasn't talking to anybody, I was surprised by how encouraging people were. Anytime I passed someone, they would say something encouraging.

One year I would like to be the runner who stops and runs with somebody for a couple of miles and talks to them and hears about what's going on in their life.

A few times, people recognized me on the course. Not so much when I was running, and definitely not when I was running at night, but when we were at an exchange or when we took a break. It was nice to be recognized, but the only bad part was it usually happened when I was standing in a really long line to use a Honey Bucket—and people kept pulling me out of line to get pictures.

I was always a little panicked when that happened because I was losing my spot in line—and I was getting ready to run.

Jeff Glasbrenner is originally from Boscobel, Wisconsin, and now lives in Golden, Colorado. In the 2000 Summer Paralympics he earned a bronze medal in wheelchair basketball as a member of Team USA. He also participated in wheelchair basketball in the 2004 and 2008 Summer Paralympics. After retiring from competitive wheelchair basketball, Glasbrenner began competing in Ironman-distance triathlons. He was a member of the Hood To Coast team The Amazing Awaits in 2008 and 2009.

I remember running next to this guy at night. I must have had a pebble in my shoe on my prosthetic running side, and it was making a clicking sound. It kept on clicking and clicking and clicking as we were running together. You could really hear the rock rattling around in my running shoe.

Finally, the guy I was running with goes, "What's going on?" I said, "It's a rock in my running shoe. I'm fine though, it's just my prosthetic!"

He was like, "No #$^&. You've got that going on and we're doing this." I told him, "I'm okay," and we got back to what we were doing.

Jay Palmer is from Bolingbrook, Illinois, and participated in his first Hood To Coast in 2017.

I value my sleep. I mean, I really value my sleep. But I remember being stuck in the back of a van that was hurtling down a gravel-strewn road. The van was bouncing up and down, just like one of those balls used to play jacks. I was trying to curl up and wondering how on earth I could get into my sleeping bag and slowly realizing that it wasn't going to happen.

The best I could do was hunch down at about a 45-degree angle and wedge the sleeping bag under my body to provide some much-needed cushioning between me and the seat.

Next to me was a woman I had met only a few hours earlier. We'll call her Nancy—because that's her name. All I could think about was how awkward this whole situation was and how much I really wanted to sleep. Then I realized how likely it was I was going to be awake—all night long.

At that point, I had a decision to make. I could either be frustrated at my less-than-comfortable accommodations, or I could suck it up, Buttercup, smile, and think about how odd and wonderful this whole deal was. Needless to say, I chose the latter.

I was the third runner in the van. We had already dropped off and picked up a couple of other runners and it was my turn to run at about 2 a.m. It was pitch black out and we were on a dusty, rocky road on a mountain. And I was going to run—not sleep, but run. Thankfully, I could see a green light strapped to the back of a runner in front of me, just like something you'd see in *Star Wars*. I considered passing him for another road kill. But then I thought, "Wait. If I pass him, then I might die on this mountain because I can't see anything."

I decided to chill and let him lead. For five miles I kept Mr. Green Light in my sights. Or maybe I should say I kept an eye on him through the thick coat of dirt that was slowly accumulating on my glasses. My watch was beeping every mile, but I wasn't looking down to check how far I'd gone. I ran one mile and then two miles, always keeping Mr. Green Light in my sights. Finally, my five miles were done!

After completing my leg I hopped in the van and maneuvered back into my spot, laughing at how the whole experience was surreal. Nancy asked how it was because it would be her turn to run soon. I told her it was the strangest run I had ever done. Things being a little less awkward now, we both laughed. At this point it was around 3 a.m. I was completely exhausted and also completely satisfied, and I shut my eyes for some much-needed rest. Thank God for the sleeping bag!

Fast forward to the finish at the beach. My buddy Steve, the guy who at the last minute invited me on this adventure, asked me how it went. Now I'm usually very thoughtful with my responses, but I just blurted out, "I'm dehydrated, I'm sleep-deprived and I had the time of my life."

Will Wise *participated in his first Hood To Coast in 1987.*

As I left the exchange to do the leg that finished at the Columbia County Fairgrounds, the volunteer at the exchange point said she was told to tell us to watch out for a particularly large cow pie in the road about a mile into the leg.

"Interesting," I thought as I started running. The moon was bright, so I turned off my headlamp to enjoy the wonderful night sky. Then from about 200 yards ahead, I heard a loud and effusive series of expletives.

As I continued along on my bucolic evening jog, I wondered, "What was that?" Then from less than 100 yards ahead I heard another scream, "%$*#&*@*+*&#!" I asked myself, "What's going on?"

Then I hit it. Not only were my new shoes covered in manure, but the manure was wet and got all over my socks and legs. It was across the entire road and several inches deep. This was no simple cow pie. It must have come from a large manure spreader taking the corner at high speed and it was nasty. "%$#$%^&*@&*+#," I said loudly to anyone within earshot.

Then, grinning ear to ear for some reason in my runner's high, I waited for it. Then it came. Of course it was another shout from about 100 yards. It was just like all the earlier ones, "%$%&#*@*+#!" Only this time it came from behind me.

I continued running and doing my duty for my team, the Dead Cheetahs. I grinned and snickered each time I heard an exclamation, steadily fainter but equally emphatic, from those crossing perhaps the largest cow pie in race history.

Sandy Dukat *is from Canton, Ohio, and now lives in Denver. Born with a congenital limb deficiency, Dukat had her right leg amputated when she was four. Between the 2002 and 2006 Winter Paralympics she won three bronze medals in alpine skiing. After retiring from competitive skiing she began competing in triathlons and captured the women's Above-Knee division of the USA Triathlon Paratriathlon National Championship four times. She was captain of the Hood To Coast team The Amazing Awaits in 2008, 2009, and 2010.*

I remember coming into an exchange in the middle of the night. At times it gets really hard to see your teammate down the road, especially at night. My boss, who was driving our van, was standing with some of my teammates around the exchange trying to find me. All they could see were the headlamps from the runners. My boss said my headlamp was moving from side to side in an unusual way. He said nobody else's headlamp was moving the same way, and he knew it was me because of the way it rocked back and forth. He said he would have put money on it being me coming down the road, and of course he was right. I really loved the fact that I could be spotted right way—especially at night—by my running gait.

The peacefulness of running at night was the other thing I remember. I thought that was a very cool experience because at that time I never ran in the dark. Part of the reason was because I can't feel if something's under my prosthetic running leg. When I was running, I would always look down to see if there was any terrain change, or a rock, or a curve in the road, or anything I could possibly step on. So for me, the race provided a moment of trust to get out and run with just a headlamp. It meant trusting my balance because the headlamp didn't really let you see everything.

Nowadays, I'm still a runner and I love early morning runs in the dark. Maybe that came from Hood To Coast.

Jim Sapp *was a member of the Road Warriors/Road Kill team that finished first in the inaugural Hood To Coast in 1982.*

We used to have night starts at Timberline Lodge. One year, my teammate Max came limping into the first exchange in the dark. He said, "I ran into one of the signs." He was talking about the big metal signs that say, "Slow, Runners on Road."

I was thinking, "Wow, that's too bad." But I was also wondering, "How the heck can you not see something that big?"

The next year I found out. I came within a foot of running right into the exact same type of sign. I was running at night, in the darkness. I was seeing all the lights from the cars on the road coming from the other direction. All of the sudden, a big patch of the sky disappeared and I saw in front of me a diamond shape of darkness. I put on the brakes just before I crashed into the sign.

I said to myself, "Okay, I understand what Max's problem was there."

Devrie Brennan *hails from Moraga, California, and now lives in Lake Oswego, Oregon. She is an orthopedic physical therapist who has participated in Hood To Coast 15 times.*

Remember the era of the Palm Pilot—probably around 2002. The guys from Team Mojo started a program that you could download to the Palm to keep track of running times. It sure beat the old clipboard with a Timex watch attached. However, in the 1970s van we were using as our mode of transportation in that year's race there wasn't even a cigarette lighter to charge the Palm.

We were running our second set of legs (13–18) on Highway 30 and were in desperate need of a place to charge the Palm. It was pitch black out. Luckily, there was a stretch on the highway with some stores and bars, as well as a gas station where we always bought lottery tickets. But since it was so late in the night almost everything was closed.

The first place we saw with lights on inside was a bar. We parked and I ran into the bar. I went straight to the bartender to ask if he could charge our Palm. His outlet was in back and he took the Palm to charge it. When he did that I finally turned around and noticed my surroundings. It was a small joint with just a few patrons drinking beers.

However, a full scan of the place revealed a gold pole on a tiny little stage in the corner. I had walked right by it on my way in and hadn't even noticed. I was so freaked out being in a mini stripper bar that I ran outside to wait in the van.

Every year we drive by that stretch of highway and look for that bar. There used to be a bronze silhouette of a bodacious female figure on a pole on the bar's front door, but we haven't noticed it recently.

I know it's somewhere near a 7–Eleven because we also stopped in there to charge the Palm—since we didn't stay very long at the bar.

Kayla Estes is from Bainbridge Island, Washington, and participated in her first Hood To Coast in 2017.

I love things like Hood To Coast where you have to push yourself physically and perform without much sleep.

I did a leg at about 1 a.m. through a forested area. We were ahead of pace, and I knew I could slow down a little bit.

Three or four times I just stopped because we had time to kill. I wasn't stressed out about stopping. No cars were passing by, and no vans were pulled over. I was just completely alone.

I turned off all my lights and just looked up at the sky and the Milky Way. It was going across the entire sky. I'd never seen so many stars in my entire life. You can see lots of stars on Bainbridge Island, but you still have the Seattle lights.

It was amazing. I did that three or four times throughout my leg. Just stopping in the middle of the road and staring up at the sky.

*Laura Friend is from Beaverton, Oregon, and her sister-in-law, **Julia Friend**, is from Camas, Washington.*

Laura: I'm super paranoid about being attacked by bears or other wild animals, especially on those dark legs when you're all alone, and my teammates were razzing me about it.

It was 2017 and we were driving in the van and I was trying not to think about it or listen to them. I was looking through my phone and came upon this picture of the eclipse that I had taken. I had been to Salem, Oregon the week before to see it.

So I said to my teammates, "If I don't emerge from the mountains, tell my family that I really loved the eclipse." They were like, "Not that you loved them? You want us to tell them that you loved the eclipse?" I guess it was just the way it came out because I was looking at a picture of the eclipse at that exact moment.

And I really did love seeing the eclipse, with my family of course. It just came out wrong.

Julia: Later, I had to change in the car after my leg, and Laura was running right after me. It was dark, she's out there running, and I'm trying to change.

Laura: You know, paranoid lady running in the dark . . .

Julia: So as we go along, in the dark, every mile, we're cheering her on, giving her a sip of water, and babying her all the way. All the time I'm trying to change in the car. We have to turn off the lights because I'm trying to change and I'd naturally like the lights off. I was still pulling my pants up when she comes running up . . .

Laura: I was yelling, "Where's my support? Where's my support?" Then they opened the door to the van and she stuck her heinie out. It was another total eclipse.

Julia: And I said, "Here's your support. Feast your eyes on this."

Ben Snyder is from Warren, Oregon, and is the captain of the Portland To Coast team Big Ben's Walkers.

In 2016 on Leg 3 I took off and immediately passed three people. I thought I was in the lead. At first I didn't see anyone behind me. Then I noticed this one flashing light.

I sped up, but the light sped up too. It was keeping pace with me. I sped up again, thinking one of the guys I passed wanted to pass me back.

As we got to the end of the leg, I finally pulled away from him a little bit. When we finished, I asked him, "Why were you trying to pass me back?" He said, "I wasn't trying to pass you back. I just didn't want to walk alone in the middle of the night."

Cindie McKenna takes a break during her 1997 solo run.

CHAPTER 15

Out Of The Ordinary

ALONG WITH THE TRADITIONAL TEAMS featuring 12 runners and two vans, there are the unique, unusual and one-of-a-kind teams that occasionally compete in Hood To Coast. It can be a solo runner trying to complete the course in less than 48 hours, or a group of accomplished wheelchair athletes. It can be athletes who take to the course on other wheels with support from a television network, a group of runners attempting to double the distance of the relay, or even talented Paralympic athletes seeking to add another medal to their collection. All those teams, and many others that are considered non-traditional, have lined up at the relay start.

Bob Foote *is the founder and chairman of Hood To Coast.*

There was a guy who wanted to run the race by himself in 1993. After looking at him I never should have allowed him to do it. He was an older guy, probably in his late 50s or early 60s, and he was not in great athletic shape. I thought to myself, "There's no way in the world this guy has completed all these ultramarathons he claims to have done." But he called his own press conference and announced he was going to run Hood To Coast solo. He was a real self-promoter.

Supposedly, he finished the race running solo. However, I soon started getting reports from people telling me he was jumping in and out of vehicles. They were telling me he was being driven around the course. He would get out on the course here or there to film some footage for TV, but basically he was just running over to his handlers who would pick him up and drive him farther along the course.

It was a total scam and really burned all of us in the organization. We decided, "Never again are we going to allow anyone to run solo."

However, that changed a couple years later when Cindie McKenna reached out to me about running solo. I knew she was the real deal. Cindie had been successfully running ultramarathons for years. Since I'd been burned by the last guy who attempted a solo run, she really had to twist my arm a bit to get the okay.

Cindie first ran solo in 1995 and really struggled. I think she finished in about 53 hours. However, she came back and ran it solo again the next two years. After her second time Cindie told me, "I learned a lot from the experience and I want to do it again. I really want do well this time."

In 1997, her third time running solo, she improved by about five or six hours over her previous best time! Her aim was to finish in less than 48 hours, and she accomplished her goal. She had people taking care of her along the way, giving her food, making sure she had a massage when needed, and things like that. Occasionally she'd stop and rest up a little bit before she got going again. But she did it in two days—which was legit. She started a day early on Thursday, just like we did with the other guy, but that was all that was provided.

At the same time Cindie was running solo, we had a two-man team run the race in 1995 and 1996. It was a father-and-son team. I know they were both ultramarathoners and wanted to run the relay as a bonding experience. It took them longer than Cindie to finish, probably because they were not elite athletes.

I still remember seeing them at the finish late on Saturday night the first year they ran. It was easy to see what the son went through because he could hardly walk across the finish line. His body was obliterated. When he crossed the finish with his father, people were literally dragging him across the beach. Those two guys just got destroyed.

I don't know why, but for some reason they decided to come back and do it a second time. After that they said, "No mas. That is it. That is it."

Shortly after that we changed the rules. We said, "From this point forward, no team can have fewer than six members." We didn't want HTC to turn into a marathon. The spirit of the race is all about teamwork and camaraderie, and we wanted to keep it that way.

Cindie McKenna was born in Van Nuys, California, and moved to Oregon in 1971. She began running shortly after joining the Air Force in 1975. In 1982 she began participating in marathons and began running ultramarathons in 1984. She ran Hood To Coast solo in 1995, 1996, and 1997 as a one-person team called Grit, Sweat and Tears.

I heard about Hood To Coast and thought it would be fun. This was before I was really running ultramarathons. In 1984 I became part of a National Guard team. I remember thinking the total mileage for each runner wasn't that much. I thought it was pretty neat—all the people and teams and camaraderie.

After that experience my friend Gunther Nemeth and I ran HTC in 1989 as a two-person team. What was memorable about that was Gunner (what I called him) was pretty sick and probably had the flu but didn't want to let me down. He ran Leg 1 down the hill from Timberline Lodge. While he was running, a friend and I mooned him—trying to make him laugh. He smiled weakly and kept running. He looked horrible and really should have stopped. We alternated each leg and he would almost crawl into the van when he finished running. But the two of us did the whole thing. Later I learned finishing as a two-person team was not as bad as finishing alone!

In the early 1990s I lived in Welches on Mt. Hood and every week I was running more than 100 miles. My week usually included running 30 miles on Sunday along with 20 miles on both Monday and Wednesday. Another day I would run about 30 miles at the Columbia River Gorge, and after that I would actually go home and do six more miles. On the other days I would just run about seven miles.

Patti Finke was my coach for several years. She and her husband, Warren, were coaches with Team Oregon and I talked to them about running HTC solo. They didn't think it was possible. But they said if I was going to try to run the event solo I didn't need to do anything different because my training already included back-to-back long runs.

Eventually I talked to Bob Foote about running solo. He said, "If anybody can do it, you can do it." Bob knew about my long-distance running history and thought it would be great. My husband, Bryon, and I thought about trying to get into *The Guinness Book of World Records* with the solo run, but we never followed through with the idea. As we looked at establishing a 48-hour course record with USA Track & Field for a solo run of that distance, Bryon and I rode bikes and measured the route, but there were a bunch of stipulations. With all its ups and downs and twists and turns, the racecourse wouldn't qualify for that type of record.

The first year I ran solo, 1995, there was quite a bit of publicity. Bob let the media and everybody know what I was trying to accomplish. I started running at about midnight on Thursday and didn't get much sleep that night or the next two.

I remember from that first year some guys came out to see me in their truck around the Coast Hills area. They said, "Wow, this is really neat. Is there anything we can do?" I said, "Yeah. I'd really like a hamburger." I was just kidding, but they drove off and went somewhere and came back with a hamburger. I still have the picture of me sitting on the tailgate of their truck eating a hamburger.

That same year, I came across a gentleman in the middle of the night. His name was Merill Klindt and he was a member of a Search and Rescue team. I'm not sure what county he was from, maybe around the Mist area. He actually found us out on the course and said he'd follow me to the finish line. He even had his wife prepare soup and sandwiches that he brought along. He was following me in his truck and we were planning to pass his house. He got ahold of his wife, although I'm not really sure how, and told her to have some pancakes ready. As we passed his house, there was a hot stack of pancakes waiting for me. I grabbed them and ate on the run. He stayed with me all the way to the finish, just like he said he would.

My goal was always to finish in less than 48 hours and get to the end before it was late at night. We ended up finishing early Sunday morning in about 52 hours when it was still dark and hardly anyone was around. My family was there and a few other people had stayed around waiting. Later I was told there were a bunch of people at the finish that knew what I was doing and were chanting my name, "Cindie! Cindie! Cindie!" I felt bad not finishing until everyone had gone home. I went through many different emotions at the finish that first year. I was tired and my feet hurt a lot, but I was just happy to be done!

The following year was similar to the first year. I finished in 53 hours. It was a real mental struggle running alone in the fog at night in the Coast Hills. There were times when it was more like I was plodding along, rather than actually running. Mike Burke, a close friend and an ultrarunner, was a strong motivator during the difficult times. He ran portions of the course with me all three years, and his patience and consistency were a tremendous help.

We decided to make a major change in 1997. Rather than starting at midnight like we did in 1995 and 1996, I began running at noon on Thursday. That helped both mentally and physiologically. It allowed my body to be more in sync with its natural circadian rhythm and allowed me to start and finish with the sun shining rather than during the evening darkness.

My third year there was a van full of nurses that came by as I was out on the course. At the time my friend Tim Farley was running with me at night. These nurses stopped their van and asked, "Is there anything she needs?" Tim, with a straight face, said, "Do you have a cigarette?" They were all like, "Oh, my God." Of course, Tim was just kidding, but it was really funny.

Tim was full of energy and a funny guy. He owned a sign company, Farley Readerboards, and my third year he put up a bunch of signs to encourage me along the way. I even recall one of his signs that said, "On the highway to the danger zone" and another said, "You are a profile in courage." Tim passed away in November 2016, a huge loss for everyone who knew him.

From that third time I also remember running on the Lewis and Clark Mainline with Tim, who ran with me throughout the race, as did Mike and Bryon. I was having a hard time and was a little irritable. I was walking and grumbling about the course, which was slightly uphill. Bryon was trying to encourage me. He said, "It's not really uphill." And I kept saying, "It's uphill." Again Bryon said, "It's not uphill." I got angry and said, "I don't want to get there after 48 hours, I don't want to be an almost." Then Bryon politely suggested, "Why don't you run!" I said, "I will!" and took off running, and did not walk another step. Tim looked at Bryon and said, "What just happened?" Later Bryon told me I ran a faster pace on that part of the course than I had the whole race.

I was not worried I wasn't going to finish—I just wanted to make sure I finished in less than 48 hours. Bryon, Mike, and Tim kept me aware of how I was doing and let me know I was ahead of schedule. It really helped raise my spirits. I was even able to pick up my pace the last few stages. Fortunately, the idea to match the start to my body clock and when the sun was out seemed to reenergize me, as I was approaching the finish in the light of day. And being among all the other teams and runners, as well as their support vehicles, really helped motivate me to reach my goal. In my third try I finally accomplished my goal, completing the course solo in 47 hours and 47 minutes.

There are many people to thank for the opportunity to run HTC solo three times. First and foremost is Bob Foote, who believed I could do it and provided me with the opportunity. Second has to be all my family and friends who encouraged and supported me and helped in ways too numerous to mention. And third is to all the people who cheered me on, waved, and offered support, not just during the relay but also when I would be out doing training runs in all kinds of weather.

Running 196 miles from Mt. Hood to the Oregon coast solo is not a simple undertaking. It took a team effort, with Bryon, Mike, Tim, and Gunner all playing key roles on the team. Bryon was responsible for the logistics and was also on the receiving end of my unpleasant moods during times when I was tired and irritable. Mike was gracious enough to provide support and pace me during all three years. Tim was a master motivator to me and to all ultrarunners. Gunner provided support and ran with me during parts of the race. The total team was really everyone who supported me, suffered along with me, stayed up throughout the night, and dealt with the multiple phases of the crazy, tired ultrarunner mood swings.

Thanks to all for such great memories.

Sandy Dukat *is from Canton, Ohio, and now lives in Denver. Born with a congenital limb deficiency, Dukat had her right leg amputated when she was four. Between the 2002 and 2006 Winter Paralympics she won three bronze medals in alpine skiing. After retiring from competitive skiing she began competing in triathlons and captured the women's Above-Knee division of the USA Triathlon Paratriathlon National Championship four times. She was captain of the Hood To Coast team The Amazing Awaits in 2008, 2009, and 2010.*

I'm the youngest of four children from a very athletic family. I watched what my brother and sisters accomplished on the playing fields and knew competing in sports was something I wanted to do. I participated in sports throughout high school, although I didn't know anybody with a physical disability playing sports. After college I moved to Chicago and quickly learned about the Paralympics.

Soon I was swimming competitively, and in 1997 I attended an event with the U.S. disabled ski team where I was introduced to adaptive skiing—utilizing one ski and a piece of adaptive equipment called an outrigger (a modified ski pole with a tip at the end) to provide balance. I was encouraged to start skiing competitively, which I did. Five years later, before the 2002 Paralympics in Utah, I made the team. I was fortunate to win two bronze medals in alpine skiing, which really unleashed in my mind that anything was possible.

In 2007 I was approaching my mid-30s and decided to retire from competitive skiing. I started focusing on training for triathlons and also found a job with The Hartford. A founding partner of U.S. Paralympics, the company was the first corporate sponsor that supported both athletes and the organization. My role was to manage the company's relationship with U.S. Paralympics and the athletes the company sponsored.

There were a lot of opportunities that came our way and one of them was Hood To Coast. At The Hartford there was a senior leader who had moved from the Pacific Northwest and had experienced the event. He thought it would be an amazing team-building business opportunity if we could put together a team that featured both our business partners and Paralympic athletes. Since that was my job, I quickly took over the plans.

I reached out to the HTC organization in 2008 and shared our story. It was after the deadline to submit an entry, but we really wanted to participate in the event with a multi-ability team that included Paralympics athletes and able-bodied runners. I'm not sure how it happened—but we were allowed to compete in the event.

We had several Paralympic athletes on the team. One teammate, John Davis, has a spinal cord injury and used both a racing chair and a hand cycle. We had two runners, Amy Palmiero-Winters and Jeff Glasbrenner, who are below-knee amputees and run with prosthetics. We also had one woman, Kelly Underkofler, who was missing her arm below the elbow. We added a few business partners from the Pacific Northwest, along with a couple company executives, and that was our team—The Amazing Awaits. In addition to organizing the team and coordinating all the logistics, I was going to be wearing an above-knee running prosthetic and be part of the team.

The whole event fit really well with my personality—I'm from an adventure and adrenaline-fueled background. It also included a lot of event planning, which is one of my best skills. I love logistics and details. In fact, I'm an over-planner, so it really fit with my detail-oriented personality. I also love competition and being a competitor, as well as being a part of a team. I'm also a big cheerleader. Participating in the race allowed me to be out on the road cheering and helping people achieve their goals and at the same time I fulfilled my own needs by running.

Rod Cruickshank *was born in Flint, Michigan, and moved to Oregon in 1968, where he attended grade school, high school, and college. He was familiar with Hood To Coast from the very beginning and competed in the relay for the first time in 1997.*

My company worked with The Hartford, a big insurance company. In 2008 they called up and said, "Hey, we've heard about this great event in Oregon called Hood To Coast and we're putting together a team with some Paralympic athletes." It was before the Beijing Olympics. They asked, "Do you want to run with the team?" I quickly responded, "It would be awesome to run with them."

We had five disabled runners on our team—and they were all amazing. They were hilarious, knew who they were, and were very comfortable with themselves. We were laughing the whole way. There were times when we'd be driving down the road and one of them would pull a leg off and just hang it out the window.

On our team were Paralympic athletes: Sandy Dukat, John Davis, Amy Palmiero-Winters, Jeff Glasbrenner, and Kelly Underkofler.

John has a spinal cord injury and used both a racing chair and a hand cycle. Amy and Jeff are below-knee amputees and utilized running prosthetics. Kelly was missing her arm below the elbow. Sandy was wearing an above-knee running prosthetic.

It was a great experience all the way around and probably the most fun I ever had running the race. The Paralympic athletes didn't see any barriers, only possibilities. Their intensity exceeded that of the experienced runners around us. It left an impression I carry to this day.

Bob Foote *is the founder and chairman of Hood To Coast.*

There was a wheelchair team that wanted to participate in the race in 1993. They were an elite group of athletes who had participated in the Boston Marathon and other big events. As far as I was concerned they were legit, and we agreed to let them compete.

What was interesting that year was the course finished with the runners heading down 12th Avenue in Seaside and then moving directly onto the beach. The course would then be right on the beach for about a half-mile until the finish line in front of the Broadway Street turnaround.

When the wheelchair team hit the beach they had to deal with making their way through a half-mile of soft sand. Of course the guy doing that final leg was pretty tired after he'd already completed most of three legs. Everyone was watching him when he got to the beach. As you can imagine, it was painful to watch because he was putting every- thing into it to turn one wheel revolution—and maybe he'd move three feet. He would push really hard again and maybe he would go another three feet. Some of the people watching were actually booing. We heard people saying, "How can they torture this guy by making him work through the sand?" It was excruciating to watch this guy inch his way, literally, to the finish line.

As a result of that experience, we determined wheelchair athletes wouldn't be allowed to compete on certain legs of the race. Of course the first two legs coming off of Mt. Hood were outlawed, along with the final leg on the beach to the finish line. We determined we couldn't let wheelchair athletes struggle like that again.

Since that team we've had wheelchair athletes on running teams—sometimes one or two on a team with runners—and we learned how to better accommodate them from the difficulties we faced that year.

Max Woodbury *is from Portland and became a C-6 quadriplegic in 1996 from a fall while working at a Superfund cleanup site. He has competed in Hood To Coast multiple times*

and captains the Pimps 'n' Gimps team that consists of both wheelchair athletes and able-bodied competitors.

Besides doing six legs on my quad-adapted handcycle in Hood To Coast, I also serve as the team captain and catalyst for raising funds for our sponsor, Adaptive Sports Northwest.

As a C-6 quad, I'm really not doing any pushing on the hand cranks. I don't have the triceps function. Instead, I spend all of my energy pulling the cranks. Because I don't have any finger dexterity or strength, I use adapted handles appropriately named QuadGrips that have shifters attached to them. I can shift gears while spinning my cranks. I also use a special coaster brake that operates without taking my hands off the cranks.

The invention of those items was important for lower functioning quads who lack finger dexterity but have the shoulder strength to use a handcycle. It was like learning to fly. Being able to keep your hands on the cranks to shift is huge because you can keep your momentum going and continuously adjust the gears as the terrain changes.

I have been hit twice on training rides by cars that didn't see my low profile recumbent handcycle. I probably could have prevented those collisions if I'd been able to stop quickly. Now that I have a coaster brake I'm a little safer on the streets. And I still wear bright clothing, use a highly visible flag, and have blinking lights on the front and back. It's definitely worth being able to cruise the streets in a human-powered vehicle, even if you're still as slow as a turtle going up hills.

In 2013 my third leg was the hardest. No doubt about it. It was all uphill for the final five miles. I basically had no sleep for 24 hours leading up to it while handcycling more than 20 miles. It was 5 a.m. and I had 11 more miles to go before finishing.

Even though it was the end of August, it was still pretty cold. As a cold-blooded quad, it's not easy to get warmed up while sitting by the side of the road in my handcycle waiting for my teammate. But that's what makes the relay so great. No matter how difficult some parts may seem, you can always think about the other 12,000 crazy people doing it. I finished Legs 27 and 28 in just over an hour and felt better at the end than in my previous four years participating.

As great as the race is, however, the finish line is a nightmare for wheelchairs. It's soft sand, mazes, and lots of people. This is where I feel most guilty, because my friends have to carry me through the sand in my chair to get to the finish line and the beach party.

After more than 30 miles of handcycling in 24 hours, I was happily exhausted. After we crossed the finish line we took some photos and headed to the beer garden, where a group of folks gave us their table—after we agreed to twerk for them.

Bob Foote *is the founder and chairman of Hood To Coast.*

In 1994, out of the clear blue, I was contacted by a woman who worked at MTV. She was a runner familiar with Hood To Coast, even though she had never run the relay. She thought it would be really cool to have the MTV rollerblading team participate in the race. She told me all the members of the team had established different rollerblading records, such as for speed, endurance, or distance. I checked it out and it appeared the team was a pretty formidable group. And the woman from MTV thought it would be cool to have the team compete in a colorful event like HTC.

They needed my permission for the team to participate. We communicated back and forth over several months and finally things came together so they could participate. I made sure to tell them all about the relay and the road conditions. We also discussed the course near St. Helens and some pretty sketchy sections of road around that area at the time. Some of the course was gravel and they would never be able to get through on rollerblades.

Before the race we decided when they got to St. Helens they would just continue north all the way to Astoria, instead of following the course route. Then they would come around down Highway 101 and merge back onto the racecourse to the finish.

I scheduled them to start in the middle of the day, in one of the regular waves with other runners. As soon as they started the first guy on rollerblades just vanished. He went as fast as you can go on rollerblades and disappeared down the hill. That vertical drop at the start is amazing, but it never really occurred to me they would push it at such a fast pace.

I caught up with the team after they finished and listened to them describe their experiences. I had chills up and down my spine, especially when they were talking about Leg 1, the five and a half miles down the mountain from Timberline Lodge. The guy who went first said he was going so fast he almost flew off the side of the mountain. He thought he was going about 40 miles an hour and said smoke was shooting off the wheels of his rollerblades. He said he almost lost it a couple of times.

As I was listening to them, I thought to myself, "Oh God. I'm glad this all worked out because they pushed it right to the limit."

Even though it turned out to be a pretty cool thing, the team decided never to come back—they said it was just too tough.

Steve Hanamura *was born in Upland, California, and now lives in Portland. He has participated in Hood To Coast more than 25 times and served as captain of the team I Hurt, You Hurt, We All Hurt for more than 20 years. Blind since birth, he is an avid runner and sports fan.*

When I run I use a bungee cord with my guide. I bought it back in 1981 for two dollars.

Most of the communication between my guide and me is nonverbal because sometimes I won't hear my guide if there's loud traffic or other noise. Although at times there is verbal communication too.

My guide and I run side by side, but the job of the guide is crucial. My guide will use the bungee cord to send me messages as we run. For example, if there's a step up my guide will move his or her hand up the bungee cord and also tell me at the same time. In certain situations there may not be time for my guide to spit out the instructions. One of my guides would say the word "uneven," which meant I needed to lift up my foot.

If my running guide pushes the bungee backward, that means, "Go behind me." When that happens I just fall in line behind my guide.

My guide and I usually try to run together side by side and get a good arm swing going, as much as possible. If my guide pulls the bungee cord toward him- or herself, I have to get closer. Maybe there's a telephone pole ahead or we're on a narrow sidewalk.

If we are on an open road I may even drop the bungee. However, when I do that my guide will definitely talk me through where we're running.

There is some training that needs to happen. The first time I'm with a guide, we just walk together. After that, we'll go to a track and practice. At the track, we'll run through different scenarios. I'll say, "Okay. Let's pretend that this is happening, and then we'll run the track." Once we get comfortable with each other we'll run on trails. Usually by the third time we're together the guide is comfortable running with me. That's how it all starts.

In a race I need someone I can really trust by my side because there's so much unpredictability. My guide has to pay attention for both of us. If I run a half-marathon, it's really going to be like a 20-mile race in terms of the energy my guide is using. The guide has to think about me and at the same time think about him- or herself. That's a lot of extra head energy.

During Hood To Coast I'll run my leg with the same partner each time, and most of the time he or she won't run any other legs during the race. Although, during my first 10 years running the race I had an ultramarathoner as my guide and she ran three legs on her own in addition to three legs with me.

What legs I run during the relay is based on the capabilities of my teammates. I've been Runner 1, 3, 4, 7, and 12, and I'll probably be Runner 10 or 11 sometime soon too. Even though I'm the team captain I don't think about myself except as to how it fits with the rest of the team. I make decisions based on who wants to run specific legs and who's capable of running certain legs. The really strong athletes are usually Runner 9.

My favorite time to run during the relay is early in the morning when it's not really warm out. It's like 5 or 6 o'clock in the morning and it's a beautiful time to be running.

One of my favorite legs is the last one for Runner 1. Another favorite is the start of the relay and the run down the mountain and past the waterfalls—that's just wonderful too. In fact, I told my wife, "When I die, I want my ashes to be thrown at the second waterfall you pass." It's just an incredible, incredible experience!

Blake Adams *is from Canby, Oregon, and a longtime member of the Transplant Trotters. He was one of the first living donors to join the team.*

The seed was planted some 20 years ago when I came across an inspiring story and photo in the *Oregonian* about a team of race walkers participating in their first Portland To Coast. All 12 walkers on the Transplant Trotters team had received an organ transplant. They all came together to deliver the message that what they had been through would not stop them from living and competing in a serious physical challenge.

I shared their passion and their interest in walking, and wondered if one day they would accept me on their team. However, there was one potential problem—I was not a transplant recipient. Having given a kidney to my then 10-year-old son, Joseph, in 1996, I was what they call a "living donor." Eventually I spoke to a team captain, who said I was eligible to join their team.

In 2000 I didn't know what to expect in my first PTC. I found the experience both challenging and rewarding. It was hard at times and exhilarating at others. Overall, it was rich in life lessons that could make me a better person.

When I became more comfortable supporting my teammates and not focusing solely on my own performance, the overall experience became better. That first year, my two legs totaled about 10 miles, but when everyone did their part it was amazing how far we could go together. On my second leg, during the middle of the night, I was feeling pain from the chafing I didn't yet know how to prevent, when I met a woman named Kathy who also was walking in her first relay. It was great to have someone to talk to as we walked. As we shared the rest of our journey together, my physical pain became easier to manage. Even though I still had to walk the same distance I saw what a huge difference it makes to be surrounded by supportive people. There really is nothing quite like taking on a challenge and realizing that you can complete it.

As exciting as it was to see our team walk the final steps together to the finish on the beach in Seaside and receive our medals, I was surprised by what turned out to be the greatest reward of all. It wasn't the final accomplishment but the journey to the finish and the opportunity to spend time with people you care about.

A lot has happened since my first PTC. Over time I've became a regular member of the Transplant Trotters. I've walked a variety of legs in both vans, and have done all the tough ones! Recently I faced my final fear—Leg 29—and the steep incline that was part of the only leg in that round labeled "very hard." I was the second to last walker in Van 1. Although I didn't admit it, I was scared as Leg 29 got close. What if after all these years my lungs finally met their match? I was tired of thinking about it and just wanted to get out there and do it. It went well, proving the anticipation was the worst part. Obviously, some of it was hard. At one point someone on the side of the road heard my heavy breathing and asked if I was all right. But I made it the same way any of us gets anywhere—one step at a time. After I passed the summit, the euphoria of the last couple of miles was like a victory lap.

The 2017 event was my 16th year as a Transplant Trotter. It was also a special occasion—our team's 20th anniversary. At the risk of sounding biased, we have a unique team. Many of my teammates received the gift of life and want everyone to know what's possible when people waiting for an organ get their second chance.

Those of us who experienced the other side of organ donation want you to know something about us too. When we gave away, say, a kidney, we did not give away our quality of life.

Steve Strauss *is from Portland and has run Hood To Coast every year since 1985.*

Hood To Coast has demonstrated that it can attract all kinds of people for many different reasons and keep them coming back, although few of them have come back as often as I have.

I've been blessed with the right combination of enthusiasm, opportunity, and consistent good health to have participated in every relay since 1985, only missing the first three years of the race because my running career was in its infancy. I was not yet integrated into the necessary running social circles. However, once I got started it was love at first handoff.

That first team in 1985 consisted of co-workers and was a mixed bag of middle-of-the-pack runners and a sprinkling of actual talent, along with a heavy dose of the adventurous spirit. We knew next to nothing about pacing ourselves for three or four legs or stretching techniques to minimize soreness, and we knew nothing about scheduling mid-course meals or the best foods to consume. In fact, hardly anyone knew that stuff back then. All I knew was the run-rest-run-rest-run cadence felt well-matched to my developing skills and I wanted more opportunities to perfect it.

I also had a strong bond with Mt. Hood, having lived, worked, and skied there for a full year after transplanting myself to Oregon from the East Coast following college.

In the early years when the relay ended in Pacific City, teams started running Friday night under a full moon. I remember one chilly morning around 2 a.m. being outside Timberline Lodge and watching the bats fly around our heads as we waited for the signal to start running. It was quite different than the carnival atmosphere of the current event's daytime and daylong kickoff.

Over our first eight years, the Standard Insurance Company fielded more teams and sometimes more capable teams. The relay was a catalyst for a growing general emphasis on corporate wellness at the company. Then in 1993 things coalesced a little differently and, without a team, I was on the outside looking in. I didn't dwell too much on having an extra free weekend in August, but it didn't last long. A phone call from a neighbor on Tuesday of race week quickly changed my status and put me back in the race to replace their unlucky teammate who had been involved in a runner-vehicle accident. Since then, I've never again considered allowing my streak of annually participating in the relay to end.

The race continued to expand and along with developing an appreciation for the history of the event, I slowly developed a connection with race founder Bob Foote. It mainly developed through my almost-annual critiques mailed to the HTC office post-race to either praise when appropriate or to make suggestions when I thought necessary.

When the urge came to me to think outside the box about how my team could approach the race, Bob was willing to listen to and ultimately accommodate my ambitious notions. First was the team UltraLords 6x6 in 2007. It was a group with marathon experience who were foolhardy enough to try and cover the race distance with a squad half the normal size. After we bested most of the full-sized teams, I knew I'd eventually want to think bigger. In 2011 the stars aligned and I sold my teammates on my most ambitious plan— forming a team to start at the coast and travel to Mt. Hood and then return to the coast. It would be a round trip, something apparently unprecedented in event history. Bob and the HTC organization took a mostly hands-off approach to our Coast To Hood To Coast team and didn't stand in the way. My main promise to them was that we would not give them a reason to regret it.

After intense research and preparation, we assembled a team called UltraLords Double Trouble of eight race veterans and one rookie. We set off from Seaside on Thursday morning with just a handful of seagulls as spectators and the goal of reaching Timberline in time to make our official starting wave for the conventional westward portion of the race. It was really interesting to see the course in reverse and enjoy the serenity, except for all the logging trucks on the roads. To our surprise and relief, all the porta potties were already in place and pristine! We cruised along, ahead of schedule, over the empty hills, and through unsuspecting towns.

It was a couple of hours before Friday's dawn when thunderstorms suddenly moved in and we could see significant lightning near the mountain. In Brightwood we encountered an early set-up crew and sheriff's patrol, who indicated the event start was in jeopardy due to some safety concerns. We cautiously pushed on. In the end there was no direct danger—and no delays due to weather.

As team captain I had given myself the honor of running the final six miles up to Timberline Lodge. I started just as the rain ceased and the first hint of daylight emerged in Government Camp. I felt both blessed and slightly delirious while effortlessly gliding through this fourth of eight eventual legs, barely noticing the rise in the road. As waves of early Leg 1 runners descended the big hill, many were incredulous at my presence. All I kept hearing was, "You're going the wrong way!" It was usually followed by some manner of encouragement. I responded in kind and kept on churning.

We reached our first finish line with over an hour to spare and after a brief celebration fell in with the masses on what was becoming a beautiful morning. Once summoned to the start, we picked up right where we left off with only minor and temporary reductions in performance. After around 45 miles apiece we still felt amazingly good as we finished strong in a combined running time of around 53 hours. To add to the satisfaction, the numerous supporters of our team had helped us raise a few thousand dollars for several charities.

Since then my association with the race has only grown. My current team, which is still company-sponsored, retains a number of core members reliable enough that we can almost prepare and compete on autopilot. This helps reduce stress, and our readiness for any surprises simply allows more time for fun.

In recent years I've had an opportunity to get to know some of the other longtime competitors. Now, more than ever, we inspire each other to keep hanging in there.

I hope they all stay a step ahead of me, in terms of seniority, for years to come. But I intend to keep chasing them. We all share an extreme fondness for this event and an unwavering willingness to help overcome any challenges to make it better—and better for all.

Lance Dayton participated in Hood To Coast several times during the first decade of the event. Later he ran the relay as part of a six-person team and also completed a roundtrip from the beach in Seaside to Mt. Hood and then back to the coast.

My first Hood To Coast was in 1984 as a member of the Portland Rugby Club. I can remember the trauma as we arrived in Pacific City only to learn all the finish line beer was gone.

We were back again in 1985. It was those first two races that prompted me to become a runner. As a rugby player I could sprint short distances, but it was the pain of those early relays that motivated me to specifically train for longer distances. I eventually competed in marathons and 50Ks, and have completed more than 90 long-distance events. I credit HTC with humbling me into shape.

The Portland Rugby Club participated in most of the first decade of the race. In some years it was comical how disorganized we were. Our most unwise vehicle choice was an Audi sedan. I recall trying to sleep sitting up in the backseat in the middle of the night and shivering. There were other years where one of our vehicles was an open-bed El Camino. One of those years, when we were in the first vehicle, after finishing we started up a Weber barbecue without legs in the back of that El Camino, cooking burgers and hot dogs as the last six legs took place. Not very smart, but it sure was fun!

Another time we lost a runner early on Friday. One of our runners was a subcontractor and he persuaded one of his crew to join us. We gave him the first leg. He blistered off the soles of both feet and was kaput. We unloaded him as we passed through Portland and absorbed his legs.

I took advantage of my parents every year and got them to satisfy our volunteer hours. Once, they ended up with a middle of the night shift, directing traffic at Columbia County

Fairgrounds. This could have resulted in me being disowned. Fortunately, the people-watching and entertainment value outweighed the abuse they took as volunteers. To this day, if I mention Columbia County Fairgrounds, they shake their heads and chuckle. The people-watching is priceless during the race.

The Coast To Hood To Coast team was a once in a lifetime experience. We planned for the better part of a year to make that trek, not knowing whether it was a real possibility. I have a strong memory of us finally kicking it off on a Thursday morning in the pre-dawn gray at the Seaside turnaround. The overriding memory was the beauty and peacefulness of the course. That must have been what it was like for Bob Foote and the early relay pioneers in1982. My second memory from that Thursday morning is of the beauty of new and unused porta potties. It was like heaven tearing the outside cover off the toilet paper roll. We all know from experience that the porta potties eventually move to the other end of the spectrum.

During that roundtrip excursion, our captain and mastermind, Steve Strauss, was running the final leg from Government Camp to Timberline Lodge. Steve was grinning from ear to ear the entire leg and enjoyed all the other runners coming down the mountain, telling him he was going the wrong way. Completing the journey from the coast to Mt. Hood and back was a huge mental victory.

We had about an hour to bask in our accomplishment in the party environment at the Timberline Lodge start. We knew we were golden having completed the first half of our run, and that the energy of the other teams would buoy us on the route back to the beach.

There was another year we did the race with just a six-person team. Six legs may not seem that difficult, but we ran them hard and not well paced. My final leg was almost eight miles and I was completely spent. I'm sure I walked much of that leg.

The relay has had a positive impact on my life and produced many awesome memories. The highlight reel of my life has some very good clips from HTC.

Bob Foote *is the founder and chairman of Hood To Coast.*

In 1997 a team from Japan came to Hood To Coast. The team was made up of a really interesting blend of teammates, some of Japan's biggest celebrities in sports and entertainment. About half the team members were television and movie actors, and the other half were athletes.

There was a comedian on the team who they told me was the Japanese equivalent of

Jerry Seinfeld. He had his own TV show in Japan with a big, cult-like following. Along with a couple big movie stars there was also a Japanese professional sumo wrestler on the team. He didn't look like much of a runner—he was a massive, strong-looking guy. There were also several athletes on the team who competed for Japan in different Olympic sports.

They turned their relay experience into a one-hour TV special that was broadcast during primetime in Japan. It was shown nationwide and was a big deal. They were trying to come up with something, from both an entertainment and publicity standpoint, which people would really enjoy. Of course they gave me a copy of the special—but it's all in Japanese—so I didn't understand most of it, except from a visual standpoint. However, they told me it had high ratings in Japan.

The footage of the course was beautiful and you can easily pick up the comedy, they're cracking each up other up and doing goofy things. I didn't have to understand it to see how much fun they were having. It was really well done.

More than a decade later, in 2012, there was a team from Toyo University in Tokyo that came to compete in the race and ended up as the overall winner of the relay. It was an elite team featuring 12 of the fastest runners in Japan. Maybe the seed for them to run HTC was planted when they watched that television special.

***Randy Gibbs** is from Portland and ran his first Hood To Coast in 1989 and his last in 2015, when he ran out of knee cartilage. He was one of the founders of the Kult Kevorkian team.*

In 1997 there were some teams from Japan competing in Hood To Coast. There was an elite team and a celebrity team.

We started the race at the same time as the Japanese celebrity team. We were up there at Mt. Hood getting ready for the start and these guys from the team from Japan came over to talk. Our team liked to fly pirate flags, and they had their Japan flags. They wanted to know about Kevorkian, who our team was named after, because they had never heard of him.

I tried to explain to them that Jack Kevorkian was an American folk hero, like Davy Crockett or Paul Bunyan. Now, the interpreter was an American and he was trying to translate what I was saying verbatim. But he was having a hard time digesting all the information I was giving him. So I tried to relate to them by explaining how Kevorkian was very much like the Japanese in that he believed in *hara-kiri*, you know, a sort of assisted suicide.

The Japanese guy was taking it all in, but the American interpreter was having a hard time keeping a straight face.

We were running with these guys off and on throughout the race, and we saw them down at the major exchange near the Spaghetti Factory. They had their flags out and were yelling at us and we got our pirate flags. And I don't know what they were yelling because it was in Japanese, but I yelled back at them, "Tora, Tora, Tora!"

Go! Fight! Winn!

Washed Up to Seaside

CHAPTER 16

Heartbreak

HEARTBREAK IS DEFINED AS CRUSHING grief, anguish, or distress. While Hood To Coast is most often associated with triumph and achievement, heartbreak also happens during the race. There are runners and teams that are not able to make it to the beach and soak in the glory at the finish line. Injuries, accidents and other health-related issues occasionally force runners to the sidelines and in some cases, to seek medical attention. As a result, in addition to triumph, heartbreak is also part of the relay's story.

Linda LaBash began running in 1990 while attending the Oregon Police Academy for probation and parole officer training. She is an original member of the Heart 'N Sole team that has run Hood To Coast more than 25 times, and has also run more than 25 marathons, including six Boston Marathons.

In 2007 Hood To Coast started out as just another fun year for the Heart 'N Sole team. It was our 17th year participating in the event. I had chosen to be Runner 12 that year, one of my favorites, especially for the final leg and the glory of the finish. My teammate Kathy Ryan had her favorite too, Leg 1, as always.

As I finished running my second leg and passed off to Kathy for Leg 25 in Mist, little did any of us know that Heart 'N Sole would not make it to the beach in Seaside or that Kathy would face a life-threatening challenge.

About five minutes into Kathy's run our Van 2 was prepared to head to Jewell School for breakfast. Traffic was really slow to get moving and we were at a standstill. A male runner came running in the direction of our parked van shouting, "1-5-5." We realized that was our team number! Runner down! That would be our Kathy!

Ardy Dunn was the first to leave our van. She's a nurse practitioner and always the first to offer aid along the course whenever needed. The rest of us got out to follow her. I was cold and wet having just completed my run. I walked up the hill to discover my friend Kathy lying flat on her back on the road with blood spilling out from the back of her head. Ardy approached me with a serious look and put her arms on my shoulders and said, "She's not breathing. She has no pulse." I didn't know what to think and must have been in shock.

Amazingly, in an instant there were two women on the ground attending to Kathy—performing CPR and rescue breathing. As fate would have it, these two women were first responder trainers with the Oregon State Police. They were two runners—Dee Rzewnicki and Terri Cassebarth—from the team Twelve Tough Mothers. Another runner, a nurse from Kansas City, was also offering assistance. For those of us who were standing around in a circle watching, wondering and waiting—the next voice we heard was from one of the first responder trainers. She said, "I've got a pulse . . . a *good* pulse. *I've got a very strong pulse!*"

I don't know how an ambulance made it through that crowd on the narrow two-lane road in Mist, but it did. I rode with an unconscious Kathy to the fire department in Clatskanie and then on to the hospital in Longview, Washington. Ardy stayed with the team. I notified Kathy's husband en route to the hospital. The team found Kathy's son, who was also running on a relay team. The entire Heart 'N Sole team, along with Kathy's husband and son, joined me at the hospital in Longview.

Later Kathy was taken by ambulance to OHSU Hospital in Portland, still unconscious. We eventually learned that that the problem was blocked heart valves, although Kathy didn't know she had heart issues. She was probably our team's strongest athlete—one who had run countless marathons in 46 different states.

Our Heart 'N Sole team usually ends our weekend at the Pig 'N Pancake restaurant in Seaside for breakfast on Sunday morning. But our fun weekend was over and Kathy's fate was unknown. So we asked the hospital staff where there was a good breakfast place in town, and that's where we went. Our team needed to end our weekend that way—supporting each other and being able to share thoughts and feelings about what had just happened.

Of course, this story has a happy ending. If you've seen the movie about the relay you know that Kathy recovered and has continued to run with Heart 'N Sole.

Peter Courtney *lives in Salem, Oregon, and has represented the 11th District in the Oregon State Senate since 1999. He is currently president of the Senate, a role he has served in since 2003.*

One of the saddest days in my life was when I broke my leg during Hood To Coast in 2013. My femur just broke while I was running. I was Runner 12 and was going to run the final leg of the relay to the finish. I was going to run along the boardwalk, and then onto the beach, and finally across the finish line in Seaside together with my team. I'd never done it before and really thought it would be a high like I had never experienced.

I remember taking off from the exchange. I was about two miles into my run when I heard something pop—and I went down. The pain was excruciating and I started to scream. I was crawling along the asphalt trying to get up, but I kept falling down. A team of women came by and they just physically lifted me up and put me in their Suburban.

It was so sad. The team that picked me up was really worried that it didn't smell too good in their van, but I knew at that stage of the race nothing smells good. They took me to the medical tent. The pain was unbearable. The medical staff provided me with pain medication which helped me make it to Monday. My orthopedic surgeon took X-rays of my leg and said, "You broke your femur. I have no idea how you put up with the pain."

That bone is still somewhat fractured and I can never run again. Unfortunately, that was the end of my running career.

One year I did serve as a volunteer during the relay. I remember my team came through the exchange where I was working, and it took so much out of me when they got in their van to head to the next exchange. I always know when the relay is taking place and know exactly what's happening with my team because they always send me updates. But, I haven't been emotionally able to go back, not even as a volunteer.

I always felt I had a special family with HTC and was really sad when I had to stop running. I'm still not over it.

Kasha Clark is an Oregon native from the small town of Lorane. She now lives in Portland and has been participating in Hood To Coast for over half her life.

In 2016, after running Leg 2, I took a bad fall while watering our team's fourth runner, as well as runners from other teams, during that seven-mile leg in the scorching heat.

I literally fell while giving water to my teammate. I was running beside her and handed her a water bottle to drink as I was also pouring cold water on her head. We were talking because I wanted to see how she was doing in the heat. As we talked, I was looking at her rather than down at the shoulder of the road where I was running. I stepped off the shoulder, rolled my ankle, and then did an endo—tumbling head over heels!

A police officer saw my fall. I had passed out. Medics came to the scene and dispatched an ambulance—my patella had shot through the skin above my knee. I came to and had the medics clean the debris from the wound as best they could and then wrap it up. I signed a release cancelling the ambulance and had my team carry me to our van so we could make it to the next exchange before our runner finished.

I didn't want my team, Washed Up to Seaside, to be delayed or to have to stop. And I knew ambulances are expensive, so it wasn't a difficult decision. I also assumed the ambulance would drop me off somewhere near Gresham, and considering my closest friends were running with me, I didn't know how or when I would be able to get home from Gresham.

After we got to the exchange at Sandy High School, I was picked up by another friend and rushed to an urgent care clinic that was close to my home in Southwest Portland. The point of impact was my patella, and I was severely bruised and had a deep wound that required stitches.

I was stitched up and joined my team in Seaside the next day. My teammates were all worried and concerned, but they were really happy to see me at the beach.

It took five months of physical therapy to recover, but one injury in 18 years isn't too bad!

Vicki King is from Gresham, Oregon, and is a member of the Soul Sisters Portland To Coast team.

It was our first year participating in Portland To Coast and I was on my first leg. I'd had a bunch of road kills and there was one more person ahead of me who I thought I could get before the end and I was focused on trying to catch up to her.

A car came along and I moved over to the side. I was still focused on the person up ahead and didn't notice that the side of the road crumbled away. I stepped off the edge and went down. I ripped all the tendons in my left leg. I sprained by wrist, broke my elbow, ripped all the tendons in my shoulder, and was covered in road rash on my hands and knees.

But I got up and finished!

I was in shock. Total shock. But I finished my leg. Then they took me away to the emergency room. I didn't finish the next day because I couldn't stand. I wanted to go to the finish line, but the doctor said, "Are you kidding me?"

It took about eight months to recover, but I was motivated to come back and do it again. I hadn't finished the race the first time and wanted to do it. I did have to take a different leg. My husband was like, "Please don't take that leg again." I ended up with a harder leg, which he didn't know.

I keep coming back because it's fun. Everyone on the team has become good friends and we have a great time.

And I want to do the original leg again!

Steve Hanamura was born in Upland, California, and now lives in Portland. He has participated in Hood To Coast more than 25 times and served as captain of the team I Hurt, You Hurt, We All Hurt for more than 20 years. Blind since birth, he is an avid runner and sports fan. Steve's wife Becky Hanamura is a longtime HTC volunteer and currently serves as the Exchange 12 leader.

Steve: Becky's first assignment as a volunteer was to pick up beer cans on the beach after the finish party.

Becky: Yes, that was my first experience as a volunteer. It was Saturday night from seven to midnight. Steve ran the race that year.

Steve: She says, "I don't think I'm going to do this anymore."

Becky: I'm a retired nurse. I said, "Okay. We're picking up garbage. Where are our gloves?" I was told by the race officials that I didn't need gloves. They said, "Just wash your hands afterward." I went over to the first aid tent, which hadn't closed yet, and got some exam gloves. After that I made a suggestion to the powers that be at Hood To Coast, and the next year there were exam gloves at all the exchanges for garbage pick-up. Since then I've done lots of other assignments and now I'm the leader at Exchange 12.

Steve: There's always stuff that happens at Exchange 12.

Becky: It's the second major exchange on the course. The exchange is located in Portland underneath the Hawthorne Bridge. It's where the last runner from Van 2 and the first runner from Van 1 meet. It's busy and chaotic. There are lots of people and plenty of vehicles. It's chaos trying to get everybody in and out with few or no incidents.

Steve: Becky's in charge of all the people who volunteer at that exchange. She assigns them to specific spots, whether it's directing traffic or directing runners or something else. She makes sure everything is running smoothly at the exchange.

Becky: There's a fire station at the exchange and I remember a few years back I watched the paramedics get on their golf cart and drive away. Before they took off, an ambulance showed up at the exchange. I went over to the ambulance driver and said, "Where do you need to be? Let me clear a path." And they said, "Well, we're not exactly sure."

They told us there was somebody under the Hawthorne Bridge, but they didn't think it was a runner. There are a lot of homeless people in that area and we all kind of assumed it was something related to that. The paramedics looked around and realized, "Well, it's apparent there's nothing here. We're going to drive around and see if we can find him."

The ambulance backed out and left. A few minutes later I saw the paramedics hop back on their little golf cart. There's a paved path all along the east side of the Willamette River, near where we were located. They drove off, four guys on this little golf cart. About that time one of the van drivers from Steve's team came over and said, "Becky, they're going to get Steve."

I saw the paramedics come back with Steve sitting in the back of the golf cart between two guys. He was just yammering away. I knew it wasn't life or death because he was sitting up and talking. They loaded him into the ambulance, and I said, "Is it okay for me to get in?" The ambulance driver I had talked to earlier told me, "I'm really sorry, I didn't know it was one of the runners."

I said, "Not only that, it's my husband." He was like, "Oh, I am so sorry."

Steve: It was pretty hot that year and I was Runner 12. It was during my first leg. I was just dehydrated and ended up in the emergency room.

Felicia Hubber grew up in Portland, moved to Montana during high school, and attended college at the University of Montana. The daughter of Hood To Coast founder Bob Foote, Felicia was just a few months old when she attended the first HTC—and she's been at every relay since. In 2006 she succeeded her father as president of HTC.

An extremely traumatic incident happened in 2008 that was probably the low point for me during all my years with Hood To Coast. It probably was as well for a lot of people involved in the race.

A runner with a High School Challenge team, Chelsee Caskey, was hit by a car. The driver was high on meth. It happened on Highway 30, just south of Scappoose.

Chelsee attended Lincoln High School in Portland, and was on the high school's team. She was running her leg at about 9 p.m., wearing a reflective vest and a headlamp. When she was struck she was on the wide shoulder of Highway 30 running with the flow of the traffic. This woman, who eventually went to jail, drove right into the back of her. Chelsee didn't see the car coming and went flying into a ditch.

She was in intensive care for many weeks with severe injuries. I remember visiting her at the hospital. She had multiple injuries and broken bones. After many surgeries, however, she amazingly made a full recovery.

It was really scary, and I felt deeply for her mom. I tear up thinking about it. I have such a close relationship with my mom, and I think about how her mom must have felt during such a traumatic time with her only child.

Although we haven't been in contact in a few years, I know Chelsee graduated from college. I remember her as being an absolutely amazing, positive, and inspirational person.

It was an extremely hard time for me because I don't ever want to see that happen to anyone, let alone one of our participants. I care for them and want to create the best possible event and experience overall that we can. It's really difficult because we want to create a safe environment for everyone, but there are unknown factors in events and in life.

Candi Garrett grew up in Portland and now lives in Newberg, Oregon. She has participated in Hood To Coast more than 25 times.

In 2017 everything was good and we were right on schedule when we got to Exchange 24. It was about 1 a.m. and we parked in the area designated for vans. One of our runners decided to go over to Tent City to sleep. I was planning to sleep in the van. Then I thought, "No, it's nice out." So we laid out a tarp and four of us put out our sleeping bags. We were excited to get about four hours of sleep. Normally we don't get more than two hours. We thought it was going to be great.

We were outside in our sleeping bags. The four of us were lined up in a row. My teammates Roger and Melissa were on the ends. My teammate Cindy and I were in between them.

All of a sudden I heard something loud. It was a guy screaming about someone stealing his truck. I heard his voice—luckily, I'm a light sleeper. I immediately sat up and saw a Honey Bucket truck barreling toward us at full speed—and I just screamed!

I don't remember how I got up and out of the way. I screamed something like, "He's not stopping. He's not stopping." And I was yelling, "Stop!" Somehow, I got up and moved away, before he ran over our tarp. I thought all my friends were dead!

Then I saw Roger and after that I saw Melissa. Then I heard Cindy screaming. She was under the tire of the truck and being dragged in her sleeping bag. I was yelling at the guy who was driving and banging on the hood of the truck. I was screaming, "Get off of her. Back it up."

The guy whose truck it was finally got ahold of the guy who had taken his truck. He didn't want to let him go, but he needed to get into the truck to back it up. The guy who had stolen his truck took off and ran away. Roger saw him run toward the bushes and got a look at him. He said the guy was wearing a hoodie and sweat pants.

We got the truck off of Cindy and there was a runner nearby who was a paramedic. He did a quick head-to-toe assessment and unzipped Cindy's sleeping bag. I was scared, wondering, "What are we going to see?" Cindy was able to move her feet, but she thought her leg was broken. They called an ambulance and Cindy was taken to Portland's OHSU Hospital.

They took the rest of us into a staff trailer, where there were a bunch of people with ham radios. It was cold out and we were able to warm up a bit. We were drinking hot beverages and they were updating us on everything happening. They asked me if I wanted to contact my team out on the course, which I did using a radio. I was able to get ahold of my team and told them, "Something's happened. You guys need to come to the Birkenfeld Fairgrounds."

When the rest of our team got there, we told them what had happened. We were all together now and it was around 5 a.m. We were then told the police had caught the guy who had stolen the truck. A K-9 unit had been brought in from Beaverton and had located him in the bushes around the exchange.

I called Cindy. She was going to be released from the hospital. It was a miracle that nothing was broken.

We drove to Seaside and got to the house we rented near the beach around 7 a.m. Then Jude (Hubber, HTC Race Series CEO) called. I've known Jude for several years from communicating with him about the race. He wanted to come by and see us. When he heard what happened he couldn't believe it was my team.

Later Saturday morning, Jude came by our house. He met the team and gave me a big hug. We all cried and it was very emotional. He couldn't believe what had happened. There had been a miscommunication and, for about an hour during the night, Jude and the race staff had believed that we were dead—and they were going to call the race. Then they found out it wasn't true.

I asked Jude, "Can we run across the finish line together? That's just very important." And he said, "Oh, you bet." He let us cross the finish line as a team and get our medals, which was cool.

Cindy is in physical therapy, and it's going to be a long recovery process. She's not able to run yet, but she's getting better all the time, and we're hoping she does get back to running.

It was an awful experience, but luckily no one was seriously hurt. It's something none of us will ever forget, but it's something that won't stop us either. We're going to continue running the race—and no one is going to take that away!

Melissa Bishop lives in Ridgefield, Washington, and is a retired Portland police officer. She first participated in Hood To Coast in the 1980s and has run in the event more than 20 times.

Every year we stop at one of the major exchanges to camp out and get some sleep. We just throw our sleeping bags on the grass and there's never been an issue. In 2017 we decided to camp at Exchange 24. One of our runners said, "Why don't you guys come with me and sleep in the tents?" And we were like, "No. We're tired and we just want to lie down here."

Four of us—my teammates Roger, Cindy, Candi, and I—laid out a tarp and put our sleeping bags down. I was on the end next to Candi, and I quickly fell asleep.

Suddenly, I heard screaming and yelling, and then felt something hit my hip. It was the tire of a Honey Bucket truck, and it pushed me along the grass. I could see a line of vans coming toward me. I started screaming and yelling. I was lucky the ground was dry and really hard. Rather than running me over, the truck just kind of slid me across the dry grass.

Then I heard Cindy yell from under the truck. That was frightening because I thought she was hurt really badly. She was hurt, but luckily it wasn't as bad as it could have been. It was scary and there was a big melee afterward. It was chaotic and crazy and frightening because we all could've been hurt very badly or even killed.

It turned out that some guy had stolen the Honey Bucket truck! Even though I'm a police officer, I had to step back and let the local police deal with what happened. To be honest, I was a little overwhelmed at that point anyway, so I wouldn't have been much help. I worked in the city, and if we were chasing someone and it was a couple hours later, there was usually little chance of finding that person.

Three hours later, we were extremely pleased to hear they actually found the guy.

Jenny Hansson began working for Portland television station KOIN 6 in 2006 and is the anchor for its morning news program. Before moving to Oregon she worked at TV stations in Tallahassee, Florida; Austin, Texas; and San Antonio. In 2013 she participated in her first Hood To Coast.

In 2017 we were at Exchange 24 when some guy ran over a runner in a stolen Honey Bucket truck. It was really scary and strange!

We were sleeping at the exchange and had just gotten up because I was getting ready to start my third leg. We heard a bunch of yelling and one guy was screaming, "What the #%@&? What the #%@&? The guy's wearing a hooded sweatshirt! He ran off into the woods!" Everyone on my team was wondering, "What's going on?" It wasn't happening right next to us, but we could hear it and it was really loud for about a minute. It was bizarre. We had never heard anything like it. Then it suddenly stopped, and we heard nothing. We decided, "Well, okay, let's keep going." We weren't sure what happened, but we were all ready to get going again.

We were in the middle of nowhere in this mountain range, and it was my turn to run. It always surprises me how alone you can be on some legs, even though there are thousands of people running. It feels strange to be alone because you always expect to be around other runners. As I was running, I began thinking about what we heard at the exchange and hoping it was nothing.

It wasn't until we were at the beach the next day when we got an alert on our phones from the station. It said there had been an incident overnight and a guy had been arrested. Someone had stolen a Honey Bucket truck and run over some runners, although no one was seriously injured. And the guy who stole the truck had been caught. We were all like, "Oh my God!"

From my experience working in news and from running the event, it's extremely unusual to hear about incidents like that happening during the relay. There's just so much camaraderie among the runners and teams. While you may be miserable at times, everyone seems to stick together.

Obviously, we were all shocked when we heard what happened, but we were relieved to hear they caught the guy and that nobody was seriously hurt.

Natalia Barwegen *is originally from Colorado and moved to Portland in 2011.*

My first year running Hood To Coast in 2014 is one I'll never forget. I was Runner 12, new to the race and a somewhat recent transplant to Portland.

I had heard about the relay, so I was ecstatic to *finally* be running. My husband and our two dogs, Olly and Guinness, came to cheer me on as I completed my first leg. It was easy for them to see me as we finished at OMSI (Oregon Museum of Science and Industry) that year. I said, 'Hi,' to my husband and dogs and then went on my merry way.

The next day my husband met me at the beach in Seaside and took me back home to Portland. It was a normal, but exhausting day. We got home and I said, 'Hi,' to my pups. Then I slumped on the couch to rest. All of a sudden, I heard my husband from the hallway of our apartment, "Babe, babe, come quick, come quick it's Olly."

We don't know what happened but that night my Olly had a heart attack and passed away. He didn't have any health problems. It's like he held on to see his mom finish this feat and decided he had completed his life's journey. I went from the absolutely highest of highs to the lowest of lows in 20 minutes. It was the absolute worst.

Many would think that the race now depresses me, but in fact it's a time for me to reflect on the amazing memories I had with my Olly. The next year (2015), I made a headband that had his name on it and everyone on my team wore it throughout the weekend. My parents in Colorado, my husband, friends in California, everyone—*everyone* wore their Olly headbands.

Now every year I wear my Olly headband with pride because HTC is dedicated to him! I never run the relay without my Olly.

CHAPTER 17

Road Kills

THE TERM "ROAD KILL" IS Hood To Coast slang for passing a runner on the course. The tradition of counting road kills dates back to the early years of the race and came to prominence during the 1984 relay.

Today, counting road kills is one of the relay's more popular pastimes. Many teams proudly display the number of road kills on the side of their van. Other teams are not fans of the term or of keeping a tally of runners passed.

Despite the different opinions about road kills, it's definitely one way for a runner to earn some bragging rights during the race. It's also worth noting that with every road kill registered, there's usually a "good job" or "way to go" exchanged between the runner making the pass and the one left behind.

Larry Dutko was a member of the Road Warriors/Road Kill team that finished first in the inaugural Hood To Coast in 1982. He later became a member of the Dead Jocks in a Box team, and is the only runner to have competed in every HTC.

By 1984 the race had expanded to the point that a staggered start had to be implemented. A mass start was no longer manageable with so many teams, runners, and vans trying to negotiate the exchanges. The increase in the number of teams required the slower teams to start earlier in the day in hopes they would reach the coast before nightfall. It also meant the faster teams would catch and pass runners during the course of the relay, which hadn't happened very often during the first two years of the race.

Given that our team name was Road Kill and that we probably made more passes than any other team back then, every time anyone on our team passed a runner it became known as a *road kill*. The term was quickly and widely adopted because it represented a way for a runner to earn some bragging rights, whether it was for passing one runner or 20 runners during a leg.

Tim Dooley *is from Gresham, Oregon, and has been running in Hood To Coast since 1989. This memory was originally published in* RaceCenter *magazine.*

A sprint to the finish does not have to be a part of every race. There's nothing wrong with sustaining a consistent pace all the way through the tape or picking the pace up a notch over the last few hundred yards. With no competitor in sight and nearing the end of my first leg in 2003, the picking-the-pace-up option seemed like the sensible way to go. That sounded very respectable for a 49-year-old veteran of the running wars who still had two relay legs left.

There I was winding my way through the tree-lined path about 400 meters from the end of my more than seven-mile leg. I was in the best condition that I'd been in for three years and had pushed the pace hard. But now my tank was close to empty. My heart rate was up and my legs were feeling the effects of the sustained push. In the distance, I spotted my teammates from Run Like U Mean It and a crowd waiting at the exchange.

That's when I heard some fast-approaching footsteps. I glanced over my shoulder and, sure enough, there was a very fast-moving runner quickly closing the gap. She must have been about 25. In retrospect, she appeared to be a cross between Jackie Joyner-Kersee and the goddess Athena. "Jeez," I thought dejectedly. "What do I do about being passed by someone so close to the exchange point?"

That's when I heard her voice. Like the echo of a loudspeaker reverberation, she bellowed, "I'm coming for you!" No kidding. Why did she have to say that? At the sound of those words some involuntary chemical reaction immediately triggered in my head. All thoughts of a humble surrender disappeared. My body disengaged from my mind as I started a flat-out, frothing-at-the-mouth sprint!

There we were side by side, Xena the Warrior Princess and the 49-year-old race veteran, sprinting for all we were worth! Xena was clearly relishing the challenge and the crowd ahead had caught sight of this sequence and was really getting into it. Xena edged ahead. At the bridge, 50 meters from the finish, I surged back beside her. My lungs felt like they were about to explode! In that exhausted state I was still somehow able to make out the faces of my teammates lining the path ahead. They were jumping and yelling for all they were worth! I would have smiled at the thought if I had the strength. I could not let up now and disappoint my teammates. Twenty yards to the finish now, Xena and the race veteran were straining for a final advantage!

Finally, it was over! I edged Xena by barely a whisker. As I staggered off the path I thought I was about to lose my lunch, but fortunately that didn't happen. The best part was my teammates' reaction. They seemed genuinely excited about the whole thing as they whooped it up, slapped my sweat-drenched back, and replayed the scene to each other.

Even Xena the Warrior Princess came by for a hug! In truth, she had proved she was the superior runner by coming out of nowhere and making up so much ground. In the process she had dragged me along on that sprint to the finish and added another great running memory to my collection.

It sure beat that sensible finish I had planned!

Jeff Glasbrenner is originally from Boscobel, Wisconsin, and now lives in Golden, Colorado. In the 2000 Summer Paralympics he earned a bronze medal in wheelchair basketball as a member of Team USA. He also participated in wheelchair basketball in the 2004 and 2008 Summer Paralympics. After retiring from competitive wheelchair basketball, Glasbrenner began competing in Ironman-distance triathlons. He was a member of the Hood To Coast team The Amazing Awaits in 2008 and 2009.

I learned about road kills during the race. Every time I'd run by somebody, I'd say, "You just got cripped!" It was short for, "Hey, you just got passed by a one-legged guy." I remember passing people and they were just flabbergasted that a one-legged guy had passed them.

That was kind of my thing with road kills!

It was also amazing to see all the really fast teams—like the teams from Nike and adidas, whose runners would blow by you like you were standing still.

I was running one of my legs and heading into the exchange. I got passed right at the end by one of those really fast runners. As I was making my way into the exchange, the guy who had cruised right by me at an extremely fast pace, put his hands to his knees and started puking all over.

I was like, "Yes! This guy is giving it his all out there, all the time."

It was really cool being around so many people driven to succeed like myself.

Scott Parker grew up in Portland and lives in Bozeman, Montana. He first ran Hood To Coast in 1998 and is the author of Running After Prefontaine: A Memoir *and* Run for Your Life: A Manifesto.

Leg 20 is five and three quarter miles consisting of two significant climbs on the gravel and dust of Pittsburgh Road somewhere in those uncanny middle-of-the-night miles between St. Helens and Mist. It was 2010 and already one of those runs that remind me why I run. The night sky was scattershot with stars and I would gladly have run uphill until sunrise.

I like to think that I run for myself—for the physical joy of moving my body through space, for the mental and emotional serenity that results from physical exertion, for the way running amplifies my sense of being a living, breathing, sweating creature who belongs to this planet—but I know sometimes I run for other runners too. Namely, the ones I'm passing.

In the darkness, the runners ahead of me appeared as stars, points of white light twinkling all around me. My road kill amassed as quickly as I could count them. I was running so easily it was as if I were flying through the night, reaching one star and letting my momentum shoot me off for the next.

So enraptured was I that I didn't notice the single point of light approaching me faster than I could escape it until I heard its carrier breathing and kicking up rocks. This guy was moving.

I reminded myself of all the profound reasons for which I ran and maturely cautioned myself against competition. So what if I got passed? No shame in that. So what if I was only the second-fastest runner for this stretch of the race? And yet, inevitably, my legs did what they would. As we crested the second hill with a little less than a mile to run I suddenly found myself in full chase.

I narrowed the gap but only to spur the other runner faster along. He denied my attempt to pass and forced me to settle in behind him. For the remainder of the leg I would not be able to regain the lead and he would not be able to drop me, and pretty soon we would cease trying. We ran—I ran—on the very edge of abandon (and probably over it). We covered dips and maneuvered curves like we had grown up on this road—lucky, because we were running it basically blind, outrunning the beams of our headlamps. Before long I came to feel that we were bound up, like our stars had fallen into mutual orbit and either without the other would lose course and vanish in the night.

And suddenly it was over. We handed off our bracelets and bent, hands on knees, gasping for air. After a moment of recovery we embraced and he showed me a number on his watch—our mile pace over the final descent—that was smaller than any I'd ever been associated with before. Immediately I latched onto that number, sharing it with my van-mates, and savoring the warm swell of pride in my chest.

But when I think of that run now, the number eludes me and so does the pride. What returns is the sense of moving so freely among the stars and gratitude for the runner with whom I shared the experience.

Lillian Mongeau Hughes *lives in Portland and is an education journalist. She first participated in Hood To Coast in 2008 as a last-minute substitute and returned in 2016 and 2017 to captain all-women fundraising teams.*

As a team we decided that we disliked the term *road kill* and especially disliked the tallies of them on van windows. It seemed crass to us, especially when a team of young, fit men had a long list on their van of all the people—most of them older and/or women— they had passed. That said, we'd be lying if we weren't keeping track ourselves and getting a little kick out of passing people. We may be polite, but that doesn't mean we're not competitive.

My most notable road kill moment came during my first leg. I spent most of Leg 4— seven miles in the sun—neck and neck with a guy I'd guess was a few years younger than me. He passed me early on, maybe at mile two, but he didn't get too far ahead. He kept breaking to walk.

When we got to the first aid station about halfway through the leg, he was still drinking water as I darted off to use the porta potty. Since I was running 26 weeks pregnant, I needed every porta potty available on the course! By the time I came out, my competitor had taken off again. I started in behind him and found that the gap closed slowly because he continued to take walking breaks and I continued to plod along at a steady pace of a little more than 10 minutes a mile.

I finally passed him again during another one of his walking breaks around mile five. But he wasn't having it and passed me minutes later. As we climbed the final hill before the exchange I closed in on him from behind. I don't think he realized it until he noticed me at his elbow, and that's when I got a big surprise. He was so intent on beating me to the exchange that he started sprinting! I matched him stride for stride for about six paces until I had to return to my regular speed.

He pulled ahead for another moment and then went back to walking as I strode by him once more. It would be hard to say exactly who "won" that little competition, but having done as well as I did against a healthy-looking young guy sure did boost my ego and mood the rest of the race. It showed me that all my years of running half-marathons and marathons prior to this particular event had paid off.

I will never be the fastest runner on any course, but I have stamina and persistence, and those two things will carry me through the unpredictable challenges that lie ahead. And that's a discovery from Hood To Coast that I'll carry with me for years to come.

Max Woodbury *is from Portland and became a C-6 quadriplegic in 1996 from a fall while working at a Superfund cleanup site. He has competed in Hood To Coast multiple times and captains the Pimps 'n' Gimps team that consists of both wheelchair athletes and able-bodied competitors.*

Everyone decorates their team vans with window paint to illustrate what their team is about or to list each individual who is participating and riding inside. Another custom for some teams is to mark on their van the number of people they pass, their road kills.

It's always fun to have a goal of catching and passing other runners. Most wheelers are faster than the majority of runners. They don't allow disabled athletes on wheels to participate in the first two legs because the steep descent is too dangerous. When the wheeler gets to roll Legs 3 or 4 in Van 1, they get to do some major sleighing. I have pedaled Legs 3 and 4 together in just over 30 minutes, averaging around 25-mph as I enjoyed the elevation drop of nearly 2,000 feet. It's a blast and easily the best part of handcycling Hood To Coast. My road kills on those legs can creep into triple digits. I almost feel guilty yelling, "On your left," as I fly by all of those runners. But I know my next legs won't be so easy.

I also do Legs 15 and 16, which include the rolling hills of Highway 30. No more cruising at 25-mph down Mt. Hood. It's payback time.

It's usually a beautiful time of day, around dusk, making the hills a bit less excruciating. I can fly going downhill in my super-low-profile handcycle and keep a decent pace on the flats. But on the slightest incline I slow to a crawl. It's just impossible to generate that much power with your arms. So now I'm road kill, slowly crawling up those hills, but at least I'm getting lots of encouragement from runners as they pass me by.

Then I gather speed after I crest each hill and start reeling all those runners back in. I cheer them on too, shouting, "I'll see you on the next hill!" as I roll on by.

Becky Hermann *is from Sandy, Oregon, and has been involved with Hood To Coast for more than 20 years. She was a longtime volunteer and participated in the event for the first time as a runner in 2016.*

Before I ever ran the race I was a volunteer. I started volunteering as a kid because my mom ran the race from almost the beginning. Every year, my dad and I would volunteer. When I got older, my husband would join us too. After my dad died, my husband and I continued to serve as race volunteers.

One of my favorite experiences as a volunteer was a last-minute shift my husband and I did for a team that we didn't know. It was at Exchange 30, from midnight to 4 a.m. It was so inspiring to be there because all the teams were amazing, and all the volunteers were amazing.

After working as a volunteer for many, many years, in 2016 I finally decided to run with the team Eternal Insanity X36. I had taken up running a few years earlier and was finally ready to participate in the event in a different way. My husband joined the team, too!

My best memory of my first Hood To Coast was running Leg 27, my final leg. I was following a runner with black KT tape on his calves. When I finally caught up to him we started talking as we ran. It turns out he was from Denmark and was running for a Nike team. It was neat to meet someone who traveled from so far away to participate in the race.

Of course the best part of my third leg was that I passed him on the uphill—and was later able to tell my teammates that I passed a Nike runner. By no means am I a fast runner, so it made my entire race!

There's no way to describe the sense of community in this relay. It's just an amazing feeling to be part of something this awesome!

Nikki Neuburger *is a Portland native and attended Oregon State University, where she walked on to the women's volleyball team and became team captain. After graduating in 2004, she joined Nike and was a longtime marketing executive at the company until early 2018, when she became the Global Head of Marketing at Uber Eats in San Francisco. She is a regular Hood To Coast participant.*

We track our road kills. It's a super fun tradition to keep track of how many people you pass on the course. But we're nice about it. Every time I pass someone, and most of the time when someone passes me, the other runner and I will exchange words of encouragement. We'll say something like, "Great job. You look awesome. We're more than halfway there. Only a mile to go." Everyone is encouraging, which is a very different vibe than you get in a huge road race with thousands of people. I think the encouragement is one of the special things about Hood To Coast.

One year when it was really hot, I was Runner 4. That set has some of the "easier" legs in the race. But the toughest leg is the first one, about a seven-mile run. The next two legs are much shorter.

It was probably 90 degrees and I'm a little bit of a wuss when it comes to running in heat or running hills. As a Portlander, I'm great in 55 degrees, and I can run in the rain all day long, but I'll pass on the heat.

I was waiting at the exchange for our runner and checking who else was going to run next. Being at Nike at the time, we knew a lot people in the running world and I saw this guy who worked with a specialty retailer. I think he had run the 1,500 meters at the Olympics in London. He was a tall drink of water, skinny, and obviously a great runner. But I think he was probably retired from competitive running and not taking things too seriously.

He went out after I started and passed me at one point. Right after that my team drove by. Then about a half-mile down the course, he stopped on the side of the road. I think he was having a bad reaction to the heat. I stopped to make sure he was okay and wasn't going to pass out or anything. I offered him some water, told him not to do anything stupid, and took off to finish my leg.

He never passed me again! So when I came into the exchange my team wasn't ready for me because they were waiting for this Olympic athlete, who was clearly going to come in before me. From then on it was always, "Nikki beat an Olympian on her leg!" That's probably my most famous road kill. That guy has no idea, but it was a really funny moment for me and my team.

Robin Balder-Lanoue *is from Monticello, Minnesota, and is the cross country and track and field head coach at the College of Saint Benedict, where she competed in those sports before graduating in 1991. She ran Hood To Coast from 1995 to 2015, and her team, Baba Yaga, was the top finishing women's team nine times, setting course records in the Women's Submasters and Masters divisions.*

We weren't one of those teams that counted road kills, but it was fun to see how many people you could pass. When we first started running Hood To Coast, we had to ask, "What's a road kill?"

It seemed as if our team was always starting late in the day and we were starting with mostly men's teams. As a result, the first 12 legs were not very much fun. We were getting passed by all the men's teams that started behind us. It wasn't until the middle legs that we would start catching people and then during the final legs we'd catch a lot of other teams.

In the early years we had a good rivalry with the women's team from the San Diego Track Club. One of those years our first runner tore her hamstring, so she barely got through her leg. I thought, "There goes our chance to win."

We had a really strong new runner that year and I had originally scheduled her to be Runner 9. I had done it in the past and knew it was really long and hard, but I knew she could do it too. When we lost our first runner, we had to bump everyone up a spot and suddenly I realized I'd be Runner 9 again.

My last leg, I told myself I was going to be smart the first half of the leg so I could finish really strong. The San Diego team was ahead of us starting the leg and their runner just took off. Of course, I was delirious before my last leg, as always, but I keep telling myself, "I'm going to be smart. I'm going to get faster every mile."

I got the decrepit feeling out of my body that first mile and then kept getting stronger and stronger. By mile five I passed the runner from the San Diego team. It was the most exciting thing I ever experienced during the race.

I started to hyperventilate, wondering if I should keep trying to go harder and harder. I knew I had to get ahead by as much time as possible because our Runners 11 and 12 were both doing four legs. We gained three or four minutes on my leg and our last two runners really stepped up and ran 6:30s, and we were able to win despite being short one person.

Knowing that everybody on the team, no matter how beat up they are, is giving it everything they have that day is a big thing. It keeps you going. That's really what it's all about.

Brian Adams *is the associate dean of graduate programs at the Pamplin School of Business at the University of Portland. He took part in his first Hood To Coast in 1992.*

I was running Leg 6 in 1992, the first year team Naked Love Pretzel participated in the relay. During my run I caught up to a woman who was decked out in full running attire. I asked her what pace she was running because I didn't have a running watch back then. She looked at me in my torn T-shirt and basketball shorts and said, "Probably too fast for you. Seven-minute miles."

I didn't know back then how fast I could run. So I thought I would try to stay with her as long as I could. When we got into Sandy and were near the exchange I decided to kick it into the next gear. I passed that woman and never saw her again. It was the first time I learned my running pace.

The last leg for Runner 6 used to be what has now become Leg 29. I had no idea how difficult it would be to run up that hill. Three of us were running together on the way up. I felt pretty good and was doing my best to pull them along. After we crested the top of the hill I started getting really tired on the way down. The other two runners then pulled me along all the way down to the exchange.

One of the best things about the race is that most runners are nice and helpful. We all want everyone to run their best and finish their legs.

One year in the late 1990s, my brother Barry ran Leg 1 with our team. He was going to finish his leg no matter what happened along the way.

It was a really hot day for the start that year and Barry probably ate too much before the race. About 100 yards from the exchange he collapsed. He then got up, ran another 50 yards, threw up, and fell again. After that he got up once more, ran fifty yards to the exchange, and then threw up again.

He had such a look of determination on his face that we knew he was going to complete the leg regardless of how many times he fell down or threw up.

Carla Pletsch *and her son* ***Andrew*** *are from St. Helens, Oregon. They have run Hood To Coast with Team Annie!*

Carla: I ran Hood To Coast for 11 years. Andrew waited to run the race until he was 13.

Andrew: My first year was 2017. At first I was going to be Runner 4. Then my mom's calf started acting up a few weeks before the race and we decided to switch. I became Runner 5, which has some of the hardest legs in the race. Not only that, I ran the most miles in my van, which I was very proud of.

Being Runner 5 is brutal. All the legs are hard. They have huge hills. I think it's the hardest. I passed 23 people—got 23 road kills—on Leg 5 alone. On my second leg I got 35 road kills. And that's not counting the real road kill I saw. Each time I would approach a person I would silently count in my head how many people I had passed. As soon as I saw someone I would speed up and try to pass them.

Getting road kills is a lot of fun. It's even more fun when you're getting some during the hardest leg of the race.

Bob Harold *is the former chief financial officer at Nike and has been competing in Portland To Coast since 1996.*

We used to track road kills during Portland To Coast. We'd put a little Nike swoosh sticker on the side of our van for every walker we passed, but it is of less importance these days.

We always have good head-to-head races with other teams. You're in a division and you see many of the same teams every year. It's never a fierce competition, but it's another incentive to push you a little bit. If you know the XYZ team is in your division and that you're competitive with them, you want to beat them. Sometimes you win and sometimes you don't.

It's all friendly, there's nothing acrimonious about it. Everybody is having a good time and is in the same boat in a way. We all want to push ourselves and do the best we can. That's the magic of competition. You see the same teams at the exchanges. We kind of get to know each other and it's all friendly competition. Sometimes I talk to the other teams, just strike up a conservation to see how they're doing, or what they do for a living, or how many kids they have, whatever. It's just small talk, but it's all friendly and all good.

You also use other people to pace yourself. There's one leg I remember on Weyerhaeuser land that goes for about seven and a half miles. I started the leg and saw this young lady ahead of me about a quarter-mile. I noticed her because she had a pony tail that flopped back and forth. I wanted to catch her by the end of the leg. We were going at about the same pace and I worked really hard to catch her. She still beat me to the end of the leg, but not by a quarter-mile—it was more like 10 yards. But she was my incentive to push myself to go as fast as I could.

Nike values fitness and athletics. The fact we field so many teams is a reflection of a culture that values fitness. We think of ourselves as runners. I think Nike employees feel it. It benefits the employees and it benefits the company. It's a reflection of who we are and what we make. If you're making shoes, you'd better run in them yourself. If you're making apparel that's supposed to enhance your ability as an athlete, then you better wear it and see for yourself.

CHAPTER 18

The Runner's Journey

NEARLY EVERY HOOD TO COAST runner has a personal story to chronicle. It's the account of the path that led them to the relay, or something that happened on the actual journey from the start to the finish. It may involve their team, teammates, or one of the legs they ran. A smooth path without any issues may be part of that journey—although that is usually the exception rather the rule.

Tilly Gomperts Willis is from London and a student at Loughborough University. A longtime track athlete, she spent most of her time focusing on sprints and shorter distances. In order to compete in her first Hood To Coast in 2017 she had to transition to longer distances.

On Friday in the early afternoon, two vans pull up outside our downtown Portland hotel. The title of our team, Coastbusters, cradled by a Nike swoosh, covers the exterior of each van. This is our cue. Six runners pile into Van 1. They're prepared to embark on the two-hour drive up to Mt. Hood in time for our team's official start at 2:45 p.m.

A few hours later, those of us who remain follow suit, assembling in Van 2 before setting off to Exchange 6, where the whole group will reunite. By that time, five of the runners in Van 1 will already have made their first contribution, collectively tackling the harsh descent from Mt. Hood.

During the first stage of the journey, the wall of tension and intrigue that sits between each team member gets chipped away. The angst of a language barrier, worry of personality clash or perhaps assumed ideologies, thought impossible to get over, are overruled. The elevated and discovered differences between these individuals seem to make them stronger.

Phones are switched off and the outside world is cut out. There's no space for distraction now. All of us in the van are concentrating on the here and now; the road ahead and the challenge to come is all that matters. No more training can be done and no further operations carried out to prepare or alter one's ability to go farther or faster.

The stresses before a 400 meter sprint are very different from how I feel in the moments leading up to my first leg as Runner 11. In track, the route, atmosphere, and inescapable pain are all common knowledge. One lap, gun to tape, out of the blocks quick and attack the first bend. Maintain the pace down the back straight and foot off the pedal. Find a rhythm to build on at the 200 meter mark. The finish line will come into view. Pain is everywhere. Lactic acid is building. Keep a strong head and grit your teeth. Your mind lifts your arms and your arms lift your legs. I'm about to run farther than I ever have before—in Oregon, the other side of the world.

It's almost 9 p.m. The runner before me will be arriving in about seven minutes. I hurry out of the van. My headlamp is fitted, race number pinned, and reflective vest jostled on. There I am, shaking out my legs and skipping in anticipation, all as my heart is pounding. I'm waiting for our team number to be called out, and for Lucas to swoop in and pass the race over to me.

I canter off into the dark, into the unknown but not the impossible. My route is straight, flat, and quiet. It is almost five miles along an off-road cycle path. The team will be there at the end, but until then I'll be alone.

The light from my headlamp puts me in a bubble. Unable to see past its farthest beam I steadily float through the first 5K with soft and even strides. The sky is clear, the air crisp but comfortable, a slight breeze sways the reeds down each side of the path, and the moon provides eerie but brilliant shadows.

After passing under a motorway bridge, a similarly lone volunteer welcomes me back into the open. "One mile to go," he cheers encouragingly. I have one mile, about 1,600 meters or four laps of the track. I begin to pick up my pace, raising my knees and putting some power into the swing of my arms. Only four laps. I can hear my breath now, realizing that for the last 35 or so minutes my breathing had been easy. I guess I was scared to put myself under too much strain this early on, still unsure how to pace or execute running "long." It's time to pick it up.

A runner who had eased past me earlier comes back into view, the red lights on their reflective jacket bobbing up and down 100 or so meters away. I settle into a quicker rhythm and feel my lungs tighten but fight to maintain the movement and fast running. I catch and pass the runner, no longer a distant target, and put my sights on the next runner only 10 meters ahead.

My teammate Ciaran is waving and shouting on the side of the path up ahead, "Tilly, let's go!" There are people milling about, waiting for their own teammates to finish. The exchange must be close. The rest of the team and Milo can't be too far away. I change up a gear again, whizzing past another runner, screaming as I go. I'm running with momentum and with adrenaline rushing through me.

Here they are. There are claps, cheers, bells, and whistles—a blur of noise erupting out of the darkness. I'm unable to see clearly, and dark moving shadows line each edge of my lane. The team hadn't been expecting me for another 10 minutes or so. Milo is on the ground tying his laces. His last static moments cut short and rushed as I arrive early. There is a second of confusion, but then the baton is in his hand, whisked away, ready to accompany him on his own adventure.

As I am doubled over, heaving to get my breath back under control, it's not only my teammates who are there to catch me. My mum is there too, my greatest friend and support. It's amazing to be able to share a moment like this with her.

I take a second to soak up the reality of an incredible group of individuals gathered around me. What a privilege to be among them. There are hugs and cheers, and excited babbling chat from me until we are back in the van.

Exchange 12 reunites both vans. The team pulls together under the Hawthorne Bridge. Speakers boom as people dance and celebrate their runner coming into view, closing the first stage of the race.

The night legs are now fully underway. Despite the harsh conditions of the dark, cold night and tired bodies, the runners are finding their strides. Perhaps becoming familiar with the atmosphere and settling into the right headspace, unfazed by the mishap of having to hop out of the van early due to the congestion of vehicles that had built up on the road.

Ciaran joins me for the 500 meters of mistakenly added distance up to the checkpoint. He directs the drills, shaking out the shivers that come with each pool of cold wind and puff of cloudy breath. We do fast feet, skips, bounds, and leaps up the center of the road, cheering the passing runners and hoping Lucas is far enough behind not to beat us to the exchange.

Shocked by the sharp evening air, the lack of sleep beginning to settle in, and visited by the inescapable fear I feel when approaching a long continuous run, I accept the importance of braving it alone. Company would provide me with a reason to announce aches and pains, vocalize the doubt and worry that fill my head. It's something I do not want to listen to.

Lucas appears out of the darkness, right on time and sends me on my way again. I venture away from my teammates with four and a quarter miles to run and Ciaran's last advice ticking over in my head. Ditch the fear of burning out. A steady pace throughout might ensure an exhilarating sprint finish, but give more from the start. Be brave, do not hold off, commit and believe all the way through. This is a long run, not a warm-up followed by a 400 meter sprint. I listen and what follows are the most thrilling 40 minutes of my life.

Chants are on repeat in and out of my head. Unlike my first leg, I can hear my breath in time with the swing and kick of my legs. I'm in control and keeping my body compact, aware of my technique. Core tight and eyes straight ahead, with the occasional glance to my surroundings, a green, rolling hillside to the right and a silky black river to the left.

While preparing for the race, I had kept thoughts of what pace I would attempt to a minimum. I had deemed the idea of overtaking people unrealistic. If I were to be somebody else's road kill, I wouldn't be disheartened. I knew my background and presumed I knew my limits. My ideal was to run all three legs without the worry of pace or time, passing over to my teammate and never slowing to a walk was the goal. That would have been enough for me to come away, head happy.

But as I continue along the winding road, twisting and turning through soft ups and downs, the dark sky and stars above begin to lighten and I find a new kind of energy. The burn in my lungs transforms into a recurring comfort, and the aches that were building in my legs are crushed and irrelevant. I'm helped along thinking about cyclist Jens Voigt's catchphrase, "Shut up, legs."

The miles are ticking down on my watch faster than ever. Every time I am notified by the buzz on my wrist I'm surprised at how quickly they're passing. With about one mile to go, I catch up with the backed-up vans crawling up to the next exchange, to my finish line. I dance down the middle of the road, hoping their passengers will catch on to my excitement. Windows are wound down and music turned up, jokes and shouts push me faster along the road and soon I am running flat out. Here was my sprint to the finish, very much connected to the long run I had just done.

A final turn before the exchange is visible up ahead. I charge into Milo and watch on as he powers off into the new day to bring the second of our rounds to an end at 7 a.m.

I steer off to the right, pacing up and down on the side of the road. Shaking every part of my body and trying to calm my heaving breath. I start to laugh as the movement continues to pulse through my body. Ciaran appears while I stutter and shake. Tears are brewing as I try to vocalize the feeling. It's just disconnected words interrupted by sharp breaths as I'm struggling to understand it myself. I jump around on the spot, back and forth, unable to stand or be still. It dawns on me how much I had been longing for that run.

Connected and in control of my body and mind. I had endured every step and heavy breath. I did not bow down to pain or doubt. I felt like a runner.

Up until that point, throughout the six weeks of training "long," I had felt lost. I missed the track and the highs that came with it. I felt as if I was training for something that did not and could not belong to me. I was an outsider waiting to be invited in.

The next exchange will set the team off on their individual and collective final battles. This is the finishing stretch—the home straight. Hugs and hype erupt as the whole team is updating each other on the past few hours that had been spent apart, although still very much together. The previous runner is welcomed back as the next gets waved on their way.

Each time the other van takes over the effort, we attempt to relax, eat, and recover. We update our road kill tally. Slips of tiredness begin to surface, but we are still going hard. Fatigue is beginning to set in, no one having slept or eaten properly in over 24 hours.

I've run farther than ever before—twice in the space of eight hours. I'm nauseated, and with that comes worry and doubt about being able to complete my final run. I'm dehydrated, hungry, tired, and agitated, and frustrated about all these facts. My second-leg high is a long way gone. I had hoped my last leg might top it.

The sheltered mountain road is left behind, leaving no escape from the scorching sun and heat of the day. Slow sips of water, deep breathes, and shuteye, along with reassurances from my teammates, begins to bring me around. We pull off the road, anticipating Sorrel and Eugen's passing, ready to give them one last show. I take the time to stretch, shake off the anxiety and tiredness that is weighing me down. Pep talks from the team, along with high-calorie energy drinks and run-throughs in my head make me certain and more determined than ever to complete my third leg. The speed and energy shown by my fellow teammates each time we passed provides me with a last touch of inspiration. At the next exchange I'm ready to give one last fight.

The first 150 meters of my last leg is a sharp climb. It's a cruel start to the finish for me. I try to remain unaffected, supporting those who are taking it slower, as well as those who are already powering away up ahead. The next 60 minutes or so is going to be one of the greatest tests of body and mind in my life. I figure it might be better to share it.

I pull up alongside another crazy person fighting her own battle. We introduce ourselves and are soon making friendly conversation, anything to distract us from the harsh reality of running on an open road in the midday heat. My legs and chest are burning, aching unimaginably from fatigue. There are shots of pain flickering through my every step. I learn this is her 10th consecutive year running the race, an impressive feat for anybody, let alone somebody in her mid-60s. Despite the pain she must have experienced in her many attempts at this race, she is yet to be put off, returning each year to grasp the practice all over again.

Another hill is coming up but the reward is in full view. My team is parked up ahead, and their shrieks lift my mind and legs as I approach. I'm drenched in cold water and now speed on by with fantastic energy. I push on. I have to leave my new friend walking behind. As I promised myself, I was not here to walk. I was here to run.

The road straightens out and in the not so far distance I can see another familiar runner. I had been one of his road kills on that first hill. I take him on and decide we should get this thing finished together. Spurring each other on, in rhythm we begin to tick off the kilometers.

It is difficult to be strangers in this sport. No matter what corner of the earth you come from, what level you compete at, or reason you get out each day to run, it's impossible not to make a friend or two along the way. We come up to the finish line together, finding our expectant friends at the end. Ciaran takes the baton and speeds away as relief floods over me. Sorrel accompanies me back to the van, ready with energy drinks and snacks, thoughtful and lovely human that she is.

Before we clambered back into the van for the last drive of the race, both of my running partners approached to offer congratulations. All of us are grateful not to have had to run alone.

My head begins to clear from the angst of another long run. The windows in the van are rolled down. I breathe, smile, and realize that the distance came, hurdles were leaped, and demons were crushed.

Steve Bence made his initial appearance in Hood To Coast in 1985 and since then he has participated in the event 28 times, split evenly between running and walking teams. In 1977 he began working at Nike and still works for the company today, while also serving as the unofficial historian for Nike's involvement in HTC.

I know there are tens of thousands of individual stories about the race, but there is something overarching that brings everyone together. That something has allowed the relay to grow so much since 1982 that now there is even a limit on the number of teams allowed to participate.

I think the key to the race is more than the funny team names or unusual team costumes that make the event fun. Or even the couples getting married on the beach near the finish line. I remember reading a newspaper article about the relay years ago that didn't really do the event justice. As I read the story, I envisioned some poor reporter being sent to the finish to write an article about the relay. The reporter probably drove to Seaside, parked, wandered around the beach, talked to a few runners, and then wrote a story about what they saw—tired runners, people limping, funny team names, interesting uniforms, and runners eating and drinking. Nothing was written about the *journey* to the beach.

Not only is the trek from Mt. Hood to the coast a huge part of the story, but the event is a story about the state of Oregon and distance running. I believe the birth and growth of Hood To Coast could not have happened anywhere else in the United States. It's not an accident that race founder Bob Foote was a runner at the University of Oregon. And the course goes right through Portland, which now could be considered the center for the sports product industry in the U.S.

Although Oregon has a relatively small population, the state has produced a disproportionate number of Olympic distance runners. In 2016 University of Oregon miler Matt Centrowitz won the first Olympic gold medal for the U.S. in the 1,500 meters in over 100 years. And he was just following in the footsteps of his father, who was a two-time Olympian also from the University of Oregon. Further back, at the 1972 Olympics, the U.S. narrowly missed medals in both the marathon and 5,000 meters when University of Oregon runners Kenny Moore and Steve Prefontaine finished fourth in their respective events. Their coaches, Bill Bowerman and Bill Dellinger, were also from the University of Oregon.

When Oregon does well, the U.S. does well in distance running. Oregon is a geographically diverse state known for its beauty as well as for running. HTC combines those elements into an authentic, difficult, competitive, athletic event. The opportunity to participate in the relay is a goal for many, just like competing in a big marathon in Boston or New York. It isn't a low-key local road race—it's a scenic, 200-mile journey.

In that context, the success of the race makes sense.

Alan Hrabal *is from Beaverton, Oregon, and has run Hood To Coast more than 16 times.*

In 1998 I ran the relay for the first time. I remember the race did not fill up on the first day of registration and there wasn't a lottery for team entries. Since then, the course route has changed periodically, and I believe most of those changes have been for the better. More recently social media has become a positive way to keep runners more aware of what's happening during the race as well as provide updates on any course changes.

Since my inaugural Hood To Coast I have run every leg of the entire race. These are the memories that have stood out over the years from having run the entire course.

Runner 1 (2004): Hitting the wall and bonking on mile two of Leg 13, along the waterfront in Portland. It felt like I had cement blocks for shoes, but I finished.

Runner 2 (2010): Getting the news of my uncle Randy's passing. My first leg was dedicated to him and my pace was under seven minutes a mile.

Runner 3 (2014): I remember seeing a team called Undertrained & Over Motivated. I should have been on that team because it totally described my training program. My favorite run was Leg 15 on Highway 30 along the Willamette River.

Runner 4 (2013 and 2016): In 2013, I ran with my friend Julie and Team Rev Up . . . but Never Nude! I had a great time. I enjoyed Leg 4, which was more than seven miles long. Its nickname, "4th and Long," says it all.

Runner 5 (2007): Oh my word! It was absolutely the hardest leg of them all. However, the toilet paper salute I received at the summit, halfway through Leg 29, was a highlight. It gave me the motivation to finish strong.

Runner 6 (2003): In my opinion, Leg 30 may be the most underrated for degree of difficulty. It was mostly downhill and scenic. I even saved a life! A rock rolled down the hillside and a van swerved to avoid it and almost drove into the path of some runners. I grabbed the girl running next to me and moved her out of the way to keep her from getting hit. Thank goodness there were no injuries, except for a disabled van.

Runner 7 (2005): Puke Hill! Leg 19 from the Columbia County Fairgrounds presented a challenge. In the race handbook it's described as having "gently rolling hills." Who are they kidding?

Runner 8 (1998): Leg 20 and the infamous hill on Pittsburgh Road. It helped to be new to the race and not know what I was getting into my first year. However, I conquered and tamed the hill, which was close to six miles and rated very hard.

Runner 9 (2012 and 2017): Leg 21 and the ditch! I hope it never gets anyone else. *Ouch*! In 2012 I ran off the road and fell into a ditch in utter darkness. I somehow managed to collect myself and finish the leg. Unfortunately, I wasn't able to run my last leg that year. We had to juggle runners and I became the van driver for the rest of the race. But I had my revenge in 2017, although little did I know the exchange point for the leg would change. I ended up with a couple extra miles on that leg, making the entire leg over eight miles of running through gravel and dust. And I still had my final leg to go with another seven-plus miles. However, having my daughter Emilie run with me that year made it all better and allowed me to forge another milestone.

Runner 10 (2006 and 2015): I was struggling in 2006 on Leg 34 when I wound up running with a woman I knew from high school. In 2015 I ran through rain and wind, and there was complete devastation on the beach at the finish line. Who would have thought there would be a tropical storm on the Oregon coast in August?

Runner 11 (2009): Oh yes, Leg 35, the Lewis and Clark Mainline, with more than seven miles of uphill and gravel—and no van support. It was just a little unnerving, especially with bear poop on the trail. This leg is rated *hard* for a reason!

Runner 12 (2000 and 2002): I really don't know why I opted to run this one twice, let alone in back-to-back events. The only explanation is the indescribable feeling of excitement as you crest the hill behind Seaside and smell the salt air before you even see the Pacific Ocean. Once that salt sea air hits, you know the finish line is within reach and your team has almost completed the journey!

Jason Humble lives in Sherwood, Oregon, and works in footwear development at Nike. He was a member of the track team at the University of Oregon and first ran Hood To Coast in 1986.

More than anything, it's the team that keeps me coming back.

Early on it was all about the race, wanting to run fast, and trying to do well. It was all about challenging myself. I ran with the Killer Bees one year and some really good corporate teams, but I've mostly run with the Dirty Half Dozen +6.

Now it's all about the guys in the Dirty Half Dozen, and getting the chance to spend a weekend with guys I enjoy spending time with and catching up.

A couple of years ago we had 10 of the originals in the race. We talk about it every year and it amazes the hell out of us that we still get together. We've managed to stay together through the years, despite having guys go to war, go through divorces, and work through other family issues. I lived overseas for eight years and was able to run Hood To Coast in six of those years. I'd just plan to be home that weekend and take home leave or vacation so I could run the race.

The first year I did the relay, 1986, I had just finished my freshman year at Cleveland High School in Portland. A bunch of kids, some who would later become my teammates at Oregon, asked me to do it. I was like, "Sure. It sounds great. What the hell." The camaraderie was special and to this day I'm still really good friends with many of the guys who were on that team. We still hang out together and enjoy each other's friendship.

That first year we weren't even old enough to drive, so our parents did the driving. We had one van with Runners 1, 3, 5, 7, 9 and 11. The even legs were in the other van. The two vans would leapfrog each other at every leg, swapping out runners.

At the time, there were a few hundred teams in the race. There was nobody at the exchanges. No volunteers. The race logo was painted on the ground at the exchange points and there might have been a sign too. In the dark, the driver and all the kids were leaning out the windows looking for the exchange marker. If you drove past it the runner would have to go that much farther.

There were no major exchanges back then and no sleeping areas. You were rolling the whole time. We kids got some sleep, but our drivers didn't, because they were going the entire way to the coast. It was a constant flow and we'd be with our team the entire way. I loved that. You didn't have to separate the vans like today. Those were really good times.

The first few years, getting up the morning after the race you were sore as hell. You'd have a hard time getting out of bed and you'd have to walk backwards down the stairs. My junior year in high school I decided to train hard all summer. I was in really good shape and got up the morning after and wasn't sore at all. It was like, "Wow, this is amazing!"

The next year, heading into our senior year of high school, I got everyone training. We were all really fit and we were all strong. We ran the race and got up the next morning and were ready to go for a run. We all felt so good. We finished second both years in the state high school cross country championships.

Nowadays, if you want to be a team that's shooting for a good time, you've got to be on it logistically. You have to understand how to navigate the race itself. It has become as much about logistics and navigation as about running. Obviously, we're getting older and aren't as fast, but we know where the bad points can be during the race and get a feel for it pretty quickly. If we have to start hitchhiking or jump out with the clipboard, we're ready for it. We've got the hitching thing down to a science.

When I was a little bit younger, a little fitter, and a little bit brasher, I always liked to do something crazy during the race. I'd cut my hair in a Mohawk or bleach my hair out, something like that.

One year I got a Russian unitard that their sprinters would wear and wore it my last leg. I got a lot of cheers from the porta potty guys when they drove by. They were honking their horns and cheering and waving. It turns out they were all Russians.

I was in Van 1 that year and we finished up near the town of Olney, just before Astoria. There's a little local bar there and, because hunting season usually opened that same weekend, it was full of hunters. We go in there and all I have on is my Russian unitard. The guy behind the bar looks at me and pretty much says, "We don't serve your kind here." Everybody on the team told me to go change my clothes. They were afraid we were going to get beat up. I went out and put on some regular clothes and a hat. I came back into the bar incognito, and everybody was talking about the idiot in the unitard.

It used to be I was raring to go when we got to the beach. Go, go, go. Now I'm always *planning* to go back down to the beer garden. I usually head to the house for a shower and something to eat and inevitably I pass out on the couch, and that's pretty much where I remain.

One time I flew back from Korea to run HTC. So I was jetlagged on top of being tired from running the race and having a couple of beers along the way, and I passed out on the couch. There's a video of my teammates trying to wake me up by banging two pots over my head. I was so exhausted I never even flinched. I remembered eating some pizza and then it was eight o'clock the next morning.

My goal is to run 100 legs. When that happens, I'm thinking of announcing my retirement on the beach. It's not that anyone would care, but it would be fun.

Jake Bittner lives in Leesburg, Virginia, and participated in his first Hood To Coast in 2017.

It was early in the morning and it was the last leg of Hood To Coast for our van. One of my teammates in Van 1, Kevin, had Leg 29, and then it would be my turn to run. We stopped at the top of the hill for Kevin to break through some toilet paper that we held across his path, and then hopped back in the van to drive to the exchange.

While every exchange seemed to be backed up with some traffic, this one was particularly bad. As the runners streamed past us, we would move a few hundred yards and then sit for quite a while, slowly making our way to the exchange. At one point, the traffic got so bad I decided to walk to the exchange. I probably had about 15 minutes to make it, and maybe a mile to go. At a quick pace I would easily make it to the exchange.

A few minutes later our van caught up to me and I hopped back in, figuring there was plenty of time to get to the exchange. As I was making my final mental preparations, and we were about three quarters of a mile from the exchange, Kevin went sprinting past us.

Our driver yelled out the window to Kevin, letting him know that we'd been stuck in traffic and that I would meet him at the exchange. Instinctively, I jumped out of the van and took off full speed down the hill after Kevin.

I ended up starting my last leg about three quarters of a mile before the exchange— in a full downhill sprint trying to catch the fastest member of our team. Not exactly the best way to warm up my sore and tired legs, but at that moment I had to do it for the team. I had a surge of energy and met him about 30 seconds after he arrived at the exchange. Kevin was surprised to see me so soon, but he passed along the bracelet and I went on my way.

I figured that surge of energy before the actual start of my leg would end up killing the rest of my run. But it didn't and I ended up having my best run of the race on that last leg. I even managed to keep up the pace I had when chasing Kevin down the hill.

Paul Raab *is from Portland and began running Hood To Coast in 1984. After his first year running the relay, he began working as a volunteer with the HTC organization, a role he still holds today. Although he is retired from a long career in medical administration, he still works as a referee at high school football games.*

It was interesting how I first heard about Hood To Coast. Bob Foote had a doctor at the time who was a physician at Portland's Good Samaritan Hospital, which is where I worked as an administrator. The hospital heard about the race from Bob and put together a team. I was running quite a bit at the time and two doctors asked me to join the Legacy Good Samaritan team.

We would get support from the hospital and wear shirts that promoted their healthcare system. They would help us with the entry fee. There were enough people on the team who had vans, so that was never a problem. We were pretty competitive and probably more on the serious side than most teams.

I didn't know how hard it would be because up until that time I'd only done a few 10Ks and one half-marathon. Running about three 10Ks in around 24 hours was certainly something brand new.

When I first started participating in the race the key for me was to know what legs I'd be running, so I wouldn't get lost. Once we got our start time, I would figure out approximately what time I'd be starting my legs. Then around three or four weeks before the event I'd go out and run one of my legs—at the exact time I thought I'd be running during the race. If my first leg was off Highway 26 on some local roads at about 2 a.m., a few weeks before the race I'd go out at 2 a.m. and run that leg. Then I'd do the same thing for my other two legs.

I always wanted to mimic what it would be like during the race because I wanted to know exactly where I was going. While it may have been unique, it certainly made it easier during the race, because even if it was the middle of the night I knew exactly where I was going. Back then the exchanges weren't like they like are now, they were marked by just some paint on the side of the road. If there was a volunteer providing directions—that was great. But if there wasn't, you had to know where the race emblem was painted on the side of the road.

The memory that sticks with me the most when the finish was in Pacific City is running up Bald Peak. When every leg was exactly five miles, Bald Peak was a steep, uphill leg that started 100 yards or so up the hill. You didn't get a good running start on a flat surface because the leg started on an incline. It was like a mile or a mile-and-a-half climb all the way up to the top of the mountain. It was just brutal, especially if you ran it in the heat of the day. After you reached the top, there would then be a downhill for another mile and a half that was almost as steep as the run down the mountain at the start.

I also remember one of my legs—my third leg along the Nestucca River—on the way to Pacific City. The river was on one side of the racecourse and there was kind of the side of a cliff on the other side. It was the middle of the afternoon and the temperature was near 100 degrees. I literally thought I was going to pass out. I hardly even remember the last half-mile or so of the run and the exchange. I just kept going straight, hoping to make it to the end. As soon as I was done my teammates took me down to the river and let me sit in the water to cool down.

In the early days we'd run holding flashlights. There were no requirements for headlamps or reflective vests or flashing lights. It was before timing chips in the shoes and the wrist wraps. We would run with a baton you handed off to your teammate. Running with a baton in one hand and a flashlight in the other wasn't easy, which is another reason I'd practice my legs.

As we got toward the coast and the finish, it got darker and darker. I remember finishing in the dark and nobody was around. The finish line was set up, but everybody was gone and there wasn't even any beer left!

Bill Schauber *is from Kenwood, California, and ran Hood To Coast from 1997 to 2013 as a member of the team I Hurt, You Hurt, We all Hurt.*

My first race was in 1997. I had met the team captain, Steve Hanamura, at a diversity workshop he was conducting for my company's senior management team. During the first break he asked me if I was a runner. When I answered, "Yes," Steve knew he had set the hook.

"Maybe not this year," Steve said, "But next year I'll give you a call to join our Hood To Coast team." Who in the world remembers to call? Eight months later, however, I get a call and Steve asked me to be on the team.

I was in good shape and regularly competed in road races. I was proud my finishes were consistently in the top of my age group. I trained on hills, and that was enough for Steve to make me Runner 9. My second leg included a gravel road along a logging trail off the beaten path. The team vans would kick up clouds of dust when they would pass and pull over to look for their runner. Then they would pass you again and there would be more dust. I thought a coal miner worked in a safer environment than where we were running.

When the leg ended, you felt like you accomplished something special. My eyes were a bit crusty and my nasal passages dried up from the fine dust, but it confirmed I was a competitor.

HTC is really an exercise in logistics. The van driver is a key team member. The driver is your mother, your father, and anyone else who might be important to you. The driver's decisions can make or break the entire running experience. Not only does the driver have to know where you can shower, eat, and get gas, it's critical that they also know how to get to the exchanges in time to drop off and collect runners.

You may be in the best shape of your life, but the relay can swallow you up if your teammates don't understand all the logistics of the course, or can't handle being in a van for 24 or 28 hours with wet socks, nasty running shorts, and underarms where you know the deodorant didn't meet the advertiser's promise.

During HTC you learn a lot about yourself. Running is a personal endeavor, but when you're one of 12, it requires you to draw on skills you weren't sure you had and discover what it means to belong to a team.

Merritt Richardson graduated from Oregon State University and worked as an auditor at an accounting firm before taking a job at Nike in 1989. After working at Nike for 28 years she recently retired. She has participated in Hood To Coast and Portland To Coast as a volunteer, a runner, and a walker.

I've always been a huge sports fan, particularly football and golf. But I've admired runners ever since I was a little kid. My dad used to run, and we would go to races to watch him compete. I was always inspired by that, even though I didn't like getting out there and running myself. When I moved to Nike I was around running all the time and people who were hardcore runners—and it was fun and inspiring.

I first heard about Hood To Coast through Nike. I can't remember the exact year, but it was probably in the early 1990s. Alberto Salazar put together a team of world-class runners to compete against the guys at adidas who also put an elite team together. There was this burning rivalry happening with elite runners in this crazy relay race that we were all hearing about. When I heard about Alberto having a team, I wanted to get involved. Through Nike you could get on a team or volunteer. Since I wasn't a runner, I thought, "I want to see what this is like up close and personal." I decided to volunteer and said, "I want to see the craziest things. Put me on a middle-of-the-night shift in the middle of nowhere." That's how it started.

I asked to be on a shift at night because I thought it would be crazy and fun. My shift was from midnight to 4 a.m., or something like that. I remember needing to drive about an hour, maybe a little more, west from Portland. It was in the woods, near logging roads and farms and stuff like that. For a while there would be nothing happening and then all of a sudden there would be these waves of runners coming through. It was dark and there weren't many lights, and there were people everywhere trying to figure out where to go, and I was guiding them into the right spot.

I have this one vivid memory of seeing a runner come in. She was yelling for her teammate to make the handoff. Her teammate wasn't there yet, so she was standing there in the middle of the night, in the freezing cold, just waiting for her team to arrive. I can't remember all the details exactly, but it was several minutes before her team showed up. As volunteers, we were wondering, "What do we do about this?" I found that really interesting and remember thinking, "Wow, this is a really complicated logistics exercise for these teams to figure out how to be in the right place at the right time while driving down dark, winding country roads and all of a sudden coming upon big crowds and having to sort their way through to find their teammate in the right spot." I thought it was just amazing.

I was a volunteer for a couple years and was amped up about the whole thing. At Nike there was a tremendous amount of enthusiasm around the relay, especially with so many of us participating on teams. I realized I needed to get in on the action.

I had a couple friends at Nike who were on teams. I also had a workout partner who I'd go to the gym with. We both had been contemplating running and we decided to join a team and start training. I was like, "I can figure out how to run." It wasn't my normal thing and I wasn't a runner, but I was going to force myself to be part of the relay. We started training—and I kept getting slower and slower. In late April or early May I realized I was getting tired for a reason—I had a baby on the way. Since I wouldn't be able to run when I was six or seven months pregnant, I just supported my team and encouraged them.

After my son was born I needed a goal. I felt like walking would be a better option than running, so I joined a Nike Portland To Coast team in 1996. It gave me a reason to work out and to be part of the relay after I had missed my opportunity the year before.

The first two years I was on a walking team we had 12 people, which meant walking two legs maybe 10 or 12 hours apart and you're done. After my second year, I vividly remember sitting on the curb outside some restaurant in Seaside with a friend saying, "This is okay, but we need to make it more exciting. What if we put together a competitive walking team for next year? We'll only have eight people on the team and we'll try to be fast."

It was kind of cool to go from a casual, leisurely team to a more competitive team. We said, "Let's kick it up. Let's be serious." We named our team the Women in Black. We took our name from the movie *Men in Black*. We also decided to wear head-to-toe black outfits because we wanted to be easily noticed by our teammates when we were out on the course. For our team logo we played off of the movie, too, and at the starting line we loudly played music from the movie.

After the start of the year we began recruiting walkers for our team. We had a couple people from the casual team who were willing to be more serious, and then we just recruited some friends who we knew were walkers or exercised regularly. We packaged up a Nike team of people willing to be serious about it. Probably around April we started meeting with a walking coach a couple of times a week. And we were sort of the silly looking women training out on the fields at the Nike campus. We were doing some sprinting exercises, and I'm sure people were looking at us like, "What in the world are they doing?"

The team we put together ended up being really successful beginning in 1996 and over the next four or five years. We got really into the training and planning. We had a coach and we designed a plan specifically for the vans and all the walkers. We couldn't follow the regular exchange plan for the vans, so we had to have a backup plan. It was very complicated, but our team loved the fact I was obsessed about our vans, including where we needed to be and who needed to be in the vans at what time.

One memory that really stands out is walking the leg where you go from total darkness to the breaking of dawn. You're out on these country roads. The mist of the coast is coming up over the farms and it's just the most amazing thing.

I was on that team for nine years before I decided to retire, but every year I was always overwhelmed by the sheer bigness of the whole event.

Jim Peterson *is a dedicated runner and high school distance-running coach from Richland, Washington. He ran his first Hood To Coast in 1984.*

I have run Hood To Coast more than 30 times on several different teams, and I have run races varying in distance from 100 meters to the marathon. HTC is the toughest and most fun of all!

Back in the 1990s I was running on the Farm-Area Racing Team. I was waiting at the exchange for my runner to come in and hand off for my third leg. Waiting with me was Alberto Salazar. It was clear that my guy would get in several minutes ahead of Alberto's Nike guy. My teammates pointed at Alberto and admonished me that I *must* hold him off. About a mile into my leg, here came Alberto. Yes, I did hold him off for at least three strides! His team set the course record, my team finished . . .

In 2008 my present team, the Fabulous Fifties, won the Men's Supermasters class. The previous year, I had been on a team that came in fifth in the Men's Masters division. However, after that fifth place finish the team decided to bump me off the roster.

A week after the 2008 race was a small local race, and for some reason I had brought my first-place plaque from HTC. I saw the captain who had bumped me from his team. I came up to him with my plaque in hand and in a loud voice said, "Hey, XXX, see this. This is what you get when you win your division. I have one and you DON'T!"

In 2017 the Fabulous Fifties won the Men's Champion Masters division. In second place were the Dead Jocks in a Box. That year was the first time we had ever beaten the Dead Jocks. At the awards ceremony both teams exchanged handshakes and congratulations. This was the same as it had been every other year, demonstrating the mutual respect and sportsmanship that is the true spirit of the relay.

Karolynh Tran *is originally from Los Angeles and now calls Beaverton, Oregon, home. She is a self-proclaimed "educator by day, baker by night, and runner through all seasons."*

Instead of getting ready for work, I was suiting up for the 2016 Hood To Coast, the relay of my life, and I couldn't stop smiling. At the same time, I was nervous out of my mind! I wanted to run some of the more difficult legs because I consider myself "tiny but powerful."

Even though I was nervous, I was ready for anything—or so I thought! For my first leg I had never run in such heat. I consumed more than enough water but was still on the brink of passing out and calling it a day. It probably looked like I was running drunk. And I also had to dance around several baby snakes as well. Luckily, my teammates were supportive hustlers. They asked how I was doing and were already hopping into the van within a minute of my response. Just the way I like to get stuff done!

My second leg was my absolute favorite because it was the most insane run I'd ever done. I had to use my "seventh sense"—although I'm not sure exactly what that is—during a run in complete darkness while inhaling and exhaling crazy amounts of gravel. It had me wondering whether I was going to either accidentally run myself off a cliff or end up with smoker's lungs. It was also my fastest run because when you're alone with not the brightest headlamp and you hear rattling in the bushes; what the heck would you do? Momma didn't raise no fool!

When I woke up from a nap between my second and third legs I was irritated because of my sore muscles and the wretched smell of funk in the van. I even said, "I'm never doing this again." However, once my grouchiness wore off, I was ready to conquer my final leg with everything I had left in the tank. It was my longest run, with plenty of rolling hills—just how I like it. I finished ahead of schedule by about 10 minutes.

Would I run the relay again? After finishing, I hounded the team captain with questions about the race the following year—so that should absolutely say something.

Nikki Neuburger is a Portland native and attended Oregon State University, where she walked on to the women's volleyball team and became team captain. After graduating in 2004, she joined Nike and was a longtime marketing executive at the company until early 2018, when she became the Global Head of Marketing at Uber Eats in San Francisco. She is a regular Hood To Coast participant.

I was actually born and raised in Portland, so I've been familiar with Hood To Coast for a very long time. The first race was held the year after I was born. My parents used to run it, and I can vividly remember the evening every summer when we would stay up all night because people were in our house getting ready for their next leg. Growing up, the race was a part of my life.

I played volleyball at Oregon State. Running was never really my sport, but as an athlete I was always around running and runners. In other sports, running is considered punishment. I didn't personally get involved with running until I got to Nike.

Then it became a way to stay physically fit and active. It also became a way to be social and do things with my co-workers because, as you can imagine, a lot of people at Nike run.

Very early on during my time at Nike I was asked to join a relay team. Since then I've run it 12 times. My partner, David, who also worked at Nike, has run it 13 times and has successfully checked the box on running every single leg. On the other hand, I serve as team captain just so I can assign myself the legs I want.

I had the great fortune—and this was one of the perks of working at a place like Nike—to be surrounded by a lot of really athletic people who participated in the race and were really great at lots of things. It's one of the reasons I got serious about running— which people I played volleyball with can't believe and think is laughable—there was such a culture of looking up. There was always a person right above you who had been doing it longer, or was a little bit faster, or had run a little farther, to help show you the ropes.

It was great to be able to train with a group of women who are my friends, who are all faster than me, and who have been running longer. It enabled me to see my own progress, and when you're participating and training with other people you rise to the occasion. You get better because you push yourself a little bit harder when you're trying to keep up with others, rather than when you're just trying to beat yourself.

Over my years running in the race I've become really familiar with the event. It's one of those races with a lot of tradition and you pass along the knowledge and culture that surrounds the race to the newbies every year. You tell your new teammates about what to eat, what not to eat, when to sleep, and about Toilet Paper Hill. You tell them not to go out too hard on Leg 1, even though you're going to feel like a champion running down that hill.

In my opinion, being Runner 12 and having Leg 36 is the very best. There's nothing like being the runner to finish the race. You could probably say the same thing about Leg 1: there's nothing like starting the race. But I like the finish because it doesn't have the body-wrecking experience of running down the mountain. I think Leg 36 is definitely special and I always talk it up to the person who gets that leg.

I've never been Runner 5 because I'm not a person who enjoys hills, although the last leg for that runner, with Toilet Paper Hill, is a really cool one to watch. The toughest people take that on and tough it out on behalf of the team. Toilet Paper Hill is really just the last of three uphill runs and the one everybody talks about, but all three legs are pretty brutal. If you're someone who's a glutton for punishment, you can't really say you've run HTC until you've been Runner 5.

The race itself ends up feeling like a whirlwind. Your first leg is over quickly. Then you're tired and sleep-deprived, and you're not really sure what's happening the rest of the race. So some of my most awesome memories are of rallying the team at the pasta dinner the night before the start, handing out the bibs and our new uniforms, along with making sure everyone has everything they need. It's where we swap stories and freak out the newcomers about what's in store for them. It's always fun because everybody's adrenaline is going and everyone is eager to start the race. Then we always stay at the beach the night afterward and have a good time.

We have to be one of the most competitive teams never actually in contention to win. There aren't many teams that show up to the relay looking for the overall win, but there are plenty of teams that show up trying to beat their time from the previous year or a rival team they've raced against in the past. We're competitive with ourselves and always try to finish in less than 24 hours.

We run fast enough to feel competitive, but not so fast that we can't have a beer before our last leg. If somebody misses an exchange, we'll still be friends, and they'll still be invited back next year. They won't be excommunicated for a mistake, which might happen on some of the more competitive teams.

The joke on our team is that Hell on Waffles has the best time *and* the best time. We're not trying to run so fast that it becomes so intense and serious that nobody likes each other by the end.

Steve Hanamura *was born in Upland, California, and now lives in Portland. He has participated in Hood To Coast more than 25 times and served as captain of the team I Hurt, You Hurt, We All Hurt for more than 20 years. Blind since birth, he is an avid runner and sports fan.*

For my second Hood To Coast I was actually in California when the relay started and had some concerns about joining my teammates.

At the time, my consulting business was booming. Three out of every four weeks I was traveling. I married Becky on August 3, 1991, and was traveling most of that month. In fact, the week of the relay I was working in Sunnyvale, California. When my team took off to make the drive up to Timberline Lodge, I was at the airport in San Jose.

My team was scheduled to start running at 2:40 p.m., and my only hope to make the race was if my plane was on time. I was really nervous about the plane being on time. But once we were in the air, I knew it was going to be fine. Of course, in those days you didn't text, so Becky was keeping track of my flight by calling the airline.

After my plane landed in Portland, Becky picked me up and brought me home. I took a quick nap, had something to eat, and then Becky drove me out to meet the team at the start of Leg 12.

I was Runner 12 and made it to the exchange in plenty of time to meet my teammates and then run my first leg. It was memorable because the timing had to be incredible. We didn't really have a plan if I didn't make it, but I guess there would have been a few extra legs to go around!

Lillian Mongeau Hughes lives in Portland and is an education journalist. She first participated in Hood To Coast in 2008 as a last-minute substitute and returned in 2016 and 2017 to captain all-women fundraising teams.

The biggest physical challenge while running pregnant was finding bathrooms along the course!

As we neared the finish, when the porta potty lines were long, people started letting me cut in line. I felt weird about doing it, but if they offered I didn't turn it down. My ankles weren't so happy about all the extra weight I was carrying, and I had some round ligament pain (ligaments that anchor your uterus to your hips), but nothing too bad.

The other challenges were more mental. For example, I had to admit I needed a little tender loving care from my teammates—which they were very eager to offer. They let me sit in the front seat most of the time, and I only drove two legs. Usually I'm the one shuffling everyone along, and this year I took a backseat (well, actually a front seat) and let them handle things so that I could focus on resting between my legs. I also chose a fairly easy set of legs, which was hard when I made the choice because only a few months before I had finished a marathon. But I'm so glad I did, because 15 total miles turned out to be plenty.

The final challenge was letting go of my normal time goal. I know it sounds nuts to think you could run at your regular pace while 26 weeks pregnant, but for a longtime runner it's very hard to cede that point. I knew from my training that I couldn't hit 8:40s, which was my original time prediction. So I decided to just shoot for 10:30s, which seems vaguely respectable under the circumstances. Over the whole course I averaged 10:40s, which wasn't too bad. And I managed to feel pretty good about it when all was said and done.

Lisa McKillips *is the assistant to the chairman at Nike and has competed in Portland To Coast more than 20 times as part of the Nike T-Wrecks team.*

The camaraderie and competition are what Hood To Coast and Portland To Coast are all about. I've always said that if you're in the right van it's a wonderful experience, and, fortunately, I've always been in the right van. I think if you're in the wrong van, with the wrong people, there could be some 3 a.m. homicidal tendencies.

For the most part, the level of competition is huge. People really get into it. The first year we did it, somebody was talking about road kills. I thought, "Well, that's really kind of tacky. You mark on the side of your van everybody that you pass? That's kind of cruel." Now road kills are huge. You see somebody in your sights and you go for it. Another road kill!

That first year we didn't have a clue what we were doing. We even had one guy walking in golf shorts and sandals. We didn't have any place to stay. We had all of our gear for the entire weekend with us in the van. We didn't know that you weren't supposed to bring your substitute walker with you, so we had a driver, six walkers, and our sub in a Suburban for the entire race. It was crazy. All I asked was that I didn't walk in the dark.

Now we do a really good job. We rent some space in Mist. We have a whole set-up there with motor homes or tents. We have a place at Seaside, and our volunteers take all of our stuff there except what we need in the van. It's a lot more comfortable than that first year.

I had a dog come after me one year. That scared me to death. I happened to be walking in the dark and we were ahead of the pack. I had two and a half miles to go to the next exchange and my van asked if I was okay. I said, "Yeah, go ahead." So I was out there alone and I saw a dog on someone's porch. It was a big German shepherd. A light was on and I could see the dog come flying off the porch. In my mind I was sure the dog was on some sort of a chain. He kept coming and kept coming, and I kept thinking, "He's going to hit his chain any second now." But he didn't. He wasn't chained up. All I had was a stupid little flashlight. In the meanest voice I could come up with, I turned and looked at the dog and said, "*No!* You go home." I was scared to death, but the dog went away. I knew there were walkers behind me and as their team vans came by I told them about the dog, and said that they had to go back to warn their walkers.

We've had some scary things like that happen, but for the most part it's funny things. It's someone going to the bathroom in the middle of the night and not bringing a flashlight, and not realizing until it was too late that the porta potty was full. It's just part of the adventure. Every year you're out there thinking, "Okay, now why am I doing this again?" Yet as soon as it's over, you're planning for the next year.

When we walked in 2015, the year of the big storm, it was our 20th year and I walked the final leg for the very first time, although it was raining and the wind was blowing so hard I missed the finish line entirely. Afterward, a lot of my teammates were saying it should be our last year because it was our 20th time. But I said, "I'm not thinking this is the last year." I would like to do every leg on the course before I quit, and I'm still a ways away from that.

I've never done the first leg. I've never walked into the fairgrounds. I've done some of the harder ones. I actually like one of the longer legs around Youngs Bay. When the sun is coming up in the morning around the bay, it's just beautiful.

One of the great things about the event is that even people who somehow feel they got sucked into joining a family team or a company team or a whatever, they go from saying, "Oh, just get me through this," to, "Oh, that was great. I can't wait to do it next year." Sometimes it takes a week or two, but eventually it's, "I can't wait to do it again next year."

Steve Spear was born in Vermont and now lives near Chicago. After serving as a pastor for 20 years, he joined Team World Vision as the Endurance Director in 2013. He participated in his first Hood To Coast in 2014.

You never forget your middle-of-the-night run during Hood To Coast. There's something very special about the quietness of the night in a part of the country you're not necessarily all that familiar with. You're a little bit sleep-deprived, but there's something unique and magical about the middle-of-the-night run that always sticks out.

You also never forget your most difficult leg. In two of the years I've run, I've been Runner 5. I remember my first year I told the team, "Give me whatever legs you want me to take." They made me Runner 5 which has some tough runs, including the final leg. My last run was Leg 29, which is pretty much two and a half miles up a mountain, and then two and a half miles downhill. When you get to the apex of the run, you feel like you've conquered Mt. Everest because it's so challenging.

When I reached the apex my team was right there, along with plenty of other teams. My teammates strung out some toilet paper across the road at the top of the mountain for me to run through. It was pretty cool running that leg and having my team there for support.

Since then, every year I'm in Van 1 I've made sure we were at the top of the mountain with a roll of toilet paper on Leg 29 for our runner to have that climactic moment.

Katherine Woltz in 2017.

CHAPTER 19

Romance And The Relay

In Hood To Coast, the participants usually love running, love being part of a team, love competition and probably love Oregon. In some cases, they also find love along the way. Or more specifically, after 25 or 30 hours together in a van, they find each other. The finish line is not just the conclusion of the race, it can also mark the beginning of a relationship—with marriage proposals frequently occurring with one knee in the sand at Seaside.

Cal Conrad is a longtime runner from Tualatin, Oregon. He has completed five marathons and been involved in Hood To Coast for more than five years.

For the 2015 race our work-sponsored team, PGE Shock Treatment, lost several team members due to injuries just a few weeks prior to the race. We were in a serious pinch and needed someone to round out our team. I knew one of my co-workers, Stephanie, ran occasionally, and she was the first person I thought to ask to join our team. I just threw it out there not really expecting her to say yes.

I explained to Stephanie that it was a really enjoyable experience. I described how much fun the legs were, told her about the costumes some runners wore, mentioned the van decorations, and talked about the exchange points. Of course I also told her how proud we are when we finish. She was hesitant, but with a little convincing from me and a few other co-workers she finally agreed to join the team.

That year turned out to be one of the wettest and craziest races ever. She was Runner 11, and I was Runner 12. The last of our legs turned into a complete stormy downpour. She had about a seven-mile leg that I told her would be relatively flat and easy. Turns out it was anything but that—it was one of the hardest runs in relay history because of all the rain and wind, along with the distance.

At the final exchange, this seemingly nice and sweet girl swore loudly as she put the wristband on my arm and looked supremely pissed off that I had even suggested she run the race. Then right as I started my run toward the beach and the finish line, the rain stopped and I had a great final leg.

We ran together again in 2016 and 2017 in the same van like we did that first year. I love running relays with her!

We went on our first date in April of 2016, the day before I left for a two-week vacation in China. While on vacation, we talked everyday—whenever I could find Wi-Fi! Eventually we bought a house together, and in February of 2018 I proposed in Portland's Forest Park—where we went on our very first run together. She said yes and we're planning on spending the rest of our lives together.

I don't know if we would have ever gotten to this point in our relationship if we hadn't shared the very real experience of Hood To Coast together.

CC Schott *lives in Charlotte, North Carolina, with her husband, Mike, and their two children. She and Mike participated in Hood To Coast in 2014.*

I first heard about Hood To Coast from my friend Emily, who had seen the documentary at a film festival before its world premiere. After hearing Emily talk about the movie, I was willing to spend a couple hours in the theater watching people train for and then run this strange relay. So that's what Emily and I, along with some other friends, did! We walked out of the theater that night in 2011 committed to actually training and running the race *ourselves*, if given the opportunity.

By the time we had entered the lottery twice without luck (2012 and 2013), both Emily and I had gotten married. Then we found out in the third year of trying (2014) that our entry had been accepted—and now we were going to run HTC! Our husbands may, or may not, have heard about the race along the way. It was then that I posed the question to my husband, Mike: "How would you like to celebrate our first anniversary in the Pacific Northwest by running for about 30 hours across the state of Oregon?" The fact that there was a team in the movie that downed a beer after each leg may have actually won him over, and he agreed to do it.

Mike was the driver for Van 2 and I was Runner 12. One of my favorite memories from the race was watching him cheer on all our runners during each leg. And Mike had a special way of showing his support. He had a unique wig or hairpiece for each one of our six runners, and at some point along the way he would put it on, get out of the van, and run alongside each team member. What made it particularly amusing was that Mike is bald—thanks to his genes and a sharp razor—so the wigs made him look *so different*! At points along the relay his hair was blond, black, and brown, and at one point he even had an afro—not to mention outlandish sunglasses, colorful bandanas, and even a pair of pink bunny ears.

I appreciated Mike serving as our driver and not getting all the glory a runner does. I also loved the way he came out of nowhere and ended up beside us to provide support and encouragement, helping pull us through certain parts of our runs. His wigs were hilarious, and his energy and enthusiasm were just what we needed to add some pep to our step!

Looking back, I can definitely say that being a part of HTC was a wonderful way to round out our first year of marriage! It's actually also a great metaphor for marriage: there are long, dusty uphill stretches; nights with little sleep; hilarious adventures; plenty of waiting, Honey Bucket kind of days; laughter; tears; and lots of encouragement because you know you're in it together!

Katherine Woltz *is a physical therapist from Frederick, Maryland, who participated in her first Hood To Coast in 2017.*

I'll never forget the 2017 Hood To Coast weekend. We chose the event because of its amazing reputation. And after more than three years of trying to get into the race we were finally going to participate.

As an avid runner but one new to relays, I was looking forward to experiencing the camaraderie with my teammates. I was also looking forward to the challenge and mental toughness required to embark on my second and third legs.

It was mentally tough, breathtakingly scenic, and it ended in the absolute best way possible. After scrambling to find parking and the rest of our vanmates, we crossed the finish line as a team—The DC Frednecks. Seconds later, standing just feet beyond the finish line, my boyfriend, Chris, dropped to his knee and asked me to marry him. Even now I can't express how excited I was. I can hardly remember the moment because I was so shocked. There were tears, hugs, and lots of "HOLY %&$#'s!" It was memorable, to say the least, and I'm so happy our close running buddies were there to witness our special moment.

All of Chris's friends on our team knew about his plan. That's why it was crucial to get Van 2 parked so the whole team could cross the finish line together. He even had one member of our team briefly stall Runner 12 at the corner just before the finish to make sure everyone was at the beach to cross the finish line together and witness the proposal.

Thanks to our teammates, we have a ton of pictures and even have a video of the proposal. I'm really glad the whole team was in on the plan. However, I have *no idea* how they kept it quiet!

It was the happiest day of my life!

Rob Rickard *is from Canby, Oregon, and has participated in Hood To Coast every year since 1983. He has also been a course marker for the event for more than 25 years.*

Except for my first two years participating, I've run on a co-ed team every year. The second year I ran the relay it was on an all-male team, and the chemistry just wasn't there. Rather than a fun experience, it was more like watch your pace and run your guts out. If your pace was five seconds slower than what you predicted, they'd wag their finger in your face.

I always thought there was a calming effect with co-ed teams. In the late 1980s I recruited a lady out of Albany, Oregon, to join our team. She was new to our team. At the same time, I had a regular runner from the city of Sublimity, Oregon.

They were both divorced and single at the time. They met in the van and struck up a relationship. About six months later, the guy called me and he said, "Hey, is it going to upset the team if I propose to her and we get married and we still want to run?" I said, "Absolutely not. Go for it." Eventually they got married and they continued running on my team.

I was in the same van with both of them. Although it was obvious they were getting along and connecting, I'm not sure anyone expected a wedding so soon.

I also remember a story about a woman on our team who was very competitive and a great runner. Her husband also ran, but he wasn't quite as competitive, so he was never a member of my team. One year, I had a guy drop out shortly before the race. I called this woman and said, "I know that we don't typically include your husband on the team because of his pace, but right now we're short one runner and we need him to fill out the team. Is it okay if I contact him?"

And her response was, "Okay, with one provision." I said, "What's that?" She responded, "He's in the other van." She didn't want her husband in the same van to question how fast she was running. That was a funny experience.

Leslie Dewar *first participated in Hood To Coast in 2001 and has competed in the event more than 10 times. She is a mother, wife, runner, and probation officer from Portland.*

In 2001 the route conveniently ran through our street in the Eastmoreland neighborhood of Portland. That year my then boyfriend insisted that I be Runner 12 and do Legs 12, 24, and 36. During my first leg he and the team went by our house to grab a tuxedo he had rented. He and the rest of our sneaky team hid it in the van until I started the final leg to the finish line. Since he'd run Leg 35, he quickly jumped in the van and did a superman-style outfit change before meeting me at the finish line all dressed up.

When I crossed the censor and ran down the chute, the announcer called out, "Team 410"—and the beach erupted in applause. Apparently, he'd already announced to everyone what was in store for us prior to my arrival! I thought all the applause was fantastic since I'd never before run the anchor leg to the beach. But then I quickly realized what was happening.

My now husband got down on one knee and proposed in front of everyone. Of course I said, "Yes." I knew that if he could love me in all the glory that comes with participating in a 30-hour, 200-mile relay race at the end of August, he'd be the one to spend my life with forever.

Two kids and more than a decade and a half worth of life experiences later—life is so good!

Felicia Hubber *grew up in Portland, moved to Montana during high school, and attended college at the University of Montana. The daughter of Hood To Coast founder Bob Foote, Felicia was just a few months old when she attended the first HTC—and she's been at every relay since. In 2006 she succeeded her father as president of HTC.*

Every year, we hear about someone who is planning to propose during the relay, or we hear a story afterward about how a proposal happened during the race. I'm guessing that since I started working with Hood To Coast full-time in 2006 we've had at least one proposal during each event for the past 25-plus years. Around 2008 or so we had three proposals at the beach party *in one year*.

I think it's an awesome culmination of the event. The feeling of, "Okay, we persevered through this entire event together. We've made it, and with the excitement of finishing this challenge together, I want to show you my love." It's that kind of mentality. There's an endorphin rush after the event, and you're spending time with the ones you love, family and friends. Maybe that's what leads to the proposals, which usually happen at the finish party on the beach.

Occasionally people reach out to us beforehand. They basically ask, "Is this all right? We just want to make sure it's okay to do." And once in a while they ask, "Can you briefly announce our proposal at the finish?" Or they want to hear something from our announcer. They're not necessarily looking for publicity, more like an acknowledgement.

Sometimes things happen that fly under the radar and we don't find out about them until after the fact. I'm sure that people have gotten married during the race as well. If they want to do it and it's not in the way of the runners at the exchanges, then it's awesome. Embracing the chaos is totally what the relay is all about.

It's this crazy thing where we have the infrastructure for the event, and we try to keep it as organized as possible within reason for a 200-mile course. However, the cool thing is all the 18,000 unique human stories, personal relationships, and emotions that come along with the race. Things like proposals are what make people sometimes stop and say, "Oh, my God, this is awesome. Where else will I witness this?"

Rich Kokesh *is from Portland and has run Hood To Coast eight times.*

In the late 1990s I was on a team with a woman who had recently broken up with her boyfriend. Apparently, he did not want her to go run Hood To Coast with all these other guys, and he followed us the entire racecourse on his motorcycle.

It was a bit odd and created a lot of drama. The woman didn't really want to get out and run her legs. Her ex-boyfriend was harassing our van and zipping around us the entire time. He was following us along the course. It was just crazy.

When we would go out and try to confront him, he would just zip off on his motorcycle. Then about 15 minutes later he'd be back tailing us again.

He followed us all the way to the finish. It was a whole lot more drama than I wanted to deal with during the weekend.

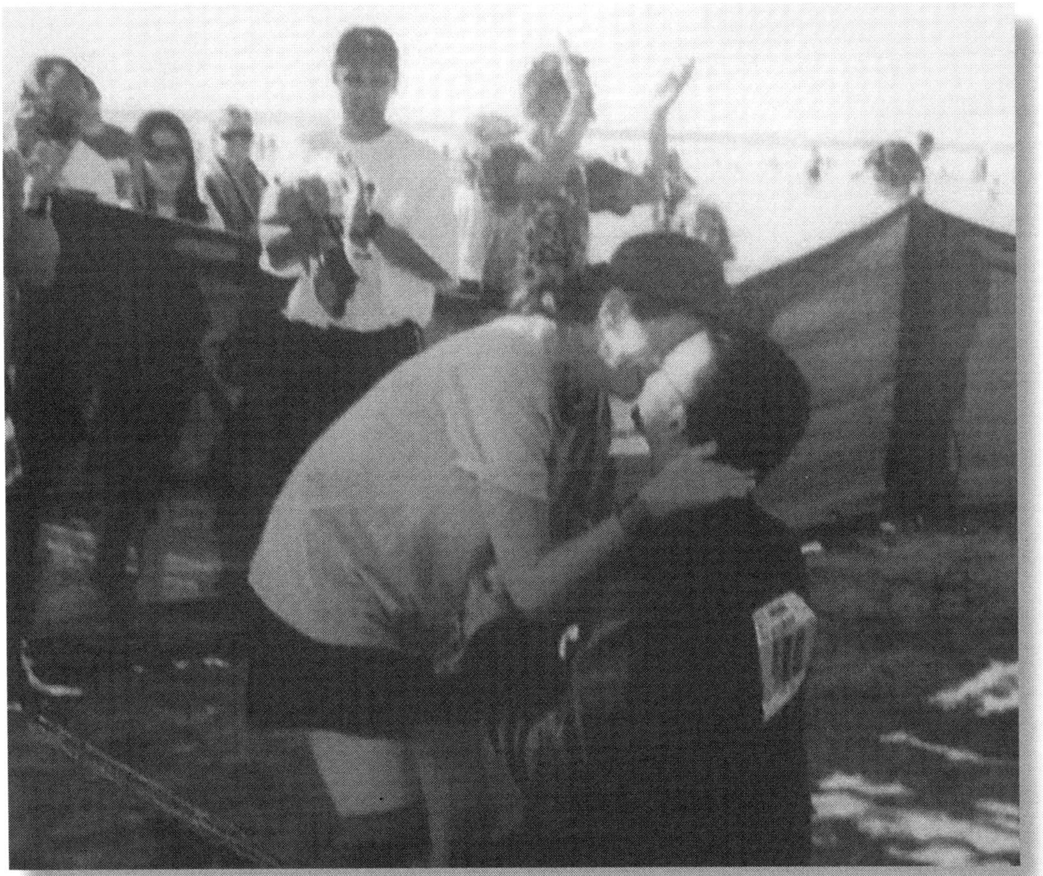

Leslie Dewar in 2001.

CHAPTER 20

Bathroom Humor

IT CAN BE CRUDE AND off-color. It can also be pretty funny, especially when packed in a crowded van, running until exhaustion and having limited access to a shower. As a result, bathroom humor is alive and well during the running of Hood To Coast.

Some of the busiest places between Mt. Hood and Seaside are the bathrooms located along the way. Whether it's the portable "Honey Buckets" or the schools and other facilities that open their doors to runners, there is always one constant. There's always a line.

Bob Foote *is the founder and chairman of Hood To Coast.*

Porta potties were an issue the very first year and really became an issue the second year with so many more teams. The runners used anybody's yard or field as their bathroom, and I started getting random complaints from the surrounding communities.

Of course, not everyone agreed. I vividly remember a letter from one participant when we were getting pressure to add porta potties to the course. The letter said, "Don't ever succumb to putting porta potties on the course. This is an adventure race and the day that you put a porta potty on the course, it'll never be enough. They'll never stop demanding more."

And he was dead right! In year three I did break down and we started to add some porta potties, a few random ones here and there along the course. But, of course, it was never enough. Never. No matter how many we add, we'll never have enough porta potties to satisfy everyone.

Steve Barger *is from Tacoma, Washington, and is the retired president of Northwest Cascade, Inc. Founded in 1968, the company installed septic systems, side sewers, and other underground utilities. In 1982 the company entered the portable toilet business with the purchase of Redford Honey Buckets.*

What does a team running 199 miles need to survive? Nutrition, liquids, camaraderie—and of course portable restrooms! During the 1980s Honey Bucket was focused on supplying portable restrooms for construction, industrial, and agricultural sites. By 1990 Honey Bucket was the market share leader in the state of Washington and looking to grow.

Luckily, the running boom that began in the 1970s was still going strong. Eventually, Honey Bucket started providing portable restrooms for local 5K and 10K events, where the restroom units were only needed at the start and finish. The degree of difficulty for our work increased when we began supplying units for the Seattle Marathon. Not only were units needed at the start and finish, but also along the entire course. In fact, our Honey Buckets were frequently used as mile markers for the marathon!

Honey Bucket continued to grow in the 1990s and expanded to Oregon, where we quickly discovered a very healthy special-event market. Given our experience with running events, we looked at the event calendar in Oregon and realized one event stood out above all the others—Hood To Coast. It was 199 miles and needed portable restroom units along the entire course. Plus all the units required servicing throughout the day and night from the start at Timberline Lodge to the finish in Seaside. Wow, this sounded crazy!

We learned that between 1982 and 1990 Bob Foote, the founder of HTC, had hired four portable restroom companies to provide units and service. Each company was responsible for a section of the racecourse. In early 1999 Honey Bucket salesman Craig Price and I visited Bob. We told him that Honey Bucket wanted to provide all the units and services required over the entire course. We told Bob about the advantages of using one company, including accountability and streamlined communications, as well as the consistency of units and services. Bob was dubious to say the least. He couldn't imagine one company capable of servicing the entire relay. We convinced him we had the equipment, people, and planning experience to pull it off.

We finally got the job when we made a bold guarantee to Bob. We told him, "If our performance does not meet your expectations, don't pay us!"

We learned that "The Mother of All Relays" really is a challenge for everyone—the event organizers, the runners, and all the suppliers. The week of the event in 1999 we had

25 employees involved in various tasks, including delivering 350 units to 35 exchanges and the start and finish line, servicing all units over 36 hours, and picking up every unit Sunday morning. It required many vehicles, lots of radio communication, and quickly reacting to special needs at some exchanges. Despite all our planning, there were some memorable surprises that first year.

At 2 a.m. Saturday morning, all the units at Exchange 32 were tipped over by vandals. Luckily, we scrambled to fix the problem before any runners arrived at the exchange.

Unfortunately, the traffic was so heavy Saturday that we were late for some services.

In Seaside, our service vehicle for the beach units got stuck in the sand—and had to be towed out by a tractor. Luckily, there was a tractor onsite to help vendors get their equipment onto the beach on Friday—and it was still around Saturday to pull our vehicle off the beach!

We had to quickly organize a lost and found station at the finish for everything we found left behind in the units. While there were plenty of shirts, hats, sunglasses, and water bottles in the units, it was amazing how much other stuff was left behind. We also found rings, bracelets, wallets, and watches, and almost anything else you can imagine. Interestingly, we did find more stuff in the beach units than at any of the exchanges—probably because the finish was where most of the celebrating was taking place!

We also forgot to make hotel reservations in Seaside for our beach crew, and every motel in the area was sold out. One of our employees, Roger Segerman, had a small motor home that he brought to Seaside from his home in Salem. Eight of us slept in it—and seven of us snored! It was actually meant to sleep two people comfortably, so every inch of space was utilized. We even had two crew members sleeping in the front seats.

That first year we had about 30 Honey Bucket units on the beach for the finish because we knew that party time also meant potty time. And as we pulled in for our last service of those units at the beach, our crew got a standing ovation.

We got paid that first year—and have been the portable restroom supplier for HTC every year since! And as the president of Northwest Cascade I continued to work on one of the race service crews every year until 2014 when I retired.

JR Inman is a vice president at Northwest Cascade, Inc. Founded in 1968, the company installed septic systems, side sewers, and other underground utilities. In 1982 the company entered the portable toilet business with the purchase of Redford Honey Buckets.

The first year Honey Bucket worked with Hood To Coast was 1999. Before we got involved it usually took two or three companies to supply the event with portable toilets because of the total number of units required, along with the staff needed for the event. Of course, the fact that the race was 200 miles long was also a factor.

It was our understanding that the race was not getting great service throughout the entire event. Maybe they had good service in one area or another spot, but not all the way through the racecourse. Our company decided to bid on the chance to supply and service toilets throughout the entire course, from start to finish.

Although I was not involved in the initial negotiations, I was part of the first operational team from our Washington headquarters sent to Oregon to figure out how to handle the event. It was extremely important to determine how to efficiently manage and staff the relay.

Did we think it was a crazy idea? We did at first, but the race quickly became one of our premier events.

We weren't familiar with any events strung out over 200 miles. Most of the events we staffed were located in one area, where everything was generally within a few miles. To my knowledge, HTC is still the geographically largest event we execute every year.

That first year we drove the entire course and took lots of pictures along the way. It was really the only way to become familiar with the race route and the overall event. We then put together a guidebook that included plenty of pictures, along with maps of the entire course, where we highlighted all the locations for our Honey Buckets.

The next step was to figure out how to deliver and service the Honey Buckets, and then pick them all up after the race. Most of our work was going to take place in a span of 48 to 72 hours. We had addresses for every Honey Bucket location along the course, but in some places we had to search really hard to find the exact locations. In our guidebook we included addresses, as well as pictures of the actual location for the toilets, landmarks near each location and what you would see on the road when approaching the location. We had to make sure our team knew exactly where to place the toilets.

In order to better manage the event we decided to break the course down into sections. We divided the course into six distinct sections, with each section having six legs. One person from our team would manage each section. Basically, we broke down a 200-mile racecourse into bite-sized chunks, which made things easier to handle.

We didn't recommend the locations for the toilets, but we did suggest exactly where to set the Honey Buckets. We also proposed the total number of portable toilets in each location based on our event experience.

That first year, a team from our Washington office staffed the relay during race weekend. I went to Oregon a week ahead of the event and stayed through the race weekend, and I worked with all the people we brought in to staff the race.

In our third year working with HTC I became the guy in charge of the overall event and started leading the event from a managerial and operational side. It was about that time we really figured out the best way to handle the event.

The race has continued to grow, and today there are 605 Honey Buckets up and down the course, and close to 1,100 services performed on those toilets throughout the event. When we began working with the event in 1999, there were 349 Honey Buckets along the course, and we performed just under 600 services.

Another difference can be seen in the number of portable toilets at the race finish. Today we have 48 portable toilets at the finish, along with sinks and holding tanks. That's quite a few more than the 30 or so Honey Buckets from our first year.

The last few years I haven't worked the event. Our company has grown and my responsibilities have changed, but I sure do miss it!

***Rod Cruickshank** was born in Flint, Michigan, and moved to Oregon in 1968, where he attended grade school, high school, and college. He was familiar with Hood To Coast from the very beginning and competed in the relay for the first time in 1997.*

Back when I started running the relay it was always about getting to the next exchange or getting ahead to try and sleep. In my early years running there weren't many services along the course. More recently people have become entrepreneurs. Now you can find anything you need along the course. I've come across everything from spaghetti stands to a porta potty in someone's front yard to a garage turned into a market with food and drinks. People have created businesses all along the route.

One year, I remembered a house from the previous year that sold food and had porta potties. When we stopped there the owners of the house were all in and had everything you could imagine! The garage was like a small convenience store with food and drinks, and their kids worked there. I remember thinking, "Man, this is great. Are you kidding me? Here I can get a hot bowl of spaghetti—on the course."

For five dollars you could also take a shower in the house. I was right there with my towel because at that point I would have paid 50 dollars for a shower. When I walked in the house I was in line with a bunch of random people, and everyone had their toiletry kits and towels.

Everybody was using the shower—and the toilet too! The house was in a rural part of the state and had a septic tank. With all the additional bathroom use, the septic tank got full and boiled back up.

It shut everything down in the entire house. As I was walking away after not taking a shower, I thought, "All the money you made, you're now going to have to pay to get the thing pumped and clean everything up."

Steve Hanamura was born in Upland, California, and now lives in Portland. He has par-ticipated in Hood To Coast more than 25 times and served as captain of the team I Hurt, You Hurt, We All Hurt for more than 20 years. Blind since birth, he is an avid runner and sports fan.

One year we left a runner behind at the exchange after Leg 5 without knowing it. My teammate Sandra was going to the bathroom. She came out of the porta potty and saw us take off in the van, but nobody realized she was missing.

When another team's van pulled up alongside us at the next exchange, they asked, "Hey, are you missing anything?" We were clueless. Then we saw Sandra in their van. They'd been nice enough to pick her up for us.

Sandra was very gracious with us. It could have brought down the whole team. Rather than blame the driver, since I was the leader of the team it was my responsibility. It was definitely a learning experience.

Now it's somewhat painful whenever I see Sandra, and not just because she's my dentist!

Laura Klink is from Portland and has been a Hood To Coast competitor for more than 15 years on various teams. In 2017 she ran with the team Cancer Crushers.

I used to work at a TV station in Portland and one of my funniest memories from the race happened while I was running on a work team we put together.

After the first night you're very sleep-deprived. It was early in the morning and there was no coffee to be found anywhere. However, someone on the team had Red Bull.

Usually during the race your stomach is a little woozy. I thought, "Oh well, I'll have some Red Bull because it's carbonated. It should help settle my stomach." And it had caffeine, which was perfect because it would help me stay awake.

Well, don't do that! I found out Red Bull was not conducive to helping my stomach. In fact, it made it a lot worse. I spent a lot of my next leg in the porta potty. Let's just say I made a lot of pit stops.

Since then I haven't had another Red Bull. Sorry Red Bull.

Scott Parker grew up in Portland and lives in Bozeman, Montana. He first ran Hood To Coast in 1998 and is the author of Running After Prefontaine: A Memoir *and* Run for Your Life: A Manifesto.

The following is a conversation between Scott Parker and his sister, Katie, about the 2002 Hood To Coast and their team, Revenge of the Nutria.

Scott: "You know what story I like?"

Katie: "What?"

Scott: "Do you remember your first Hood To Coast?"

Katie: "Not this story. I'm still pissed about this one."

Scott: "Seriously?"

Katie: "No. That was a joke."

Scott: "Right."

Katie: "I like this story. You and Brian are the ones who come out looking like idiots."

Scott: "Come on. We made it to the exchange."

Katie: "Barely. Luckily."

Scott: "It all worked out."

Katie: "I'm having the best run of my life. It's sunrise. The fog is burning off in the trees. I'm doing like seven-minute miles and feeling great. About half a mile from the exchange you two are standing on the side of the road yelling at me to slow down because everyone else in your van is asleep in some field."

Scott: "You'd rather we didn't tell you?"

Katie: "I would have rathered you'd been at the exchange already."

Scott: "Not our fault you guys ran so fast. But, for the record, no way did you run seven-minute miles."

Katie: "Seven-somethings."

Scott: "Right. . . . Anyway, we did see you coming. We did get our runner up. We did make it to the exchange more or less on time."

Katie: "First of all, less than on time, not more. Second of all, you only saw me because you were wandering around looking for a garbage can."

Scott: "I like to keep a neat van. The point is we saw you."

Katie: "That's no excuse. I should have never let you back on the team after that."

Scott: "Damn, Coach!"

Katie: "You wanna be on the team, you gotta be at the exchanges early."

Scott: "Too bad you aren't as strict when it comes to hygiene."

Katie: "Hygiene? It was just a little pee."

Scott: "A little pee? You run into a van exchange, hand off the bracelet to our runner—who, I emphasize, was there no more than twenty or thirty seconds after you were—and then barrel through the crowd of runners shouting, 'Out of my way! I pissed myself!' I think maybe you were still peeing at the time."

Katie: "I was not still peeing."

Scott: "I don't think I can really trust you on this."

Katie: "It wasn't even a full pee."

Scott: "Half a pee?"

Katie: "Less than half—like a quarter."

Scott: "What does that mean—a quarter of a full bladder?"

Katie: "Yeah, a quarter of a bladder."

Scott: "If it was a quarter of a bladder, why didn't you just hold it?"

Katie: "Wasn't worth it. It would have slowed me down."

Scott: "You wanted to piss yourself."

Katie: "I did not. Why would I want to piss myself?"

Scott: "I don't know. Why did you come in shouting about it? No one would have known."

Katie: "I was covered in piss. Of course people would have noticed."

Scott: "It's Hood To Coast. Your piss would have been covered by a dozen worse smells."

Katie: "Are you telling me you've never pissed yourself during a leg?"

Scott: "That's right."

Katie: "Then I hate to tell you this, but you've never really run Hood To Coast."

Jennifer Masi is originally from Portland, but participated in her first Hood To Coast when she was living in Connecticut. She has since relocated back to Portland with her family.

My first time participating in Hood To Coast was 2014. Being from Portland, I knew all about the race and flew out to Oregon from my home in Connecticut to navigate and be the driver for Van 1. Little did I know when I made the commitment to my teammates that on race day I would be six months pregnant.

While there is so much I remember from that first race (I've done three more as a runner since then), I particularly remember the middle-of-the night drive after all our runners had completed their second legs. We were headed into the infamous Exchange 24 at a snail's pace because traffic was backed up for miles. There were loud snores coming from the back of our van. My co-pilot was doing her best to stay awake but was fighting a losing battle. To top it off, I had to pee—bad—which as any pregnant woman knows is its own special kind of torture.

We were finally coming up on the exchange and I was plotting the fastest route to the Honey Buckets. I began to make the turn into the large van parking lot when a volunteer told me it was full and we would have to drive on to the next exchange. Well, that didn't go over well with this beyond-tired, bladder-bursting, hormone-fueled mama-to-be.

I continued to slowly edge the van forward into the parking lot as I spoke with the volunteer, unwilling to take no for an answer. Our van was parking in this lot, and I was getting to a Honey Bucket—pronto. As I pleaded my case, I spotted an open parking space on the front row right next to the road! Afraid someone else would take the spot, I yelled at one of my teammates to get out and save it. He jumped over some bushes and claimed it. I then informed the confused volunteer that someone was saving a space for us and drove past her before she could ask any questions or tell us no again. Carefully, but quickly, I drove through a ditch, around a stretch of orange tape and into my awaiting parking space. More importantly, I jumped from the driver's seat and found the nearest Honey Bucket. Success!

Steve Hanamura *was born in Upland, California, and now lives in Portland. He has participated in Hood To Coast more than 25 times and served as captain of the team I Hurt, You Hurt, We All Hurt for more than 20 years. Blind since birth, he is an avid runner and sports fan.*

During the relay you can stop at some of the high schools along the course to take a shower. Different organizations do it as a fundraiser. They'll charge a couple dollars to take a shower and a couple dollars for a towel.

One year we stopped at a school to grab a shower. I was in the locker room with my teammate David. He said, "You better wait for me. I'll take you into the shower." Well, I told him I could get there by myself and started walking.

I was walking down toward the shower and I accidently bumped into somebody. The guy I bumped into started going off on me. He was yelling, "What the hell are you trying to do to me?"

David ran over yelling, "He's blind. He's blind. He can't see." But this guy's biggest fear was I was going to make a move on him or something.

I just bumped into him by mistake. David had to intervene. The guy wanted to punch me out. I thought it was kind of humorous.

"The dude can't see, man. The dude can't see," is what David kept telling the guy.

There have been some really funny blind experiences during Hood To Coast, and my team always gives me a lot of crap about it in a fun way. We just have a really good time with it.

Amado Lumba *works in corporate events at Nike.*

Although this wasn't very funny when it happened during the relay, now looking back it's pretty funny.

There's a product called Body Glide that runners apply to prevent chafing. The container is similar to the packaging for a stick of deodorant. In my race toiletry kit, I had all the essentials, including Body Glide, deodorant, and Icy Hot. All three looked alike.

We were at the Columbia County Fairgrounds and I was getting ready to run my second leg. Before my turn to run, I always applied Body Glide. However, this one time I accidently applied Icy Hot on my sensitive parts. It made for an interesting warm-up, in more ways than one!

Everyone in our van got a good chuckle too!

CHAPTER 21

Helping Others

EVEN THOUGH HOOD TO COAST is a competitive event, there's also a sense of camaraderie among the teams, runners and walkers participating in the relay. Many people talk about the *spirit* of the relay, the kindness that exists among perfect strangers, great friends or family members. Everyone faces a challenge during the relay, and there's usually someone there to provide encouragement during a steep climb, companionship during a middle of the night run or some water when a thirst needs to be quenched.

Lark Asbury was born in Portland and grew up in Hillsboro, Oregon. She works at Nike and has been involved in Hood To Coast as either a runner or a volunteer for more than 10 years.

At Nike, if you're a runner, it's typical to go for a run at lunch. One of my very good friends, who joined me on these regular lunch runs, was Ted Winn. In May 2014 Ted was diagnosed with brain cancer. It came totally out of the blue. He was a super healthy guy who could run me under the table any day and who had participated in Hood To Coast more than 15 times. He had a tumor that needed to be removed immediately. All his friends and Nike teammates were shocked.

As a mom I always want to fix things, but I couldn't help Teddy. Then I decided to contact a colleague at Nike, Amado Lumba, and ask him if there were any Nike team slots still available for HTC. I knew the answer was probably going to be no, especially since it was May and the relay was in a few months. Amado said Nike didn't have any spots open, but he knew Teddy and liked the idea of putting a team together as his support system.

Amado reached out to HTC and connected me with Mickey Godfrey, who worked at the race at the time. Mickey contacted me and said, "A fundraising team just backed out and we'd love to give you that slot because of the reason you're running." Usually, fundraising teams are supposed to raise a minimum of $10,000. Mickey added, "I know you can't get there, but how about you commit to $2,000 and I'll give the slot to your team."

I opened my mouth and said yes without having a team of 12 behind me. I had six people I knew would drop everything and run, but I was very, very nervous about following through on the fundraising commitment. When I put the word out to Teddy's friends and people who were part of Teddy's running group and explained what we were doing, people changed their summer plans to join the team. People who didn't run the relay but were marathon or half-marathon runners said, "I'll do it. Throw me in." We also had people who were non-runners who switched from cross training to running to join the team.

We then started brainstorming fundraising ideas. We ended up with a team of 12 Nike employees who took part in our lunchtime runs and, more importantly, were all friends of Ted. We said, "Let's do it! Let's fundraise for Providence Cancer Research in Teddy's name and see if we can at least get two grand."

We quickly created a fundraising account and collected product from the different teams and categories at Nike. Between holding a sample sale where we sold the donated product and the fundraising account, we were able to raise more than $23,000 between May and August.

We went through 2014 really driven by Teddy. His family had come up with the motto "Go, Fight, Winn"— and that's what we named our team.

We were all thinking about Teddy as we were running. We knew if Teddy could fight brain cancer, we could endure running through the middle of the night, leg cramps, and sleeping in a stinky van.

It was impactful and empowering and very emotional because we were all close with Teddy. While we were running, he was actually at Oregon Health & Science University Hospital having his 16th round of chemotherapy. We sent him pictures and videos of us out on the racecourse trying to keep his spirits up because he was bummed out he wasn't running. When he was diagnosed in May, Teddy said, "I'm on the team. Count me in. I just need to beat this thing first."

After the race we framed our bracelet and bibs from the relay and took it to him in the hospital. Teddy was humbled by what we did. I told him, "Why are you so surprised? You're our friend." He said it meant so much, and he told us getting our videos and pictures from the event made him feel like he was out there.

In 2015 we again ran the race. Teddy wasn't able to run because he didn't have his strength back. However, he joined us on the team in 2016. He had only about 75 percent of his energy level back and definitely wasn't in running shape, but to see him at the starting line and complete every single one of his legs was awesome. For someone who used to run a mile in a little more than seven minutes, it was probably humbling to do a mile in 10 to 12 minutes.

We lost Ted in March 2018. He fought hard and never gave up, nor did he ever lose his laughter and passion for life. The cancer was incurable and became too aggressive for his brain to fight off any longer.

Teddy lived life to the fullest and impacted all those around him. His zest and zeal for life and his passion for encouraging others never stopped.

Our team was founded in his name when he was first diagnosed to spread encouragement and inspiration in his fight. Yet he was the one who inspired us to keep going, to give back to others, and to keep putting one foot in front of the other. We will continue to participate in the relay and to fundraise for different organizations. We will carry Teddy with us as we run the race and we will continue to "Be like Ted."

As Teddy once said, "It's not about me. It's about friends coming together and making an impact in the community and helping others we don't even know. It's about showing support and compassion."

Morgan Powers is from Beaverton, Oregon, and participated in the relay several times before taking a job with the Hood To Coast organization as the director of design and development.

I work throughout the year with the 80 or so fundraising teams that have committed to each raising $10,000 or more for the Providence Cancer Center. In return, those teams get a bunch of benefits, including guaranteed entry, preferred start times, a waiver on providing volunteers, and a private party area at the beach.

In 2017 we had 82 teams committed to raising the $10,000. Our goal in 2018 is $850,000 total, and it will be a million dollars in 2019. The main reason the fundraising program has been so successful is it's the only way for a team to automatically get in the race and bypass the lottery.

Providence has been a great partner. They're a nonprofit hospital and Hood To Coast provides another way for them to get their name out there and to create awareness about all the great work they do.

On race day I start the event at the special check-in area at Timberline Lodge for all the fundraising teams. At first, being at the mountain working and not running was hard. It was difficult seeing all the runners with their excitement and enthusiasm. It made me want to go run with them.

After all the fundraising teams start, I follow the course and stop at a couple exchanges to see if the teams need anything. Then I head to Exchange 18 at the Columbia County Fairgrounds, where the fundraising teams have a VIP tent with food, drinks, and sleeping cots. I try to make sure everything is going well for all the teams.

The plan then is to go to the beach and catch a few hours of sleep. However, that part of the plan can change quickly, like it did in 2017 when we had to switch an exchange in the middle of the night. You have to be able to adapt. I happened to be in the area when I heard about the exchange switch on the radio. I was about two miles away, so I rolled on over to see how I could help.

There was a cement barricade there that we had been told would be removed by race weekend. However, it was still there and blocking a bunch of parking at the exchange. The Portland To Coast walking teams had gone through the exchange and it was functional for them, but we knew when the majority of runners came through in the middle of the night there would be no place for them to park.

So we drove up and down the road for about six miles looking for a place to move the exchange. We found one house with a big lot in the back and someone working in the yard with a backhoe. We pulled in and asked, "Can we use your lot for race parking in about two hours?" He said, "Sure, just let me level out the dirt and you'll be good to go." We piled all the exchange signs and cones into the back of our cars and moved them. We have all these exchange schematics that are planned months in advance, but we drew one up in about five minutes and made it work. That was definitely a thrill!

At the finish we have a VIP area for the fundraising teams, and I welcome all the teams to the beach. It's so much fun to see the teams come through feeling like they've really accomplished something. Of course everyone who does the race has this feeling of accomplishment when they finish. But not only did they finish the race, they raised $10,000 or more for cancer research. They can pick up a nameplate with their team name and put it on a sign that says, "Finish Cancer." That's usually the moment they feel like they really finished the race.

Many of the teams don't necessarily have a personal connection to cancer. However, some of the teams do have that connection to cancer and it's really special to see them finish. There are always a lot of tears, along with a lot of smiles. I remember recently there was a team with a mother who had lost her son, and she was embraced by all her team-mates when she finished. I'm sure she could definitely feel his presence and she was really happy to have that experience.

It's a big thing in the running world. People want to run races themselves, but they also want to help others or a cause. That's a huge part of the relay and I love HTC because of it.

Sherry Willmschen is from Portland and is now retired after working for years in social services. After participating in Portland To Coast she took a job with the American Cancer Society as a patient navigator.

I participated in Portland To Coast on the team Christine's Dream for four years beginning in 2001. I had never walked so far in my life, and as a breast cancer survivor I was empowered to complete all my legs.

The funds our team raised were donated to the Komen Foundation. I still have fond memories of waiting for my teammates, finding friends on other teams, meeting many wonderful survivors, and taking the team picture at the finish line. Our annual tradition once we finished was to stop at the Camp 18 restaurant on our way back to Portland.

What a blessing!

Gwenn McGill grew up in Bend, Oregon, and now lives in Portland. She has her own event management company and has also worked as a race announcer for many years. In the early 1990s she was a member of a Hood To Coast team and in 2014 she began announcing the Portland To Coast start.

I was not a big runner when I was young. It wasn't until I was in my late 20s or early 30s that I started running. It was just recreational. My sister was more of a competitive runner and at that time was on an all-women's Hood To Coast team called The Heartbreakers.

Through her I'd been following the relay for a few years, but I never participated in the event until one year when the Heartbreakers needed a runner and they asked me to be a part of the team. It was a fairly competitive team, and I wasn't a fast runner. My first response was, "You mean you want me to drive the van, right?" They said, "No. No. We really want you to run." So I ran, and despite my being slow we actually won our division.

One of my fondest memories of that first year took place during the middle of the night while I was out running my second leg. I can't remember exactly where it was, but I think it was around St. Helens. Wherever it was, it was dark and it felt like I was in the middle of nowhere. I remember feeling like, "Oh my gosh! I'm really alone out here." No sooner did those thoughts go through my head than seemingly out of nowhere two other runners—a couple guys—came up on either side of me. I immediately got nervous and thought, "Oh, God! I'm here in the middle of nowhere and I don't know these people. What if they're not really runners?"

Of course, you go through that panic wondering what if something happens. It turned out they were legit runners and they could see that I was just a bit nervous. They were much faster runners—I mean they caught up to me and nobody was around when I began my leg. But rather than charge ahead and leave me all alone, they chose to stay with me throughout the remainder of the leg.

There were still a couple miles left to run, and during that time we started talking. "Where are you from? Why are you running?" They were keeping me going and it made time go by quickly. It almost felt like I was carried to the exchange by their companion-ship and conversation. They were my little angels that just sort of popped up out of nowhere and then stayed with me throughout the remainder of the run. It was pretty cool.

Unfortunately, I wasn't able to connect with them later and tell them how much I appreciated what they did. (Although, I'm not sure I would have recognized them—it was pitch black when we were running!)

I felt my way of thanking them would be by paying it forward, which I did a year later.

The following year, I noticed a woman who seemed to be struggling throughout the various legs of the event. On the final leg, she was really, really struggling, so I slowed down and stuck with her throughout the reminder of that last leg so that we could finish together. I can't imagine having thought to do that without having the experience from the previous year and knowing what that felt like. She gave me a big hug at the finish and I gave her a big hug back. I was so happy she made it, and I think she was really thrilled to have me run with her to the end.

We never did see each other again, but who knows, maybe she was able to pay it for-ward the next year. I know those things happen all the time during the race.

Sandy Dukat *is from Canton, Ohio, and now lives in Denver. Born with a congenital limb deficiency, Dukat had her right leg amputated when she was four. Between the 2002 and*

2006 Winter Paralympics she won three bronze medals in alpine skiing. After retiring from competitive skiing she began competing in triathlons and captured the women's Above-Knee division of the USA Triathlon Paratriathlon National Championship four times. She was captain of the Hood To Coast team The Amazing Awaits in 2008, 2009, and 2010.

One thing that really stood out was all the support we received during the event. It was really evident at the exchanges. It was pretty easy to tell when one of our Paralympic athletes was getting close to the exchange because the crowd would erupt. It began as a polite applause, but before long there were plenty of loud cheers and just an amazing amount of support filling the exchange. It was something we didn't really notice with many other runners. However, everyone knew when we were coming to an exchange.

Out on the racecourse there was a lot of support too. The amount of respect we received was amazing. While we were running, there were a ton of other runners giving us high-fives or thumbs-ups or telling us, "Way to go!" A lot of the participants recognized how hard it was because they were doing it, and we were right there with them on a prosthetic leg or in a chair doing the same thing. It really helped build more respect for us among the running community.

It's amazing how hard you can push that last little bit when you hear all the applause. Initially you think, "Why is this happening?" It was definitely motivation for me because I'm a competitor and wanted to go as fast as I could. I also wanted to demonstrate that I could keep up with my teammates. It also enabled me to be myself on the course. And it was great that we were able to show a larger running audience what we were doing.

I had my game face on before I started Leg 1 at Timberline Lodge, and inside I was completely focused. I remember a lot of runners at the start talking to me, but it was more like, "Oh boy, are we ready for this?" It wasn't specifically, "Oh wow, you're sitting up here on a prosthetic."

At the start there was a whole lot of energy for everybody and it was really encouraging—whether you had a disability or not. That's what really set the tone for the event—the huge support at the top of the mountain!

It was also perfect that I ran Leg 1 because that's where I'd train in the summer when I was skiing. It was thrilling that my sports experiences were coming together in one place. It was a reminder of all that I had achieved and all that's left to accomplish. On many levels being on Mt. Hood meant so much to me. Competitive ski-racing and running are two things I never thought I'd do in my life—and this mountain was about to become the place where I did both!

Rob Rickard *is from Canby, Oregon, and has participated in Hood To Coast every year since 1983. He has also been a course marker for the event for more than 25 years.*

The first year we participated in the relay we were just a bunch of running friends who got together and said, "We've seen the flyers for this event, let's go out and do it." We had no idea what we were doing.

In those days the teams were made up of 10 people. We had one van and all 10 of us headed out in it. We had a great deal of fun just getting started. Then we realized we hadn't packed any water or food.

On my third leg I got into a real hot stretch and our van was nowhere to be found. Another van came up—it was an old Volkswagen van—and the guys had the slider door wide open. They asked if I needed some water. Oh, did I need some water.

Their runner was about 200 yards ahead of me. They watered me down and then they moved up and watered their guy. This kind of rejuvenated me and I started reeling in their runner. They then dropped back and gave me some more water. It didn't bother them a bit that I was gaining on their runner. Eventually, I passed him.

But that was a great example of the Hood To Coast spirit, which I think is, *Help me, help you. It doesn't really matter if we're running against each other. How can we help each other?*

For 35 years I've enjoyed that experience.

Amado Lumba *works in corporate events at Nike.*

I've run the race at least 10 times, but I don't think I've ever done it in back-to-back years. After each one there was a break, often of a couple years. Each one is memorable in its own right because there are quite a few things that happen in the 26 to 30 hours you're crammed in a van with five other people.

The first time I ran Hood To Coast was in 1996. It was with a good buddy who I worked with in Portland. At the time, I was a long distance runner, which is how my buddy and I bonded. We were avid runners who would run together, either in the morning or the evening, or sometimes both.

He presented the idea of running the relay to me. I said, "I don't know, man. I don't know if I could do that." It seemed daunting at the time. However, there was really no reason for me to shy away from it, and I'm glad I didn't.

I even designed the T-shirt for our team that year. It featured a shoe with wings, and it was a Nike with the Swoosh, even though I wasn't working for Nike at the time.

My buddy and I, along with his dad, were together in the van. I was Runner 5. One of my best memories is of running Leg 29 that year. It was my last leg and it basically had me on a major incline for the first three miles, and then the last three miles were downhill. No matter how well I thought I had trained for the incline, I was still not prepared.

What was cool is on the way up there were quite a few other runners having just as tough a time as I was, and we all encouraged each other. It turns out the old adage is true: misery does love company. There was actually a really fast woman who blasted past me, but then she came back and offered me a drink from her water bottle. It was pretty neat because she certainly didn't have to do that. It was also cool to see, on my last leg, all the camaraderie among the runners.

Todd Russell lives in the Portland area. Although he's a runner, he doesn't participate in Hood To Coast, working instead on one of the ambulance crews for the event.

About eight or 10 years ago I had a friend who died in his 40s of a brain tumor. Every year he would run Hood To Coast, and he truly loved the race.

After he passed, his wife spread his ashes in multiple spots along the racecourse, from beginning to end. She did it during the off-season because she didn't want to interfere with the race itself. I know it was a cathartic event for her, and I know my friend would have liked it because he loved to run the relay.

I'm a runner but haven't run the relay myself. I usually work on one of the ambulance crews for the race. I've carted a few people who have had heat issues off to the hospital, but luckily, nothing worse than that.

It's always been a great experience, and I look forward to it every year.

Steve Spear was born in Vermont and now lives near Chicago. After serving as a pastor for 20 years, he joined Team World Vision as the Endurance Director in 2013. He participated in his first Hood To Coast in 2014.

At Team World Vision, we partner with different events across the U.S. to raise money for clean water in Africa. One of those events is Hood To Coast. We started our partnership with the race in 2013, the same year I ran across the U.S. For 150 straight days I ran about a marathon every day and helped raise close to a half million dollars for clean water in Africa. After my run was finished I joined Team World Vision.

During my cross country run, I would occasionally talk on the phone with Michael Chitwood, the founder of Team World Vision. In one of our conversations, Michael said, "I'm bummed you'll be finishing your run and won't be able to join us at Hood To Coast in Oregon. It's going to be a great thing." He was telling me all about the event and how five Team World Vision teams were participating.

A few months after I finished my run Michael asked me, "Since you resigned your church position to run across the U.S. and don't have a job now, do you want to work for Team World Vision?" So at the end of 2013 I joined the staff and one of my responsibilities was to manage the HTC program. Michael said, "Not only do we want you to oversee the program, we want to increase the participation from five to 10 teams in 2014—with each participant having a fundraising goal of $10,000."

I responded, "I don't know anything about the race. I've never been there and have only heard you talk about it, but I'll totally do it." Afterwards, I was thinking, "How difficult will it be to get people to run a relay race of 199 miles?"

One of the first things I did in was to interview the people who participated with Team World Vision in the 2013 race. I talked to almost every person that ran on one of our five teams. I needed to get my brain loaded with information about the relay, along with enough ideas and stories to recruit double the number of runners in 2014. I needed to have a strong feeling for what the event was all about. Soon I realized it was a special event. Every person I contacted said it was epic or amazing or unforgettable. Using the stories I'd heard, I started recruiting runners for 2014—and quickly had enough people signed up to field 10 teams.

When I ran the relay for the first time in 2014, I saw why everyone was so pumped and charged up about the event. It was a glorious mix of a running race, an "all-nighter," a moving party, summer camp, and a music festival— taking place in a beautiful part of the country. After that first year, I thought, "This thing is absolutely epic." Now I understood why so many people told me the race was the most fun event they've ever done.

We've had 10 teams participate in HTC every year since 2014. In 2017, we had a couple of people fall out at the last minute and needed to recruit a few runners. One of the guys I recruited to fill in was Jay. After we finished, he found me while we were hanging out at the beach. Jay said, "I've got to tell you a couple of things. I'm sleep-deprived, I'm dehydrated, I'm 45 years old, and I just had the time of my life."

Bob Foote (HTC founder) was actually walking around the beach not long after I talked to Jay. I relayed to Bob what Jay said because I thought in a couple sentences he nailed what the relay is all about.

CHAPTER 22

The Storm Of 2015

IN 2015, EVERYONE INVOLVED IN the relay battled a variety of inclement weather conditions along the course—from rain, to thunder and lightning, to severe winds. These weather conditions were prevalent throughout the race, especially along the second half of the course. Runners were advised to use extreme caution. The weather in Seaside was so bad many of the structures erected for finish line activities were damaged and the traditional post-race beach party was canceled for safety reasons. Even the actual finish line was relocated. Seemingly everybody involved in the 2015 race has a memory they will never forget.

Matt Kenchington *is from Annapolis, Maryland, and now lives in Los Angeles. He participated in the 2015 Hood To Coast.*

Legend had it, it hadn't rained in Oregon in months, but this night in August of 2015 was different. The apocalypse was upon us. I don't remember exactly which number the leg was, as I've tried to block as much of it out as possible, but it was an intense incline on a dirt and gravel road. It was my second leg and I was ready to rock and roll—until I wasn't. Everyone got quiet as the van headed to the drop-off point. The wind was blowing like no other; in fact, I believe Dorothy's house flew past us. The rain was just starting. The lightning strikes were beginning, and the "one one-hundreds" between them and the thunderclaps were getting shorter and shorter. As we pulled up to the exchange, I got all my gear on and quickly hopped out. With fear in their voices, my teammates said, "Good luck, Matt. You'll do great."

I was waiting (impatiently) for my teammate Nate to show up with the magical wristband, but I could barely see anything as the rain had grown significantly stronger. After a minute or so of searching, I heard my name being called, "Matt!" However, it wasn't a normal call; it was a call from someone who was in desperate need of shelter. He passed the wristband and gave me a please-don't-die pat on the back. With that, I was off into the dark distance.

The beginning of the run wasn't too bad. The air, though wet, was fresh and smelled nice. I didn't need to cover my face with a mask as suggested because the dust was non-existent. Also, it wasn't hot. The temperature was perfect. I kept my eyes on the ground in front of me to make sure I avoided any natural obstacles that might appear out of nowhere. Little did I know obstacles would be coming from places other than the ground. I found this out when I was suddenly hit by a branch flying through the wind. This is when I knew it was going to be a different run. In fact, it wasn't a run anymore—it was a fight for survival. Like Rocky versus Drago, or David versus Goliath, or Matt versus ninth-grade teasing.

As I fought my way up an increasing incline, I was all alone and running out of steam. Not just from pushing against the gale-force winds but also because I was completely unprepared for this run (although that's a different story). Then, I heard footsteps behind me. I was about to be passed, but it was great to see someone else sharing this experience. The ripped and shredded runner looked at me, the look of agony in his eyes, and said, "This sucks!" I agreed and continued my trek to the top. Many more runners passed me along the way and I made sure to make eye contact with all of them. No one was really having fun, but we all made a connection. At least I think we did.

When I saw the lights of the exchange growing closer, tears of joy began to run down my face. (Something had actually gotten caught in my eye, but I like to call them tears of joy.) I started my sprint, which is what most others would call a light jog, and made it to the handoff. I couldn't find my teammate at first, but she soon appeared. I passed her the wristband and wished her luck, feeling like a winner. Well, a survivor more than anything.

My other teammates quickly found me and brought me to the van, where everyone had towels waiting. Relief spread across their faces as they saw my body intact and a smile of pure relief across my face. Everyone stayed quite silent for a while as each of us processed the event in our own way. I made sure to make eye contact with everyone in the van. The silence was broken when Frank said, "Dude, I didn't want to make you anxious, but I really got scared as we were driving up the hill." Everyone else in the van added, "Me too!" We all smiled in agreement, and the van was on its way to the next stop. After a few more moments of reflection, I said, "That was the single hardest thing I've done in my life. And . . . It. Was. Awesome!"

Smiles spread across all our faces, knowing we had just experienced the experience of all experiences. And *that* is what it's all about!

Tim Dooley *is from Gresham, Oregon, and has been running in Hood To Coast since 1989.*

The three of us were about six miles from the finish line in 2015. We were running directly into a 70-mph gust—and howling defiantly at the weather gremlins that were trying to torment us! In the pouring rain, numb from our windy beating, our pain had given way to determined solidarity and total disregard for the tempest that surrounded us. We were unconquered! Nothing was going to stop us from finishing!

My good friend John and I were escorting John's daughter Sarah as she neared the finish of her leg of seven miles. That morning Sarah had turned 21. This was her first Hood To Coast. The time we'd spent earlier bracing ourselves against the wind and the rain while waiting for the beginning of Sarah's turn to run had taken its toll. Sarah broke down and began to cry. Just as John and I were discussing emergency substitution options, our next runner came in and handed off to Sarah. We asked, "Sarah do you want to continue?" She responded, "I have to," as tears streamed down her face and she turned to run.

That scene left both John and me sick with worry because Sarah's leg would take her down a seven-mile path that provided no access to motor vehicles. She was on her own. What dad could sit back and leave his daughter to battle that challenge alone? As soon as we drove to the next exchange point, where Sarah was to finish, John jumped out of the van and began to run down the trail in her direction. A little later I followed. As I stepped out of the van into the typhoon, it was really ugly. Tree branches were falling everywhere, and people were seeking shelter. I didn't know what I'd find when I tracked Sarah and John down, but when we saw each other in the distance it was amazing! John's unexpected appearance had bolstered Sarah, and in his company the emotion had swung all the way back from despair. Now the two of them were invincible! And when I joined them, I too was absorbed into their invincibility. When John saw me he began to cry tears of great joy and friendship. Together we were going to pull through again!

What a father-daughter experience! I was so happy for John because I've been blessed by so many similar experiences with my girls. My two daughters, Andi and Carolyn, were running with me again this year. I milked every moment of the special time with them, reveling in their teasing banter, proud of the women they had become.

I've been running this race since 1989, and the core of our running team has remained amazingly constant since those early days. In the mid-1990s we added Carolyn to our crew when she was just a 15-year-old gangly colt. I only let her run two legs that year, and I did four. Now she was an adult and we had come full circle. Both my girls were now stronger runners than I, and I would have done well to let either of them run my third leg.

My legs felt dead as John, Sarah, and I made our way up the gravel road. I thought of my dad, whom we had recruited to run with us when he was 61. I couldn't help but smile at the thought. He was a pretty frisky old guy. Now 61, I wasn't feeling as frisky as my dad, and at this point in the race I resembled one of those quickly fading old guys. With that knowledge I had made up my mind during my second and third legs that this would be my last race. I was feeling the effects of some recent medical challenges, and it was time to pass the torch.

Now I just wanted to finish in style, but the weather was not cooperating. In previous years, I had run the first leg down Mt. Hood in a lightning and hail storm; I had run a half-marathon with my dad directly into a 50-mph wind; and I had run two marathons in 87 degrees. However, this final HTC chapter had them all beat. This weather was crazy!

Suddenly we spotted our teammates waiting for us in the distance! Our pal Ted, who had at our earlier urging briefly contemplated surrendering to the raging typhoon, was now bouncing around getting ready for the handoff. Ted would never have quit. And who could give up now after Sarah's feat? Determination! And what a crew! The faces of that group reminded me of what has kept me coming back for this historic trek over and over again. It's the people. The connection we have is more like that of a family than of a team. We care about each other and enjoy each other's company tremendously. And every year at our pre-race pasta feed we catch up on each other's lives and toast team members like "Sunny" Tim McLeod, who may not be running with us but will always be part of our team and in our hearts.

As Ted took the handoff and headed slowly into the howling storm, there would be none of the usual finish line festivities awaiting him. The beach was closed and all the tents at the finish line had blown away, now replaced by a make-shift finish marker on the Seaside Promenade. In spite of the horrendous weather, and 29 hours and 15 minutes after our Timberline Lodge start, Ted came limping down the Promenade toward the finish line. Every finisher was truly a winner in this storm. Fifty yards from the finish, Ted was joined by 11 other very boisterous members of our running family, the Return of the Asphalt Warriors. We were whooping it up. We had prevailed in what we'd later refer to as "the year of the hurricane!" Our pain had subsided and our spirits soared! Twelve friends had gone the distance *together* once again.

David Stewart *was born and raised in Portland. He has been participated in Hood To Coast seven times.*

It was 2015, the year of the storm. Anyone who ran that year will have a version of this tale. The finish line blew away. On my second leg, lightning and thunder crashed down all at once. The wind howled and trees cracked under its pressure. I ran through pouring rain, half expecting a van to drive by and tell me to get in. Race cancelled.

It didn't happen. As I passed other runners, I didn't say, "good job." Instead I screamed, "Run faster! Let's get out of this #@^%!"

As the early morning light was revealed through the gray skies and a steady deluge of yet more rain, my teammates and I sat in Van 2 tired, defeated, and smelling somewhat like old socks. We were prisoners in our Sienna minivan with a seven-foot yellow Power Ranger stuck on the side.

The rain pounded on the roof. Some of us tried to sleep. Ivan, who was our Runner 12, succeeded and his six-foot, five-inch body was sprawled out across two rows of van seats, much to the discomfort of his fellow vanmates.

As I stared blankly out from the driver's seat of our minivan I began to sing. It was terribly out of tune.

Ooh-oo child
Things are gonna get easier
Ooh-oo child
Things'll get brighter

One voice joined in. Then two voices were singing with me. Soon it was three of us. And next the whole van was singing. Even Ivan half opened his eyes, managed a smile, and joined us for a couple verses.

Then, as if a sign from God, the clouds parted and the rain stopped. The sun shone down on our van as if to say, "Don't give up, things will get brighter."

And then it immediately started to rain again.

Wind and rain battered us the rest of the race. Ivan ran through a makeshift finish line in Seaside. Our Van 1 teammates were celebrating in Portland. They were told to go home.

We were, too, but after the night we'd been through, there was no storm that could keep us from finishing.

Candi Garrett *grew up in Portland and now lives in Newberg, Oregon. She has partici-pated in Hood To Coast more than 25 times.*

During the storm in 2015, Melissa was running Leg 29. She was close to reaching the top of the killer hill as the rain was coming down sideways, and there was thunder and lightning and branches flying all over. When Melissa reached the top of the hill, she had a huge smile on her face and her arms were raised in the air. And we were right there holding a roll of toilet paper for her to run through as we cheered. That run is tough in normal weather, but during that storm—Melissa was a beast to battle all the elements!

Later on, when I talked to my husband in Seaside, he told me they had closed the beach. I was like, "No way. That's unheard of." But, sure enough, they had closed down the beach. The tents on the beach were blowing all over. It was just wild.

Although the conditions were awful, we never even considered stopping or not finishing. A team from where I work didn't finish. When I was talking to them afterward I said, "What? That wasn't even an option." We just had to tough it out!

Lark Asbury *was born in Portland and grew up in Hillsboro, Oregon. She works at Nike and has been involved in Hood To Coast as either a runner or a volunteer for more than 10 years.*

In 2015 we thought that it was going to be really hot during the relay, so we were all training in the heat to make sure we would be ready. And then the storm came.

That was also the year I chose to be Runner 5 in Van 1 and do Leg 29, one of the hardest uphill runs of the relay. I said, "You know what? I'm going to do it. I'm going to run Toilet Paper Hill. I've got this." I specifically remember running up that hill for three miles with rivers running by my feet the whole time and branches hitting me in the face, and I was just laughing hysterically.

It was a crazy year. We found out that the finish party at the beach wasn't happening and teams were not completing the race because of the weather. As we finished our final legs and were getting ready to hand off to Van 2 for their last legs, they were in a really low spot. They had a really rough time with the weather and didn't even think they could keep going.

Even though our Van 1 was finished running, we were still a team. Everyone in Van 1 said, "We're going to be with you every single leg, and if you need one of us to run with you, we'll do it. We will complete it as a team." Our Van 1 went to every single exchange with Van 2. We were there when they started and with them when they finished, and we cheered for them the whole time.

It was awesome to be able to help them get to the finish. Even though the finish had been moved off the beach, the whole team ran to the finish line together. Afterward, all of us went to dinner—soaking wet. It was an awesome time we will never forget.

To this day we still talk about it when we go out running together. Someone will say, "Do you remember when we ran through that storm during Hood To Coast?"

Kirk Helzer is from Tualatin, Oregon, and is a longtime competitor in Hood To Coast with the Dirty Half Dozen +6 team. His father, Richard, ran in the very first HTC in 1982.

Starting up the Coast Range in 2015, the weather was incredible. Our runner was going up this gravel road and we were trying to get through in the van. We were going through some of the most surreal countryside. Thunder was cracking, there were 30-mph winds, and it was alternating between super heavy rain and hail. Images of those conditions will stay with me for a long time.

It was an epic event. We were all wondering if they would actually stop the race. We were sitting in the vans with our fingers crossed saying, "Please let us keep going. We've come this far. We're not going to let a little wind and rain stop us from finishing."

It slowed down every team on the course, but we were determined not to let it stop us. We started seeing local law enforcement officials coming out and were thinking, "Oh no, don't shut it down." We even began working on our logistics, in case they told us we had to backtrack. We'd find a way to get back on the course and finish it anyway.

That's the mentality of our team, and it explains why we enjoy Hood To Coast so much. Each year is a different adventure. The reason some of us do this is to put a hurdle in front of ourselves. It's about overcoming adversity. It's about clearing that hurdle. We crave that in some respect, and to some of us that's what this event represents. It's still a run from a ski resort down to the ocean, but invariably something beyond the control of anybody involved happens. We'd been waiting, knowing there would come a year when the weather was that challenge.

I got lucky. We were through the worst weather when it was my turn to run. It was sunrise, but it was still dark and stormy, so we had to use our headlamps and all the vans were still fully lit up. My last leg was still run in 25- to 30-mph headwinds and a steady rain. It was uncomfortable, but it was not unbearable.

I remember thinking while I was running my leg, "We got this." We only had another seven or eight legs to go and we were close enough to the coast that I knew we were going to finish. The weather wasn't going to stop us.

Van after van after van went flying by us. Those were the teams that decided they weren't going to complete the last set of legs and were driving to the coast. I remember thinking, "I'm glad I'm here. I'm glad I'm on this leg. Even though it sucks and the weather is terrible, I wouldn't want to be any place else." One way or another, our team was going to finish.

Coming into Seaside, everything on the beach had been torn down by the weather and the finish line had been moved to the road by the turnaround. There was no crowd and zero fanfare at the finish. We all looked at each other and nodded, knowing nothing could stop us.

I take my hat off to the HTC organization. They did what needed to be done to keep the event open and the teams moving forward. We understood and we felt for them. The weather had destroyed a big revenue opportunity for them and the other vendors at the beach, and we knew it must have been very difficult for them.

Nikki Neuburger *is a Portland native and attended Oregon State University, where she walked on to the women's volleyball team and became team captain. After graduating in 2004, she joined Nike and was a longtime marketing executive at the company until early 2018, when she became the Global Head of Marketing at Uber Eats in San Francisco. She is a regular Hood To Coast participant.*

Everybody who ran the race in 2015 has a crazy story. It was the wildest weather ever. Over the course of five miles, I had a headwind that was crazy, a tailwind that was crazy, and a side wind that was crazy. I couldn't tell where the wind was going to hit me next.

I was Runner 7. I was running my second leg in the middle of the night and it was pouring down rain with lightning and thunder. It got to the point where the lightning and the thunder were so close, people were getting scared and jumping into the bushes because they thought they were in danger, which wasn't actually the case.

It was like running in a video game. You're sleep-deprived. It's three in the morning. And you're in the middle of nowhere. Most of the time when you're running for about

24 hours like our team instead of 16 or 17 hours like some of the top teams—you don't see a lot of people on the course. So when you're out there alone with the lightning and thunder, you start running faster because you're a little scared about what's going to happen.

I ran three miles with a total stranger because it was so scary neither of us wanted to be out there running alone. Things like that add to the folklore of why the race is so special and cool.

I'm sure some people had a bad experience, but most of my teammates run all the time, and crappy weather wasn't going to deter them. It made the race more memorable. When you've done it more than 10 times, the races kind of bleed together and you can't really remember one year from the next. The 2015 race will always stick out as one of the craziest moments of my life, especially that middle of night run during the storm. It's something I'll remember forever.

The only real bummer was they had to cancel the festivities on the beach because it was too dangerous. The feeling was like, "We finished, but nobody's here." Everybody usually gets together and celebrates at the beach. As a result, the finish was a little bit anticlimactic, but they were just trying to get us out of the way so we wouldn't get hurt.

All in all, it was a pretty extraordinary race. Hood To Coast prioritized the safety of the runners, and most people understand that should be the top priority.

Sally Showman *worked as a meteorologist and reporter at Portland television station KOIN-TV.*

I tried out for volleyball my freshman year in high school and got cut. I wanted to do something athletic, so I tried cross country. It was one of the best decisions I ever made. Once you start running it's hard to give it up. It gets in your blood. I've run my whole life and have probably done about 30 half-marathons, in addition to competing in Hood To Coast.

Going into 2015 I said I wanted to spearhead a KOIN team. I was willing to be the captain and organize it if the station would give us permission to do it, which it did. We had about 25 people who wanted to do the race. With only one team, it turned into a lottery. I actually pulled names out of a hat to select our team.

I remember it so vividly because that was the year of the big wind storm. I was a meteorologist and did the weather on the morning show. I had been watching that storm all week long. I was getting more worried each day as we were seeing the forecast models come in and it looked like it could be a big one.

We went live on Friday morning from the race start at Timberline Lodge and I was there in Van 1. I was excited because there's so much energy at the start, it's just incredible. It was a really nice day, a beautiful sunrise, although I remember telling the reporters back at the station I was worried about the wind at the coast on Saturday morning. At that time there were high wind watches for the Oregon coast that would eventually transition into a high wind warning. But mostly I was really excited. We had a great group of people in our van and off we went.

I did my first two legs, finishing my second in St. Helens. I remember going to the Safeway store to get my dinner and noticing that my phone was blowing up. The station was wondering what I was thinking about the race and the windstorm. Dan Floyd (HTC COO) called and was wondering the same thing.

I had been kind of out of touch because your cell phone battery runs out so fast on the racecourse. As we started up into the Coast Range my service started getting super patchy. I told them what I could, but I wasn't able to check weather models or even get on any kind of website to see what was happening. At some point Friday afternoon or evening, the national weather service pulled the trigger and issued the high wind warning. That's when the race organizers and all the meteorologists in town got really concerned.

I remember going to an exchange to try and sleep, but I was too nervous. I couldn't sleep. I was afraid someone was going to get hurt. I was thinking, "Oh my gosh, this could be a total nightmare." The Coast Range is so wooded, and with all that wind I was petrified someone was going to get hurt by a falling tree limb or a falling tree.

All through the Coast Range I didn't have any phone service. I didn't know what was going on. I didn't know how much the winds had picked up at the coast.

Leg 29 takes you up over the top of the Coast Range. Once I started down the other side, the winds began to pick up and there were tree branches breaking off. When we had the transition with the next van it became apparent that the winds were strong and we began to get gusts of up to 70- and 80-mph I began to get text messages from people at the finish letting me know it looked like a hurricane had blown through. Everything had blown everywhere.

We got there and all of the sudden it was a news story. I called the station and told them to get a news crew out to Seaside because of all the damage. Wind storms like that are pretty much unheard of for the end of August. In the winter we have those storms and it's not all that uncommon, but to see it at the end of August during the race was unbelievable.

I remember hearing brutal stories from team members who ran the last six legs about running against that wind. It wasn't the same after-party we'd had in the past, but it was totally understandable. I think we got really lucky that no one was hurt. And everybody on our team said we had to do it again next year so we could have a great after-party at the beach.

Sure enough, we did it again the next year and the after-party was great.

I always feel personally responsible for the weather. There's this "weather person's guilt" that you have. I'm not all that recognizable in my baseball hat and greasy hair that hasn't been washed in two days, but everyone who recognized me that day wanted to know what the heck was going on.

Every time I do the race, while I'm doing it, I think I'm not going to do it the next year. And then the day after, I'm like, "Okay, when do I sign up? I've got to do this again."

David Warden has served more than 20 years in the United States Navy and is currently a Senior Chief Petty Officer in the Navy Reserve based in Portland. He was an Exchange Leader during the 2015 Hood To Coast, overseeing volunteers at the final six exchanges.

In the Marines there's a saying, "Embrace the suck!" That pretty much describes what the 2015 Hood To Coast was all about.

Moving to Oregon in 2013, I'd heard about the relay and after some research, realized it was a huge event that also gave back to the community. I wanted to get involved and worked several military-themed events for them. When they asked me to take on a role with the race, it was a no-brainer. That's a great team to work with and for, and I was excited to be a part of the event coordination.

I've always said the more arduous the race, the sweeter the victory, and 2015 was a bear. I compare the weather to the time when I was aboard the USS Paiute, off the coast of Cape Hatteras, North Carolina. The vessel was just over 200 feet long and we were getting pounded head on by 30-foot waves. All topside decks were secured—you don't go outside in weather like that. You don't do anything but go to your rack, stand your watch, and try your best to keep your lunch down.

The weather during the 2015 race was horrendous! There was wind, rain and cold, all the perfect conditions for quitting. There were 60-year-old, mature trees bending and tossed about like they were bushes. It was nuts and our volunteer support was waning because of the weather. Along the route, I pulled at least four huge branches off the road and at times enlisted others, including runners, to help drag the branches off the road. Some branches were so big, it took three or four people to move them.

Only winners run, operate or volunteer in that weather. Admittedly, it was a bit treacherous at times, but I wasn't going to quit. I'm no quitter. I wasn't worried that my shoes were completely soaked or that my socks were so muddy they looked like brown church socks. I didn't care what my breath smelled like, the condition of my clothes or my appearance. My mission was to give those runners, supporters and families their money's worth, the experience everyone comes to expect from the relay. I wasn't going to let the weather stop it. I'm not that guy. I was going to make it the best experience I could for the participants and volunteers.

At every exchange I visited there were miserable volunteers, shaking with chills, and I think every one of them was ready to quit. It was my job to motivate them, to pump them up. I'd pull up to an exchange, keep my truck running and look for the volunteers who seemed the most miserable. I'd relieve their stations, encouraging them to warm up in the truck. I think that went a long way in building camaraderie among the volunteers

I remember pulling into the last exchange before the beach. The party had already been cancelled and the sweep truck was clearing the course. There were 12 runners still on the course and I said to their supporters that their teams were what the spirit of the race was all about. I shared that same passion with the volunteers and they all agreed that because of those teams, the weather didn't matter. Our biggest "why" for keeping this exchange and the race open was so they could hold their heads up, knowing they'd likely endured the worst running conditions of their life. This went deeper than a beach party. This was a true victory on the part of staff, runners, supporters and volunteers. Those volunteers dedicated their energy to ensuring each runner to the very last had someone there cheering for them.

There are 11 General Orders to the Sentry and number five is, "To quit my post only when properly relieved." I was not going to quit my watch. I know it's silly to get emotional, but I was not going to quit until I knew every single runner was safe. It was my duty. When chaos hits, I simply apply the military training instilled in me and things seem to normalize, no matter the circumstance. The Navy grew me up and made me the man I am. Some may think it's just a stupid race, but it was more than a race. It was about keeping every last person affiliated with the event safe. Even the last runner has a family, and maybe kids. If my kid were out there running, I hope a volunteer is there to ensure their safety.

Those volunteers were amazing! Sometimes when you have a whistle and an orange vest there can be this air of superiority, but that wasn't the case. Their attitude was, "You're running and I'm doing everything I can to give you the best experience."

The experience is incredible whether you're a first-time runner, a van driver, vendor or part of the volunteer squad. The 2015 event solidified for me that inside all of us is a seed of amazing. Seeing thousands of runners, drenched, exhausted and still running— they were all champions to me. They had the hearts of champions and I expressed that belief to each runner or supporter that crossed my path.

To me, HTC exemplifies what teamwork is all about. It should be, "Hood *Team* Coast."

Cassie Negra *is the Hood To Coast office manager and oversees the registration lottery for the race. She previously handled marketing and sponsorships for the organization.*

The year of the wind and the rain, 2015, was just my second year on the job. Everything about the relay was still pretty new to me.

I had been talking with a woman whose husband was on a Nike team from Europe coming over to run the race. She was going to travel with him to Oregon, just to visit and do some sightseeing. And she really wanted to serve as a volunteer at the race. I told her to find me when she got to the beach in Seaside and I'd figure out something for her to do.

When she arrived at the beach we were all running around like chickens with our heads cut off, trying to figure out what to do because of the stupid weather. I told her to just stick with me.

At one point the weather forced us to change the finish so the runners would not end on the beach. Jude (Hubber, HTC Race Series CEO) then asked us to help direct traffic. He needed us to tell runners to keep going straight on one street, rather than turning at the corner.

I took this woman from Europe who wanted to be a volunteer and another woman and we headed down to the corner. We all had on raincoats and other wet-weather gear. The wind was so strong we had to link our arms together or we would have been blown away. It was grueling standing there because the wind was just pounding us.

I couldn't even imagine what it was like for all the runners and walkers in that weather. It was just crazy!

Jude Hubber *is the Hood To Coast Race Series chief executive officer.*

I was with Dan Floyd (HTC COO) and Felicia Hubber (HTC president) in the command center at our old office on Friday trying to decide what the hell we were going to do. It was the proudest I've ever been while working at Hood To Coast. We didn't agree on everything, but we weren't fighting either. We were sincerely trying to get stuff done and to get it done quickly.

We were starting to get reports that trees were blowing down and stuff like that. At that point, however, runners were spread out so far along the course that stopping the race was basically impossible. We went through all the different scenarios for the race, including whether we should consider cancelling it. We were constantly checking with our safety people and the police, but I don't think we ever really got close to actually cancelling the event.

We sent out a message on social media basically saying, *If anyone feels like quitting, don't worry about it, stop. We'll have you back next year. Don't feel like you need to finish this race.* We knew some people were going to get the message, but because service is spotty in some areas on the course, not everyone would.

Once the decision was made to continue the race, around 11 p.m., we got in a car and drove to Seaside. As we were driving, we weren't really in much of the bad weather we were hearing about. We could see lightning off in the distance and we were hearing some stories about the weather over our radios. But people get pretty amped up during the race and sometimes someone out at one of the exchanges might say it's pretty windy when it's not too bad. So it wasn't totally clear yet to us what was happening.

Saturday morning, however, we were up really early and everything was blowing down on the beach in Seaside. I was like, "Oh, this is crazy." When you see it in person and all of a sudden tents start blowing away, that makes it real. We didn't allow anyone on the beach because it was just too dangerous. We were just letting everything break loose and blow away. At one point I remember hanging over the edge of the wall trying to cut things away so they could blow in the wind. It was just insane!

Then we decided to change the course and had to come up with a new design for the finish, since we couldn't end the race on the beach. Someone came up with the idea to finish by making a left from the Promenade onto Broadway Street, rather than a right onto the beach. I went out and ran it and it seemed to work. It was chaos and the staff was spread all over, so I was grabbing volunteers and having them run with me and putting them on street corners to direct runners.

Ironically, that was probably the happiest many our participants have ever been. You'd think they would have been angry or unhappy. But people were saying, "I just ran through a hurricane." Not many people can say that. They appreciated the fact that we still had a finish line, and most of them just went with the flow.

Christina Fuller *is co-owner with her husband, Tyler, of Portland-based Fuller Events. The company has been producing the Hood To Coast finish line activities in Seaside since 2013.*

In 2015 we had probably the best weather we've ever had for setup at the beach for

Hood To Coast. It was a gorgeous week. Warm and blue skies, it almost felt too good to be true. And of course it was.

Our setup was right on schedule. We're always watching the weather and we heard about the wind and the possibility of a significant storm coming in. We started monitoring it early in the week and touched base with our rental companies regarding their tents and their structures, along with the things on their end that might be susceptible to wind.

We were in touch with the HTC team several times a day, making real-time adjustments and talking about a Plan A, a Plan B, and a Plan C.

We were unsure of the magnitude of the storm, where it would hit or when it would hit. I don't think any of us really expected downtown Seaside and the finish party to be the epicenter of the winds. Five miles north and five miles south they didn't have what we had. So it was hard to predict what would happen. But we were planning the whole time to adjust as needed.

As the weekend moved closer we were in conversations with the HTC team every couple hours to see what they had heard. We were checking all the weather websites, looking at NOAA (National Oceanic and Atmospheric Administration) forecasts, using all the resources available to us to see how we could adapt our schedule and production plan.

About 5 p.m. on Friday—which is normally when we're chasing the last few hours of daylight to get a lot of the finishing pieces in place so we're ready to welcome the first runners—we stopped production. We stopped building anything further, realizing that it looked like the storm was going to hit Seaside. At that point we spent the last few hours of daylight reinforcing some things, putting backstays and additional supports on the stages and tents. We were also releasing and loosening things like banners that could turn into sails and blow off somewhere and cause an issue. First and foremost, our number one priority was safety. How do we keep everyone safe? That was a pretty clear priority for us.

The storm started to come in at nightfall. At that point the runners were running and headed toward town. We were hearing stories of some downed trees along the course and different scenarios here and there.

Of course it was a sleepless night for Tyler and me. We were in our rental house in Seaside and the wind was just whipping. By 3 a.m. we decided to just go down to the beach. It was still dark and we were standing on the Promenade, looking out onto an empty beach that was pretty much ready for the festival.

About 5 a.m. we decided not to open the beach party for now. At that time the wind was beginning to really come in. Everything was staying pretty solid, which felt good, but it was getting a little wild as the sun was coming up.

The decision wasn't hard to make, realizing the storm was hitting and it wasn't going to be safe. It would be a bigger challenge to evacuate people from the beach than to never let them on in the first place. We knew we had the support and the respect of the HTC team and if we said we didn't feel it was safe they would have our back.

Trying to be optimistic, we were hoping that by lunchtime maybe the storm would roll through and we could open up. But it became pretty clear before long that wasn't going to happen. You would be walking along the Promenade at midday and you couldn't make any headway. With the wind and the rain, it was quite a spectacle.

We never looked back on not opening the beach party. We never questioned it. We started going through our vendor phone tree to make sure everything was safe and that they had done everything on their end. We repositioned security, which is normally posted throughout the event, to man new positions limiting beach access for safety reasons. We had to move the finish line timing mats and their infrastructure and their technology, which ended up being the first of four times we moved them during the course of the day.

Necessary services, including timing and first aid, also had to be relocated. We moved them to the Shilo Inn and other locations in the area near the roundabout.

Since there was nowhere to go, all the runners and their families and friends who were meeting them at the finish line moved into the streets. The city worked quickly and closed down Seaside's Broadway Street to accommodate the crowd. Everyone had the same end goal, safety, and it worked out very smoothly.

We got pretty lucky in terms of actual equipment lost and damaged. All the big infrastructure pieces stayed pretty much in place. The stage was strong. Some of the equipment ended up a quarter-mile down the beach and we found it as we were cleaning up the next couple days.

The tent companies probably took it the hardest, as a few of the tents got toppled. A lot of the signage and banners got ripped and torn, so those were a loss. The catering company took it pretty hard too. They had everything stocked for a full day of food booths, which they never got to open. All of their food went to waste, whether it was hot dog buns blowing down the beach or sand in the chicken sandwiches.

We had no injuries, however, and we really did weather the storm pretty well. That's a tribute to the vendors making appropriate preparations at the last minute when we could see the storm was coming. It turned out to be a doozy and its own source of entertainment, just watching the storm hit the event site.

Everyone was so supportive, including the runners. Most didn't feel like they were getting slighted because we didn't have a finish party. They realized it was a responsible move not to let anyone down on the beach.

Overall we did well to minimize the impact. We emphasized safety and were able to communicate with most of the attendees. It solidified the professionalism of the event, the quality of the vendors and sponsors and producers. Everyone was on the same page and really had a dialed-in response during this time of crisis.

Bob Foote *is the founder and chairman of Hood To Coast.*

My toughest year for the race was probably 2015, when we had the terrible storm. It was a heartbreaker. I take so much pride in our beach party. Now that I don't have any real responsibilities during the race, other than the start area, the beach party is my favorite part of the whole weekend.

At the beach after the race I have a chance to talk with hundreds of teams. They tell me their war stories and they're so buzzed and pumped up. I live the whole feeling of the finish experience vicariously through them. It was a real bummer to have that experience taken away in 2015. I consider the beach party the culmination of the event and the real spirit of the race, and we lost it that year.

You never know exactly how many people attend our beach party. The guys that pump the porta potties have made a pretty exact science out of knowing how the volume of usage equates to a specific number of people. They say the beach party attracts about 100,000 people, including participants, spectators, locals, and everyone else who comes by. That probably makes our beach party the biggest held on the West Coast. As far as I know, there's nothing else even close, all the way down to Southern California.

To have a party of that magnitude washed out was a heartbreaker for me. It's a celebration of your accomplishments. Runners bust their butts the whole race to get to the finish and they want to celebrate the achievement. That's what the beach party is all about.

Besides the disappointment of the beach party being cancelled because of the weather, my other memory from that year involves my wife, Alyda. She walks on a Portland To Coast team every year. In 2015 she had the last leg and took her exchange up in the Coast Range. Her teammates wanted to pull out, but she said she was going to do her leg and charged off.

I was standing on the Promenade by the finish when some of her teammates came running up. They were fearful for her safety and said we needed to go look for her. I said a couple of choice words and then added, "No. She's tough. There's no way she'll back down because of the weather."

Just then she rounded the corner, and I could see she was in her finishing kick. She had on a windbreaker with her hood tied so tight only a little of her face was exposed. And she was grinning. She was just loving it—loving the pain! She was just barreling along. And as soon as she crossed the finish line she said, "I beat the hurricane! I beat it! I won!"

The celebration at the Seaside race finish.

CHAPTER 23

Reaching The Beach

THE HOOD TO COAST FINISH on the beach in Seaside signifies the end of the journey. It's where teams reconnect and cross the finish line together. Medals are distributed, pictures taken and team celebrations begin. There's a tremendous sense of accomplishment from a group of tired, hungry and worn out runners.

Adam Morris *is an attorney from Wayzata, Minnesota, who participated in his first Hood To Coast in 2014.*

Hood To Coast finishes in the town of Seaside, south of Astoria, which is where the movie *The Goonies* was filmed. The beach is dotted with hotels, like all beach towns. Most of them look like their heyday was in 1985, the year the movie came out, if not decades earlier. There's a giant rock outcropping along the ocean, south of town. It looks somewhat like those Thai outcroppings—without the shimmering heat, of course—in the James Bond movie *The Man with the Golden Gun.* In contrast to Thailand, though, the Pacific Ocean in Seaside is frigid.

All this is to say that the beach-town vibe of Seaside isn't like thousands of famous beach towns in America. Still, Seaside is a perfect place to finish the relay. For one thing, its beach feels like it's about a mile wide, and it's flat as a football field. The sand near the water feels compact, and the beach is wide and long enough to probably land a 747. An entire high school cross country team could easily do their training on the beach running side by side.

The softer sand near the boardwalk—really a cement Promenade—is dotted with small sand pits and charred wood, apparently left by campers who fit perfectly into the funky Oregon culture. In addition to natural beauty, a throwback, laissez-faire vibe draws people to Seaside. And on the last Saturday in August, what draws people to Seaside are more than 10,000 smelly, exhausted, limping revelers.

Because Seaside is small and somewhat hard to get to, or leave, and because many of the runners have been up for more than 30 hours, the race's finish teems with people. This may seem an odd observation to a non-runner or even to many runners, but at many big races the huge finishing areas seem far too crowded for comfort. And in most races, runners more or less clear out after getting their medal, water, and a snack, and perhaps greeting a friend or family member, simply because there is not much reason to stick around.

In late August in Seaside, however, there's nowhere to go and not much else to do but drink IPAs, listen to music, share stories, and check the race results. Everybody is giddy to be there because for nobody is the experience ho-hum. Grizzled veterans of many marathons and old-hands express surprise at how much fun they've had in the race. Thirty-year runners of the race compare the freebie T-shirt and medal with their other 29, and they know the years by sight and description. Cover bands play on a giant stage, and runners ask each other, "What leg were you?" Everybody knows that Leg 5 also means Legs 17 and 29. And everybody knows that Leg 29 is a bitch.

It's not Seaside's natural beauty that ultimately moves people to hang out—it's the fact that all 12,000 just participated in a race that seems impossibly long and difficult.

Christina Fuller *is co-owner with her husband, Tyler, of Portland-based Fuller Events. The company has been producing the Hood To Coast finish line activities in Seaside since 2013.*

My husband and I had been working together in Portland in the event scene and obviously knew of Hood To Coast. It's an iconic event in the area. As an event planner you're always looking for something challenging, interesting, and outside of what you're doing, so in my mind I was always thinking, "Man, that would be a fun event to work on."

We thought the loyalty of the participants and the community rapport that exists around the race made it one of those cool bucket list events to work on. We'd worked with Dan Floyd (HTC COO) in his previous job on the Portland Waterfront Blues Festival. He was familiar with our services. They were looking for a new finish line producer and reached out. It was a real pinch-me moment.

We do large events all the time, but the relay is unique. It's a real challenge to produce something on a beach. There's the sandy surface. And it's a public space that people want to enjoy all summer, so you need to work around them. That makes it both fun and challenging.

The Oregon coast isn't like a parking lot, which you know will be the same year after year. It's organic and changes every year. We go out and check the site every year prior to setup to see what adjustments we need to make. To see how the winds have changed the sand dunes and how the grass has shifted.

We also check the tide tables to see how far the tides will come in. We've had some close calls. One year the water got about 10 feet away from one of our generators, but so far we've been spared.

The setup starts on the Sunday or Monday in the week leading up to the event and we're working all the way until the first runner rolls in. We have a team of about 10 during the week, which ramps up to about 20 by the event date. That doesn't include the dozen or so partners and vendors and their extensive teams that it takes to build that finish line village. We have teams that water down the sand to make it compact so we can move vehicles. And we have a stage-build team, a tent rental company, the Honey Bucket team, and the sponsor activation teams. Once you include everybody, we probably have a hundred different folks working to build that party area.

Teardown takes about a day and a half to two days. It's amazing how quickly everything can go away. We're usually done by the end of Monday, if not sooner. We're out of there and it's back to being a regular old beach.

The sand obviously presents a lot of challenges. Most vehicles can't navigate it. So we have to get creative with loading in, whether it's using Gator-type carts or all-terrain forklifts. Even big 4x4 pickup trucks can get stuck in the sand because it's so soft.

We have only one access point where you can drive in and out, which is also unique. Usually you have a couple of different areas. We've got the one loading dock right there on Seaside's Avenue A. It also serves as the emergency fire lane for the fire department and lifeguards. We basically have just two parking spots that we can use at any one time to load in the event, which is very, very limited. So we choreograph the vendors and the teams and work very closely with Seaside to make sure it's as well-oiled a machine as possible. We need folks to stick to their load-in times and we need to keep those forklifts and Gators moving all day, every day, to help vendors unload and get their stuff to where it's going.

The race really does take over the entire city for those couple days. We work diligently with the city, the police department, the fire department, and the local businesses to make it as an enjoyable process as possible. For us it means doing what we say we're going to do. If that means keeping the fire lane clear so they have great access, then that's what we do. We try and go out of our way, which usually means more work. But they lend us their city to host this amazing event, so we want to be very good stewards of the city and the beach. Over the last several years the city has been very supportive of us and the event and it has really turned in to a great partnership.

The level of the sophistication of the activations on the beach continues to increase and the sponsors are doing some awesome build-outs and creative booths. That added complexity requires time and energy, however, and adds another whole layer to an already complicated load-in schedule.

But it's the best office you can get. Talk about an office with a view!

The number of people attending the event is astronomical. When you have that volume of people it keeps you on your toes. Seaside is a busy destination—I read where it was recently voted the number two summertime beach destination in the country—and that means we've got our work cut out for us. What we see as our jobsite, someone else sees as their playground, so we have to work around them. As kids are seeing the ocean for the first time and building sandcastles and running on the beach, we're coming through with a massive backhoe or a forklift or something like that.

We invite anyone who wants to come to attend the beach party. The event is free and open to the public. We always say if you're in town on Saturday come by, there's a band playing, and it's a great party.

We're really proud to work on this event. It feels like part of the fabric of Oregon and the running community and the outdoor community. To be able to plan a party at the finish is very meaningful to us. We get to see our friends and family there too. It seems like the least we can do is provide a really well-executed and organized event.

Felicia Hubber grew up in Portland, moved to Montana during high school, and attended college at the University of Montana. The daughter of Hood To Coast founder Bob Foote, Felicia was just a few months old when she attended the first HTC—and she's been at every relay since. In 2006 she succeeded her father as president of HTC.

My mom, Patti, carried me around in a little backpack as she sold merchandise during the early years of the race. My dad said I liked sitting on stage during the awards presentation and would hold onto his leg as he walked around.

My own earliest memories of the race are of being at the finish in Pacific City. I was born in 1982, the year of the first race, and the finish was moved to Seaside in 1989, so it was probably in the mid-1980s that I remember being at the simple, quaint beach party, sitting at a picnic table with all the runners, and eating spaghetti on a paper plate. I remember at that young age looking around and wondering, "What is this party all about?"

At the finish one year, there was a giant inflatable Spuds MacKenzie—the Bud Light dog. I remember thinking that was pretty funny. I also recall participants running down a paved road that led to a dead end in a parking lot next to the beach. I would sit there with my grandma or mom and watch as all the runners would cross the finish line.

My mom and grandma would help out with the race, and I would hang out with them. In the early years, my mom handled all the data entry—inputting the names, addresses, and all the other information for the participants. She also was responsible for selling apparel at Timberline Lodge and the beach.

I always seemed to be with my mom or dad and doing what I could to be of help. When I got a little older, maybe six or seven years old, I would do the carbon copies for credit cards when people bought apparel, unpack or move boxes, or put labels on thousands of mailing envelopes and folders.

At our house in Portland we had a basement room that was originally supposed to be used for a pool table or game room. Instead it was the race storage area. The fairly large room was stacked from the floor to the ceiling with boxes of merchandise and posters and every other miscellaneous item for the race you could possibly imagine. You could barely open the door. I'd climb around in there and make forts with my friends. We made that place a really cool place to play!

After the race ended and we cleaned up from the finish party, my mom, dad, and I would always take a short camping trip. We had a camper van, and every single year after the race we would pack up our things for a trip down the Oregon coast. We'd find a unique camping spot we'd never explored before and spend two or three days hanging out together as a family, camping and enjoying a few days of rest.

I always enjoyed that trip after the race.

John Hammarley *is the longtime and only public address announcer for Hood To Coast. He is responsible for introducing every team at the race start and as they cross the finish line. Hammarley is a former television news reporter in Chicago, New York, Dallas, and Portland, who now lives in Bend, Oregon. He received six Emmy Awards during his television career.*

My annual tradition after the last wave of runners head out is to get in my car and drive to Seaside. Nobody rides with me, which is probably a good thing because I couldn't carry on a conversation after introducing more than 1,000 teams. Even I'm sick of my voice! I probably couldn't talk even if I wanted to because announcing all those teams is a pretty big strain on my vocal cords. So from the moment I get into my car Friday night at Timberline Lodge, until I start announcing the finish at the beach on Saturday morning, I'm pretty much silent.

I take my time driving to the beach and don't follow the racecourse. Once I get to Sandy, I often pull off to get something to eat and drink. It's usually two cups of hot chocolate—I'm not a coffee drinker—and about three Taco Bell beef burritos. Both the hot chocolate and burritos feel really good on my throat!

Especially in the early years, it was a long, lonely drive from Timberline to the beach in the dark of the night. There were many years where I had the radio blasting and the windows rolled down as I drove across the Coast Range. It's just another part of the job and I haven't had problems with that trip over the years.

On Saturday morning I get up and have some more hot chocolate. I start talking to myself in my hotel room to warm up the vocal cords. Then I get ready for another long day. I get to the announcer's tower at the finish a little before 10 a.m. There has been an announcer there in the early morning hours for the Portland To Coast walkers, then I get the microphone and start announcing teams as they finish.

The atmosphere couldn't be any more different between the start and the finish. While the finish is as vibrant as the start, it's also more celebratory and a little more relaxed. I'm proud to announce each team coming across the finish line because it's a heck of an accomplishment, especially for those teams who've never done it before. And regardless of how many years each team has done it, it's always a good feeling for them to hit the sand at the beach and know they're finished. My tone at the finish is somewhat joyous, but not necessarily, "Okay, let's get out there and do it again." For one thing, everyone is tired. Some runners haven't taken a shower and others haven't slept. They're done and they want to find the beer garden or have some decent food or take a shower.

At the finish my responsibilities change significantly. While I control the start in terms of a predetermined group of runners leaving every 15 minutes, the finish line is completely different. There's always an hour in the race on Saturday afternoon when it's total gridlock at the finish. Usually it's late in the afternoon, between 4 and 6 p.m. There are so many teams coming across the finish line then that I'm just announcing one team after another. In the early years the last teams would finish around midnight. Now it's gotten progressively earlier, to where I'm really shutting the course down at 8 or 9 p.m.

The challenge is to stay ahead of the game. Having a spotter on the Promenade to give me a heads-up regarding what team is about to finish is extremely helpful. In the announcer's tower there's also an antiquated computer system, where I can punch in a team number and hopefully it will show the team name.

While my voice isn't the "official" finish, it does signal to each team their work is done. For many people it's the end of a new experience. Hopefully, it's also the start of a year's worth of stories they can tell their family and friends until the next year or the next relay.

I also have to be careful about the amount of joking around I do at the finish because for many runners their nerves are somewhat frayed, to say the least. Sometimes I can hit a nerve and they don't really appreciate it. Over the years I've found it necessary to be careful how much good-natured fun I aim their way. A lot of the runners are impatient. They're tired and dirty, and they don't need some wise-ass announcer making fun of them.

There's never been another race announcer and there's not another race that I announce—it's just Hood To Coast!

Steve Hanamura was born in Upland, California, and now lives in Portland. He has participated in Hood To Coast more than 25 times and served as captain of the team I Hurt, You Hurt, We All Hurt for more than 20 years. Blind since birth, he is an avid runner and sports fan.

One year I was running Leg 36 to the finish. When you get to the boardwalk in Seaside and start running down toward the finish, people are everywhere. My guide has to be really direct with me because people are sometimes in the way. They're over here and they're over there, and sometimes I have to run in between them.

My first running guide had no mercy. She would just yell, "Blind runner. Get out of the way." Then for emphasis she would add, "Blind runner coming through. Blind runner coming through." She was just ruthless. And if you were in her way, she would let you know.

I actually thought it was kind of funny. At that point, I'm not bothered by anything. I'm just totally focused on doing what I'm told, and running through people is hard and takes focus.

It's also thrilling because I get applauded a lot. If I'm truthful, I probably get a little extra applause because of the blindness. I can really feel the warmth from the people when they do that.

It doesn't just happen at the finish. Basically, I probably get applauded more than other competitors even just running into any exchange, and that's a part of Hood To Coast too.

Martha Estes is from Bainbridge, Washington, and has been part of the Portland To Coast team Mr. Toad's Wild Ride for about 15 years.

What brings me back year after year are my teammates. We have a great time together. Everybody just gets silly. We have a competitiveness among ourselves that's fun.

We don't set out to win, although we've done well on several occasions. We have people who want to be part of our team again and again. It's just a really great weekend.

The feeling of coming across the finish line after your whole team has worked so hard to get there is very special. And having the crowd there at the end and knowing that you did it as a team is really exciting, too.

We try to give everybody a chance to walk the last leg. Each year someone new who hasn't crossed the finish line in the past gets the opportunity.

I had the opportunity to do it about eight years ago. You're exhausted. You don't think you have anything left in you. Then you hear the crowd cheering and urging you on as you're coming down the sidewalk along the beachfront and it just re-powers you.

You know your entire team is waiting at the end to join you and cross the finish line. It's just a great feeling and a real high. We look forward to it every year.

John Hammarley is the longtime and only public address announcer for Hood To Coast. He is responsible for introducing every team at the race start and as they cross the finish line. Hammarley is a former television news reporter in Chicago, New York, Dallas, and Portland, who now lives in Bend, Oregon. He received six Emmy Awards during his television career.

One story that sticks out from all my time announcing the relay happened several years ago. It was at the finish in Seaside. Most of the gridlock had come and gone, and most teams had already finished. The sun was setting and it was getting dark. A women's team was coming off the Promenade and was certainly within earshot of my voice.

I announced their team name and then said something like, "Well, ladies, what do you have to say for yourselves now?" And they didn't say anything. They just all lifted up their tops and presented me with a nice, bare-chested salute to recognize their accomplishment. It was one of the best finishes I remember.

I'm surprised in all my years announcing the race that's the only time I recall being "flashed"—or whatever you call it when you pull up your running top—but that's the one time I remember having naked women or men coming to the finish.

Will Wise *participated in his first Hood To Coast in 1987.*

My dad turned 60 on May 6, 1988. I told him I admired his career and our friendship, and to celebrate his 60th birthday I would take him up Mt. St. Helens or to hike Oregon's South Sister, or do something else epic—just father and son. He thought about this for a bit and told me he'd like to run that goofy running relay race that I had started doing.

For the next six years Pops would run Hood To Coast with the Dead Cheetahs. He loved it and flew in from Michigan every year to do it. And he always brought along a big cooler full of sandwiches for the van.

After one of these race adventures we got a room at the Turnaround Motel in Pacific City. I had lived in Pacific City for a couple summers and was familiar with the area. The hotel was cheap, but it was right on the beach. After the race we were looking forward to doing some ocean fishing around Haystack Rock and exploring Cape Kiwanda.

Exhausted from the race, we had a martini and went to bed.

About 3 a.m., two huge, bearded guys came barging through the door into our hotel room. My dad and I were both up in an instant, and we had a stare down with these guys. Then these guys explained—in a congenially, albeit lubricated fashion—that their friend who owned the motel had given them the key to our room. It was just in case they felt after a night at the nearby Sportsman Bar they shouldn't drive home.

Pops let them have it and informed them that they were not spending the night. They slouched back to their pickup and waved goodbye.

We slept well the rest of the night.

Linda LaBash *began running in 1990 while attending the Oregon Police Academy for probation and parole officer training. She is an original member of the Heart 'N Sole team that has run Hood To Coast more than 25 times, and has also run more than 25 marathons, including six Boston Marathons.*

Since the very first year Heart 'N Sole participated in Hood To Coast, we've always had breakfast together at the Pig 'N Pancake restaurant in Seaside on Sunday morning. It's an annual tradition that started for our team in 1991 and begins with us attending the race awards ceremony before breakfast.

Besides our annual breakfast at the restaurant, our team has another longtime connection to Pig 'N Pancake. When Evelyn Bonney first organized the team, she invited women runners 40 or older to join the team. One of the original team members was Linda Poole, and her parents owned the Pig 'N Pancake.

For the first 10 years our team ran the relay, the owners of Pig 'N Pancake, Bob and Marianne Poole, sponsored our team. In addition to sponsoring us, they hosted us in their home Saturday night after the race, fed us dinner, and treated us like royalty. And on Sunday morning they would reserve a table for us at the restaurant.

Nowadays, the restaurant is always crowded the day after the race, with many runners waiting for a table. Sometimes the wait can be more than an hour. We always get on the list and wait, hoping the circular "family table," which can seat 13, is available. When that table isn't available, the staff always tries to accommodate us by moving a few tables so we can all sit together.

Now we even know each other's special breakfast order. Kathy gets a Dungeness crab omelet, Marita orders buckwheat pancakes, Susan has the gluten-free protein plate, and Sandy gets oatmeal and fruit. And almost everyone gets pancakes. It seems natural to know what everybody orders after so many years together.

Our annual race weekend always involves four events—the race, a Saturday night slumber party, attending the awards ceremony, and breakfast at the Pig 'N Pancake. Breakfast together before leaving Seaside is a positive way to end another adventurous weekend.

Heading down the Seaside Promenade toward the finish line.

Christoph Baaden

CHAPTER 24

That's Entertainment!

HOOD TO COAST IS FULL of entertainment. There's music at the start and finish and throughout the racecourse, some of it coming from vans and other vehicles outfitted with blaring sound systems built specifically for the race. There are runners and volunteers wearing costumes and vans full of decorations inside and out. Celebrities occasionally participate and there are also well-known athletes that compete. Even a documentary film was made about the race, featuring four teams attempting to successfully navigate the course. It's all entertainment and it's all a part of the relay.

Christoph Baaden is originally from Germany and now lives in Los Angeles. He is the producer and director of the documentary Hood To Coast, *which was released in 2011. His wife, Anna, is from Portland and served as a producer on the film.*

When I proposed to Anna, I asked her, "Where do you want to get married?" There wasn't any discussion. She said, "I've always wanted to get married on Mt. Hood." Anna's entire family is from Portland, and she grew up skiing at Mt. Hood. Her family has a strong generations-old connection to the mountain and Timberline Lodge.

As a film buff, I had of course seen the movie *The Shining*, and was thinking, "Getting married there is so crazy." But when I saw Timberline I thought it really was a beautiful place, and in August 2006 we were married there. It was the week before Hood To Coast and we saw all the equipment there ready to set up the race start. I asked my father-in-law about the relay. At the time I wasn't a runner and really didn't care much about running. After hearing about the race, I thought it sounded painful but that the concept was interesting and hoped their discomfort was fun.

Over the next year, I wanted to start exercising but I hated going to the gym. We live in Los Angeles, where it's always 75 and sunny, so I picked up running in a very casual way. In 2007, a week before the relay, my father-in-law, Bill, called and said, "Our team just had a runner drop out. We need somebody to fill in. Can you please run with our team?" I told him, "I'm not a runner. I do maybe two miles every two days." He replied, "Trust me, it's going to hurt, but you can do it."

All I knew before Bill's call was that the race was the world's oldest relay, it was 200 miles long, and it started at Mt. Hood and went to the ocean. I didn't know anything else. I hadn't heard about Leg 1, and I had missed the part about running in the middle of the night, never mind in the freezing cold, and sleeping outside or in the car. I basically went into the race blind but enthusiastic.

The team made me Runner 1 and said jokingly, "It's all downhill." I remember flying out of the start, or at least what felt like flying out of the start for a non-runner, feeling all the adrenaline of the top of the mountain. Halfway down the mountain, our van caught up with me and they were flagging me down. My teammates were yelling at me to slow down. I was thinking, "Why should I be slowing down? Aren't we racing?" As the van passed, my teammates kept telling me not to go "full power." I'm not sure why they didn't think to tell me before I started that, as we say in the film, Leg 1 is famously brutal.

My teammates brought me ice packs after I finished the first leg saying, "You'll really need these." I told them, "Why would I need ice packs? I feel fine." I survived my second leg during the middle of the night, but sure enough, by my last leg it felt like my legs were falling apart. However, I was weirdly, incredibly happy anyway.

It sounds crazy, but about halfway through my first leg I started thinking how cinematic everything was, how wonderful the energy and enthusiasm on the course was, and how it all pointed to the possibility of a film. I told everybody in our van, "This is so cool, there's something here." You push through the night, that's where the meat of the story is in act two, and then I vaguely remember finishing my rather painful last leg and realizing, "That's the climax, there's a film here." What ultimately sold me on the idea as a filmmaker is that I gravitate toward underdogs and characters slightly outside their comfort zone, characters that can't or shouldn't accomplish something but ultimately succeed.

About a week after I ran the race, I reached out to Bob Foote (HTC chairman and founder), Felicia Hubber (HTC president) and Jude Hubber (HTC Race Series CEO) with an email. Anna and I drafted a lengthy letter explaining who we were, and why we'd love to make a film about the race. They said, "We have gotten many proposals to make a film, but we've never given anybody the green light. How would you approach it if we allowed you to make a film?"

We didn't want to make just another sports movie: the race had become personal and we wanted to make a film about the people who participate in the race, not a film about the sport of running. We wanted to highlight runners and teams that overcome obstacles and succeed. Our goal was to honor the race and make the film a love letter to Oregon, but we didn't want to smooth out all the rough edges that make the event so memorable, the painful bits. We sat down with Bob Foote, and he listened carefully to what we had to say. It was clear that no one had approached it this way before. We sent them a formal proposal and were delighted and surprised when they very quickly turned around with a "yes," given how understandably protective they are of the event.

After they gave us the go-ahead, in February 2008, I moved to Portland. My co-director, Marcie Hume, and I were literally living in my in-law's basement.

For the first two months, Marcie and I met with at least 100 different teams. We had two or three meetings every day, talking to team captains and runners. We were looking for underdogs who maybe shouldn't be running the race but who were pursuing it and might actually succeed, and stories that stuck with us after we met them. After heavy deliberation, we started filming interviews with seven or eight teams, and then ultimately we made the call to highlight just four teams' stories.

We were so lucky that the storylines fell into place. We also found that ultimately the race wasn't just the backdrop for the film. It was a character in its own right.

Making *Hood To Coast* was by far one of the hardest projects I've ever done and probably will ever do. In hindsight, it was one of those films that if I looked at it on paper and were 20 years older and more experienced I never would've taken it on. It was simply a massive endeavor to capture something so epic. But fortunately, I didn't know any better, was incredibly gung-ho, and simply went for it—there was no turning back.

We approached the filming of the 2008 race with the precision of a military operation. The biggest challenge we faced was how to move along the course and cover 200 miles, despite the fact that our four teams wouldn't start the race at the same time. We also had to deal with almost half the racecourse not having cell phone reception, parts of the course where no vehicles were allowed, and traveling with three extra people in already crowded vans (a camera operator, sound person, and field producer). Between interviews and filming with our four teams, we effectively took six months to plan for two days of shooting.

To top it off, it was also a difficult week to get an experienced crew to work on the film. The same weekend as HTC in 2008, the Summer Olympics *and* the Democratic National Convention were taking place. So many people in the film industry were booked shooting those two events.

On race weekend we had 117 people working to make the film, which is unheard of for a documentary. We had to plan for crews embedded with all four teams, five "floater" crews with specific instructions, two cranes, and a helicopter, not to mention food and water delivered to our crews in the middle of nowhere. The night before the race started we gathered the entire crew together in one room. I walked into the room, looked around, and realized more than half the people in the room I had never met in person. All of the sudden our entire film as well as hundreds of thousands of dollars in investor money were in their hands.

We had done everything we could to prepare. We put together a detailed "production bible" for the film, a book explaining how the race worked and what they could expect to see the next day with photos, maps, and everything we could think of. None of the crew had run the race or even heard of it before, with maybe one exception. We included pictures of all the team members and their uniforms, the race start, and the finish line. We highlighted key areas along the course and provided details about all the legs and specific landmarks, estimated schedules and arrival times, along with possible team cross-over opportunities. We included multiple pictures of all four teams and all their members so our crew, who had never met them, would recognize them right away. The guide was distributed to all 117 crew members.

Because we obviously couldn't be with all the different camera teams over the race, we spent a huge amount of time marking the areas along the course where we wanted crews to shoot with pink ribbons. We actually drove the entire course over three days, tying the ribbons to trees, signs or fences that we thought provided good sightlines and nice shots. Unfortunately, I'd say only about 30 percent of the ribbons worked. Some ribbons blew away in the wind, others were ripped off by people, and a number of them were missed just because people were standing in front of them along the course.

Before we began, however, I knew that I had to empower everybody working on the film to work on their own and trust the crew. "Look for the people you have pictures of," I told everybody. "They are the people whose stories you are here to tell. Use our pink ribbons as a guide. If you don't see any pink ribbons trust your gut and use your talent and what you're trained to do to make a good film."

Our crew had to improvise constantly, "We don't see a pink ribbon. Let's figure out what to do. Maybe we'll film something different. We didn't get this one handoff, but we'll get the next one." Documentary filmmaking is a little bit like playing jazz. You have to be a good improviser. We didn't have to cover everything all four teams did, but we definitely needed each team at the start and the finish.

We ended up with 800 hours of film from the 12 camera crews that continued rolling throughout the race. That included between 10 and 12 hours of interviews and training with the four teams featured before the race began, but everything else was from the two days of the race itself. It took me more than three months to simply see all 800 hours and more than a year and a half to edit the film. I had a little office set up in our house and watched 10 hours of footage every day for three straight months. There was no other way to do it, because you never know what gems you'll find until you watch everything. To this day, I'm the only person who has seen all 800 hours.

After that labor of love, we were thrilled when the film had its world premiere in 2010 at the South by Southwest Film Festival in Austin. Some of the team members were able to join us, which was incredible. And seeing it with an audience on a 60-foot screen, when you've been agonizing for months over a 17-inch monitor during the edit, seeing it perfectly mixed and beautifully colored on a giant screen, capturing the race we loved so much already, was very different and emotional.

Seeing the film embraced by the audience in Austin, where very few had probably been to Oregon, let alone were runners or had heard of the race, was a huge relief. We were so proud of what we had accomplished because we could see it and feel it right there in the room. We were getting the response we had hoped for. It was a big test for us to prove the film would appeal to both people who had run or knew the race and the average documentary lover. That was huge!

We purposefully picked a way to distribute the film with race participants and fans in mind. What usually happens with a documentary is you're approached by a distributor with an offer. We had a distributor who said, "What we're going to do is put it in 10 theaters across the country. If it does well we'll go to 20 theaters, and if it does really well we'll do 30 theaters. Maybe we'll get to 40, but that's kind of it."

We also had an offer for a one-night only event, but the film would be shown in 500 theaters. It was a huge deal. We wanted it in every major city in the U.S. so even if it was a 30-mile drive you could still get to a screening. It was the right call and something we really wanted to happen.

We knew the premiere had to be in Portland, and for the large rollout we needed to have a live event broadcast with the film. In January of 2011 we did a live red carpet, which was broadcast from Portland to all 500 theaters showing the film. And because of the huge popularity of the event in Portland, we had to pick the largest theater in Oregon where we could host a live premiere. The best place turned out to be the Keller Auditorium in downtown Portland, which has almost 3,000 seats. We added a little twist to the movie premiere. We made it a red carpet gala because we wanted everyone to dress up, but we asked everyone to also please wear sneakers! We needed to have that running spirit there.

In one day we sold out the first screening and added four or five other theaters in town. The film was broadcast in Portland theaters that night and played to audiences across the country.

The entire experience, while exhausting, was life changing, just like the race itself. Somebody in the film says, "Hood To Coast is like Woodstock on wheels."

That's the best description we've heard, and we embrace it.

Emily Spiegel *is from Charlotte, North Carolina, and is the captain of the Hood To Coast team Agony of Da Feet.*

In March 2010 I was at the South by Southwest Festival in Austin for work. I knew South by Southwest was a music festival, but I was also interested in everything else happening there, especially the film festival. During my downtime from work, I was determined to see at least one film screening. After checking the film festival schedule, I discovered there was one movie playing during the window of time I had available. It was called *Hood To Coast*, and the description made it sound interesting. While I had never heard of the race before, I'm a runner and thought it would be worth my time.

Boy, was I right. The opening scene sucked me in, and I was captivated the entire time. I laughed and I cried, and I loved every minute of the film. After the screening, the director and some cast members, who were on the teams featured in the film, participated in a question-and-answer session with the audience. It was fun to hear their personal stories. It added another dimension to the experience.

After walking out of that theater I immediately started thinking about how I could run this race. It was something I just had to do. In a couple hours, I went from not knowing anything about Hood To Coast to being obsessed with running it. I made a note of when the movie premiere would be playing across the country, and made a mental list of everyone to invite to the screening. Once my friends saw the film, I knew they would all want to run it too.

Fast forward ten months to a cold and snowy January night in Charlotte. I had purchased a dozen tickets to the only theater in Charlotte showing *Hood To Coast* during its one-night engagement, and convinced a bunch of friends to come with me. The roads were icy and the snow was piling up, and southerners don't drive particularly well in the snow. But I was determined to see the movie again and wanted my friends to experience it too. Despite the weather, I was not taking no for an answer. My friends, who had heard me talk about it for ten months, were intrigued. We found the best drivers, who clearly were not native North Carolinians, and piled into a few cars to drive across town to the theater. My boyfriend (now husband) was working out of town, and I was disappointed he was missing the movie.

As we sat down in the theater, I was nervous I had over-sold the film. Would anyone be as excited as I was about this amazing race? Would anyone want to travel literally across the country to run 200 miles through the state of Oregon? Would anyone be interested in running in the middle of the night and sleeping in a van? Maybe they would. I grinned the entire time the movie played because I could tell everyone was enjoying it along with me.

As we walked to our cars after the movie, I could feel the energy. Everyone was *in*. The conversation turned to when we should enter and how many of us should complete an entry, as well as what the odds were that we would get in through the lottery. My goal was a step closer to reality. And then we waited, and waited, and waited for October, when the applications were due. I read the instructions on how to complete the team application probably a dozen times. When do I mail the application? When does it need to arrive? Should I trust the postal service? No, absolutely not. FedEx would be the only option.

We did not get selected in the lottery that first year—or in the second year. Then we followed the process for early entry for teams that had been rejected previously. I still vividly recall receiving an email the third year we applied and learning we were *in*. I was working in my office and let out a loud scream. Several of my colleagues came running into my office to make sure everything was okay. I was so happy. I immediately called my husband and teared up when I told him the news.

As silly as it sounds, it felt like a dream come true. I'd been thinking about the race and wanting to do it for four years, so the fact it was really going to happen was a bit surreal.

We quickly put a team together. My husband and I were the first two, along with several friends from Charlotte who had attended the movie premiere with me three years earlier. A colleague, who grew up in Portland, agreed to run. But when she found out she was pregnant, she became one of our van drivers instead.

We filled out our team of 12 easily. One of my favorite things about the race is the connections that lead to the formation of each team. When we needed extra runners, a friend's brother and sister were added to our team roster. Another friend knew a couple from Tualatin, Oregon, who also joined our team. And finally, a casual acquaintance my husband and I unexpectedly met at a race expo filled the last spot when we told her about the race.

As relay newbies, we put so much time and energy into the planning for the 2014 race. Once we had our team, 12 runners and two van drivers, we did numerous conference calls to discuss logistics. We scoured websites and blogs for tips and tricks and advice. We talked about the race nonstop. What should we pack? Are there supplies we will need? What will we get when we arrive in Oregon? We were all so excited and took training very seriously that first year, following relay training plans very closely. My husband and I even went on several late-night runs to test our headlamps and reflective vests. Looking back on that first year, I laugh because our preparation these days is not quite so rigorous.

When the calendar finally turned to late August, it was time to head west to Oregon. I'll never forget trying to fall asleep the night before the race in our room at Timberline Lodge. The nervous energy and excitement, along with the anticipation, were overwhelming. I couldn't believe it was really happening and didn't sleep a wink the night before the race start.

Now HTC has become an annual tradition. Our team hasn't missed a race since 2014. The race is all I hoped for and more. It's a part of every summer that I look forward to. I love piecing our team together each year, and the friendships that develop as a result. I also think our planning has reached "expert" level. We book our vans and our lodging—both at the mountain and at the beach—for the next year even before we leave Oregon after the race. We save our grocery list every year, along with the paint to decorate the vans. It is a well-oiled machine.

While I have many great memories from the race, my favorite things by far are the two meals our team shares together—a Thursday night pasta dinner at Government Camp, and a pizza and beer gathering in Seaside after the race. That's another area where we've become experts. We learned after the first year, when we waited three hours for our pizza, that Van 1 calls in the order as soon as it gets to Seaside.

For most of our team, we see each other only once a year, during the relay. Thursday night is spent catching up on what has happened during the past year. It's also the time when we figure out who has trained and who hasn't, and who is familiar with their legs and who hasn't even looked at the handbook. It's also the time to get to know our new team members.

By Saturday afternoon, we've become family. There's nothing better than all of us sitting around, sharing stories, recapping all the ups and downs of the past 30 hours, and laughing until it hurts. It could be Dennis telling his story about being pulled over by the police for driving too slow or Matt recapping his run in the middle of the night up a mountain during a hurricane. Or it could be Ashley talking about hearing Kevin yelling her name at the exchange while she was in a Honey Bucket or Frank fighting a stomach bug and running in 117-degree weather fueled only by Pedialyte. There are countless other stories. I look forward to sharing them every year. There's nothing like it.

And later that night, as I fall asleep after our team celebration has ended, I always think back and I'm so thankful that all those years ago I decided to see a film about a race I knew nothing about called *Hood To Coast*.

Tim Dooley is from Gresham, Oregon, and has been running in Hood To Coast since 1989. This memory was originally published in RaceCenter *magazine.*

I never pictured myself on the red carpet at a movie premiere, but amazingly there I was posing for a photo at Portland's Keller Auditorium showing of *Hood To Coast*. Okay, maybe the photo was just a souvenir shot. And thankfully there were no television personalities on hand to critique my attire—a University of Portland baseball hat and down jacket to fend off the freezing January rain. All the same, I and a couple thousand other Hood To Coasters decked out in everything from black tie to running costumes had shown up in force to see the movie of our beloved relay race!

My wife and two daughters had surprised me with tickets at Christmas. It was great to have their company at the event. In addition to being my daughters, Carolyn and Andi were also my teammates. I had raised them on the relay! It was only fitting that my wife, LeAnn, was with us too because years earlier she served as a volunteer and was with us on many occasions at the Seaside finish line.

As we exited the red-carpet area, Andi embarked on a mission to get her new running book autographed. Scouring the lobby she asked, "Where's Bart Yasso from *Runner's World*?" It was at that point that Carolyn voiced the million-dollar question. "What does Bart Yasso look like?" Our perplexed looks provided the answer, but in true detective style we opened the flap of Andi's book and our running guru's likeness was quickly revealed. Shortly thereafter it was Carolyn who triumphantly found Bart, and both daughters quickly corralled their autograph prey!

We eventually made our way to our seats in the theater. I felt relaxed and primed for the movie, especially after the team with the great bird hats sat behind us instead of in front of us. And what a movie it was! I was reeled in hook, line, and sinker by people and scenes that repeatedly reminded me of my more than 20 years of race adventures. Greeting out-of-town runners at the airport, reveling in the pre-race carbo-loading dinner, rising above middle-of-the-night fatigue, the van camaraderie—the flood of memories kept coming. Over and over again I found myself poking LeAnn and saying, "There's my leg!"

Four teams were featured in the movie, and each had a different story. Like many race participants, I saw my relay running life reflected in those stories. I suspect that many of us could relate to the rookies who wonder, "What have we gotten ourselves into?" Somewhere along the way, like me, they found their answer in the transforming magic of going the distance on the HTC trail. I could also relate to the "tribute team" that ran in the memory of a fallen friend and family member. It made me think of Tom Makarowski, my enthusiastic teammate and friend, taken from us all too soon.

Of course I related to the veteran team. My race memories date back to 1989, when I was "a young lion." Now, the "old lion" has slowed down but is still striving to go the distance! Finally, I surely related to the Heart 'N Sole team. Like runner Kathy, I've experienced medical setbacks and my doctor scrutinizes my race involvement every year. But Kathy said something that summed up the race for me and it remains my battle cry! She said, "I'm alive! I feel good! And I have to be there!"

John Hammarley is the longtime and only public address announcer for Hood To Coast. He is responsible for introducing every team at the race start and as they cross the finish line. Hammarley is a former television news reporter in Chicago, New York, Dallas, and Portland, who now lives in Bend, Oregon. He received six Emmy Awards during his television career.

About 12 or 15 years ago I started creating a music playlist for between the waves of runners at the start—for when I'm not yapping and introducing teams. I pull together what I think is an energetic playlist. Now during the time between one Hood To Coast and the next it's one of the things I enjoy the most. I pull together six or seven hours of music to play at the start. I collect all that music because I don't want to subject everyone at the start—the people checking in teams and the volunteers and the vendors—to the same songs over and over and over again.

I'll start creating a playlist probably the week after the race—in early September while my memory is still fresh. I'll take the top 10 songs from the race start—the songs that really got the crowd raucous—and put them in the music playlist for the following year. Then during the year leading up to the next race I'll listen to all different types of music to figure out what to add. When I find a song that may work, I think how the crowd will respond at the start. I just have this inherent sense where I know what's going to capture people's attention and get their feet moving.

What I discover every year is there are maybe five new songs that people love. People want to dance and move around before their wave takes off, and music just gets them ready to run. Through the years there's been quite a range of what people respond to at the start. Sometimes it's classic hip-hop. That's always a favorite. Some good driving rock and roll from years back is always a winner. There's nothing really mellow and not anything too heavy. Maybe there's a song from AC/DC or something from KISS, but not really too much metal.

When I'm putting together the music I'm thinking about being in the announcer's tower and wanting to see people smile. Some people start dancing right away and others are snapping their fingers. It's really fun for me to play the music and see a bunch of older men and women, who are kind of buttoned-down, start moving. It's like gold to get them moving!

John Hughes is a police officer from Tigard, Oregon. He is an avid runner who has participated in Hood To Coast five times.

It was hot and humid for the last leg of the race in 2017. We were making our way to Seaside and blasting music from our van through ice cream truck speakers mounted to the roof. It was awesome pulling up behind runners as they were slogging through their last leg. When they heard our music, smiles came to their faces and they pumped their fists. Some of the runners even started dancing!

We've all had difficult moments during our legs, which made lifting people up with music my favorite moment.

Bobby Brown is from Vancouver, Washington, and is the lead DJ for Hood To Coast.

I've been working as the Hood To Coast DJ for more than 17 years now. I've got 14 DJs who work for my company and 30 sound systems. We do all types of events all over the place, but the relay is my favorite.

I used to do the start at Timberline Lodge. Now I work the Portland To Coast start under the Hawthorne Bridge for the walkers. Then I finish up on the main stage at Seaside.

Sometimes I go for 40 hours straight. It can be close to 20 hours in Portland. Then I head down to Seaside. I sleep in the back of my truck for awhile, get up at 6 a.m., and do it all over again, all day long.

We play anything from the 1960s until now. Anything you can imagine, as long as it's upbeat. We know we're going to play disco. We know we're going to play classic rock.

And we know we're going to play all the top-40 stuff. Really, just anything that makes people dance.

I always take requests. Whatever the girls want I'll play. I try and give everybody exactly what they want. That's what makes it fun for me.

Felicia Hubber grew up in Portland, moved to Montana during high school, and attended college at the University of Montana. The daughter of Hood To Coast founder Bob Foote, Felicia was just a few months old when she attended the first HTC—and she's been at every relay since. In 2006 she succeeded her father as president of HTC.

When I started working for the relay in 2006 it was strange because we didn't have a tagline or slogan for the relay. I came on board thinking we needed to create a cohesive and consistent brand message. The relay had been around for many years, and it seemed odd that we didn't have one.

Jude (Hubber, HTC Race Series CEO), my dad, and I started tossing around different ideas and came up with what we thought were some catchy and interesting ideas. Initially, I thought of using the phrase the "Granddaddy of All Relays." That idea may have come from attending the Rose Bowl, which is known as the "Granddaddy of Them All." My dad and I are big football fans and we went to the 1995 Rose Bowl to watch the University of Oregon play Penn State.

For about six months or a year we floated that tagline around before I decided maybe it wasn't a great idea. My next thought was, "What if we take that idea and spin it off in a feminine direction?"

After doing that, I asked my dad, "What do you think about the tagline 'The Mother of All Relays?'" We felt it worked because Hood To Coast spawned the entire relay movement around the country. It seemed to really make sense. It represented what we were and what we were going to continue to be, while also acknowledging the event's history. It was simple, cohesive, and represented what the event continues to be. And it just felt right!

We started getting the word out by branding our website with the tagline. At the time, we were doing all the race apparel in-house and started branding everything with The Mother of All Relays. It was rather informal and grassroots—we basically just started putting it on the website and on apparel.

People seemed to love and embrace it almost immediately. Participants and media started using the expression right away—almost like it had always been around. Everyone began using the slogan in media publications and with their teams—on team apparel and team vehicles. It just stuck.

It had a very simple and organic origin, but it has stayed with us through the years. It's emblematic of what we encompass and what the race embodies as a relay and bucket list experience for many runners worldwide.

Jenny Hansson began working for Portland television station KOIN 6 in 2006 and is the anchor for its morning news program. Before moving to Oregon she worked at TV stations in Tallahassee, Florida; Austin, Texas; and San Antonio. In 2013 she participated in her first Hood To Coast.

I've lived in Portland since 2006. The first time I ran the relay was in 2013. We always cover the event at the TV station, and I'd done many stories about the relay on the morning news. Every year our station has a reporter at Mt. Hood for the start and, since I anchor the morning show, I always talk to that reporter.

I was on the cross country team in high school and ran casually throughout my life, but I'd never run anything more than a 5K. When the station decided they were going to have a team, called the KOIN Newshounds, someone asked me to join. I'd never run a relay before and wasn't sure how much I'd have to run. People tried to explain it to me, but I didn't really understand it. I agreed to do it not totally knowing what I was getting into. However, I heard from people at work who said, "It's so fun. You really get to know people. There are some hard times, but you'll love it."

Sometimes I get recognized because so many people who run the race are from Portland. It also helps that our vans are decorated with quotes from the movie *Anchorman*, along with all our names and the station logo. Before we start running, we usually do some live interviews with our morning show and there are cameras from our station at certain points along the course.

It's a cool way to meet people who watch our show but whom we wouldn't normally meet. If people approach me, they usually know who I am. We take pictures with some people; others just want to talk. I've worked in the Portland market for more than 10 years, so after awhile people come up to me and ask, "Hey, aren't you that lady?"

It's funny, but people recognize me more when I look my worst out in public, like during Hood To Coast. I don't know what that says, but I can hear people whispering, "Yes, that really is her."

I was really disappointed about missing the relay in 2015. Sally (Showman), the station's meteorologist, ran, and our traffic reporter also ran, along with several other reporters at the station. Three of us on the morning show wanted to run, but I ended up having to sit it out. My boss at the time said I had to work. It was a bummer, but that boss isn't at the station any longer. Hosting the morning news that year and having to "throw it out" to them for a live report with our team at Timberline Lodge was really tough.

That was the year of the big storm. I tried to make myself feel better about missing it afterward by focusing on how rough the conditions had been. At the same time, it would have been cool to say I survived the weather.

Every year when I finish, I say, "I'm not doing this again." I'm usually tired when I say it, and can't imagine tackling it again. Then after some time, I always want to do it again.

Felicia Hubber grew up in Portland, moved to Montana during high school, and attended college at the University of Montana. The daughter of Hood To Coast founder Bob Foote, Felicia was just a few months old when she attended the first HTC—and she's been at every relay since. In 2006 she succeeded her father as president of HTC.

We found out about comedian Kevin Hart running in the race about two weeks before the 2016 race. When we heard, all of our staff basically said, "The Kevin Hart?"

Jude (Hubber, HTC Race Series CEO) knows a guy at Nike who works with their athlete celebrities. He had Jude's contact information and approached him. He told Jude, "Hey, Kevin Hart wants to run Hood To Coast. Can we make it happen?" And Jude's response was, "Of course." We always save a couple of spots for last-minute teams.

I think Kevin heard about the relay through Nike. He has his Move with Hart initiative with Nike, which has a goal of getting more people involved in physical fitness throughout the U.S., and making it a fun, attainable experience.

I can't speak for him, but Kevin's a runner and probably thought along with his Move with Hart staff and team, "This is a great platform for me to be able to get the word out about my initiative."

I saw him at the finish, but I didn't want to go introduce myself or anything like that. He was surrounded by an entourage. I heard he had an epic experience and, of course, saw his post-event YouTube videos praising the race. You can't ask for much more than that!

Announcer John Hammarley (right) sends another group of runners off at the start.

Johanna Olson nearing the finish line in 2004.

CHAPTER 25

In Memoriam

HOOD TO COAST HAS BECOME a place to honor and recognize those who have passed away and once had a special connection to the event. The race now regularly includes teams that are paying tribute to someone who has lost their life. In some cases, the team wears gear that features and honors the individual. In other instances, the team is carrying the deceased's remains and may even scatter some of the ashes along the course.

Angenie McCleary grew up in Portland and has lived in Sun Valley, Idaho, since 1999. She participated in Hood To Coast five times before forming her own team in 2004, and she has served as the captain of that team every year since.

Since I grew up in Portland and always loved running, I was interested in Hood To Coast from a very young age. Starting in middle school I ran cross country and track, and I continued running in high school. As I became more involved with running, I remember waiting eagerly to see who would win the relay and whether it was a Nike or adidas team. I even remember when an elite Nike team set the Women's Open record of 18:49:54 in 1996.

While in school I committed to one day putting together my own competitive women's team. In 2004 my friends and I decided to form our own team, and the Girls Just Want to Have Fun team was born. I always knew I wanted to be team captain but had no idea of how meaningful the experience would be. Competing in the relay is so much more than just running and spending hours together in a van.

Since our team was formed, with runners from the Seattle area, California, Idaho, and Massachusetts, we laugh about the running being the easiest part of the race. Over the years, we've faced many obstacles. We've run out of gas, gotten a flat tire, missed an exchange, ended up lost on the course, and been stuck in traffic forcing our runners to hitchhike to the next exchange. We've also had teammates get injured, become sick, and suffer heat exhaustion. However, experiencing all those difficult moments has definitely made us stronger.

Over the years, our team has developed deep friendships and supported each other through difficult times in our lives. For me, the race has been a staple through many years of change and growth. What I find most remarkable is that not only do we experience challenges and unknowns every year during the race, but we also really get to know our teammates and share life's ups and downs together. We've seen each other get married, have children, excel in careers, and experience health challenges and injuries, as well as many other highlights and difficulties. We've been able to support, inspire, and celebrate each other, and every year we all look forward to coming together for the race. It reminds many of us of our school days running cross country, when we only dreamed about running HTC.

Every year after the relay I return home more motivated and inspired. It always amazes me that after running three times in 24 hours, staying up all night, riding in a van for hours, and serving as the team captain, I still return home after the weekend renewed and rejuvenated. The power of running on a team with an incredible group of women is truly amazing.

Most importantly, our team is now a tribute to one of our founding members and my best friend, Johanna Olson. She ran with us for our first eight years as a team before she passed away from brain cancer.

I first met Johanna at the 2000 NCAA Division III national cross country championships in Spokane, Washington, when she won the individual title—shortly after completing radiation following her first brain surgery. We later became best friends and training partners when she moved to Sun Valley in 2002. She would eventually participate in the 2004 and 2008 marathon Olympic Trials.

One of my favorite memories of Johanna involves our first year running the race in 2004. She was our anchor, running Leg 36 to the finish. Unfortunately, when she took off to start that leg she forgot the wrist wrap. We realized it after our van turned in a different direction than the runners. Although we tried to catch Johanna, we just couldn't. I hopped out of the van and started screaming. I remember running faster than I ever thought possible to catch her and give her the wrist wrap. We didn't lose any time and won the Women's Open class that year.

In 2013, after we lost her, we decided to honor her by changing our name to Team

Joha, which was her nickname. Johanna was first diagnosed with a brain tumor in 1996 in college, and suffered from a grade four brain tumor her last four years running with our team. Despite two brain surgeries and chemotherapy, she joined us at HTC every year and always had a huge smile on her face.

Johanna always inspired us! Her enthusiasm and love of life were contagious. Our first year as Team Joha we again won the Women's Open division. She was definitely with us that year and we run in her honor every year. The relay now has an even deeper importance to us and allows Johanna's memory and spirit to live on through our team.

Peggy Paul *was a member of the Aching Calves Hood To Coast team for eight years beginning in the early 1990s. She can now be found cheering during the event as runners pass by her home in Boring, Oregon.*

I'm not sure how to capture seven or eight years of Hood To Coast memories. The race represented *much* more than just a relay. It was a way to have fun and stay fit, as well as to get some sun on my shoulders. And many of my most cherished memories are from the race.

It was an event that I ran with my family and closest friends—and that charted a course of camaraderie, courage, strength, and inspiration. Some 20 years later, the picture from our first race still hangs on my bulletin board. From my more than 35 years of running, I have some big relay memories, right up there with running the 100th Boston Marathon, the New York City Marathon, and the Marine Corps Marathon. The HTC years hold that big of a place in my running memory vault.

For seven years, beginning in 1994, I co-chaired our team with my sister-in-law Lori. We ran with sisters and brothers, cousins and co-workers, neighbors and nannies. We ran through pregnancies, injuries, crises, and more. While there were a few team members along the way who we wanted to dump in Olney or Mist, by and large we loved being the Aching Calves.

We claim the start of the whole cowbell phenomenon. Many of us worked for the Oregon Dairy Council at the time, so we were the Oregon Dairy Council's Aching Calves. We outfitted each van with *real* cowbells and rang them at exchange points, in the moonlight of Scappoose, under the sunshine of Seaside, and along almost every mile of the course. We ran in our cow shirts and were *moooooo'd* along the way. And year after year we heard other teams proclaim, "The cows are back!" Our vans were decorated with Holstein spots, tails, and plenty of cow swag. We loved being the Aching Calves!

Every emotion was felt at some point along the course—exhaustion, frustration, and elation. We laughed when the five-gallon Gatorade cooler tipped over in the van our first year and spilled the sticky syrup everywhere. We cried in Jewell the last year during a particularly touching talk about life and cancer and friendships. We slept on the floor of the gym in St. Helens, nearly ran out of gas along Highway 26, and got yelled at by neighbors as we blasted Springsteen's "Born to Run" and the theme song from *Rocky* through the quiet streets of Eastmoreland. We were road-killed by Alberto Salazar and the Killer Bees under a full moon and, yes, we mooned our teammates and others! We made run-through tunnels for each other, waved flags, did the Macarena, and sang "Sugar, Sugar" by The Archies until our throats were raw.

Mostly, my memories of running the relay center around my now late sister-in-law Lori, who passed away more than 10 years ago due to breast cancer. Every year she ran—through chemotherapy, surgeries, remission, recovery, and through the recurring, metastatic year. Each year, the finish line represented a victory for Lori. It was our whole team's focus to watch Lori finish another year.

It was her escape. Together we painstakingly planned all the exchanges, meals, and sleeping spots, and did so around the kitchen table months in advance of the actual event. It was a simpler time, more old-school, before Wi-Fi and cell phone coverage, before easy electronics and emails, before GoPros and Fitbits. Instead, we ran with clipboards and cameras and boomboxes and batteries—and oh such joy.

I haven't run the race since Lori passed away. I'm not sure I could do it without her. Instead, I'm a spectator now—and the self-proclaimed best spectator ever! Each year, our family and friends cheer from our driveway along Brooks Road, now part of Leg 8. How fitting that after hanging up my running shoes the racecourse would shift near the turn of the century and pass right down our homestead road in Boring. How lucky am I?

Each year we put out lawn chairs, barbeques, coolers, hoses, Tiki torches, and signs, and make the most of one of my most favorite nights of the year. Recently, a race official drove past us, checked out our fanfare, and decided we all deserved volunteer T-shirts as a thank you for all our cheering and HTC love.

As I've said to my family numerous times, the relay is like my Christmas. It's my favorite holiday and most-treasured night of the year!

Susan Corden *lives in Baltimore. Her father, Walker Lindberg, was born and raised in Seaside, where she "spent many a summer."*

It was the proverbial dark and stormy night.

My three precious children were out running through the Oregon wilderness in the Pacific Northwest's first storm in many months. And they were doing it because they wanted to!

They had planned, invited others, traveled across the country, and brought their kids. They had spent lots of money and cajoled others to do the same for the privilege of running the 2015 Hood To Coast.

The team of runners trickled into Oregon in late August from Baltimore, Philadelphia, Orlando, and Seattle. The team included a lawyer, a financial adviser, a nutritionist, and a banker, among others. Some athletic, some not. Some serious runners, some not. All were determined to get my father—their grandfather—Walker Lindberg, home.

The reason this team, Running Walker, was carrying Walker's cremains in a fanny pack is that he hadn't yet found his final resting place, in the area known as the Cove, in Seaside.

Seaside is on the Oregon coast, where the race ends with great fanfare. Seaside also was Walker's birthplace, as well as the birthplace of several other members of the family of the Running Walker team. Seaside was the village that raised my dad. He and my mother, Shirley Scott, were Seaside High School sweethearts.

Walker loved happenings. This love had its origins in Seaside, where as a little boy, when he wasn't delivering newspapers at The Tides, logging in the woods, or lifeguarding on the beach by the turnaround, he was scouting out "happenings"—especially those with food. He could be found at every festival, church spaghetti dinner, cookout, or clambake, with plate in hand.

In his mind, the south end—the Cove, The Tides—was the best. It has been a traditional meeting place for family vacations, reunions, weddings, and funerals. We kids (sisters, cousins), who are now grandparents, grew up riding the ocean waves with air mattresses and no wetsuits, hiking Tillamook Head to Indian Beach, where crab salad was the reward at the end. And sandcastles! We built the best sandcastles. Many family members' remains have ended up in the Cove among the rocks and seaweed at the base of Tillamook Head.

When it came time to put Walker, this restless energetic soul, into the Pacific, his restless energetic granddaughter Evynn and her husband, Kurt, schemed, planned, and organized to give him one last big happening, a trip from Mt. Hood to Seaside.

In 2015, because of the storm, the finish for Running Walker was very different from the normal race finish, which is sunny and festive, with music and food. Just the kind of happening Walker would have loved.

In a way it was a gift, although I'm not sure the runners who braved the storm would agree. All the festivities were literally blown away. There were no stages, no music, no booths, and no food. All were cancelled. But looking back, the way our ceremony unfolded seems entirely appropriate and part of the amazing memory.

After a brief but wonderful celebration at the Promenade turnaround, with the runners who had worked so hard to plan and then run through the stormy night, Walker was carried on his last trip down the Promenade to the Cove. The rain stopped, but the ocean roared. The wind blew the sand over the beach. The clouds were still dark, big, and billowy. Family and friends convened at The Tides, now our summer home. A bagpiper began to play. Our gathering walked over the rocks and onto the beach. The atmosphere was otherworldly. Mystical.

My sisters, Jani and Emily, and I looked for a quiet tide pool among the rocks and waves. The ocean was unpredictable due to the storm. We found what looked like a good spot and proceeded to gently pour him in. Ashes blew in the wind. Waves crashed. We giggled as we do in all kinds of situations. Our quiet tide pool was suddenly overcome with ocean. And into the Cove he went.

Heading back to The Tides, the runners decided it was time for them to take a dip. Suddenly they were all running again, straight toward the ocean. I know Walker loved that whole happening. It continued into the evening after warm showers, lots of food, lots of love, lots of family and friends.

Walker Lundberg was born January 8, 1925. He passed away October 18, 2012. He was put to rest in August of 2015.

He lived a very full life and was loved by almost everybody.

Evynn Overton *lives in Baltimore and in 2015 put together a Hood To Coast team to honor her late grandfather.*

My husband and I are serious runners and have made a lot of close friends through running. Kurt ran in high school, but I didn't start running until I was in my 20s. I needed a way to exercise because I wasn't on a team anymore. After we began having kids it became even more important. We were always busy and tired, but running seemed to help with all of that. Now we've got three kids and they're all very active, and my husband and I still run because it helps sustain us.

A bunch of us had our eyes on Hood To Coast because it seemed like a really exciting event. My grandfather lived in Seaside, and we planned to spend some time with him at the end of the race. My friends knew I was originally from Oregon and still had family there, and many of them had met my grandfather during his visits to Baltimore.

We tried to get into the race for three or four years, but our entry was never selected. After my grandfather passed away we tried to get in the race for a couple more years. Finally, in 2015, we were selected for the relay as a charity team.

It was amazing how quickly the team came together. Almost everyone was from the East Coast, from Baltimore, Pennsylvania, and Florida. We also had one couple join the team from Seattle. The race has a mystique among serious runners everywhere, and most of our friends had heard about the relay and were excited to run. It was incredible to have friends willing to fly all the way to Oregon to run a race. They're dedicated runners and friends, and everything just clicked into place.

My husband had the idea of carrying my grandfather's ashes along the route to where he lived, The Tides, in Seaside, and then to an area at the foot of Tillamook Head known by the locals as simply the Cove. All of his family's ashes are in the Cove. My grand-mother is there, along with his sister and mom. That was always the plan. The idea was pretty out there, so we weren't sure how everyone on the team was going to feel about it. My mom and her sisters weren't against it. They hadn't laid him to rest yet and thought this would be a wonderful way to do it.

My grandfather's name was Walker Lundberg, and my youngest brother came up with the team name Running Walker. My grandfather loved living life well and was very charismatic, the kind of person you remember and who always had a sparkle in his eye. He liked any big gathering, and this seemed right up his alley. He would have loved it!

My mom's youngest sister, who had the ashes, kept saying, "Ev, the ashes are really heavy. I don't think you can run with all of him." She was right. Instead, we had a fanny pack with some of his ashes. At each exchange we didn't just slap on our wrist band. We buckled the fanny pack on the next runner, too.

The challenge of the weather that year was just part of the magic. We had torrential rains and crazy winds during some of our legs, but everybody just powered through. Everything was just amazing between the camaraderie among my teammates, running through Portland, the excitement of running during the night, and that route to the coast. It was all incredible.

It couldn't have been more magical on the beach. The wind was incredibly heavy. The sand was blowing. We were all bent over walking from The Tides to the Cove. Nothing needed to be said. It was so windy my mom and her sisters poured my grandfather's ashes right into the ocean so they wouldn't get blown away. It was just beautiful. Afterward, a bunch of us jumped into the Pacific Ocean, and then we strolled slowly back to The Tides and enjoyed time with family and friends.

I'll always cherish that time as one of the most amazing things to ever happen in my life. It was such a great way to bond, and I think our friends and family feel the same way.

Jeff Boly *is from Tacoma, Washington, and has been competing in Hood To Coast since 1985. He is a co-founder and captain of the Mr. Mojo Risin' team now running in the Men's Supermasters division.*

We had this guy on our team for many years, Brook Boynton. Because his name is Brook, somebody along the way called him Brook Trout and then he became just Trout. He was an amazing guy, one of nicest guys you'd ever meet. He was always the force of benevolence and never had a bad word to say about anyone. He was also an amazing runner, a phenomenal six-minute miler at 52.

Unfortunately, in 2009 he was driving home from work in Southern California and he was hit from behind by a car going 90-mph and we lost Brook. It was a horrible moment for the team. We had to do something to commemorate him because he loved this race as much as anyone.

He was cremated, so I created a little mini urn that fit on a slap wrap bracelet like the one Hood To Coast gives out every year. We hiked up to this place above the start on Mt. Hood and put down some of his ashes and set up a little pile of rocks. We carried him all the way to the finish and sprinkled some of his ashes in the Pacific Ocean.

We have that ceremony at the start every year to connect with him. The pile of rocks stays there because it's covered with snow most of the year—it's nicely preserved.

When we first started running, in order to differentiate our team from other teams, we wore bandanas. Back then it was whatever bandana you could find; a crazy hodgepodge of colors and bandanas. Now we hand out one of his bandanas to every member of the team and when we run, we run in his bandanas. We collect them all at the end, wash them, and bring them back the next year. We also honor Trout on our clothing every year by writing, "Trout 1957 to 2009."

Robin Balder-Lanoue *is from Monticello, Minnesota, and is the cross country and track and field head coach at the College of Saint Benedict, where she competed in those sports*

before graduating in 1991. She ran Hood To Coast from 1995 to 2015, and her team, Baba Yaga, was the top finishing women's team nine times, setting course records in the Women's Submasters and Masters divisions.

As a coach, I tell my teams this all the time: after you graduate from college you can continue to run on your own, but it's not the same as being on a team.

It was two or three years after I graduated college, around 1993, when one of the guys from my conference contacted my best friend and me about a team running competition in Oregon called Hood To Coast. They were putting together a co-ed team of six men and six women and asked if we'd be interested.

I was still running in road races and stuff like that, but I missed being part of a team and decided to sign on. So did my friend. The guys were in charge of naming the team and they came up with the Flaming Buttafuocos. Hopefully you remember Joey Buttafuoco. Our T-shirts had a black-and-white picture of Joey Buttafuoco giving the thumbs up.

It was just awesome being part of a team again and running through the night. Afterward, we started looking at the women's results and thought we could put together a pretty good women's team. It took a couple of years, but we finally organized a team of women runners.

First things first, we needed to come up with a great name. There was a book out called *Women Who Run With the Wolves*, and one of the stories was a Russian folk tale called "Vasalisa," about a woman who meets a witch named Baba Yaga. The story is about facing your inner fears and how you become stronger and gain strength by facing those fears. As runners, we felt it was about the challenge of running and the inner strength and soul that it takes to be a runner.

To us, the relay represented Baba Yaga and that became our team name. Just surviving each year makes you stronger. Over 20 years I don't think we ever had a year when something didn't go wrong. There are just so many things that are uncontrollable, but overcoming those challenges makes you stronger.

In 2010, Cindy Brochman, one of our runners, passed away from cancer. We decided to go after the Women's Masters course record to honor her. She was always Runner 1 and took so much pride in it. Her saying was, "Balls to the wall, girls, balls to the wall."

We were in the second to last group to start that year, probably around 5 p.m. Our first runner ended up going into oxygen debt because of problems with the altitude. We lost about 20 minutes on that leg. Then there was an accident on the course that held up all the runners. By Leg 11, we were the last team on the course. It was the middle of the night and we were all alone.

We were sure we'd lost any chance of setting a record, but we kept going, doing our best, and having fun. At the finish, we were standing on the beach and had just buried the bracelets we had worn to honor Cindy. We were sad because we didn't set a new record for her. Then we realized it was the pace per mile that counted toward the record, because the course changes every year. We looked it up and realized we had beaten the record pace by a few seconds a mile. We went from tears of sadness to tears of joy. It was just incredible.

The relay is really all about the people you are with on the journey. My teammates filled up my soul and rejuvenated me. The race is exhausting. You don't sleep for two days and you're doing three 10Ks as hard as you can, but when it's all done your soul is filled.

There were years, especially when we had really close races, that right before the third leg—when you're sleep-deprived and have already run really hard for two legs—I was almost in tears. I was wondering, "How am I going to do this? I've got nothing left." Everybody has that moment when you question whether you can do it.

Then you have that logical discussion with yourself, "You've done it before. You've done this." And you get out there and do it. You just keep pushing and some-how you do it.

Charles Conrow *is from Long Beach, Washington, and ran Hood To Coast with the PDQ Lemmings team more than 20 times.*

My wife, Brianna, and I had been doing Hood To Coast for about 20 years. She ran with the HOST to Coast team, which was a non-profit organization I helped found.

HOST is an acronym for Homeownership a Street at a Time and was formed in the late 1980s when serious gang problems plagued North and Northeast Portland. Deteriorat-ing housing values had put home owners in negative equity without the ability to maintain or sell their homes.

We helped improve, rehabilitate, and build housing in underserved and distressed neighborhoods, lifting up those neighborhoods by improving enough of a distressed area to form the basis for the for-profit market to take over. Usually this involved a whole street being improved at the same time, hence the name.

HOST built more than 400 homes, and Brianna was the project manager and the glue that held us together on a day-to-day basis. After running on the HOST team, she volun-teered with the PDQ Lemmings every year, even when she came down with ovarian can-cer. Everyone on the team knew her well. She volunteered and worked during the race for our team, all the way until 2015, which I thought would be my last year running in the event.

In 2016, she was able to come to Seaside to cheer our team across the finish line and attend the awards ceremony. She passed away October 3, 2016.

I decided to come back and run the race again in 2017, basically for her. I felt her with me all the way, reliving many special moments and memories from past races. I was Runner 4, which is a set of legs she did several times and knew well. I could feel her with me here and there, especially when slogging through the night and at the exchanges she worked.

It was a tremendous experience, one I won't ever forget.

Lauren Larson *is from Portland and works for Columbia Sportswear Company.*

We were walking for Kat Coker in 2017. Our team name was #TestedToughforKat. She did Portland To Coast a couple of times with our all-women's corporate team. She was diagnosed with leukemia and passed away in April 2017. We were walking for her and in her memory.

She was a big believer in charities and did a ton of charity events. Kat loved life, lived it fully, and gave from the bottom of her heart. Her big thing was the Make-A-Wish Foundation and she'd spent more than 15 years helping wishes come true. She loved unicorns and we passed out about 50 little unicorns during the race with a link to her giving page as a reminder for us and others to do the same and to give back to those around them.

We talked about her a lot during the race. She was a very special woman. She was a super positive and super happy person. She loved doing this event. She even moonwalked her way across the finish line in 2016. She always had a really fun time with PTC. Everyone remembered her and her spirit.

Debbie Harth *is from The Dalles, Oregon, and is a member of the Awesome Power Portland To Coast team.*

We first started doing Portland To Coast about 20 years ago to improve our health and build camaraderie with other women. I was about 45 years old when we started.

It has turned out to be so much more.

We have a great sisterhood. We've had divorces and we've had marriages. We have a teammate who had cancer. There are a lot of things that we've been through together. We have teachers, nurses, and people from all walks of life on our team. Some people have dropped off and we've added others, but we have a real core group of us.

I lost my daughter and keep her ashes with me. She had always been very supportive of me competing in this event.

Usually when I'm walking at night by myself I think of my daughter. I look up at the stars and it's so beautiful. It's a very peaceful time.

Or I think of her if I hear someone playing a Michael Jackson song. She loved his music. Sometimes when I'm out there by myself and it's very quiet, somebody will go by and I can hear a Michael Jackson song playing on their headphones and I think, "Thank you."

Acknowledgments

WITHOUT THE SUPPORT AND ENCOURAGEMENT of our wives, Emily Spiegel and E.J. Garner, we would never have undertaken this project. Family has always played a key role in our lives, and thanks from Marc to Andrea, Peter, Ben, Eva, Eddie, Merrill, Kate and Sam. Marc would also like to thank his "family" in Portland, Scott and Dana Reames, and Jennifer and Dennis Masi, as well as all his Agony of Da Feet teammates over the years. Art would like to thank Bonnie, Bill, Jim, Sylvia, Anna, Emma and Katy.

Marc and Art would like to thank the entire Hood To Coast organization, especially Bob Foote, Felicia Hubber, Jude Hubber, Dan Floyd, Cassie Negra, Ross Hubber, Morgan Powers, Luke Vanoudenhaegen and Brandon Nelson. When we initially presented this project, they were open to the idea and supportive every step of the way. Throughout the process, they were extremely helpful, assisting us with contacts, patiently answering questions and quickly providing information or confirming facts. This book would not have become a reality without their help.

Dan Wickemeyer expertly designed this book cover, and was more than tolerant with all our requests and changes.

Scott Parker, in addition to providing us with his own memories, served as our copy editor. He helped with the consistency and continuity that can sometimes be a challenge with so many entries from multiple sources.

We were fortunate to connect with Wendy Gable who skillfully crafted the interior of this book.

Many of the images included are from individuals who contributed memories to the book. Additional images were provided by Full Sail Brewing, Honey Bucket and Hood To Coast.

You don't put together this many memories without an incredible amount of help. In addition to those agreeing to share their stories, to whom we owe a debt of gratitude, there are many others who agreed to interviews, had suggestions regarding who we should contact, helped arrange conversations, provided background information and confirmed facts. No matter how many we mention here, we're sure to miss some.

Among those we turned to were Brian Alfano, Christoph Baaden, Steve Bence, Peter Courtney, Matthew Cox, Mike de la Cruz, Sandy Dukat, Larry Dutko, Ashton Eaton, Brianne Theisen-Eaton, Nelson Farris, Dave Frank, Christina Fuller, Jeff Glasbrenner, John Hammarley, Becky and Steve Hanamura, Jenny Hansson, Dave Harkin, Bob Harold, Amado Lumba, Patti McDonald, Lisa McKillips, Cindie McKenna and Bryon Frenyea, David Murphy, Nikki Neuburger, Paul Raab, Rob Rickard, Joe Rubio, Steve Spear, and John Truax.

And of course we would be remiss without thanking all the participants, teams, volunteers, event organizers, sponsors, partners and others who have made Hood To Coast what it has become today. Without all of them, we wouldn't have been able to share these stories.

About the Authors

Marc B. Spiegel first participated in Hood To Coast in 2014 with the team Agony of Da Feet and has run the relay four times. His first book, co-authored with Art Garner, was the Amazon bestseller *Indy 500 Memories: An Oral History of "The Greatest Spectacle in Racing."* He is a sports marketing and communications professional with more than 25 years of experience working with a variety of global brands. He lives in Charlotte, North Carolina, with his wife, Emily—the Agony of Da Feet team captain. Follow him on Instagram and Twitter (@marcbspiegel).

Art Garner is the award-winning author of the Amazon best-sellers *Indy 500 Memories: An Oral History of "The Greatest Spectacle in Racing"* (with Marc Spiegel) and *Black Noon: The Year They Stopped the Indy 500.* In 2014 *Black Noon* won the Motor Press Guild's Book of the Year award and was a finalist for the 2015 ESPN/PEN award for literary sports writing. Art spent more than 35 years in automotive public relations and now lives in Olympia, Washington, with his wife, E.J. Follow him on Twitter (@artpgarner).

23239971R00224

Made in the USA
Columbia, SC
10 August 2018